INDIA

Pranay Gupte is an award-winning columnist for *Newsweek International*, and is also a contributing editor at *Forbes* magazine, one of the most influential business publications in the United States. Earlier, he was a reporter and foreign correspondent for the *New York Times* for fifteen years. He spent three years in Africa and the Middle East as a foreign correspondent for the *New York Times*, covering the hostage crisis in Iran, the war between Iraq and Iran, the Soviet take-over of Afghanistan, the assassination of Prime Minister Indira Gandhi, and assorted coups and crises in many countries.

Pranay Gupte is the author of two previous books, *The Crowded Earth: People and the Politics of Population* and *Vengeance: India After the Assassination of Indira Gandhi*, of which *India: the Challenge of Change* is a completely revised and expanded version. He is a frequent talk-show guest on radio and television, and lectures widely at universities and various institutions on foreign-policy and Third World matters. He recently became managing editor of the International Commentary Service (ICS).

Pranay Gupte is married, with one son. He and his family divide their time between New York City and India.

Reviews of *Vengeance: India After the Assassination of Indira Gandhi*:

'This native son has given us an interesting and up-to-date account of India after Indira Gandhi.' *New York Times*

'*Vengeance* attempts the more difficult, and more rewarding, effort of explaining truths about contemporary India that are more vivid and powerful than any myth. It is this depiction of the real India that marks *Vengeance* as a major work.' *Wall Street Journal*

INDIA: THE CHALLENGE OF CHANGE

PRANAY GUPTE

With a foreword by
JAMES W. MICHAELS

METHUEN · MANDARIN

A Mandarin Paperback

INDIA: THE CHALLENGE OF CHANGE

First published in Great Britain 1989
Reprinted 1989
by Methuen · Mandarin
Michelin House, 81 Fulham Road, London SW3 6RB

Mandarin is an imprint of the Octopus Publishing Group

Copyright © 1984, 1985, 1989 by Pranay Gupte

Some portions of this book, in another form, have appeared in *Vengeance: India After the Assassination of Indira Gandhi*, *The Crowded Earth: People and the Politics of Population*, *Forbes* and *Newsweek International*.

Photoset by Rowland Phototypesetting Ltd
Bury St Edmunds, Suffolk
Printed in Great Britain by Cox and Wyman Ltd
Reading, Berks

British Library Cataloguing in Publication Data

Gupte, Pranay
  India: the challenge of change
  1. India (Republic). Politics
  I. Title
  320.954

  ISBN 0-7493-0030-2

CONTENTS

This book is for Anand and Malati Lal, with my love and gratitude.

ACKNOWLEDGEMENTS

This book is based partly on my reportage for two previous works relating to India, where I was born and brought up. Much of the material here, however, is new. This volume is not merely a revised version of the earlier books, but one that draws largely on fresh reporting and analysis in India, the West and the Third World at large. The story of India is one of continuity yet change, and I have tried to record this in my new book. I might add that recent developments in the subcontinent have been so dramatic that any author attempting to keep abreast of these changes is left bewildered and even dazed.

My task was made considerably easier by scores of people who assisted enormously during the research, writing and production of this book. Some of them would prefer not to be identified for various reasons. Anonymous or not, their help was critical; the errors in the book are solely mine.

Fortunately, there are several people whom I can publicly cite as having been indispensable in the creation of this book. To start with, my warm thanks to James W. Michaels, editor of *Forbes* magazine, for the wonderful foreword to this book. Few people know India as intimately as Jim Michaels does, and few Westerners understand and love this vast land as he does. I feel privileged that Jim agreed to take time off from his frenetic editing schedule to write his essay for my book.

Romesh and Raj Thapar of Delhi, two of the loveliest and warmest people I've had the privilege of knowing, shared with me many insights and gave me a lot of their time. They are both gone now, but they live on in the hearts of their vast numbers of friends – and in the work of hundreds of writers and journalists around the world whom they inspired and guided.

My special thanks also to Dr Rajni Kothari of Delhi's Centre for the Study of Developing Societies, who spent long hours with me and offered detailed analyses of the contemporary scene in India.

Also in Delhi, my thanks to: H. Y. Sharada Prasad, former

information adviser to Prime Minister Rajiv Gandhi, and now in charge of the Indira Gandhi Memorial Trust; Salman Haidar of the External Affairs Ministry (and now India's deputy high commissioner in London); Manmohan Singh, chairman and managing director of Frick India; Harji Malik; Nandita Narain; Ambassador Kris Srinivasan and his wife Brinda; Ajai and Indu Lal; Vijay and Bunty Dhawan; Khushwant Singh; Chancal Sarkar; Professor Ashis Nandy of the Centre for the Study of Developing Societies; Professor Dharma Kumar; Arun Bhatia, of the United Nations; K. K. Modi, of the Modi Group; M. J. Akbar; Pandit Ravi Shankar; Rajpal Singh Chowdhury; Gerson da Cunha; Meher and Kuldip Saran; Vichitra Sharma of the *Hindustan Times*; Zahed and Laila Baig; Hugo Corvalan of the United Nations Population Fund; Ashok Birla; Prabha Krishnan; P. A. Nazareth, formerly secretary of the Indian Council for Cultural Relations, and subsequently India's consul general in New York; Rajeev Sethi; Pavan and Renuka Varma; P. J. Anthony of the *New York Times* bureau; Rami Chhabra; Inder Mohan and Rani Sahni; and Babulal Jain.

In Andhra Pradesh, my warm thanks to Anand Mohan Lal, my father-in-law, for his suggestions and his insights into the Indian condition; and to my mother-in-law, Malati Lal, for her encouragement. Special thanks also to Pramila and Lessel David for their time and their assistance in arranging for visits to the countryside. And thanks to Chief Minister N. T. Rama Rao; to Ramoji Rao, publisher of *Newstime*; and to Potla and Nandita Sen, also of Hyderabad, for their trenchant assessments of the Indian scene; and to Santosh and Asha Reddy.

In Bangalore: my appreciation to T. J. S. George, the veteran journalist who is resident editor of the *Indian Express*, and to his wife Ammu. In Kashmir: C. B. Kaul of the *Indian Express* was enthusiastically helpful in setting up appointments and in providing expert assessments of the local political scene. Thanks also to Begum Abdullah and to Moulvi Mohammed Farooq, the religious leader of Kashmir, who generously gave me his time and thoughts.

In the Punjab: Inder Mohan and Anjali Khosla; Janak Raj Seth; Bhagwant Singh Ahuja, Mickey Ahuja and the entire Ahuja clan; Jagjit Singh Hara; the late Lieutenant General Gowri Shankar; the late Dr M. S. Randhawa; Karuna and Satish Mahajan; and Raman and Rajeev Mehta. They all went out of their way to help me. My profound gratitude to them.

In Cochin and Madras, my thanks to T. C. and Bhavani Narayan; and N. Ram, associate editor of *The Hindu*. In Bombay: Rahul Singh and Niloufer Billimoria were generous with their time, as were Vir and Malavika Sanghvi. My gratitude to Prabhakar Korgaonkar and his sister Tai. And thanks to: R. V. Pandit, editor and publisher of *Imprint* magazine; Sailesh Kottary; Dr Rusi H. Dastur; Dr Mahendra Jain; Bakul Rajni Patel and her son Sanjay; Khalid Ansari and Anil Dharker of *Midday*; Geeta Kanar, Devinder and Kanwaldeep Sahney; Dhiren Bhagat; Shobha De; H. P. Roy; Bhaichand Patel; Anil and Jaymala Bhandarkar; Arun and Gayatri Bewoor; Dilip and Bina Thakore; Vasant and Asha Sheth; Shyam Benegal; Shashi Kapoor; Tina Khote; Nalini Singh; Dom Moraes and his wife Leela Naidu; Ramchandra Moray; Murli and Hema Deora; Hari Jaisingh; M. A. Manuel; Nani A. Palkhivala, one of India's most distinguished lawyers and thinkers, who generously shared with me his thoughts on the Indian scene; Dr M. R. Srinivasan, the eminent physicist, and his wife Geeta; and to Vidya Nayak Root.

In the United States: special thanks to Professor Ralph Buultjens of New York University and the New School for Social Research, who offered his assessment of Indira Gandhi, his close friend over many years; John Darnton, Warren Hoge, A. M. Rosenthal, Robert B. Semple Jr. and Howard Goldberg of the *New York Times*; Thomas A. Blinkhorn, Shahid Javed Burki and Frank Vogl of the World Bank; Frank Karel III, Dr Rogers Beasley and Susan Spadone of the Rockefeller Foundation; William Burke; David F. Squire; Prakash Shah; Rajan Pillay; the late Rafael M. Salas, executive director of the United Nations Fund for Population Activities (UNFPA); Jyoti Shankar Singh, director of information and external affairs for the United Nations Population Fund; A.E. R. Kerner, formerly of UNFPA, and now a roving ambassador for the Oslo-based Worldview International Foundation; Lucy Komisar; Selig Harrison of the Carnegie Endowment for International Peace; Professor Maya Chadda of Rutgers University; Sudha Pennathur; William H. Draper III, and J. Russell Boner, of the United Nations Development Programme (UNDP); and Bradford Morse, former administrator of the UNDP.

Also in the US: Mohan and Nita Shah; David Toufic Mizrahi, editor of the *MidEast Report*; Talat Ansari; Kamal Dandona; Tushar Kothari; Ajit G. Hutheesing; Ponchitta Pierce; Cecilia

Corpus; Madhur Jaffrey; Shehbaz Safrani; Ranjit Sahni and Neville P. Bugwadia, who read the manuscript and saved me from egregious errors; Tarzie Vittachi, formerly of UNICEF; Ray and Jenephur Moseley; Allan Dodds Frank and Lillian King; Victor J. Menezes; Tim Ferguson, Melanie Kirkpatrick and John Fund at the *Wall Street Journal*; Kantic and Manju Dasgupta; Professor Jagdish Bhagwati of Columbia University; Janki Ganju; Ilene Barth and Mark Howard of *Newsday*; Tennyson Schad, who taught me some very important things about law and writing; and Homei Saha.

I also want to express my profound gratitude to Julian Bach, my literary agent in the United States, for his support and many kindnesses.

To my journalistic colleagues in New York, a very special thanks for their help: Kenneth Auchincloss, Richard Steele, Steven Strasser, Jerry Footlick, Mathilde Camacho, Patricia Mooney, Joan McHale and Ellen Lambert at *Newsweek International*. And at *Forbes*: Sheldon Zalaznick, Lawrence Minard, Jean Briggs, Harriet Miller, Jerry Flint, Everett Halvorsen, Roger Zapke, Ronit Addis, Alexandra Gregson and Ray Healey Jr.

In Britain, my thanks to: Ann Mansbridge and Alex Bennion at Methuen London; Michael Thomas, my literary agent at A. M. Heath and Company; Dilip Hiro; Shyam Bhatia, Lorana Sullivan and Cameron Duodu at the *Observer*; and Elizabeth Ohene at the British Broadcasting Corporation.

While this is mostly a book of personal experience and reporting, I have freely raided the scholarship and research of several writers. I have shunned the use of such scholarly paraphernalia as footnotes because this is a reporter's book, not an academic tome. Most of my sources are acknowledged in the narrative and bibliography, but I ask forgiveness for sins of omission.

I am deeply grateful, as always, to my wife Jayanti. Her critique of my manuscript was immensely helpful. And appreciation is in order for our nine-year-old son Jaidev, who has had to contend with a father who was absent more often than present – and even when he was present, he seemed absent from parental duties because of the exigencies of deadlines. Jaidev's India will be considerably different from the country his father grew up in. I hope this book will, in time, help him understand the extraordinary changes occurring in an extraordinary land at a particular point in time. I hope that Jaidev's India will be a better and happier India.

INDIA AND ITS STATES

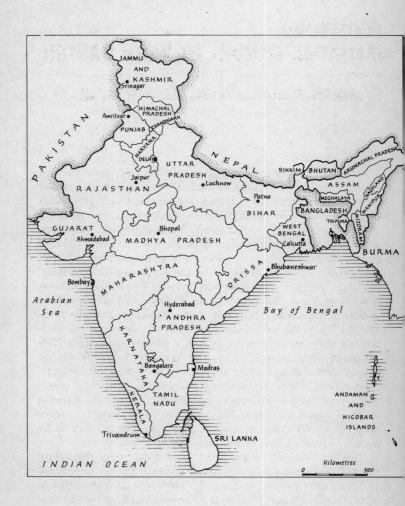

FOREWORD: MAHATMA GANDHI TO RAJIV GANDHI

BY JAMES W. MICHAELS (EDITOR, *FORBES* MAGAZINE)

I am a relic, one of the few still-active American newsmen who covered the events leading to Indian independence, knew the personalities involved, and stayed on to report on the bloodshed and on the gradual settling-down that followed independence in 1947. Moreover, I have visited India frequently in the years since and followed her progress both through reading and through personal contacts. I have interviewed three generations of India's ruling family – Jawaharlal Nehru, Indira Gandhi and Rajiv Gandhi.

However, my intent in this introduction to Pranay Gupte's book is not to reminisce, but to draw upon my very personal experience to help readers transcend the cultural differences between India and the West. The differences are profound; but so are the similarities, the common ground. India is a political democracy. Toleration of cultural diversity is not a foreign importation to India but deeply rooted in its culture and history. A Westerner's first impression of India is: how different this place is. But closer observation yields a quite different insight. Democracy in India is a living reality – blemished, but reality usually is. In India, as in most of Western Europe and the United States, people are free to be people – providing they do not too flagrantly break the law.

Here are 800 million people, half of them under the age of twenty. They do not have a common language. It is not exceptional in Delhi and elsewhere to see a South Indian speaking in English to a North Indian waiter because it is the only language they have in common. Religions? Hindu and Moslem have a history of strife that makes Catholic and Protestant in Northern Ireland seem like a couple of neighbours squabbling over a back fence. Yet the polyglot, polyracial, polyreligious mass of people has maintained under ferociously difficult conditions what I believe to be the only freely elected government among the dozens of countries which shed imperial rule after the Second World War. India's army has left its barracks only to fight foreign enemies or to restore order when the police were overwhelmed. Unlike in next-door Pakistan, the army in India does not pretend to embody national legitimacy; it exists only to defend that legitimacy. No matter how you cut it and for all her flaws, modern India is a magnificent and humane accomplishment.

My personal passage to India began forty-six years ago. It was the India of the British Raj, of colonial subjugation. The late Paul Scott has described the last days of British rule far better than I could, and television viewers have glimpsed that period in the magnificent series *The Jewel in the Crown*, based on Scott's *Raj Quartet*. In those four novels, and in a fifth, *Staying On*, Scott has brought a dead society back to life and shown the strange mixture of arrogance on the one hand and genuine idealism on the other that differentiated British rule in India from colonial rule in most other places.

The significant thing is this: while Indians finally rose against the worst features of British rule, they ended by adopting some of the better features of British democracy and fair play. Why did this happen in India when so many other former colonial countries fell back into one form or other of autocracy? I think because Hindu culture, which is dominant in India under the veneer of Westernism, is basically tolerant and respectful of individual eccentricity; it is thus extremely fertile ground for democracy. (Many of my Indian friends would prefer me to say 'Indian' culture is tolerant, but I see no evidence of democracy taking strong hold in Islamic nations.) India was not a *tabula rasa* on which the British etched new patterns. In a major sense the British simply helped make legible again that which was already written there.

Like most Westerners, my first impression of India was of uncrossable, unfathomable gulfs.

I first had a sense of crossing these gulfs on a stifling pre-monsoon morning in Delhi more than four decades ago. I awoke that sweltering morning in Delhi to the news that President Franklin D. Roosevelt had died in Hot Springs, Virginia. The pre-eminent leader of the Free World was gone. What did his passing mean to the world? Indeed, what did it portend for me?

I was one of the tens of millions whose lives had been disrupted and changed by the Second World War, which caught me on the eve of my graduation from Harvard and deposited me, at twenty-two, in India, a country of which I knew almost nothing. In 1943 and part of 1944 I served as an American Field Service volunteer ambulance driver with the British–Indian army that was slowly pushing the Japanese back into Burma. Later I moved from the mud and blood of India's eastern frontier in Manipur to an interesting but scarcely taxing office job for what was then the United States Office of War Information in Delhi. From the small room I shared with another American in the old Cecil Hotel ('Europeans Only') I bicycled daily the four miles or so to the USOWI office in New Delhi's Connaught Circle area. My path took me through the crowded Chandni Chowk, Old Delhi's 'street of moonlight'. Then as now Chandni Chowk was framed on one side by the crowded bazaar, but in those days, when India's capital had scarcely 10 per cent of its present population, the broad street opened on the other end to a stunning vista of the red sandstone Mughal fort, the Lal Qila, across what was then a vast parade ground.

I had already experienced two years of India and had, like Kipling's Kim, travelled the Grand Trunk Road from Bombay to Calcutta. I had even learned enough Hindi – in the military mode – to converse with ordinary Indian soldiers. For all this I as yet knew only a little of the country or its culture. It was British India then, and as an employee of the United States government I was discouraged from mixing socially with Indians; our British allies, not yet reconciled to the loss of the jewel in the King Emperor's crown, did not like our doing so. Franklin D. Roosevelt had already irritated the British Tories on the subject of India's freedom; so much so that FDR's personal emissary to India had been booted out by the British authorities. FDR's Four Freedoms had nourished the growing hope for independence in the minds of those Indians literate enough to know what was going on. The American press was loudly and sometimes ignorantly critical of British imperialism. The last thing the imperial authorities wanted was a lot of naive young Americans running about and getting the natives stirred up.

Yet, as far as I could do so without endangering my job and without seeming odd to my fellow Americans, I quietly made a few Indian contacts. A charming pundit, whose family was steeped in Delhi history, and whose mouth was red from betel-chewing, came weekly to my room to give me Hindi lessons. He brought with him Indian food – then almost unobtainable by foreigners in this heart of India – from the bazaar. Over a bottle of sherry, which he loved but could not himself afford, we talked about Indian history and culture and the virtues and vices of British rule, then in its last few years. These evenings were, for me, a rare and almost forbidden pleasure. By and large, Indians and Westerners felt clumsy in one another's company, and remained so well after independence.

And so, though I liked the few Indians I had got to know, I was not at all prepared for what happened as I cycled to work on that sweltering morning of 15 April, forty-four years ago. Chandni Chowk was always crowded in the morning, a time when the temperature was still only in the low 90s. This particular morning it was extraordinarily crowded. I had to get off my cycle and push it. Only slowly did it dawn on me why the street was thicker with people than usual. A hero was dead. I suddenly realized: people aren't ignoring me as usual. Recognizing by my uniform that I was an American, people were offering condolences at the death of my president. A grizzled, burly, middle-aged man blocked my path. What did he want? Only to embrace me, tears in his eyes. In his few words of English he said: 'We have lost a friend.' That done, he let me pass. Other Indians were crying. People wanted to touch me, to show me, any American, their sorrow at the death of the English-speaking statesman who championed their cause against that of his own British allies. A common sorrow united us. FDR had plucked the same sympathetic strings in those 'strange' Indians as in so many Westerners. We were divided by culture and economic status but united by the Four Freedoms. For the first time, I sensed that Indians and Americans had more in common than was commonly supposed.

At this time Mahatma Gandhi and his protégé Jawaharlal Nehru were agitating furiously for Indian independence from British colonial rule. Like many Americans at the time I was ambivalent about Indian nationalism. It was bred into Americans that one nation ought not rule another and the arrogant discrimination against brown skins seemed irritating and stupid to most of us.

But there was another side to British imperialism, at least in those twilight days. The unfairness, the irrationality of one nation ruling over another was tempered by the British sense of fair play and respect for law. From a political point of view such rule is no longer acceptable, but this much can be said for it: respect for individual and human rights in British India was of a far higher order than respect for individual rights is today in many so-called Islamic and Marxist–Leninist states.

Individual rights were not the main issue in India then. Political freedom was. In the middle of the Second World War, when both the Western powers and the Soviet Union were in mortal battle against an evil enemy, the Indian National Congress declared that independence came before cooperation in the war against Hitler. Without a firm promise of freedom Indians would not only not support the war effort, they would impede it. And impede it many of them did. But with few exceptions, there was no sympathy for the Axis powers: it was America's – Roosevelt's – call for freedom that Indians in general responded to, not to Japanese propaganda about Asian solidarity. When the British finally conceded Indian independence, there was, therefore, surprisingly little bitterness in spite of the sometimes brutal history of British rule.

Mahatma Gandhi, Jawaharlal Nehru, Maulana Abdul Kalam Azad, Vallabhbhai Patel. All dead now, these were the men who led India to independence and to a reconciliation with the former colonial master. In 1946 and later, as a young reporter for United Press International, I met them all, these founders of independent India. Gandhi, who knew how to sway simple peasants and rouse them to a sense of nationhood. Nehru, Cambridge-educated, smooth, a graceful writer and speaker in English, urbane – Gandhi's seeming opposite yet his choice for leading independent India. Azad, a courtly, neatly bearded Moslem who represented the Indian soul of the Indian Moslem and opposed the creation of Pakistan. Patel, ugly as a toad, but tough and smart, and to some observers the most able of the nationalist leaders; Patel lost in the power struggle to Nehru because he seemed to represent Hindu India rather than the secular India which the more cosmopolitan Nehru stood for. I shall never forget the day when, from a distance, I watched Mahatma Gandhi gently shaking his finger at Patel, who like a child hung his head. Gandhi opposed the creation of Pakistan, but once it was a fact he insisted that India carry out her agreements with Pakistan to the letter. Patel advocated a tough line with Pakistan but relented under the Mahatma's scolding.

The two nations were born, India and Pakistan, amidst terrible bloodshed – bloodshed directed not towards the departing colonialists but inwardly, Indian slaughtering Indian. For the Indian revolution took a strange turn. Not only did the colonial rulers leave of their own will, they actually sent one of their most influential and charming personalities, Lord Louis Mountbatten, to make sure that independence did not get delayed by bickering among the endless shades and gradations of Indian nationalism.

Had the British suddenly seen the error of their old ways? It wasn't just that. They had lost the will to empire and had a war-battered economy to rebuild – and did not want to get caught in the middle as the various factions struggled for the prize of power that was now sure to fall. The British may not have left willingly but they left gracefully. In scenes unparalleled elsewhere at a time when colonialism was unravelling throughout the world, the last viceroy, Lord Mountbatten, drew cheers from the Indian crowds almost rivalling those for Jawaharlal Nehru. The British left India, not with the lion's tail between his legs, but proudly and with general good grace.

Unfortunately, independence did not come peacefully. Deflected from resentment of the former oppressors, revolutionary ardour turned inward; Moslems and Hindus did some settling of ancient scores. Millions were uprooted from ancestral homes and literally hundreds of thousands died in cruel, senseless mutual slaughter. Pakistan, which was first conceived as little more than a bargaining chip in a grab for power by the brilliant and enigmatic Mohammed Ali Jinnah, was torn from India to hasten the independence timetable; it was as if the mothers in the King Solomon tale had agreed to settle their differences by putting the baby to the knife. Jinnah, the father of Pakistan, was not even a good Moslem; he smoked, drank, ate pork and emulated the English gentleman. Never mind that he didn't really represent Moslem India as Maulana Azad did; he understood power, understood that he could capitalize on Britain's desire to get out and on the nationalist mainstream's desire for democracy. Pakistan made no sense geographically, historically or economically, but there it was and there it is.

Would this truncated, bleeding India hold together? Probably not. Could it develop in relative peace? The chances looked slim. But it wasn't my problem. For me it was a thrilling opportunity to practise my journalistic trade on a grand scale at an early age. I was just a greenhorn journalist but I was recording history. Good fortune had me on the scene at Birla House in New Delhi within minutes of Mahatma Gandhi's assassination and UPI broke the story to the world press. Trekking through the hills and mountains of Pakistan, I became the first foreign journalist to report from the spot the fighting between India and Pakistan over Kashmir in 1947, a conflict that smoulders still. Born in bloodshed, it seemed that India would not last long.

But India did hold together. It has had wars with Pakistan and China, a runaway population growth, an oil crisis, and riots and separatist movements based both on language and on religion. Corruption festered, encouraged by the bureaucratic socialism that breeds corruption wherever it exists. Resources were wasted on grandiose state projects. Yet the centre held. There were no *coup d'états* – just free elections. India made huge advances in technology, industry, trade. The statistics show only modest economic growth since independence. I do not believe the statistics, which I believe to be vastly understated in a society where nobody quite trusts the bureaucracy which gathers the statistics. Low though it still is on average, the Indian standard of living has made huge leaps forward since independence, and a huge middle-class has been created where hardly any existed before. Upward mobility is strong now in a society which for a millennium was in the static grip of caste. Though the government's economic policy was, by and large, atrocious, the natural industry and talent for business of the Indian people managed to shine through.

It is March 1977. Thirty-two years have passed since I wheeled my bicycle through the crowds in Chandni Chowk on the morning after FDR's death. Except for the grand old imperial buildings and the still resplendent uniforms of the President's Guard, Paul Scott's India is gone. Delhi is no longer British and Mughal. It is all commerce and politics now, a sprawling industrial centre as well as the capital. It is a Punjabi city now, its character transformed by the hundreds of thousands of Hindu and Sikh refugees who fled east after Pakistan was carved from India's flesh. I am dining at the home of old Indian friends. They have a visitor, another old friend who lives to the north in the hills above Almora. There he owns a small fruit orchard, employing about three dozen workers. The man from Almora is puzzled. All the polls, all the newspapers, are predicting that Indira Gandhi will win the general election, that her party will win in a landslide.

The prime minister had been ruling under a State of Emergency which gave her government extraordinary powers to arrest, to censor, to punish, and to suspend civil liberties. By and large, these powers were used sparingly but there were certainly abuses. Indira's youngest son, Sanjay, had launched a powerful campaign to bring down India's birth rate. This was not a brutal dictatorship as we see it today in so-called Marxist–Leninist countries, but neither was it the usual Indian state of live-and-let-live. India was flirting with totalitarianism. Just flirting, mind you. Stung by criticism of her use of the new powers, Mrs Gandhi had called the election, confident that the masses would be sufficiently pleased by her government's somewhat heavy-handed progress against crime, corruption and inflation that they would forgive the relatively minor infringements against personal liberty.

Which was why my friend from Almora was puzzled. 'Everybody' thought Mrs Gandhi would win, but the illiterate men who tended his orchard told him privately that they intended to vote for the opposition. Why? Well, they said, they appreciated all Mrs Gandhi had done for the country but they were disturbed that the police had come one recent night to a neighbouring village and carted off the village schoolmaster, who had, apparently, been openly critical of Sanjay Gandhi's male sterilization campaign. My friends wondered: could the polls and the experts be wrong? Could Mrs Gandhi possibly lose?

Lose she did, and overwhelmingly. Indira Gandhi even lost her own seat in Parliament. Her party was swept from office. The experts were scarlet-faced. But would she accept defeat? Would she mount a *coup*? She went quietly from office. I later spoke to several fairly ordinary Indians. How did they feel about the election results? A significant number said the same thing: they had voted against her only to teach her a lesson; they did not want her to lose but they did not want her to win so strongly that it would go to her head and give her and her son too free a hand.

So the 1977 elections showed clearly that India was no pushover for totalitarianism, even when it was exercised in the name of the

masses. The voters firmly rejected it. They were not about to follow
anyone blindly, not even the tough daughter of Jawaharlal Nehru,
hero of independence. There clearly would be no Khomeinis in
India, no Castros, no Ghadafis. Indians had reacted to a power
grab, no matter how moderate, pretty much as Western Europeans
and Americans would.

The opposition, now in power, made a terrible mess of things and
Indira Gandhi was prime minister again in 1980. But she had
learned a lesson: in her comeback period she ruled democratically,
ruthless where she had to be, but always recognizing now the
limitations to her ability to exercise power. In the end she was
removed from power undemocratically – by traitors' bullets. Even
this tragedy did not seriously damage democracy in India. After a
brief outburst of brutality, the country regained its balance as surely
as the United States did after the assassination of John Fitzgerald
Kennedy. Mrs Gandhi's successor, her older and sole surviving son,
Rajiv, was confirmed overwhelmingly by the voters, and he, too,
has learned the limits of power in a democracy.

A strange kind of democracy, you may say. One family has ruled
for forty of the forty-two years since independence. Rajiv Gandhi
succeeded his mother; Indira Gandhi, after a lapse of a couple of
years, succeeded her father, Jawaharlal Nehru, as prime minister;
and Nehru reigned from independence until his death in 1964.
Nehru's father, a wealthy Allahabad lawyer named Motilal Nehru,
had been head of the nationalist party long before independence.
And although Mohandas Gandhi, the Mahatma, had stirred and
roused the masses to clamour for freedom, he never exercised real
power, giving instead his blessing to Nehru. A royal family?
Four generations of them. But Westerners would do well to
remember how close the US came to making the Kennedys a royal
family. We should remember, too, that even Nehru had to live with
the constraints and frustrations that democracy and the rule of law
impose.

How will history judge Indira Gandhi? Her flaws were obvious: her
tendency to surround herself with unthreatening nonentities, her
ruthlessness. She was political to her very soul; while campaigning
on an 'eliminate poverty' platform, she did little to stimulate the
economic growth that can alone reduce poverty in a developing
economy. Politics interested her; economics was secondary.

Grant all this, but examine the other side of the balance sheet. This fragile woman held India together. Given the centrifugal tendencies, she may have been right to emphasize politics over economics. She had a shrewd sense of timing, rarely making major moves until she felt the swell of public opinion behind her. When she did move, it was with overwhelming force. Take the war with Pakistan over Bangladesh: she held her hand while millions of refugees poured into India, while Pakistani troops committed atrocities in what was then East Pakistan; she seemed to remain passive despite the clamour for action from the electorate. But she was not being passive; just waiting for her case to build. India won an overwhelming victory.

Indira Gandhi has been criticized, unjustly I believe, for the Indian army's bloody and partly bungled attack on the Golden Temple in Amritsar. Whoever was to blame for the political impasse between the Sikh community and the government, by the time she sent the army in there was really no alternative to the use of overwhelming force. The place was no longer a temple; it was an arsenal and a hiding place for assassins and cut-throats. The worst element of Sikh terrorists had taken it over; these terrorists were sallying forth to kill women and children and old men, then scurrying to the Temple for refuge. People now say that she perhaps used excessive force, but at the time the Hindu majority and the moderate Sikhs were wondering what she was waiting for. In the event, the attack on the Golden Temple cost Indira Gandhi her life. To have failed to act would have cost her and India worse: a total breakdown of authority.

I interviewed her in early 1984 when she had less than a year to live. She was in a philosophical mood, dwelling on the difficulties of achieving needed change in an ancient, impoverished society. I shall never forget her words: 'Although India doesn't present the tidy picture we would like to have, you can't deny the forward movement.' No, you can't. Nor can you deny her dominating presence in that movement.

One of the greatest obstacles to forward movement is what Indians call communalism and we, in slightly different context, call racism. Both are more often swear words than accurate descriptions of attitudes. When an Indian deplores communalism he means the practice of favouring one's own community over other communities, putting community before nation. Communalism, carried to extremes, leads to bloody riots. In practice, the term is almost always coupled with 'Hindu', since the Hindus, making up 80 per cent of the population, are expected to be more tolerant than the minorities – for whom one is supposed to make allowances. One is supposed to be particularly gentle with Moslems and solicitous of their sensibilities. Since the central government is bound by the very Constitution to secularism, any assertion of Hindu rights or of Hindu virtues tends to be regarded as communalism.

Thus we see the spectacle of an overwhelming majority having to behave with great restraint in its own land. When Sikh extremists massacred innocent Hindus in the Punjab, throwing bombs into wedding parties and pulling travellers from buses and hacking them to pieces, a devotion to secularism forced many Indian intellectuals into a position of criticizing Mrs Ghandhi's government for ignoring the 'legitimate demands' of the Sikhs – although nobody articulated with any precision just what these demands were. But when Mrs Gandhi sent the Indian army into the nest of murderers that the Golden Temple had become – well, some people considered that a communal act.

Ridiculous as these arguments sometimes become, there is virtue in them. They force the majority to lean over backwards to protect the rights of minorities. That India's overwhelming Hindu majority accepts, though sometimes grumblingly, these restraints is one more sign of how basic is India's underlying commitment to tolerance and to democracy.

Nobody can negotiate with the IRA provos, the Red Brigades or Khomeini terrorists – and nobody could conduct rational negotiations with the Sikh killers. Too bad that so many innocent Sikhs suffered; their real tormentors were fellow Sikhs.

Remember this about the Sikhs: they are not a downtrodden minority but a group who by dint of hard work and common sense have earned an economically and politically privileged position in India. They are an admirable people ill-served by a rotten leadership; one is tempted to think of Germany in the 1930s. What is said is that many Sikhs in Britain and North America, secure in their sanctuaries, egged on and financed the fanatical leadership and helped bring suffering on their people in India.

Moving to the international field, the recent dramatic events in the Soviet Union, pointing to real hope of a relaxation in the forty-year Cold War, may finally remove an old irritant in India's relationship with the United States and to a lesser extent with Britain. Under Jawaharlal Nehru, under Indira Gandhi, and now under Rajiv Gandhi, India has interpreted neutrality in ways that many Westerners have seen as tilting heavily towards the Soviet Union, especially in the United Nations. To many of us in the West this has seemed hypocritical – a democracy siding with totalitarians.

India has seen it differently. To India, the Soviet Union has been a friend, trading on terms favourable to India, supplying advanced arms that were often denied by the US. And this is undeniable: US foreign policy has favoured Pakistan over India, encouraging India to balance that powerful support for an enemy by enlisting support from the Soviet Union. But if tensions ease between the US and the Soviets, India may no longer be called upon to take sides. Then the US and India can deal on a basis where the Cold War no longer matters. The Soviet withdrawal from Afghanistan is a good sign. Meanwhile, I, for one, hope that the US will in the future be less anxious to side with Pakistan, thus diminishing what is probably the main issue pushing India in a pro-Soviet direction on foreign policy.

From the Indian viewpoint, the so-called East–West struggle was never the primary issue. The primary issues are the political vulnerability of India's geographical position, its struggle for economic development, and a deeply felt if possibly exaggerated desire to continue to be militarily much stronger than Pakistan. In the long run, India's survival as a democracy is more important to world freedom than Indian support for US or UK policies in the United Nations.

What of Rajiv Gandhi? It is unfortunate that India seems unwilling to give political legitimacy to anyone who is not descended from Motilal and Jawaharlal Nehru – but that is the way it has been. Rajiv Gandhi is not the statesman his mother was, nor does he have her highly developed political instincts. But he is an attractive personality and if he can learn to surround himself with stronger and better associates, he could yet play a major part in leading India into the highly competitive world economy. This much can be said for him: unlike his grandfather and his mother, he has no taste for state socialism.

It is almost impossible to end an essay like this without comparing India with China, ancient civilizations both, similarly afflicted with too many people and too little capital. China has gone the Marxist–Leninist way, India the democratic way. Which has done better? By just about any standard I would say India. We currently see the Chinese moving cautiously towards a freer economy, pulling back, moving again. In the meantime, India has managed to avoid paying the terrible price in human suffering that China had to pay during the failed 'Great Cultural Revolution' of the 1960s. So far as economics is concerned, I see no evidence that China's industrial and agricultural progress has been faster than India's. Totalitarianism has brought China more misery than benefit; democracy has cost India a certain amount but has brought great benefits.

Much is hopeful in the Third World's only major working democracy but the population figures are sheer horror. With the obstetricians and midwives working overtime, with the population growing 15 million souls a year, will the generation that Rajiv Gandhi represents be able to maintain democracy? In the chapters that follow, Pranay Gupte tries to provide some answers.

Born and raised in India, Gupte moved to New York, where he distinguished himself at a relatively young age in the highly competitive business of newspaper and magazine reporting and book writing. As an author, and as a *New York Times* foreign correspondent, he has travelled and reported widely in Africa, China, Iran, Cuba, and just about any other place you can mention. As a contributing editor at *Forbes*, he has travelled the world to cover the news where economics and politics intermingle.

Like Rajiv Gandhi, who belongs to the same generation, Pranay Gupte represents a new and worldly India. He and I disagree on a number of points, the Sikh troubles being one. Our differences are not so much philosophical as generational. He, being younger, is less patient with injustice and corruption; and I, being older, tend to take a longer view. Yet I firmly believe that what he reports here on the human face of democratic India is of great importance to those of us who are both worried and hopeful about the future of the free world.

INTRODUCTION:
THE CHALLENGE OF CHANGE

The everyday drama of democracy and grassroots development in India is presented only fitfully before foreign audiences. With 800 million people and a vibrant multi-party system, India is the world's biggest free nation. More Indians qualify to vote in their elections, which have been held mostly on schedule every five years for the last forty years, than the combined populations of all the industrialized democracies of the world, including Britain, the United States and Japan.

Unlike many Third World nations, India is an open society where foreigners and locals alike can go where they wish. Little men in little cars or bullock carts do not follow foreign correspondents around, monitoring all their movements – as frequently happens in other developing nations which do not share India's commitment to democratic values and institutions, and to human rights. The Indian government does not censor transmissions to outside news organizations. Access to sources in India is rarely a problem: indeed, Indians and their officials are garrulous to the point of verbosity. The Indian press is arguably the freest in the world, with more than 5,000 daily and weekly newspapers, and another 5,000 monthly magazines, in a variety of languages.

India is an ancient land, but it is also one of the giants of the modern post-war era. Among the myriad nations of the Third World, it is widely regarded as the first among equals. Since achieving independence from Britain in 1947, what was once a colonial territory consisting of 400 princely states has become the world's tenth most powerful industrial country, producing cars,

computers and satellites. India possesses the world's biggest group
of scientists and engineers after the United States and the Soviet
Union; India's military is the fourth biggest in the world, after the
US, the USSR and China; India has exploded nuclear devices; and
it produces more feature films – nearly 1,000 annually – than any
other nation. Ancient culture, modern nation.

Change has come with bewildering speed in the post-colonial
period; yet, age-old customs and traditions remain a vital part of
everyday life. Marriages are still arranged in many parts of India;
elders are still venerated, not shipped off to nursing homes for the
aged; religion reigns, if not supremely, then still powerfully. Colour
television is enjoyed by the masses in the remotest regions, but the
most popular programme on the airwaves is the *Ramayana* – a
series about a mythological Hindu king, his travails and triumphs.

I had long felt that this aspect of India – change in the midst of
continuity – wasn't fully conveyed to their audiences by journalists
reporting out of India. I was aware, of course, that Western
audiences weren't entirely unfamiliar with India. Headlines about
the Indian sub-continent raced across the front pages of British,
American and other Western publications whenever there were
natural or man-made tragedies. Communal riots were a special
favourite of Western television and radio producers – nothing like a
good story on bride-burning to win viewers. As with many other
Third World nations, India was 'news' mostly when there was bad
news to report. An adapted version of Gresham's Law seemed
especially applicable for India: the bad news drove out the good.
And the availability of such news? Plentiful.

There are serious journalists who argue that, even under the best
of circumstances, India is a difficult place to cover. The sheer size of
the sub-continent poses a formidable challenge. Local transportation facilities aren't always reliable; the climate can be
debilitating. Long ago, Jawaharlal Nehru wrote: 'To endeavour
to understand and describe the India of today would be the task
of a brave man – to say anything about tomorrow's India would
verge on rashness.'

Still, I resolved long ago to write a book that showed how one
Indian-born journalist saw his country, a sympathetic book but one
that also accurately, fairly, yet critically reflected contemporary
reality. Because I lived abroad, I felt that my geographical distance
from my homeland offered a special perspective – that of loyal but

critical observer of the Indian scene. But how to go about it, how to structure a book about so large and diverse a land? Ideas came and went, ambitions rose and fell, reporting trips to various parts of India were undertaken – but still there was no clear sense of what my India book would ultimately be.

On a balmy October morning in 1984, I found myself in Bombay, where I was born. I had flown in from my home in New York to visit my father, who was seriously ill and confined to a hospital room. On that day, 31 October, the news of the assassination of Prime Minister Indira Gandhi by two of her trusted Sikh security guards hit us all like a thunderbolt. Later that day, my former employer, the *New York Times*, telephoned to ask if I would travel up to the Punjab and report from there for the newspaper. The caller was John Darnton, the deputy foreign editor (and now the metropolitan editor), who knew that I was in Bombay.

Darnton, a veteran foreign correspondent and a winner of the Pulitzer Prize for his reporting from Poland, diplomatically did not point out that for security reasons foreigners were forbidden to travel to the Punjab since the Indian army's invasion of the Golden Temple in Amritsar, in June that year, to flush out Sikh terrorists who had obtained sanctuary in Sikhism's holiest shrine. This meant that the newspaper's American staff members couldn't travel to this troubled state. In my case, of course, it helped to look Indian in India and also to carry an Indian passport – facts that were implicit in Darnton's request and which would enable me to journey without hindrance to the trouble-torn Punjab, the home state of Prime Minister Gandhi's assassins.

When I told my father about Darnton's request, he urged me to speed up north at once, never mind his condition, for this was history in the making.

In the event, I was the only correspondent representing a foreign publication who was able to report from the Punjab in the wake of the assassination. Even while I was in Amritsar, innocent Sikhs were being massacred in Delhi and elsewhere in northern India by Hindu-led mobs, supposedly to exact retribution for the Indira Gandhi murder. Yet there was a strange calm at the Golden Temple, where I worshipped in the company of Sikh friends. As I visited Sikhs and non-Sikhs around the Amritsar area, it struck me that a book was finally taking shape in my head.

I decided that I would write not only about the assassination of Indira Gandhi and its aftermath; I would write about where Indians, who had gone through a remarkable seventeen years of her political rule, now saw their country going. I would write a blend of narrative, anecdote and analysis. I did not wish to be a soothsayer, but I did want to find out from ordinary Indians and from their leaders what sort of future they thought lay in store for them. And so I embarked on a fresh series of travel.

That reporting trip took me between November 1984 and June 1985 from the northern Indian state of Kashmir to Kerala at the southern tip of the country. I travelled to India's great cities and booming towns, and I journeyed to rural areas, where more than 70 per cent of India's population lives. I interviewed politicians and peasants and political scientists; I talked to young professionals, movie stars, teachers, farmers, businessmen, technocrats, journalists, musicians, artists, village artisans and social workers. Most of all, I looked up ordinary Indians.

I wanted, if not a portrait, then at least a sense of where my country stood at a particular point in time. I wanted to write about the great changes that had occurred in national life during Indira's time – and about what lay in store under her son and successor. I talked to people of many religions and ethnic persuasions. I observed firsthand the December 1984 national elections in which Rajiv Gandhi's ruling Congress Party won 401 out of 508 seats contested for Parliament, an unprecedented achievement for any political party since India became independent from Britain in 1947.

I rediscovered the hugeness of my land – 1,269,340 square miles, or two-thirds the size of the continental United States, as large as all of Europe, its 800 million people constituting a fifth of all humanity. I heard the cadences and cacophonies of India's fifteen major languages and of many of its estimated 874 regional dialects. India stretches 2,000 miles from the Himalayan heights of Kashmir in the north to the beaches of Kerala in the south, and 1,700 miles from the tea gardens and oil fields of Assam in the east to the scorched plains of Gujarat in the west. India's coastline is more than 3,500 miles long; its borders with Pakistan, Nepal, China, the Soviet Union, Burma, Bhutan and Bangladesh ramble over 8,300 miles of deserts, mountains and tropical forests.

Everywhere there were crowds: when India achieved independence there were 350 million Indians; now there are more than twice that number. And in fifty years' time, there will be more than 2 billion Indians. Indeed, India has already become the world's most populated country, after China, which has 1.1 billion people. Everywhere there were also cattle: India has 200 million of them, or a quarter of the world's bovine population. More than seven-tenths of Indians depend on farming for their livelihood, but although agriculture constitutes almost 45 per cent of India's gross national product of $200 billion, farmers enjoy a *per capita* income of considerably less than the national average of $250.

I found out that fewer than half of India's 576,000 villages – where 70 per cent of the country's population lives – have electricity. Literacy is also low in villages: only one woman in four can read and write; only half of India's males have gone to primary school. I was told that more than a third of the world's illiterates live in India. Despite the widespread availability of primary health care, the infant mortality rate in India is 129 per 1,000 – one of the highest in the world – compared with 92 in Brazil, 56 in China, 28 in the Soviet Union, and 14 in the United States and Britain. Life expectancy is fifty-four years, according to the government, but Indians in many parts of the country survive fewer years than that.

I discovered that there are 100 million 'untouchables' in India, the economically backward and socially shunned people whom Mahatma Gandhi called Harijans, or God's children. Of India's current estimated population of 800 million people, 85 per cent are Hindus and 10 per cent are Moslems; there are also 20 million Christians, 14 million Sikhs, 5 million Buddhists, and almost 4 million Jains, members of a sect who abhor violence so much that most wouldn't even dream of crushing a cockroach.

As a traveller in those months following Indira Gandhi's death, I was struck by the high hopes that many Indians had for her son and successor. People were liberally garlanding their new leader with goodwill. I was encouraged by their general optimism concerning Rajiv Gandhi, who was widely perceived as a young and fresh-faced man untainted by the corrosive political practices of his predecessor and mother. Rajiv had an extremely telegenic family in his wife, the Italian-born Sonia, his daughter Priyanka, and his son Rahul. I was also encouraged by the fact that in a period of general political decline, missed economic opportunities and authoritarian tendencies under Mrs Gandhi, popular Indian culture none the less flourished: the fine arts and performing arts were thriving; and several grassroots organizations had sprouted to serve the everyday needs of deprived people in towns and villages, whether such needs concerned the supply of potable water or the provision of legal advice or the generation of employment for village artisans.

Part of my reportage first appeared in a book entitled *Vengeance: India After the Assassination of Indira Gandhi*, which was published in the autumn of 1985. I was convinced at the time that the Rajiv Raj would truly usher in a new era of peace, prosperity and general progress not only in India but in the whole South Asia region. Gandhi, after all, was starting with a clean slate; his view of politics was global, not parochial; his economic instincts were centrist, even favouring free enterprise over public-sector statism. He seemed keen to play a decisive role in resolving numerous local conflicts in the region. And Rajiv was anxious to make his mark quickly as a world leader, initially through the mechanism of the Nonaligned Movement, whose three-year chairmanship he inherited from his mother.

Within four years, however, the political landscape of India had altered dramatically.

The early promise of Rajiv Gandhi had withered. Gandhi's bold plans for economic liberalization were stymied by India's bureaucratic behemoth – and by his own lack of drive. For decades India prided itself on the fact that, almost alone among major developing countries, it had not piled up major foreign debts. Since October 1984, when Gandhi became prime minister, India's foreign debt had grown from $23 billion to $35 billion. Why? Mostly because of rising imports and lavish borrowing to finance showcase projects. Inflation was heading towards double-digit figures. Economic policies were bedevilled by inconsistencies of approach, frequent reshuffling of key aides entrusted with carrying out Gandhi's vision, and by Gandhi's own failure to provide strong, committed direction.

By 1989, Gandhi's leadership was also being increasingly challenged by opposition leaders who were emboldened by a series of corruption scandals featuring Gandhi's associates and friends.

One of the biggest scandals involved the secret, illicit payment of $100 million in commissions by the Swedish arms manufacturer, Bofors A. B., allegedly to people close to the Gandhi circle. Bofors, a subsidiary of Nobel Industries, had been awarded a controversial $1.3 billion contract to provide India with 155mm howitzers. The Indian media, ever eager for a hot story, and Gandhi's political opponents seized on the story – at least in part because Gandhi's supporters had made such a big deal of his 'Mr Clean' image. The scale of the Bofors affair suggested that political corruption had become more extensive than ever before and had also deepened its roots in the body politic.

The arms scandal wasn't the only unpleasant story on the Indian scene. In the strategic border state of Punjab, Sikh separatists escalated their terrorist campaign to establish a theocratic state called Khalistan. Where did the Sikhs get their weapons? The Gandhi administration accused neighbouring Pakistan of being a conduit for arms, and also of providing sanctuary to the rebels. Moreover, Indian intelligence officials seemed convinced that money raised by affluent Sikh expatriates in Britain, the United States, Canada and Western Europe was being used to buy sophisticated weapons for the terrorists. These officials believed that the Sikh terrorists' 'hit list' included not only Rajiv Gandhi but also his wife and children. The children, in fact, were taken out of school by the Gandhis and began to be tutored at home.

By 1988, virtually the entire South Asian region was in the throes of turmoil. In Afghanistan, the Indian government had supported the Soviet invasion of December 1979. Pakistan, meanwhile, had joined hands with its patron, the United States, in backing the mujahedeen, the so-called 'freedom fighters'. More than 3 million Afghan refugees (out of the 5 million who had fled their country) were camped in Pakistan. The Soviet invasion of Afghanistan proved to be of unusual value to Pakistan: Washington began to perceive Pakistan as a frontline state against Soviet expansionist ambitions in Asia, and funnelled more than $2 billion in economic and military assistance to the mujahedeen through the Pakistan government. Moreover, the US initiated a six-year, $3.2 billion aid package to Pakistan in 1981 – a package that included forty F-16 fighter-bombers – and in 1988, after considerable debate, the US Congress agreed a second six-year aid package, this one amounting to $4 billion.

By mid-1988, the Soviet Union's reformist leader, Mikhail Gorbachev, had decided to pull his troops out of Afghanistan, where 13,000 Soviet soldiers had died in guerrilla combat with the mujahedeen, and another 37,000 had been wounded. The incursion into Afghanistan had obtained for Moscow widespread inter-national condemnation, especially from the Islamic countries. More-over, despite the massive investment of manpower, munitions and money, the Russians weren't able to sustain a strong local government in Kabul, the Afghan capital.

The dynamics of Gorbachev's policies of *glasnost* and *perestroika* obviously meant that the Afghan adventure had to end soon. Better to cut one's losses and exit gracefully. Gorbachev's 'saviour' turned out to be the United Nations, which had tried for six years to end the Afghan war. On 14 April 1988, an agreement was signed in Geneva under the aegis of the UN; the agreement was guaranteed by both superpowers. Under its terms, the Soviets agreed to pull their 115,000 troops out of mountainous Afghanistan; the US and the Soviet Union, however, reserved the right to resume military assistance to the mujahedeen and the Kabul government respect-ively. Because India (under Indira Gandhi as well as her son) had been such a strong supporter of the Soviet-backed Kabul régime, there was now a general feeling that if the mujahedeen resistance leaders grabbed power in Kabul, India's influence would be diminished as far as Afghanistan went.

It wasn't just India's western border that Rajiv Gandhi had to worry about. In the south, shortly after a peace treaty had been signed by Gandhi with neighbouring Sri Lanka in July 1987, India sent 'peace-keeping' troops to help resolve a bitter civil war be-tween that island-nation's majority Sinhalese and minority Tamils. The exercise proved costly, and by no means conclusive: more than 1,000 Indian troops were killed by the Tamil separatists, who had earlier received alms and arms from India. Some of Gandhi's critics were calling the Sri Lankan situation India's Afghanistan or Viet-nam. To the east, in Burma, students clamoured for democracy, and after some initial concessions the military was once again in charge, bloodily crushing dissent.

In November 1988, Rajiv Gandhi despatched Indian troops to crush an attempted coup in the Maldives, a string of islands in the Indian Ocean. The attempt by renegades to overthrow the Maldives Islamic government hardly posed a security threat to India – but Gandhi showed that he did not appreciate the concept of power-by-*coup d'état*, and he showed that India was perfectly willing to impose its will in the region.

Even if the Maldives *coup* attempt had succeeded, it would

hardly have affected the region's security in any serious fashion. But clearly, Gandhi must have been mindful of the fact that other countries, geographically much more contiguous to India, had, by 1988, seemed candidates for *coups* because of internal uncertainties. In Nepal and Bhutan there were now challenges to feudal monarchies. The military-led government of Bangladesh was mired in corruption, and the country's economy continued to be bedevilled by natural disasters and inept management.

The overall geo-political situation in South Asia had changed considerably since my reporting trips of 1984–5. Two of the most dramatic developments occurred in 1988: President Mohammed Zia ul-Haq of Pakistan was killed when his plane blew up. Despite being a military dictator who couldn't resist the occasional sabre-rattling at India, Zia was essentially a moderate man who did not feel that war was the best way to arrive at an accommodation with his huge neighbour. He was a shrewd and masterly politician who held his ethnically tumultuous country together for almost twenty difficult years.

In Sri Lanka, President Junius Richard Jayewardene decided in September 1988 that he would retire from public life, thereby ending one of the most remarkable careers in Third World politics. His retirement created another imponderable in India's relationship with this troubled island neighbour. Jayewardene had shifted from an anti-Indian to a strongly pro-Indian stance in recent years, bringing Sri Lanka's foreign and domestic policies into alignment with India's strategies. However, Jayewardene's expectations that this démarche would ease the separatist and other tensions in his country remained unfulfilled – more than 5,000 Sri Lankans have died in the civil war since 1985. India now had no guarantee that Sri Lanka's new leader, Ranasinghe Premadasa, would be as well disposed towards Delhi as Jayewardene, creating another grey area of uncertainty for Indian policy-makers.

These recent developments restructured an entire region that had become increasingly important in world affairs, a region increasingly wooed by the superpowers because of its strategic location and its potential as a huge market. More than a quarter of the global population, which was squeezed into this region, now faced the 1990s with uncertainty and insecurity. The speed and fluidity of local developments illustrated how quickly things change in regional and world politics; the changes underscored the need for local and world leaders to act swiftly and shrewdly to cope with exigencies and emergencies.

Perhaps more than ever before in the post-war, post-colonial era, the sub-continent now constituted a test case as to whether Third World countries could construct a satisfactory life for their people in a world where economic growth and social progress are increasingly hard to fashion. But by 1988 it was by no means clear that the countries of the region were meeting their challenges. It was amply evident that the new rulers of India, who had promised change, were confounded by it.

It seemed to me that 1989 would be an especially critical year, a time when vital concerns, issues and a clash of heritages would converge. The axis of confluence would of course be India's general election, which constitutionally has to be held during this year – the greatest political show on earth when more than 500 million voters will pour their frustrations, concerns and hopes into the ballot box. The noisy clamour of democracy at work will be, in truth, a vast referendum on the future direction of India and the performance of its present rulers. The 1989 election, coming as it will at this juncture of Indian history, will produce either an indictment or an endorsement of Rajiv Gandhi and his policies for a New India.

I thought I should end this introduction on a personal note.

My father died not long ago. The eldest son of a Hindu family is required by tradition to light his father's funeral pyre, and I flew from New York to Bombay to discharge my duty. I am an only child; in addition to comforting my widowed mother – who herself died eight months after my father – there was much to be done by way of organizing the religious rites, and attending to such matters as death taxes and property settlements.

My father, a lawyer and banker, had left behind a modest amount for my mother, and I had to journey through a nettlesome bureaucratic labyrinth to ensure her financial security. I discovered that the Indian bureaucracy was as inflexible in its attitudes and accommodations during someone's bereavement as at other times: my father's cremation was held up for more than an hour because some obscure clause in the local municipality's rule-book called for the filling-out of a certain form; but the municipal office had run out of blanks, and I had to wait until the remaining one could be photocopied. In India the bureaucracy rules supreme in death as it does in life.

A Brahman priest invited me to chant Sanskrit hymns. On the plane to Bombay, I had read up on the origins of these hymns. In lyrical language that goes back to ancient Aryan times, these hymns invoke the blessing of the gods for the soul of the departed. They ask the gods not only to forgive him for his mortal sins but also to release him from the cycle of death and rebirth.

In the thirteen days of mourning that were to follow, I volunteered for every religious *pooja* and ritual that Hindu sons traditionally perform in India – not because I felt obliged to go through the motions but because these ceremonies revealed to me the significance of symbolism in everyday Indian life. I sat through rites before tiny mounds of rice and sweetmeats, which were symbolic offerings to the soul of my dead father and to the spirits of my ancestors over the millennia; I washed the feet of the officiating Brahman priest in acknowledgement of the Brahmans' centuries-old stewardship of Hinduism; and I poured milk and rose-water over coconuts to solicit the blessings of my own male forefathers for continuation of the male line in the family (the coconuts symbolized the collective bodies of my ancestors). They were complex rituals, and the priest, a cheerful man named Pandurang Gulwani, patiently explained the significance of every one of them.

As I lit the sandalwood heaped on my father's funeral pyre and watched the flames soar towards the clear blue February skies, I thought about what extraordinary changes my father had seen during his lifetime. He was born in the first decade of this century, when India was a colony of an imperial power that wasn't greatly interested in the economic well-being of its subjects. My father lived through the founding and flowering of India's nationalist movement, through two world wars in which Indian soldiers served heroically, and through a time that saw the rise and triumph of men like Mahatma Gandhi and Jawaharlal Nehru. Indeed, I was conceived the morning after India achieved her independence from Britain – my parents, who had been married for nearly a decade by then, were determined that their first child be born in a free India.

My father, who believed in destiny, lived to see the establishment of modern India's great political dynasty – Nehru, his daughter Indira Gandhi, and her son Rajiv Gandhi. He was proud of this dynasty's achievements, and I always felt that he was a trifle disappointed that I did not share all his enthusiasms. On that breezy February morning after the cremation, I gathered my father's ashes in a small brass urn and consecrated them to the high tide of the Arabian Sea, on whose shores my father would take me for long walks when I was a child. During those walks he would often tell me how proud he was that I would grow up in a free India where men could dream limitless dreams. He would talk about the certain possibility that in my lifetime I would see more change than he and all his forebears combined.

Such change would bring with it great challenges, my father often said when I was a child and in his subsequent letters to me after I had settled abroad. But he would always add that it was not the change that really mattered, nor even the resulting challenges to the traditional ways of an ancient land. What mattered was the capacity of Indians to deal with the change and challenges.

About that capacity there was – in his mind, and now in mine – a big question-mark. And so, when I think about the legacy of my father, what comes to mind is not only his warmth, his gift of love and caring, his profoundly moral conviction that work is the best form of worship, and his belief that good will ultimately triumph over evil.

I also reflect, especially in these times of head-spinning change in India, on the questions he often raised during his remarkable lifetime. Are we, as Indians, really capable of meeting the challenges to our timeworn attitudes and lifestyles? And can we seize the time and transform our society to ensure a better life not just for the privileged few, but for everybody? The rhetoric of politicians and the penmanship of journalists often overlooks the fundamental fact that Bombay and Delhi alone do not constitute India: the vast majority of Indians live in small towns and villages, and many of these millions have not had the opportunity to participate in the progress of the past four decades.

Not long after my father's death, I was going through his papers when I came across an ancient notebook. It was a diary that he had kept during the independence struggle. He had jotted his impressions about the titans of his time – Mahatma Gandhi, Jawaharlal Nehru, Maulana Azad, Sarojini Naidu, Vallabhbhai Patel. It was a time of excitement, and it was a time of hope. I moved down the pages to the post-independence entries, and one particular section caught my eye.

'Indians are clamouring for deep, constructive change,' my father had written in Marathi, his native language. 'They have suffered for so long, but they are a patient people. How much longer will they suffer, how much longer will they be patient?'

He wrote those words just around the time I was born, some forty years ago. In the four decades since India's independence, people's threshhold of patience has been steadily lowered – but perhaps never more alarmingly than in the years following the murder of Indira Gandhi.

Her murder was the most momentous event of recent Indian history – an explosion that ended an era closely linked to an earlier generation and brought forth a new leadership and a new approach to India's modernization. The murder of Indira Gandhi in her own garden by two trusted Sikh security guards on 31 October 1984 changed for ever the political landscape of India, and arguably of the Third World as well. It touched off a holocaust in which thousands of innocent Sikhs in northern India were massacred by Hindu mobs who were blessed, if not led, by factotums of the ruling Congress Party. The very idea of secularism, ardently espoused by Mrs Gandhi's father, Jawaharlal Nehru, and so eloquently enshrined in the Indian Constitution, was suddenly threatened. Government in the capital city of Delhi was paralyzed.

The question on everyone's mind then was: will India, the world's biggest democracy, survive as one nation?

Now, five years after Indira Gandhi's assassination, that remains the central question as India rolls into the last decade of this extraordinary century and prepares for the next millennium.

CHAPTER ONE:
THE ASSASSINATION OF
INDIRA GANDHI

On the morning of Wednesday, 31 October Indira Gandhi woke up, as usual, at six o'clock and rang for her valet, Nathuram, who fetched her a customary pot of piping hot tea. Mrs Gandhi, barely a month short of her sixty-eighth birthday, then quickly scanned several local Hindi and English-language newspapers – another daily practice. Many of the papers carried front-page articles about her journey, the previous day, through the eastern state of Orissa, where she had made a number of appearances at political rallies.

It was dully cold in her bedroom – few Delhi homes, including Mrs Gandhi's, are equipped with central heating – and the portable electric heater seemed to work unsatisfactorily. Mrs Gandhi rose and spent a few minutes on limbering yoga exercises, bathed, put on a bright orange saree, and joined her grandchildren Priyanka and Rahul, and their mother Sonia – Rajiv Gandhi's wife – for breakfast. Rajiv was in West Bengal that morning on a political mission for his mother, the prime minister, who was widely expected to announce soon the date for India's national parliamentary elections.

The morning meal consisted of toast, cereals, freshly squeezed orange juice, eggs and tea. After that the children would set off for school. Mrs Gandhi asked Rahul and Priyanka how they felt. The previous evening, the car in which they were travelling was rammed by a van that shot through a red traffic light not far from the prime minister's residence at One Safdarjung Road in Delhi. The children weren't hurt, and the prime minister's security staff reported that there was nothing sinister about the accident.

As Mrs Gandhi talked to the children, who seemed in good spirits, two aides entered the dining-room. One was Rajendra Kumar Dhawan, a short, pleasant 47-year-old man with slickly oiled hair that appeared permanently plastered down on his scalp. Dhawan had served Mrs Gandhi for almost twenty years and was probably her most trusted subordinate. It was nearly time to leave for her first appointment of the day, Dhawan told the prime minister. She nodded, then kissed and hugged her grandchildren, and walked into her small study to flip through a pile of government files that Dhawan had already placed on her desk.

On her desk was something that Mrs Gandhi had written in her own hand. It was a sort of last will and testament. Of her aides, only Dhawan had read it, even though the document wasn't quite complete. He had once asked her about it, and Mrs Gandhi had shrugged the question away. But Dhawan, like some others who worked in close proximity to the prime minister, was aware that she had recently seemed rather distracted. A longtime friend and adviser, Professor Ralph Buultjens, had even heard her reflect about the possibility that some harm might befall her.

Mrs Gandhi's mood worried people like the New York-based Buultjens, and Dhawan, who had been concerned about her safety since the Indian army's assault in June 1984 on Sikhism's holiest shrine, the Golden Temple in Amritsar. The army had flushed out Sikh terrorists who had been holed up in the Temple, but not before hundreds of men, women and children, who had come as pilgrims to Amritsar, died in the crossfire between the terrorists and the military. Mrs Gandhi had been determined not to yield to the terrorists' demand for a separate nation, which they wanted to be carved out of the north-western state of Punjab, India's granary. Although the majority of the country's 14 million Sikhs did not support the separatists, the army's action in Amritsar was widely deplored in the Sikh community, not only because of the loss of lives but also because of extensive damage to the Sikh shrine.

Among Mrs Gandhi's aides, as among Indians all across this vast country of 800 million people, there was, since the Amritsar event, a growing conviction that it would be only a matter of time before Sikhs took action against the prime minister. They feared that Indira Gandhi would be killed in vengeance.

Was she herself seized by some premonition?

Dhawan glanced quickly at the handwritten note. This is what Mrs Gandhi had written:

I have never felt less like dying, and that calm and peace of mind is what prompts me to write what is in the nature of a will. If I die a violent death, as some fear and a few are plotting, I know the violence will be in the thought and the action of the assassin, not in my dying – for no hate is dark enough to overshadow the extent of my love for my people and my country; no force is strong enough to divert me from my purpose and my endeavour to take this country forward.

A poet has written of his 'love' – 'How can I feel humble with the wealth of you beside me?' I can say the same of India. I cannot understand how anyone can be an Indian and not be proud – the richness and infinite variety of our composite heritage, the magnificence of the people's spirit, equal to any disaster or burden, firm in their faith, gay spontaneity even in poverty and hardship.

Dhawan reminded Mrs Gandhi of her first appointment of the morning, which was with Peter Ustinov, the British actor. Ustinov planned to produce a documentary about her and, indeed, had accompanied the prime minister during some of her travels across India. The feature on Mrs Gandhi was to be part of a series tentatively called *Ustinov's People*. Now he had scheduled a final interview with Mrs Gandhi and was waiting with his film crew on the lawns behind the Safdarjung Road residence, on the side facing Akbar Road. Mrs Gandhi had a special fondness for men and women of the arts, and Peter Ustinov was one of them. Moreover, Ustinov, a stout Santa Claus in mufti, was heavily involved in a cause that the prime minister herself vigorously supported – improving the plight of children. In fact, Ustinov had come to India wearing two hats: as a film producer, and as a fundraiser for UNICEF, the United Nations Children's Fund. Later Ustinov would say that he had wanted to ask Mrs Gandhi how as an only child she came to terms with loneliness.

Ustinov's interview was scheduled for 9.20 a.m. He thought the Akbar Road lawn would be an ideal spot because of its picturesque location. It was a cool, late autumn morning, with just a nip in the air, and the roses in Mrs Gandhi's garden were in full bloom. Behind the lawn was the prime minister's residential office, where she often received visitors in the morning before her usual journey to the ornate, more formal prime ministerial office in South Block, near Parliament House; this building, and a tall hedge next to it, separated the Akbar Road area from Mrs Gandhi's living quarters at One Safdarjung Road.

At 9.15, Mrs Gandhi stepped out of her home, with Narayan Singh, a Delhi policeman, holding an umbrella over her head to shield her from the sun. Dhawan followed. Behind them were Rameshwar Dayal, a local police sub-inspector, and Nathuram, Mrs Gandhi's valet. She walked briskly, as was her custom, towards the Akbar Road office. As she neared a hedge, she spotted Beant Singh, a Sikh policeman who had been part of her security guard for six years. She smiled at the 28-year-old Beant, a tall, bearded man. The prime minister had resisted pleas from aides to have him transferred in the wake of the assault on the Golden Temple. 'I have nothing to fear from Sikhs,' Mrs Gandhi told them.

Beant moved up to Mrs Gandhi, whipped out a pistol, pointed it at her, and fired three shots into her abdomen. Without a word, Mrs Gandhi started to fall to the ground. There was a nonplussed look on her face. But before her body slumped, another Sikh guard, Satwant Singh, twenty-one years old, emerged from the hedge and opened up with a Thompson automatic carbine. Mrs Gandhi's body was nearly lifted from the ground by these powerful bullets; she was spun around by the velocity of the bullets, and then she crashed to the ground. In the space of twenty seconds, thirty-two bullets had been pumped into her small, frail body. By the time Indira Gandhi's body fell on the ground, she was quite possibly dead. It was now 9.17 a.m.

The body lay on the ground for nearly a minute before anyone took action. Her bodyguards had dived for cover. Rameshwar Dayal had been shot in the thigh from the round fired by Satwant Singh. When Dhawan and the others rose, they saw Beant and Satwant standing with their hands raised; they had dropped their weapons.

'We have done what we set out to do,' Beant Singh said, in Hindi. 'Now you can do whatever you want to do.'

But no one attempted to grab the assailants. Mrs Gandhi's aides looked at her body and started shouting orders to one another. At this point, Sonia Gandhi ran out of the house barefoot and still in her dressing-gown, her hazel-brown hair still wet from a wash.

'Get a car!' Sonia shouted. 'Get a car!'

'Madam, there is an ambulance here,' someone responded.

A specially equipped ambulance was parked near the Safdarjung Road exit; the vehicle was kept there on a twenty-four-hour stand-by for emergencies. But on this morning, with Mrs Gandhi bleeding profusely and bits of her bones and flesh spattered on the ground, no one could find the ambulance driver. Someone said he had gone off to get some tea; someone else said the driver hadn't reported for work at all – there were no keys in the ignition switch.

Sonia Gandhi and Rajendra Kumar Dhawan then lifted Mrs Gandhi's body, with the assistance of Narayan Singh, Nathuram and Dinesh Bhatt, a security official, and carried her towards an Indian-made Ambassador car that was parked nearby. She was placed on the back seat, with Sonia cradling her head while crouched on the floor. Dhawan, Bhatt and an aide named Fotedar, also got in. Dhawan ordered the driver to rush to the All-India Institute of Medical Sciences.

The Institute was a good twenty minutes away by car in moderate traffic; there were other medical facilities closer to the prime minister's house, such as the Ram Manohar Lohia Hospital on Baba Khark Marg. But the Institute, known locally as AIIMS, kept a special supply of Mrs Gandhi's 'O' group Rh. negative blood type; her complete medical records were also maintained there. The Ambassador car darted towards AIIMS, but the traffic this morning was heavier than usual, and it was not until ten o'clock that the vehicle finally reached the hospital, some four kilometres away from the prime minister's home. Dhawan tried to administer artificial respiration, but he could already see that there were few signs of life in Mrs Gandhi.

Back at One Safdarjung Road, meanwhile, it had not occurred to anyone to telephone AIIMS to warn hospital authorities that Mrs Gandhi was being brought there. Various security guards scurried about the area where Beant Singh and Satwant Singh still stood, their weapons on the ground. Then someone suggested that the two men be arrested. They were led off to a nearby guardhouse by members of the élite Indo-Tibetan Border Police. Within twenty minutes, shots were heard inside the guardhouse. Beant and Satwant had both been shot by their guards; Beant died instantly, while Satwant suffered serious injuries to his spine and kidneys. It was later explained by the government that the two Sikhs had tried to wrest away their guards' weapons in an effort to escape. But at least three officials present at the scene have testified that the

Indo-Tibetan guards abused the Sikhs verbally and then shot them.

When the prime minister's car arrived at the emergency entrance of the All-India Institute of Medical Sciences, there was no reception committee. In fact, it took the sentries more than three minutes even to open the gates leading up to the emergency section, for the guards hadn't been informed that a VIP was in critical condition. Once at the emergency unit, Dhawan and Fotedar jumped out to alert medical personnel that Mrs Gandhi lay gravely wounded outside. But no stretcher could be found. Someone got hold of a hospital trolley.

As the body was placed on the trolley, the young intern in charge of the emergency room became hysterical.

'Madam! Madam!' he started shrieking, nearly collapsing over Mrs Gandhi's crumpled, blood-covered body.

Another physician who was present in the room said to himself: 'This cannot be Indira Gandhi. She looks like a child wrapped in a washerman's sheet. Is this really the prime minister of India?'

This doctor rushed to a house phone and dialled the number of the Institute's senior cardiologist. Within five minutes, a dozen of the Institute's top physicians gathered in the emergency room, including Dr J. S. Guleria, a veteran professor of medicine, and Dr Bal Ram, the senior cardio-thoracic surgeon on duty that morning. They tried to massage Mrs Gandhi's heart. An electro-cardiogram test showed faint traces of a heartbeat.

'Her pupils were dilated – so we knew that her brain was already affected,' one physician recalled later. 'Even if we had clinically revived her, there was already permanent brain damage.' There was no pulse. One medical aide inserted an endo-tracheal tube – a rubber tube that is pushed down the mouth and windpipe – to pump oxygen to Mrs Gandhi's lungs, mainly to keep the brain alive. Two intravenous lines were set up for blood transfusion.

At this point, the decision was made to take Mrs Gandhi to the eighth-floor operating-theatre. There, in Operating-Theatre Number Two, surgeons laboured to remove bullets from her body. More than eighty pints of blood were pumped into her, four or five times the body's normal blood content. The surgeons linked Mrs Gandhi's body to a heart–lung machine, which assumed the function of pumping and purifying her blood. The surgeons wanted to ensure that her body's metabolism rate slowed down and that her blood pressure dropped – this was done through the heart–lung machine, which cooled the blood from the normal 37 degrees Centigrade to 31 degrees.

Present in Operating-Theatre Number Two were the finest of the physicians and surgeons attached to the All-India Institute of Medical Sciences, which has long been the country's showcase medical teaching and research facility. In addition to Dr Guleria and Dr Bal Ram, there were cardio-thoracic surgeons P. Venugopal and A. Sampat Kumar; and general surgeons Shukla, Dhawan and Kapoor. The anaesthetist was G. R. Gode. They found that the bullets Beant Singh and Satwant Singh pumped into her had ruptured the right lobe of Mrs Gandhi's liver. There were at least twelve perforations in the large intestine and there was extensive damage to the small intestine. The heart was intact, but one lung was shot through. Blood vessels, arteries and veins had burst. Bones and vertebrae were shattered. The spinal cord was severed.

Nothing that the surgeons could do would bring Indira Gandhi back to life. 'She was already far, far gone by the time she was brought to the Institute,' one surgeon said later. 'In fact, Mrs Gandhi was probably dead by the time she hit the ground in her garden at Safdarjung Road.'

At 2.30 that afternoon, five hours after she was shot in her garden, Indira Gandhi was officially declared dead.

On the morning of Wednesday, 31 October Vichitra Sharma was preparing to leave her home in Delhi's Maharani Bagh for her office in Connaught Place, the capital's bustling downtown section. Sharma, then thirty years old, lived with her parents in one of Delhi's wealthy residential neighbourhoods; it is uncommon for single women to live away from home, even in sophisticated urban India, and besides, Delhi was at the time experiencing a dreadful housing crisis.

Vichitra Sharma was what her colleagues call a 'star'. Her star shone at the *Hindustan Times*, one of Delhi's leading English-language dailies. At the *Hindustan Times*, Sharma's star was a fiery one, because she often challenged governmental policy at a newspaper widely known for its general allegiance to the ruling Congress party.

She was a small woman, with large expressive eyes. Her

reporting assignments had taken Sharma all over India, but in the last year or so she had been especially focusing on labour and political issues in Delhi. She had recently written an acclaimed series of articles on medical politics at the All-India Institute of Medical Sciences. For that series, she was to win one of India's most prestigious journalistic awards.

At 10.30 on this morning, Sharma was about to step out of her parents' two-storey house when the telephone rang. The caller was A. R. Wig, Sharma's immediate superior and the newspaper's chief reporter. Wig asked Sharma to go immediately to the All-India Institute of Medical Sciences.

'Indira Gandhi's been hurt,' he said. 'We think she was taken to the Institute. You know a lot of people there. Why don't you try and get in there and see what you can find out?'

Sharma's first reaction to Wig's call was that perhaps the prime minister had been injured at some political rally. Sharma was scheduled to cover one of Mrs Gandhi's forthcoming campaign visits through the neighbouring state of Uttar Pradesh, and a colleague at the *Hindustan Times* had cautioned her to expect stone-throwing incidents in that politically volatile province, where Mrs Gandhi was not universally popular.

Sharma hailed a taxi outside her home. The thirteen-kilometre ride to the Institute took nearly thirty minutes. There were no signs of any unusual activity at the hospital's gate; no crowds had gathered. Sharma wandered for a few minutes around the Institute's academic block, hoping to spot a familiar face. She spotted a young physician who had been a source for her recent articles on the Institute. He told her that he'd just come out of the emergency room, assisting the surgeons who were trying to revive the mortally wounded prime minister.

'Look, the whole eighth-floor area has been sealed off by security guards,' the physician, Dr Rizvi, said to Sharma. 'If you want to go anywhere near the area where Mrs Gandhi is, then go as a blood donor. We badly need the 'O' group Rh. negative type blood.'

'She's not dead, then,' Sharma said.

'She's in very bad shape,' Dr Rizvi said.

Vichitra Sharma slipped into the Institute's main building. She was stopped by a security guard on the main floor.

'No one allowed,' the guard said.

'But I'm going to give blood,' Sharma said.

'Then you may enter,' the guard said. 'The blood bank is up ahead.'

Sharma knew enough about the building's layout to circumvent the blood bank and head towards the stairwell that would take her to the eighth floor. Over the next ten hours this stairwell, which, surprisingly, was unmanned by security guards, would be Sharma's repeated route back and forth from the eighth-floor operating-theatre to the main floor, where Delhi's VIPs would gather.

As Sharma climbed the stairs, she ran into a woman who was rushing down. The woman was in tears.

'She's gone, she's gone!' the woman cried.

'How could it be?' Sharma said.

'I saw it upstairs. The doctors have given up.'

Once upstairs, Sharma found the eighth-floor corridor outside Operating-Theatre Number Two filled with guards and various hospital personnel. No one tried to stop her. She surreptitiously took notes. Now there was a crescendo of murmurs. Delhi's VIPs had started arriving. Sharma recognized a woman named Shehnaz Hussain, Mrs Gandhi's personal beautician. Miss Hussain wore a long, flowing yellow evening dress. Sharma also recognized several members of Parliament belonging to Mrs Gandhi's Congress Party. Socialites started showing up; some junior cabinet ministers followed.

Sharma decided to check out the scene downstairs on the main floor. There she found that many senior cabinet ministers were ensconced in a conference room. Some of them were weeping; most seemed numb.

Outside the conference room someone tapped Sharma's shoulder.

'Excuse me, but can you do me a favour?' a man asked Sharma. 'My boss, the health minister Shri Shankaranand, is in that room. Can you tell him that his driver is waiting outside and wants to know if the boss will come home for lunch?'

'Why don't you go in yourself?' Sharma said.

'I cannot do that. I am only a lowly employee.'

Sharma delivered the message, but Shankaranand seemed too distraught to understand what she was saying. It struck Sharma that these cabinet ministers had slid into a kind of collective coma.

'What kind of men were these?' Sharma would say later. 'I realized then that she had made puppets out of every one of them –

and now she was no longer around to pull the strings. In her years of power, she'd taken away the manhood from every one of these men – so now they were like zombies, not knowing what to do, no initiative coming from them. It occurred to me how propitious a time it was for some determined military man to seize power at this very moment.'

Upstairs, the surgeons kept pumping blood into Mrs Gandhi's body. They went on furiously trying to remove the bullets, trying to revive her – knowing full well that she was long dead. But no one had ordered them to desist – so they kept up their efforts.

At four o'clock in the afternoon, Rajiv Gandhi, Mrs Gandhi's son and heir-apparent, arrived at the All-India Institute of Medical Sciences. At the time when Mrs Gandhi was brought into the eighth-floor operating-theatre, the forty-year-old Gandhi had been more than a thousand miles away in Contai, in the state of West Bengal. It was an hour or so later, on his way to yet another political rally, that Gandhi's motorcade was stopped by a police jeep at a place called Heria. It was there that a police inspector told him about the assassination attempt.

A number of Congress Party workers around him started to weep, but Rajiv Gandhi kept his poise and even comforted some of them. A police officer told him that an Indian air-force helicopter was waiting at a place called Kolaghat to transport Gandhi to Calcutta or some nearby military air base from where an air-force jet would speed him back to Delhi. But when Gandhi's motorcade reached Kolaghat, there was no helicopter there. Apparently it had already been despatched to Mahisadal, which would have been the next destination on Gandhi's schedule that morning. A policeman rang Mahisadal to ask for the helicopter to be sent back to Kolaghat.

While he waited, clad in a *khadi* homespun flowing white shirt called the *kurta*, and in loose pyjama trousers, with his trademark Kashmir woollen shawl draped around his shoulders, Rajiv Gandhi appeared to the men and women around him a picture of cool composure. He fiddled with the dials of his portable Sony transistor radio and finally raised the BBC. The British Broadcasting Corporation's overseas service was already saying that Indira Gandhi was dead, but Rajiv Gandhi had also turned in alternately to All-India Radio, the government network, which was playing Hindi film music.

'It's all very confusing,' Gandhi said, to no one in particular.

There was confusion, too, at the All-India Institute of Medical Sciences when he eventually arrived. Government officials were fluttering about like pigeons, arguing among themselves whether the government-owned radio and television networks should announce the prime minister's death. There were angry comments about Sikhs in general, and about Mrs Gandhi's Sikh assailants in particular. There was some discussion also about whether Indira Gandhi's body should remain at the hospital or be taken back to One Safdarjung Road.

Rajiv Gandhi stayed inside Operating-Theatre Two until about six o'clock in the evening. By now the corridor outside was thick with Congress Party workers, cabinet ministers and their families, and assorted hangers-on.

Vichitra Sharma stood next to a group of wealthy Delhi socialites.

'I must go inside to show my face to Rajivji,' one of these socialites said. 'He must know we took the trouble to come here at a time like this.'

Sharma thought: in India it is so important to be seen doing the right thing in front of the powers-that-be.

When Rajiv Gandhi left, the corridor was quickly emptied of people. A physician who knew Sharma told her that Gandhi had said he would return at 7.30 p.m. to collect his mother's body.

By 9.30 p.m., he hadn't come back. Sharma went into the operating-theatre to look at the body. Indira Gandhi lay there, alone and dead and unattended, on a cold steel table. No family member was present, just some curious medical orderlies who would occasionally slip into the room.

'I was in tears,' Sharma said later. 'Here was a woman who ruled India, who was so powerful until that very morning. And now she lay there cold and lifeless. And no one was there to pay her the courtesy of guarding her body. It was pathetic.

'I felt numb. Before me lay a woman who was once so majestic. Now she was a mere body, crusted with blood and surrounded by ugly tubes and bottles and equipment. Right before my eyes I saw that an era had ended, that something had gone from our lives for all time.'

CHAPTER TWO: 'WHAT NOW?'

On the morning of Wednesday, 31 October I was getting ready to visit my 76-year-old father, who was in hospital in Bombay with an ailment of the oesophagus.

It was a typical Bombay morning: the sky was cloudless and blue, the sunlight was strong and the humidity heavy. The roar of automobiles, scooters and lorries, accompanied by the tinkling of a thousand bicycle bells, rushed in through the open windows of a friend's apartment where I was staying. I could hear polyglot hawkers outside, proclaiming the fine virtues of their fruit or fresh fish or vegetables, and there were also the dull drumbeat and rhythmic mantras of a *sadhu*, a mendicant who had brought along his sacred brahma bull for makeshift worship by Hindu pedestrians as they trudged to their offices. Somewhere in the neighbourhood, a muezzin's voice was being broadcast by a public-address system perched on a mosque's minaret: faithful Moslems were being summoned to prayer. The fragrance from a magnolia tree outside floated into the apartment as well, mixed with the fumes from the traffic.

I had slept badly. The air-conditioning had stopped working, and someone in an adjacent apartment in this ancient block of flats had played cacophonous Hindustani film music throughout much of the night. The first order of the day was, as it is for every Hindu, the morning ablution, and as I showered away the night's accumulated sweat from my skin, the telephone rang.

A frisson of fear rode up my back; I thought it was someone calling with bad news from the hospital. But the caller turned out to be Malavika Sanghvi, the wife of one of my closest friends, Vir Sanghvi. Vir was then the editor of *Imprint* magazine, one of the country's most respected monthlies, and Malavika herself was fashioning a formidable reputation as one of the liveliest young writers in India.

'Can you come over?' Malavika said. 'It's quite important.'

'Are you both all right?' I said.

'Yes, yes, we are okay,' she said. 'There's nothing wrong with us. But come over if you can. I can't tell you over the phone, but I think something terrible has happened.'

The Sanghvis lived several miles away on Carmichael Road, in one of the smartest residential neighbourhoods of Bombay. I dressed hurriedly, dashed out of the apartment, and hailed a taxi. The driver was a jolly man of the local Maratha community, called Ramchandra Moray. Like most Bombay taxi-drivers, he was used to breakneck driving, which is to say that there was no need for me to tell him that my journey was urgent. Moray cheerfully cursed the thick traffic in his native language of Marathi, he cursed in Hindi, he even cursed in pidgin English. He very nearly ploughed into a bullock-cart near Marine Drive, the long, curving corniche that links south Bombay to the northern, hilly neighbourhoods of Malabar Hill and Carmichael Road. Moray challenged other taxis in a series of spurts through the dense traffic. I held on to the worn leather handles of the back door, too terrified to think much about why Malavika Sanghvi had called me. Each time I tried to reflect on my brief conversation with her, Moray would jerk his taxi to within millimetres of a major accident. Moray deposited me in front of the Sanghvis' building in eleven minutes flat. I never wanted to ride with this man again, but I nevertheless asked him to wait for me, for taxis were usually hard to get in this part of town during the busy morning hours.

Malavika Sanghvi, a tall, striking woman of twenty-six, was ashen-faced when she opened the door of her apartment.

'Indira Gandhi has been shot,' Malavika said.

I looked at my watch, a reporter's habit. It was ten-fifteen.

'What? How do you know this?' I asked her.

'A family friend telephoned my father,' she said. 'My father phoned me. Vir left for an appointment before my dad's call, so I thought I'd see if you could find out more about this.'

'How did this family friend get the news?'

'She's the wife of the foreign secretary and she happens to be in Bombay at the moment. Her husband phoned her from Delhi. She didn't tell my dad anything more. All she knew was that Mrs

Gandhi was shot in her garden just after nine o'clock this morning. Can you find out more?'

I reached for my briefcase, which I always carry – another old habit – and retrieved my phone book. I looked up the number of Hari Jaisingh, the editor of the Bombay edition of the *Indian Express*, the country's largest English-language newspaper. He, if anyone, would have the latest news. I had his direct number at the newspaper office; Jaisingh answered the phone himself.

I identified myself.

'Where are you?' Jaisingh asked.

'In Bombay,' I said.

'Welcome, welcome,' he said, ever the gracious Indian.

'Thanks. Now tell me, is it true that Mrs Gandhi has been shot?'

There was a slight pause.

'Yes, we just got the news on the ticker. Two security guards. We think they were Sikhs, who else? But no confirmation yet. Come over to the office, if you can. We should soon know more. But I must tell you, it's pandemonium here.'

I asked Malavika where we could reach Vir.

'He's probably already reached his astrologer's office by now,' Malavika said.

'Vir believes in astrology?' I said. I hadn't known about this aspect of my friend's life.

'Devoutly.'

'Let's call him.'

Malavika dialled the astrologer's number. Vir was summoned to the phone.

'Vir, we've heard that Mrs Gandhi was shot just a while back,' I said.

'You're joking,' Vir said.

'No,' I said. 'I just talked with Hari Jaisingh at the *Express* and he said the news is already on the ticker.'

'You're joking.'

'No, really.'

'God, I don't know what to say.'

'Let's meet later in the day. I'm off to the *Express* office to get more details.'

'I'm absolutely stunned,' Vir said. 'I just don't know what to say.'

'Ask your astrologer what's in store for India,' I said, and immediately regretted my flippancy.

We agreed to meet for lunch at one o'clock at Chopsticks, a Chinese restaurant in the Churchgate area, not far from Vir's office. Chopsticks was favoured by many Bombay journalists. Malavika promised to join us there.

Downstairs, Moray was listening to his transistor radio. A small, plump man with a handle-bar moustache and betel-leaf-stained teeth, he was drenched in sweat, and for a moment I thought he'd heard the news on the radio. But it was the humidity. Moray had been enjoying music on All-India Radio. It would not be until six o'clock that evening that India's government broadcasting network would formally announce the death of Mrs Gandhi, almost nine hours after the prime minister had been shot. The agency's bureaucrats waited because none of their superiors would take the initiative and give the go-ahead to broadcast the dreadful news until a cabinet minister had personally given permission – but, as it happened on this day, the entire cabinet was paralyzed with fear and numbness in Delhi.

I was tempted to tell Moray what I'd heard, but I resisted the impulse. Had I said anything to him, he would no doubt have asked me how I knew, and then I'd have to explain and elaborate, and my Marathi was simply not good enough to sustain an entire conversation – I'd lived in America for twenty years, and this had considerably eroded my native vocabulary.

I directed Moray to the *Indian Express* building at Nariman Point, a good five miles from Malavika Sanghvi's apartment. I also asked him to drive more slowly this time. I wanted to observe the scene, I said.

'Scene? Sahib, what is there left to see in Bombay?' Moray said. 'The city has become so ugly. All tall buildings, no space left. Ugliness everywhere. Too many people. Eight million, nine million people, and still growing. You want to see scenery? I will take you to the Hanging Gardens on Malabar Hill. About the only open space left in this city. You wish to go to the gardens?'

'Never mind,' I said. 'Please drive slowly. I just want to think.'

'What is there to think?' Moray said. 'Just listen to my radio.'

He drove, the radio on low volume. Still no word about Mrs Gandhi's condition. Indira Gandhi shot? Had Malavika Sanghvi and Hari Jaisingh together been playing a practical joke on me? But how would Malavika have known that I would telephone Jaisingh for confirmation concerning the shooting? As the taxi grunted along, I thought about the fact that the news had not quite fully hit me. So far I had reacted as a reporter would: find reliable sources, get the facts, be cautious, do not leap to conclusions. There simply had been no time to react at a personal level; it was too soon to react as an Indian. But one thought kept turning in my head: she may not have been very good for the country, and she may even have been disastrous, but she was always a splendid woman.

There were rivers of people on the pavements of Bombay, men and women and children and beggars and *sadhus* and urchins. They cascaded through the streets. Spindly men pushed two-wheeled carts laden with cartons and crates. Cats scratched in garbage mounds. When my taxi stopped for red lights, miserable women would come running towards my vehicle, thrusting at me babies with bloated bellies and watery eyes. 'Babu, a *paisa* for food,' the women would say, each echoing the other in what seemed to be a rehearsed refrain. An occasional mangy dog tried to cross the flood of traffic, only to return frightened and yelping to the pavement.

The small readymade-clothes shops in various neighbourhoods were brightly lit inside, and even at this relatively early commercial hour seemed to be packed. Salesmen and customers were haggling, and as I drove past they seemed like characters in some pantomime; the *mithai* shops, with their garish handpainted signs, had already begun attracting clientèle lured by their assortment of greasy, *ghee*-dripping sweetmeats. There were no anxious knots of people gathered in the street around a transistor radio, as happens in India when some momentous event is being announced on the air.

Life seemed to go on as if nothing had happened. And why should it not? How many of those people would have heard about the shooting? In most Third World countries, the radio is about the only instant source of news for most people – and in most of these countries the radio network is usually operated by the government, which is not inclined to broadcast unfavourable news with any alacrity. As Moray took me down Hughes Road, then through the access road leading into Marine Drive, I saw newsboys peddling the early editions of *Midday* and the *Free Press Bulletin*, Bombay's afternoon tabloids. I strained to see the headlines as we passed the urchins, but there was nothing about the shooting.

Shooting? It seemed very unreal. Sikh assailants? A death in the morning?

I suddenly remembered that I had promised to visit my father at the Bhatia General Hospital. I asked Moray to turn in the direction of Tardeo, the neighbourhood where the hospital was located. Moray shrugged, and spun the taxi around. We were caught in a minor traffic jam near the Gowalia Tank area. Moray cursed. Then he drove through a red light. A policeman, clad in a shabby khaki uniform, blew his whistle in protest, but Moray happily disregarded the warning. It struck me that if Indira Gandhi had indeed been shot, and if she were to die or be incapacitated, I should scratch my travel plans, no matter what my professional commitments in New York. I would be witnessing history here.

Bhatia Hospital was an aging, six-storey building of no particular distinction. The sentry at the main entrance saluted me smartly. (I had given him a few rupees the previous week to mark Diwali, the Hindu New Year.) The elevator wasn't working, so I walked up to the fifth-floor ward where my father had taken a private room. Someone was playing a transistor on one of the floors, filling the corridors with music – Hindi film music, what else? My parents were waiting for me. I decided to give them the news.

'What I'm about to tell you is very confidential,' I said, still breathless from climbing the stairs, 'but I just heard that Indira Gandhi has been shot.'

'We already know,' my mother said.

'How?' I said, disbelievingly.

'The doctor was just in here. His sister called to tell him. Apparently her husband is in Delhi on some business and he heard the news there, so he phoned her immediately. It's a wonder he got through on the phone.'

My father was furiously tapping a pen on a writing board. Since his tracheotomy – undertaken to ease the pressure on his windpipe and enable him to breath through a tube inserted under his neck – he'd been rendered voiceless. He was reduced to expressing himself through writing down all his communications. He pointed to a sheet of paper on which he'd written something.

'I knew this would happen,' my father had written. 'It was destined on the day she launched the attack on the Golden Temple. This is vengeance.'

'Vengeance?' I said.

'What do you expect?' my father wrote out on his shiny white pad. 'You send in troops to the Temple, you take untold lives. You don't know how fanatical Sikhs are. What is the Biblical saying – an eye for an eye, a tooth for a tooth? This is one life avenged for a thousand lives taken in June. But this life was worth more than all of them. This life was priceless.'

He was referring to the Indian army's invasion of the Golden Temple in Amritsar. Indira Gandhi had sent in her troops to flush out the Sikh terrorists who had taken sanctuary there. The terrorists, led by a fanatical fundamentalist named Sant Jarnail Singh Bhindranwale, had launched a campaign to carve out an independent theocratic Sikh state out of the Punjab, one of India's wealthiest provinces and the granary for much of its population of 800 million people. The Sikh separatists planned to call their new nation Khalistan.

Bhindranwale's men had gunned down some of the moderate Sikhs who opposed them and also some Hindus around Punjab state. The basis of the Khalistan campaign was, as Bhindranwale himself often thundered out in speeches, the claim that Sikhs were being discriminated against by India's majority Hindus – an argument that ran counter to the fact that India's Sikhs had become just about the country's most affluent ethnic minority community. There was widespread anguish among India's 14 million Sikhs over the army's action, which resulted in Bhindranwale's death and the destruction of some parts of the historic Golden Temple. And in the wake of the military operation, on 6 June 1984, there was also a widespread conviction among Indians that Sikhs would exact revenge by killing Mrs Gandhi.

My father stopped writing and signalled to a nurse in the room, who wheeled in a suction machine, attached a rubber tube to my father's trachea, and flushed out his lungs so that he could breathe without gasping.

'But how do you know that she is dead?' I said, presently. 'Perhaps she will live.'

'Vengeance,' my father wrote, slowly. 'When you shoot someone in vengeance, you shoot to kill. She must be dead. What a tragedy, what a loss to this nation. Nehru's daughter dead.'

Then he started crying, this very frail old man. It was the first time in my life that I had seen tears in my father's eyes.

On the morning of Wednesday, 31 October Ramchandra Moray was in a particularly good frame of mind. The previous day, he'd paid off the last instalment of a 60,000-rupee – the equivalent of about $6,000 – bank loan he had taken out to buy his Fiat taxi, and now the vehicle was no longer, as Indians like to put it, 'hypothecated' to the Bank of Baroda; the car was all his. The previous week, Moray's wife had given birth to a boy they named Santosh – their first son, after six daughters – and Moray, who had recently turned forty, was convinced that the stars were finally aligned just right for him.

Moray lived with his wife, Anasuya, and their children in the Colaba section of Bombay, a neighbourhood of fashionable apartment buildings in whose shadow sit block upon block of squat, squalid tenements, known locally as chawls. The Moray family occupied two rooms in one of these chawls; their apartment was squeezed above a small restaurant off a street named Allana Marg. The restaurant specialized in *idlis*, the rice pancakes favoured by many people in South India, where rice is the main crop. Ramchandra Moray had no particular liking for *idlis*; he was a good, robust consumer of mutton and chicken dishes, which he insisted that Anasuya prepared for breakfast.

On this morning, there was no Anasuya around to prepare breakfast. She was a hundred miles away in her hometown of Alibagh, where she'd given birth. Also with her were the six Moray daughters – aged from sixteen to seven – and Ramchandra was alone in his dwelling. He woke up at eight o'clock, which was an hour later than usual for him, pumped the kerosene stove in the alcove kitchen and made himself a strong brew of tea: he put so much sugar into his teacup that the spoon was virtually cemented into place, erect. He then bathed in the tiny communal bathroom just outside his apartment, lit several *aggarbattis*, or joss sticks, at the small altar above his bed and prayed for fifteen minutes before the pictures of the Hindu gods Krishna and Shiva. The prayers were of gratitude over the fact that he was now the father of a son: the Moray family name was now assured of continuity. At the end of his devotional session, Moray applied a little *tikka* on his forehead, a dab of red vermilion which signifies that a Hindu man has performed a religious duty.

Ordinarily Moray left home at about eight o'clock every morning. He checked the engine of his taxi, lit another *aggarbatti* in front of a small picture of Shiva on the dashboard, and was off. He drove till noon, returned home for lunch, took a nap for an hour, and was back driving his taxi until seven or eight in the evening. This effort netted him about 200 rupees every day, or the equivalent of $15. This was a relatively handsome income in a country where the *per capita* income statistically was $250, but where annual incomes of less than $100 were the lot for most people.

On this day, Moray decided to relax. He slipped on a pair of *chappals*, the hardy, thonged sandals favoured by many Bombayites, and went for a walk. Around the corner from his home, on Colaba Causeway, he stopped at a roadside newsstand and bought a copy of *Navakal*, a local Marathi-language newspaper. One of the articles on the front page was about Prime Minister Indira Gandhi. She had toured the eastern state of Orissa the previous day and visited a number of military facilities. At a place called Gopalpur, she laid the foundation stone of a new military school for guided-missile training.

That same day, Moray read in the newspaper, Indira Gandhi spoke at a rally in Bhubaneshwar, the capital of Orissa State. It was a typical political rally, which is to say that hundreds of thousands of people had gathered in an open-air parade ground to get a glimpse of her and to applaud her, no matter what she said. Many of these people had been brought from their remote rural homes in buses hired by the local Congress Party. The party always seemed to have plenty of cash for such things; it was also blessed with a cadre of skilled political aides who travelled from state to state ensuring that Mrs Gandhi's public appearances went off well.

In her thirty-minute speech in Hindi, Mrs Gandhi spoke about the dangers of communalism and about external threats to India's security. Then she recalled that in some quarters there was considerable political hostility to her and that sometimes the situation got out of hand. She recalled that only the previous day someone had hurled a stone at her at a rally.

'But I am not afraid of these things,' the newspaper quoted Mrs Gandhi as saying. 'I don't mind if my life goes in the service of the nation. If I die today, every drop of my blood will invigorate the nation. Every drop of my blood, I am sure, will contribute to the growth of this nation to make it strong and dynamic.'

Moray, not a man to be especially moved by political rhetoric, shrugged as he read the newspaper. He did not think that Indira Gandhi's seventeen-year tenure had been all that beneficial for India's poor; she certainly hadn't done much for his own hometown, Alibagh, where farming was on the decline because of high production costs – a situation that forced people from peasant backgrounds, such as himself, to flee from India's 576,000 villages to big cities like Bombay in order to earn any kind of living. Moray had been lucky in being able to buy a taxi and become self-reliant; but some of his folk from Alibagh hadn't even found permanent jobs, drifting from one household to another as temporary *naukars*, or servants.

Moray walked back to his taxi and drove off. At about ten o'clock, at the point where Colaba Causeway meets Sohrab Bharucha Lane, a man in a brown safari-suit furiously flagged down Moray's taxi. I was that man.

As I entered Moray's taxi just outside the Bhatia Hospital, I found him fiddling with the dials of his transistor radio. He seemed agitated.

'I am trying to get some foreign station called the BBC,' Moray said.

'Why the BBC?' I said.

'These young fellows who were just walking by a minute ago said the BBC is saying that Indira Gandhi has been shot. Do you know how to get the BBC?'

'Does your radio have a shortwave band?'

'What is shortwave?'

'If you don't know what shortwave is, then your radio probably doesn't have it.'

I was right. No BBC would be available on Moray's transistor, which had only the local radio bands. The BBC world service had broken the news of the shooting within minutes of the event. By eleven o'clock, the BBC was saying that Mrs Gandhi was dead.

'Is it true?' Moray said.

'Is she dead?' he asked solemnly.

'I don't know if she's dead. But she was shot a little while ago in her garden in Delhi.'

'What fate! I was reading only a little while ago in *Navakal* about her speech yesterday in Orissa. She said something about not minding death in the cause of the nation. Do you believe in fate, sahib? All these things are ordained.'

I nodded, intrigued by the speech Moray referred to. He had already discarded his copy of the Marathi newspaper.

'Did the Sikhs shoot her?'

'That is what's being said.'

'Are you going to Delhi?' Moray suddenly asked.

'No, why should I? I would now like to go to the *Indian Express* building.'

'If the Sikhs shot her, there will be bloodbaths everywhere. I hope for the sake of the Sikhs that whoever shot Indira was not a Sikh.'

'I agree.'

'Sahib, do you think the Sikhs are really Indians?'

'Of course they are. Why shouldn't they be?'

'Then why did they kill Indiraji?'

'We don't know for certain if she was killed by Sikhs.'

'Tell me, sahib, if the BBC is a foreign station, how did they get this news so fast? My All-India Radio station is still playing Hindi songs.'

I told Moray that the BBC had the best radio news service in the world, that it had painstakingly carved for itself over the years a reputation for being impartial and fair – and for often being first with the news. The BBC, although a British government corporation, was rarely partisan.

Such was its reputation that officials in Delhi frequently called up the BBC's India correspondent, Mark Tully, for information and insights concerning political developments in the country! While the BBC and Radio Australia – each of whom had excellent local sources in Delhi – were broadcasting details about the Gandhi assassination, All-India Radio's executives were still awaiting orders from superiors about when to release the news of the death. But these superiors themselves did nothing until a new prime minister was selected.

As I spoke with Moray, I could not have known anything about the paralysis that had gripped the capital of Delhi, a thousand miles to the north. Moray drove in silence the rest of the way to the *Indian Express* building. I looked for signs of unusual crowd activity. The street pedlars and beggars and urchins and cart-pushers were still busily going about their business. The shops were still open. Bombay was still its usual self.

Moray drove me along Marine Drive. We passed six-and-seven-storey buildings where Bombay's wealthy live, their bedrooms and balconies facing the vast expanse of the Arabian Sea. We passed the open *maidans*, or grounds, of the Hindu, Islam and Parsi gymkhanas, the clubs set up by ethnic community leaders well before India's independence from the British in 1947 to counter the whites-only policy of the Britons' own exclusive recreation establishments. We passed the Bal Bhavan, the children's centre, where my father would bring me when I was a toddler so that I could be exposed to books and games and educational films. How the years had flown – the Bal Bhavan remained to nourish and nurture successive generations of children, but I had fled India.

At one point, there was a traffic jam: one of Bombay's 26,000 black-and-yellow taxis had come to grief against a lamppost, and a crowd had gathered out of curiosity, even though no one seemed to have been hurt. I was merely seeing one of some 5,000 traffic accidents that occur daily in Bombay, a city of 8 million people and a million vehicles. Moray told me he'd never been involved in a major accident.

'How can I afford to bang up my car?' Moray said. 'It provides me my livelihood. I have to save up for the sake of my son, Santosh.'

'Why are you already worried about your son? He's only a week old.'

'Yes, but they grow up so fast – and the cost of living moves up even faster,' Moray said. 'I went to my village last week to see the boy after his birth – and do you know how expensive the *mithai* was? But I had to distribute the sweetmeats. It is the tradition, especially when a son comes into the family. I feel very happy, sahib – a son after six daughters.'

The offices of the *Indian Express* were located on the second floor of a skyscraper known as the Express Towers. The skyscraper was situated in Nariman Point, on land that was reclaimed about ten years ago from the Arabian Sea. The newspaper was published daily in English at ten centres around the country, but Bombay's was clearly the flagship edition. The paper's owner, Ramnath Goenka, was a cranky man in his eighties who seemed fitter and more youthful than many of his far younger employees. Perhaps that was because he paid them badly. When Indira Gandhi imposed her 'Emergency' in 1975 and subjected the Indian press to censorship, Goenka was one of the few media barons who continued to criticize her. It took courage to do so, and Goenka suffered a great deal of harassment – his books were frequently audited by the tax authorities, his buildings were raided by the police, his presses were sometimes stopped in mid-edition.

His building had not aged well; large shards of plaster had peeled from its outer walls, creating an unintended illusion of rust. The stairwells were so thoroughly soaked in urine that the tiles had eroded. The elevators creaked. In many places the electrical wiring lay exposed. Across the street from the newspaper's offices was the Hotel Oberoi, a luxury facility whose coffee shop, called Samarkand, was a favourite of *Express* staffers. Many an *Express* employee, shouted at by Goenka or his irascible henchmen, had sought refuge in a beer bottle, or two, or three, at this coffee shop.

On this morning, the Samarkand was empty. India's bush telegraph was already at work, and those who could manage it had flocked into the news-room of the *Express*. By the time I reached Express Towers, security guards were posted at the entrance to the paper's offices. I elbowed my way through a thick throng struggling to get into the premises.

'No one allowed now,' a burly guard in a brown beret said, standing squarely in the middle of the doorway to the news-room. He tried to push me back.

'I have an appointment with Mr Hari Jaisingh,' I said.

'In that case, welcome!' he said.

There was a murmur in the crowd behind me.

'Why is that man being allowed in?' someone shouted, in Hindi. 'We all have appointments with this Mr Jaisingh. Let us in!'

'Go away!' the guard shouted back.

'But our prime minister has been shot,' someone protested. 'All we want is the real story. Is that too much to ask of a newspaper?'

By this time, I had slipped past the guard and was well into the cavernous news-room. I could see at once what Hari Jaisingh had meant when he told me earlier on the phone that it was 'pandemonium' there.

Virtually everyone in the room had gathered around the bank of teletype machines. People yelled every time a fresh bulletin appeared on the ticker. Sometimes they gasped. Hari Jaisingh was frenetically trying to get some of these people to leave the teletype area and return to their desks.

'Come, let's sit in my cabin,' Jaisingh said to me, giving up on the idea of re-establishing his authority in the news-room. 'What's the use of shouting at them? People will be people.'

Jaisingh is a large man with a broad forehead and tired eyes. He wore a grey safari-suit that morning, and it was badly ironed. He was a bit agitated, but he did not overlook his hostly duties: he gave me a cup of tea.

'A very high-up source just telephoned me from Delhi with very sad news,' Jaisingh said, presently. 'I am afraid that she is no more with us. Indira Gandhi is gone.'

I started to say something, but Jaisingh had swivelled his chair around to face the window. He looked out at the vast blue sea, then said:

'The question is, What now?'

Chopsticks was crowded. Among those who were enjoying ersatz Chinese food were a couple of movie actors; there was Rekha Mehta, a local writer and editor; and there was Rauf Ahmed, an amiable local publishing executive. The restaurant was abuzz with conversation. I walked in at about one o'clock, and this was what various people were saying:

'There will now be a massacre of the Sikhs.'

'Rajiv is sure to become prime minister.'

'Rajiv will impose another Emergency – a permanent one this time.'

'Will we still be a democracy tomorrow morning?'

'Maybe she's not really dead. All-India Radio is still playing music.'

'She must be dead. No one can survive after being shot at such close range.'

'How do you know about the close range?'

'The BBC said so.'

'She'll be a martyr. Maybe Rajiv will win the elections now.'

'That's right. Indira would never have won the next election.'

'Can you imagine? A pilot as our leader?'

'He's not become PM yet. Maybe they'll pick someone else.'

'Who? Who is there? They're all old farts. He's the only decent chap.'

'How could she have let Sikhs stay on as her bodyguards?'

'Sheer stupidity of her staff. They should all be arrested.'

Vir and Malavika Sanghvi were already seated at a table toward the rear of the restaurant and were eating soup. Chopsticks was one of their haunts, and because they knew my tastes they'd already ordered from the menu for me. Neither looked especially

distraught; Malavika, in fact, now appeared a great deal less pale
than when I last saw her in the morning. I filled them in on what
I'd picked up at the *Indian Express*.

Vir Sanghvi, a slim man with an intense face and large, soulful
eyes, was a whiz-kid of Indian journalism. A product of Bombay's
exclusive Campion School and Ajmer's Mayo College, he went on
to the Mill High School in London, and then obtained a master's
degree in politics, philosophy and economics at Oxford University's Brasenose College. He had started writing for Indian publications while he was still an undergraduate at Oxford. Upon his
return to India, Sanghvi helped start Bombay's first city magazine,
one modelled vaguely after the *Tatler* and *New York Magazine*.
The magazine, which he guided for three years before moving on to
the editorship of another magazine, was called *Bombay*. (It is still
flourishing as a guide to this cosmopolitan city's arts, entertainment
and trend-setting activities and activists. People still call up Sanghvi
pleading to be featured in the magazine, even though he moved on
to the editorship of a far more serious journal, *Imprint*, which ran
long, thoughtful articles on national affairs and enjoyed a dedicated
readership all over India. Sanghvi later became editor of *Sunday*,
India's biggest weekly news magazine.)

'Are you going to miss Indira?' I asked.

'I think it's fair to say that most people of my generation were
ambivalent about Indira Gandhi,' Sanghvi said. 'In 1966, when she
first became prime minister, we were too young to realize what she
stood for – I was only ten then. But by 1971, when she fought a
national election and won by a landslide – after having first broken
away from the Congress Party bosses who'd installed her in the first
place – we were all on her side. Then she won state assembly
elections all across the country in 1972 and established her creden-
tials as India's most powerful leader – one who did not need the
support of any party machine.

'My disillusionment came later. By 1974, things had begun to go
badly wrong: inflation, lawlessness, corruption – these were all on
the rise. Still, I retained a sneaking admiration for her until 1975,
when she declared the Emergency and suspended the Constitution
and jailed thousands of her political opponents. Even then, I was
prepared to buy her story: that the opposition, through its unruly,
disruptive agitations, had left her with no choice. By late 1976,
though, when her younger son Sanjay rose to be heir-apparent, it

was impossible to defend Indira Gandhi. She was clearly establishing a dynasty, and this became even clearer after Sanjay's death in an air crash in 1980 – Indira insisted that Rajiv give up his pilot's career and enter politics, even though he seemed extremely reluctant to do so at that point. For most of the last eight years of her life, I was opposed to Indira Gandhi and much of what she stood for.'

Did he feel any sadness at all at her death?

'Of course,' Sanghvi said. 'An old woman was shot to death in her own garden. There is sorrow in that. Indira did contribute to India. She provided firm, strong leadership, she ran a shrewd and intelligent foreign policy, and she believed in India as an entity, often rising above caste and communal divisions.'

What impact did she have on Indian life, I asked Sanghvi, how would he assess her legacy? I realized that it was probably much too early to ask such a question, but I wanted to try it out on him.

'She did a lot of damage,' Sanghvi said, as if he'd already expected the question. 'In retrospect it seems clear that she either destroyed or subverted most of the institutions of Indian democracy. She pretty much killed the Congress Party, which was one vehicle, especially under her father, Nehru, of ensuring that a vast country like India was ruled by consensus. She destroyed the powers of state chief ministers and damaged the federal structure. She pressurized the judiciary and sapped its independence by appointing mediocre judges and transferring to inconsequential and uncomfortable outposts those judges who dared to assert their independence. She damaged the independence of the bureaucracy by calling for a 'committed civil service'. She politicized the army by using it for civilian purposes and by manipulating promotions. She turned the cabinet into a joke by vesting unprecedented and sweeping powers in her personal staff and in her sons. And she prevented any rivals from emerging within the party – peopling it, instead, with thieves and scoundrels, in comparison to whom her elder son, Rajiv, seems positively angelic.'

What impact did Indira Gandhi's life have on his own life, I asked Sanghvi?

He reflected on that a bit, fiddled with the fried rice on his plate, then said: 'I feel tremendously let down. I came back to India with great hopes and a sense that good would prevail. But what I encountered was a cynical leader whose only concern was political survival.

'I think people now, and certainly myself included, simply have no faith in their national government. We've seen how corrupt those in government have become. It seems to me that if Rajiv becomes prime minister, he will simply have to institute major political reforms – he will have to fashion a new climate of hope and political cleanliness – if people are to trust their leaders again. I don't think his task is that difficult. Unlike a lot of other Third World countries, we still have such institutions in place as a judiciary, a parliament, a strong press. We have the two-thousand-odd officers of the Indian Administrative Service who can be galvanized into selfless service. The answers are already there – no need for Rajiv, or whoever becomes prime minister, to appoint commissions to search for solutions. I say, stop interfering with the judiciary, depoliticize the bureaucracy, lift the stifling controls over industry – and stop trying to run every little thing directly from the prime minister's office in Delhi. Let people be.'

Malavika Sanghvi had been listening attentively to her husband. I asked her how she viewed Indira Gandhi's death and the likely ascension of Rajiv Gandhi to India's political throne.

'I can't help but feel in my bones that exciting times lie ahead,' she said. 'I know, of course, that Indira herself had a wonderful opportunity back after the 1971 elections to bring about massive changes. She blew it. So I'm cautious about the prospects of any leader to succeed. But there is one side of me that desperately wants Rajiv – and I hope it will be him in the prime minister's seat – to succeed. After all these years of bad news, we need good things to happen in India.'

CHAPTER THREE:
THE SUCCESSION

At 9.40 on the morning of Wednesday, 31 October Murli Deora was saying farewell at Bombay's cavernous Victoria Terminus to nearly a thousand elderly citizens who were about to board a train for the northern city of Allahabad. They were all 'freedom fighters', men and women who had struggled alongside Mahatma Gandhi and Jawaharlal Nehru and Indira Gandhi against India's British colonial rulers. On this morning, they were about to travel to Mrs Gandhi's hometown of Allahabad to observe the fiftieth anniversary of the founding of their particular freedom fighters' unit. In his capacity as president of Bombay's Congress Party organization, Deora had arranged the financing of the trip.

Deora was a short, slim man with a ready smile and quick wit. He was a self-made businessman who parlayed his high-school savings into a personal fortune that was said to run into millions. He had served as Bombay's non-executive mayor. Married to a former interior decorator named Hema Phansalkar – who bore him two sons – Murli Deora was seen at every event that mattered in Bombay, especially those events that attracted the city's political and commercial élite, whose darling he had become, and from whom he raised money to finance election campaigns not only in Bombay but elsewhere in India for the ruling Congress Party.

His popularity with this élite, Deora often told visitors with a twinkle in his eyes, was largely because of his own personality and charm. Not so. Bombay's high-and-mighty were fully aware of Deora's powerful connections in New Delhi. He was very close to Indira Gandhi; and he had taken her son, Rajiv, to participate in management seminars in Western Europe, where Deora had business associates. Deora maintained an extensive national and international network of contacts, which benefited the Congress Party as well. He stayed in touch with key people of this network through regular telephone calls, personal letters and, of course, greeting cards during festive seasons. Moreover, Deora often took time out to visit constituents in hospitals, and he made it a practice never to miss a funeral in his election district. As a result, this whirling dervish of political energy and commitment frequently put in eighteen- or twenty-hour days.

That Deora had survived as a Gandhi friend was the subject of much discussion in Bombay society. Normally, those who billed themselves as 'close' to Indira Gandhi seldom lasted long in that category after the characterization came to Indira's attention. She had a way of exiling from her inner circle those who excessively capitalized on their friendship with her. And there was no shortage of such people. A former chief minister of Maharashtra State, A. R. Antulay, even collected millions of rupees for a dubious social-welfare society, telling his industrialist donors that his friend, Mrs Gandhi, had blessed his endeavour. Antulay was eventually cut adrift by the prime minister. But Deora was a shrewd political operative who always managed to stay on the right side of most issues – and of his political patrons, the Gandhis.

On this morning, Deora mingled with the 'freedom fighters', and addressed the group briefly in Hindi.

'You are going to a historic place to observe a historic anniversary,' Deora said. 'You are going to the very home of Nehru and our beloved leader, Indiraji.'

The group applauded vigorously. Deora wished them well in their journey, and left for his business office in Khetan Bhavan, a large building in Bombay's commercial district of Churchgate. He ordered a cup of tea, then settled back in his chair to scrutinize the morning's mail. Behind his chair was a large montage showing a sylvan setting of green woods and sunrays streaking through foliage. The office had a yellow sofa and armchairs to match, and little else. A friend had once suggested that Deora instal a book-case, but the Congress Party boss had replied: 'What for? Books are not part of my personality.'

At 10.15 a.m., one of the four telephones next to Deora's desk rang. It was Girilal Jain, then the Bombay-based editor-in-chief of *The Times of India* chain.

'I've just learned that the prime minister was shot in her home,'

Jain said. 'She's not dead, as far as I know. I thought I should inform you.'

Deora leaped out of his chair.

'Thank you for telling me,' he said, replacing the receiver in the cradle.

As Deora recalled later, his first reaction was of total disbelief. He thought of telephoning a local physician friend, Shantilal Mehta. The physician had long ago operated on both Nehru and Mrs Gandhi, and was still occasionally consulted by the prime minister. Deora reached Dr Mehta at Bombay's Jaslok Hospital and gave him the news.

'You are familiar with Indiraji's health,' Deora said to Mehta. 'Perhaps you can be of assistance to the doctors in Delhi.'

The two men decided they would fly to Delhi at once. Deora told Mehta that he would collect him at the hospital in thirty minutes, and that meanwhile he'd book them both on whichever flight was available.

As it turned out, while Deora was on the phone to Dr Mehta, someone called Deora's office on behalf of two key Gandhi aides, Dr P. C. Alexander, her principal private secretary, and Dr Krishnaswamy Rao Saheb, the cabinet secretary. These two men happened to be in Bombay that morning, and now a special Indian Airlines plane was being readied to transport them to Delhi. The caller urged that if Deora wanted to fly to Delhi, he should be at Bombay's Santa Cruz Airport no later than eleven o'clock.

Deora informed his wife Hema that he was on his way to Delhi. She herself had just heard the news of the shooting from a family friend, Harry Cahill, who was the United States consul general in Bombay, and she'd been trying unsuccessfully to reach Deora by phone.

Deora collected a small overnight suitcase that was kept fully packed with clothes and accessories in his office closet, then drove off to Jaslok Hospital, where Dr Mehta was waiting for him, with his own overnight attaché case. Deora's driver sped to the airport, but by the time they reached Santa Cruz, which is located in the northern suburbs of Bombay, some thirty kilometres from Deora's South Bombay office, it was almost 11.20. The Boeing 737 chartered by Dr Alexander and his colleague had already taken off. No regular flight from Santa Cruz to Delhi was scheduled until 5 p.m.

Deora found out, however, that there was a Kuwait-bound flight

out of nearby Sahar Airport – the international wing of Santa Cruz –
that was scheduled to stop in Delhi. That Air India flight would
leave at 1.30 p.m., so Deora and Dr Mehta rushed to Sahar.

There they found an assembly of local VIPs who had already
booked themselves on the flight to Delhi. Among those gathered at
the check-in counter were Vasantdada Patil, the chief minister of
Maharashtra State (of which Bombay is the capital), and Margaret
Alva and Saroj Kharparde, both members of Parliament.

'Somebody had a transistor on, but All-India Radio was still
giving no news about the shooting,' Deora recalled later. 'They
were still playing Hindi film songs.'

The men and women gathered at the airport exchanged
views about the shooting. There was general agreement that the
assassination attempt was part of a conspiracy by the Sikhs.

'Among us, there was gloom, sadness – and growing anger that
something like this had been allowed to happen,' Deora said later.

Everybody aboard the Air India flight was tense during the
ninety-minute ride to Delhi. Deora walked up to the cockpit several
times to request the pilot to radio for additional news concerning
Mrs Gandhi. Virtually everyone on board refused the meal offered
by Air India's stewardesses.

'When we landed in Delhi, the atmosphere of gloom at the
airport was so heavy that I just knew she had died,' Deora recalled.
'I just broke down and cried.'

Dr Shantilal Mehta, who was almost thirty years older than
Deora, put his arm around the younger man and consoled him.

'We just have to accept what happened,' the physician said.

The two men were driven by Saroj Kharparde in her car to the
All-India Institute of Medical Sciences. It was her driver who had
told them about Mrs Gandhi being taken there. Deora saw that
several foreign embassies, including the United States embassy,
had already lowered their flags to half-mast – but the flags at Indian
government offices were still flying loftily. Huge crowds had
gathered in front of the Institute. Security guards were using
lathiis – the bamboo sticks used by Indian policemen – and batons to
keep people from entering the hospital's compound. But in India,
VIPs such as members of Parliament enjoy divine status, and so
Mrs Kharparde's car was allowed to enter the premises.

It was 4.15 p.m. Deora, Dr Mehta and Mrs Kharparde went up to
the eighth-floor operating theatre where surgeons had tried to

revive Mrs Gandhi. They were informed that the prime minister had been officially declared dead at 2.30 p.m. Deora was crying without control. He saw Rajiv Gandhi disappear into Operating-Theatre Two, where Mrs Gandhi's body was kept, and then re-appear to comfort some friends who waited outside in the corridor.

'But I just did not have the heart to go up to Rajiv,' Deora recalled.

Deora composed himself and continued to linger in the area outside Operating-Theatre Two. At 5.15 p.m., there was some commotion. President Zail Singh, who'd been in North Yemen on an official visit, had arrived directly from Delhi Airport. Rajiv Gandhi greeted him and escorted the bearded Sikh head of state into the operating-theatre. Deora spotted Karan Singh, the Hindu former Maharaja of Kashmir, and Pupul Jayakar, India's cultural czarina and probably Mrs Gandhi's closest friend. He saw Rajiv Gandhi's close friends and aides, Arun Singh and Arun Nehru.

'Rajiv Gandhi was the most calm and collected person there,' Deora recalled. 'Everybody else was weeping or howling. He was comforting others.'

As Deora waited, he thought about the last time he'd seen Indira Gandhi alive. It was during her visit to Bombay on 5 October. He had arranged a public rally for her, and then, before she left for Delhi from Santa Cruz Airport, he accompanied her to the home of her elderly uncle, Gunottam 'Raja' Hutheesing. Hutheesing had married Nehru's sister, the late Krishna, and was grievously ill and confined to his home in Navroj Apartments on Altamount Road.

'He will be very happy to see you,' Deora said to the prime minister. 'With someone as old as he is, you never know what can happen, how long he will last.'

'You're right,' she said to Deora. 'You never know what's going to happen to any of us. Let's go and see him.'

The prime minister hugged Hutheesing warmly. As she left, after a ten-minute visit, she said to him: 'Get well soon!'

Was it a premonition of her own death that made her decide to squeeze in a visit to Raja Hutheesing? Deora pondered this as he waited outside Operating-Theatre Two, where Indira Gandhi's body now lay.

It was now well after six o'clock. Saroj Kharparde suggested to Deora that they go to her home so that he could rest for a while. Deora decided instead that he would stop off at the Taj Mahal

Hotel, where a room had been booked for him by his Bombay office. He showered, napped briefly, then went to Maharashtra Sadan – the Delhi office of the Maharashtra State government – to meet Chief Minister Patil. At around 10.30 p.m., the two men drove to One Safdarjung Road to meet Rajiv Gandhi. They didn't know that he had already been sworn in as the new prime minister of India.

'He was very composed,' Deora recalled. 'He was consoling every visitor. I thought to myself: what class! The torch had been passed to a new generation.'

Gandhi told Chief Minister Patil that he should at once return to Bombay.

'I want every state chief executive to be at their station,' the prime minister said. 'If any trouble occurs around the country, I want you all to be back where you belong.'

The directive obviously applied to Deora as well, for he was head of the influential Bombay unit of Rajiv Gandhi's Congress Party.

As Patil and Deora left One Safdarjung Road at around 11.15 p.m., they ran into B. K. Nehru, an uncle of Gandhi's and a former ambassador to the United States. Many years ago, One Safdarjung Road used to be Nehru's private residence when he held a government post in Delhi; Nehru was now governor of the western state of Gujarat.

'Why did she reinstate those Sikh guards?' Deora recalls Nehru asking. Mrs Gandhi had insisted that the two men who later killed her, Beant Singh and Satwant Singh, be brought back as her personal security guards after they had been transferred in the wake of the Indian army's assault on the Golden Temple in Amritsar. Indian intelligence officials believed that a plot to kill the prime minister had been devised by radical Sikhs following the army's action on 6 June 1984 – as vengeance for the hundreds of Sikhs who died in the military operation.

That night, at the luxurious Taj Mahal Hotel on Mansingh Road, Murli Deora slept fitfully. He was, of course, pleased that his friend Rajiv had become prime minister, rather than anyone else, but Deora wondered what sort of chief executive Rajiv Gandhi would make. He worried that there would be a backlash against India's minority Sikhs. Would there be trouble in Bombay? And in Delhi?

Deora fell asleep not knowing that the massacre of Sikhs in India's capital city had already started.

At about the same time that Murli Deora fell into his troubled sleep, Swraj Paul was disembarking from Air India's Flight 104, which had brought him non-stop from London to Delhi.

The journey had taken ten hours, and Paul had sat through most of it in uncharacteristic silence. He was ordinarily an extrovert, an irrepressible man, given to loud laughter and chatter. At fifty-three, he had established himself as one of the wealthiest Indian immigrant entrepreneurs in Britain; he bought steel mills and foundries, and was now involved in electronics, publishing and shipping. But it was not because of his self-made millions that Paul had become well known in both Britain and India. His fame – some would say notoriety – was more the consequence of his much-publicized friendship with Indira Gandhi and her family.

There were those who saw something sinister in that friendship, whispering that Paul was the foreign-based manager of the Gandhi family's ill-gotten fortune. But Swraj Paul would insist that he did nothing illegal on behalf of Indira Gandhi, and there was no evidence to prove him wrong. He often said that he simply demonstrated unswerving loyalty to the Nehru–Gandhi dynasty because he believed in its greatness. His explanations did not silence critics, some of whom wondered in print whether Paul's close ties with the Gandhis had resulted in any financial gains for him; some uncharitable critics said that Swraj Paul did nothing for anyone unless there was a heavy measure of personal gain in the transaction, a charge which Paul cheerfully refuted with ready references to his many acts of generosity.

Indira Gandhi's relationship with Swraj Paul was advantageous for her. Between 1977 and 1979, when she was out of office and a political pariah during the opposition Janata Party's years in power, it was Paul who invited her abroad and arranged many public appearances for the former prime minister. Those appearances helped sustain her confidence in her own appeal as a public figure; Mrs Gandhi also used the trips to keep abreast of international affairs. And the foreign trips gained her widespread media coverage, always a restorative for a politician's spirits, especially a politician who was then being vilified in her native land by politicians who did not have a fraction of her experience and class.

At 4.45 that Wednesday morning, the phone had rung in Swraj Paul's bedroom in his fourth-floor apartment in Portland Place.

'Swraj, I have bad news to tell you – the prime minister has been shot,' the caller said.

Paul's first reaction was to assume that Prime Minister Margaret Thatcher of Britain had been shot. Then it occurred to him that the call sounded like a long-distance one. He was right. The caller was a friend named Ralph Buultjens, who was telephoning from New York. Buultjens was at least as close to Indira Gandhi as Paul was; Buultjens, in fact, was widely said to be her most influential foreign-policy adviser, even though he was born a Sri Lankan. He made his living as a university professor, lecturer and author in the United States, and had heard the news of the shooting on American television at around 11.30 p.m. in New York on Tuesday night (Eastern Standard Time is generally ten and a half hours behind Indian Standard Time).

Swraj Paul woke his wife, Aruna, who had slept soundly through his brief conversation with Ralph Buultjens. Her response to the news was one of disbelief. She suggested that Paul at once telephone New Delhi.

Paul direct-dialled the prime minister's residence. The phone was picked up by Mrs Gandhi's information adviser, H. Y. Sharada Prasad.

'Is it true?' Swraj Paul asked.

'Yes, I'm afraid so,' Prasad said glumly. 'The news is very, very bad.'

Paul recalls that he took this to mean that Mrs Gandhi was dead, although even as Prasad spoke to him the prime minister was being attended by physicians at the All-India Institute of Medical Sciences.

Paul started to cry. So did Aruna. They both decided to catch the next available flight to Delhi. Later that morning, Aruna was still so overcome with emotion that she could not make the journey to Delhi.

Air India's Flight 104 left London's Heathrow Airport at 9.35 that morning. As Swraj Paul lowered his six-foot frame into his first-class seat, he wondered if Rajiv Gandhi had been selected by the ruling Congress Party to succeed his mother.

A special car from the prime minister's house awaited Paul at Delhi's international airport. Paul went straight from the airport to One Safdarjung Road. He saw Rajiv Gandhi and embraced him. Not a word was exchanged between the two men.

Paul was led by a Gandhi aide to the dining-room, where Mrs Gandhi's body now lay, smothered in flowers. Incense wafted from joss-sticks. Paul thought about the last time he had met Indira Gandhi. That meeting was in August 1984, when he had flown in from London to present Mrs Gandhi with a copy of his pictorial biography of her.

'I hope you like the book,' Swraj Paul said to Mrs Gandhi.

'I'm sure I will,' she had replied, with a soft smile, turning the pages of the lavishly illustrated volume. 'I appreciate what you have done here.'

The conversation had taken place in the same dining-room where Indira Gandhi now lay lifeless.

On that Wednesday morning, Ralph Buultjens, like Swraj Paul, spent many hours remembering Mrs Gandhi.

Swraj Paul's friendship with Mrs Gandhi was of relatively recent vintage: in 1969, she had helped with arrangements to transport Paul's young daughter, Ambika, to London for treatment of leukaemia (Ambika subsequently died). But Buultjens had known the Nehru family for nearly thirty years, ever since he travelled to New Delhi after his education in Colombo to obtain an interview with Mrs Gandhi's father, Prime Minister Jawaharlal Nehru. So close did Buultjens and Mrs Gandhi become that they would speak on the phone several times a week: Buultjens says he has voluminous notes of their conversations.

They would meet up in Delhi, which Buultjens visited frequently, or during one of Mrs Gandhi's periodic travels abroad. They discussed not only foreign affairs and politics but also history, literature, poetry and the theatre. Buultjens would arrange for Mrs Gandhi private meetings with Western intellectuals, whose company he says she relished. Buultjens, a tall, striking man with a high forehead, thick greying hair, and a tendency towards heaviness, was often conspicuously near Mrs Gandhi whenever she made public appearances in Britain and the US. Unlike others who enjoyed far less access to her, he never flaunted his relationship with Indira Gandhi. In fact, even with close friends Buultjens seemed reticent about discussing his dealings with the Nehrus and Gandhis.

Buultjens did not need to exploit his access to the prime minister because he was never dependent on this privilege for his livelihood.

He taught political economy and comparative religion at New York University and at the New School for Social Research in New York, and was a distinguished visiting professor at many institutions around the world. The 46-year-old Sri Lanka-born scholar was regarded by his peers as one of the most brilliant political scientists of his generation. His views on world affairs were frequently sought by business and social leaders. Buultjens was also often invited by international figures to offer his advice on and analyses of global topics. His writings appeared regularly in the opinion pages of such major publications as the *New York Times*. And Buultjens had also written nearly a dozen books on international affairs.

When Buultjens first heard a bulletin about the Gandhi shooting in New Delhi – where it was already Wednesday morning – on late-night television in New York on Tuesday, he could not believe the news.

He thought: this is a very bad joke.

But then a producer from the American Broadcasting Corporation telephoned him, asking him to appear on a television news show on Wednesday morning. Shortly afterwards, a producer from the National Broadcasting Company called, and after that someone from the Columbia Broadcasting System. On Wednesday, Buultjens, who was already known to television and radio producers as an authority on the Indian sub-continent, would be one of the most sought-after sources for the American media.

In between the media queries Buultjens telephoned friends in India to get the latest news concerning Mrs Gandhi. His phone bill for the night of 30–31 October eventually amounted to nearly $900.

'I kept wondering what was going to happen to the whole region now,' Buultjens said later. 'I was always telling Mrs Gandhi during our phone conversations to be careful.'

He recalled being in her Delhi office on 1 June, when the prime minister was giving her generals the go-ahead for Operation Bluestar – the army assault on the Golden Temple in Amritsar. Mrs Gandhi had said to Buultjens: 'You know, this is the most difficult decision of my political career. This is war on your own people.'

A couple of months later, Buultjens had accompanied Mrs Gandhi to Delhi's Red Fort, from whose ramparts she delivered her annual Independence Day speech on 15 August. He noticed that the 67-year-old prime minister became breathless as she climbed the steep stairs to the rostrum.

'It must be very tiring to go up all those steps,' Buultjens said to Mrs Gandhi.

'I may never have to do it again,' she replied, cryptically.

And only two days before the assassination, Buultjens had spoken to Mrs Gandhi about the continuing controversy concerning the army action in Amritsar. Although Sikhs generally hadn't supported the terrorists, there was almost universal condemnation in the Sikh community of Operation Bluestar.

'We're all besieged,' Mrs Gandhi said to Buultjens. 'But we will pull through this one.'

And a few weeks before that conversation, Buultjens had telephoned the prime minister to relay the news that he had been chosen to receive the prestigious Toynbee Prize, which is given annually to an outstanding social scientist. Buultjens requested Mrs Gandhi to present the award formally (a similar request had already been sent to her office by the Toynbee Award Committee, which is based in Paris).

'I'd be delighted,' Mrs Gandhi said. Then she mysteriously added: 'But I may not be around to give it to you.'

On the morning of Wednesday, 31 October Ralph Buultjens told a caller that he thought the real test of a political leader was how he or she tackled his society's problems. 'Did the leader leave his country behind in better shape than when he found it?' Buultjens said. 'In a larger sense, Indira Gandhi meets this test well.'

Buultjens said that under Mrs Gandhi's helmsmanship, India coped well with many difficulties: the Bangladesh War of 1971, the global oil crisis of the 1970s, the economic slump that followed, the Emergency of 1975–7. 'She managed to keep the unity and integrity of India under great pressure,' Buultjens said. She was responsible for making India a self-sufficient country in food, he went on, and she instilled in the country's poor a consciousness that they had the right to a better life. Mrs Gandhi, Buultjens said, took personal interest in promoting such things as science, technology and higher education, items she saw as the 'bedrocks' of India in the future.

'She was also a real secularist,' Buultjens said. 'She really believed that people of all religions could co-exist within the boundaries of a modern state.'

'She was the single most exposed and heard political figure in all of history,' Buultjens said. 'Just think of the millions in India who saw her at rallies, on television, who heard her voice on radio. And think of her own life – she met virtually every major political figure of this century: Gandhi, Nehru of course, Churchill, De Gaulle, Adenauer, Monnet, Kennedy, Eisenhower, Stalin.'

It was largely because she was her father's daughter, of course, that Mrs Gandhi gained such exposure. Between 1947 and 1964, she served as Prime Minister Jawaharlal Nehru's official hostess. Her mother, Kamala, had died in 1936. Nehru never remarried, although he had liaisons with a number of women. Indira Gandhi's own marriage in 1942 to a Parsi named Feroze Gandhi floundered: she and her two sons, Rajiv and Sanjay, lived with Nehru at the prime minister's official residence in Delhi, while Feroze Gandhi camped in a house reserved for parliamentarians (he died in 1960, of a heart attack).

Those years at Nehru's side, Buultjens recalled, were invaluable for Indira. She learned statecraft. As president of his Congress Party, she played a leading role in forging a coalition in Kerala that defeated that state's ruling communist government. She travelled the length and breadth of India, getting to know grassroots party workers everywhere. She often accompanied her father on his frequent trips abroad; she attended summit meetings, she sat in on his sessions with the group of Third World leaders, such as Tito of Yugoslavia and Nasser of Egypt, who had formed the Nonaligned Movement. This experience more than made up for her lack of a completed university education.

Buultjens, who plans to write a biography of Mrs Gandhi, pointed out to questioners that it was not until after Nehru's death in 1964 that Indira Gandhi fully came into her own. She was selected by Nehru's successor, Prime Minister Lal Bahadur Shastri, to serve as minister for information and broadcasting. Shashtri died in Tashkent of a heart attack on 10 January, 1966; fourteen days later Mrs Gandhi was sworn in as prime minister.

She was initially chosen, Buultjens said, because the Congress Party's aging but still powerful leaders – known collectively as The Syndicate – thought Indira Gandhi would be extremely amenable to their manipulations. No one suspected her of possessing a steely will. She out-manoeuvred these party bosses, broke away from the old Congress to form her own Congress Party, and flourished.

The years in office were not free of controversy, however. She imposed a national 'Emergency' in 1975, contending that Opposition leaders had brought India to the brink of disintegration.

Thousands of her political opponents were incarcerated during the two-year Emergency, when the Constitution was suspended. When she decided to hold a general election in March 1977, her party was routed. During her three years in political exile, she meticulously planned her return to office. The Opposition Janata Party, which had defeated the Congress, collapsed because of internecine squabbling, paving the way for new elections in January 1980. Once again, Mrs Gandhi became prime minister of India.

How would Indira Gandhi be remembered?

'As a political giant,' Buultjens said, on one of the television programmes on Wednesday morning. 'As a superb political strategist. As a leader who genuinely cared for her people and worked selflessly for them.'

That evening he boarded an Air India flight for Delhi. As the Boeing 747 took off from New York's Kennedy International Airport, it struck Buultjens how Orwellian a year 1984 had turned out for India: there were communal problems in Assam, there were growing tensions in the Punjab, there was the army assault on the Golden Temple, there were assorted political crises in Kashmir and Andhra Pradesh; and now there was the assassination of Indira Gandhi.

And as the plane roared into the night, Buultjens thought of something else. How ironic it was that once again, as at independence in 1947, people were asking aloud if India would survive as one nation. History, Ralph Buultjens thought, had come round full circle.

By 2 p.m. on 31 October, All-India Radio's hourly news bulletins began referring to the fact that Indira Gandhi had been shot in the garden of her home and that she was being treated at the All-India Institute of Medical Sciences. By four o'clock that afternoon, a large crowd had gathered in front of the Institute's main entrance.

Dev Dutt, a Delhi-based journalist, was in that crowd. This is his account of what happened that afternoon:

'There were slogans mostly in praise of Mrs Gandhi, and a few slogans threatening revenge, but there was no tension. There were a number of Sikhs in the crowd. Their faces showed no fear or apprehension. We talked to some of them in order to gauge their state of mind. The Sikhs seemed to be supremely confident about the goodwill of their Hindu brethren. It seems they nursed no suspicions against the Hindus. They did not show any traces of nervousness of any kind. The non-Sikhs in the crowd did not seem even to notice the presence of Sikhs and took their presence as normal.

'While this crowd waited patiently, the flow of traffic and the normal business around nearby kiosks continued. I was standing near the street-crossing in front of the Institute when thirty or forty young men emerged out of the crowd and formed a neat column three or four men deep and ran towards the crossing near a traffic island. They caught hold of a scooter that was parked on the other side and set it on fire. Then these young men moved toward some nearby buses that had been slowing down on account of the fire. They began to pull Sikhs out of buses. They started to pull off their turbans and beat them relentlessly. I saw five turbans burning in a row on the road.

'There were no policemen in the area. The group had a free hand. After about twenty minutes, a group of khaki-clad men arrived and began to chase away the miscreants.

'It is difficult to explain the sudden eruption of violence in the Institute area that afternoon. But the question is: who were these people who came out of the crowd and went on a rampage?'

The incidents near the All-India Institute of Medical Sciences were the first in Delhi in which Sikhs were targeted and man-handled. By late evening, non-Sikh mobs were rampaging through Sikh neighbourhoods elsewhere in the capital. Led by men identified by some of the victims as local Congress Party leaders and Delhi administrative officials, these mobs burned down houses, raped women, looted homes, and murdered Sikh males. A senior member of Mrs Gandhi's cabinet was seen directing some of the rioters.

Not long afterwards, when I visited Sikh neighbourhoods in Delhi, it was hard to believe that people in a country that calls itself civilized were capable of inflicting such gruesome atrocities on innocent men, women and children.

Dhanwat Kaur, a 28-year-old woman in Delhi's Trilokpuri section, recounted for me how the rampaging mobs invaded her one-room tenement home, dragged her husband Manohar Singh by his genitals, and hacked him to death in front of her. Her three small daughters and a son were present when this brutality occurred. For an hour afterwards, the son, three-year-old Jasbir, clutched what remained of his father's body and refused to let go.

Dhanwat's neighbour, Amir Singh, a carpenter, told me how he had gathered a group of women and children and hidden them in a nearby Sikh *gurdwara*, or temple. But a large group of marauders set fire to the temple. Most of the women and children managed to escape, Amir Singh said, but a dozen Sikh men remained trapped inside the inferno and perished. 'The sad thing was, the people who set fire to our temple included those very men who had helped us to raise money for building the temple,' he said.

Over the next four days, more than two thousand Sikhs were reported to have died at the hands of these mobs in Delhi. Most died terribly: they were often burned alive, or were hacked to pieces while female members of their families were stripped and made to watch. Pre-pubescent boys were castrated by mobs. The carnage spread to neighbouring states as well. In Uttar Pradesh, more than a thousand Sikhs were reported to have been killed in the cities, including Kanpur, Lucknow and Ghaziabad. In Haryana, the death toll exceeded a hundred. In Bihar, the toll rose to three hundred. Sikhs were also slaughtered by well-armed mobs in Madhya Pradesh, West Bengal, and parts of Himachal Pradesh. Most of those states were governed by the Congress Party.

It is impossible to say with certainty how many Sikhs died in the five-day period following the murder of Indira Gandhi, but officials of the Delhi-based People's Union for Democratic Rights (PUDR) and the People's Union for Civil Liberties (PUCL) – who investigated many of the incidents in the capital and who produced a well-documented report – say that the national death toll probably exceeded three thousand. While the actual property loss may never be known, many estimates suggest that between 31 October and 5 November, more than $250 million worth of property was destroyed in Delhi alone.

The organization's report was entitled *Who are the Guilty?* It sold briskly. The report suggested that the Delhi government had in effect encouraged Hindu and Sikh communalists to 'feed upon each other' in the Punjab, and that the repurcussions of the Punjab situation were being felt in Delhi. The Sikh community must be reassured in the aftermath of the holocaust in Delhi, the report said.

Investigators from the PUDR and the PUCL found that the

attacks against Delhi's Sikh community were hardly spontaneous expressions of grief and anger over Mrs Gandhi's assassination – as the Delhi authorities have asserted they were. The rampaging mobs were well-led, well-armed and well-informed about just where Sikh families lived. Congress Party leaders were seen turning up not only in poor localities such as Munirka, Mangolpuri and Trilokpuri, but also in rich neighbourhoods such as Friends' Colony and Maharani Bagh, with lists of residents. Thugs – or *goondas*, as they are commonly known in India – turned up in Delhi Transport Corporation (DTC) buses, or in vans and trucks and jeeps ordinarily used by local Congress Party workers.

The PUDR and PUCL investigators found that there were two distinct phases to the violence against Delhi's Sikhs.

The first phase was marked by three rumours that were spread around the capital on the evening of 31 October: Sikhs were reported to be distributing *mithai* and lighting oil-lamps to celebrate the demise of Mrs Gandhi; trains containing the bodies of hundreds of murdered Hindus were said to have arrived from the Punjab at the Old Delhi Station; and Delhi's water supply was said to have been poisoned by Sikhs.

Subsequent inquiries showed that no one had actually witnessed the sweetmeat distribution. There had been no train-loads of dead Hindus coming in from the Punjab – but Delhi policemen had actually been cruising in vans through certain neighbourhoods and announcing by loudspeaker that such trains had indeed arrived at the Old Delhi Station. The policemen also announced that Sikhs had poisoned the city's water supply.

The second phase, the PUDR/PUCL report said,

began with the arrival of groups of armed young people in vans, scooters, motorcycles or trucks from the night of 31 October and morning of 1 November at various places like Munirka, Saket, South Extension, Lajpat Nagar, Bhogal, Jangpura and Ashram in the south and south-east; the Connaught Circus shopping area in the centre, and later the trans-Jamuna colonies and resettlement colonies in other areas in the north. With cans of petrol they went around these localities and systematically set fire to Sikh houses, shops and gurdwaras. We were told by local eye-witnesses that well-known Congress leaders and workers led and directed the arsonists and that local cadres of the Congress Party identified the Sikh houses and shops. A senior police official pointed out to us: 'The shop signs are either in Hindi or English. How do you expect the illiterate arsonists to know whether these shops belonged to Hindus or Sikhs – unless they were identified to them by someone who is either educated or a local person?'

In some areas, like Trilokpuri, Mangolpuri and the trans-Jamuna colonies, the arsonists consisted of Gujar or Jat farmers from neighbouring villages, and were accompanied by local residents, some of whom again were Congress activists. In these areas, we were told, Congress followers of the Bhangi caste (those belonging to the Harijan, or 'untouchable' community) took part in the looting. In South Delhi, buses of the Delhi Transport Corporation (DTC) were used by the miscreants to move from place to place in their murderous journey. How could the DTC allow its buses to be used by criminals?

The attacks in the resettlement colonies of Trilokpuri and Mangolpuri, where the maximum number of murders took place, again displayed the same pattern. The targets were primarily young Sikhs. They were dragged out, beaten up and then burnt alive. While old men, women and children were generally allowed to escape, their houses were set on fire after looting of valuables. Documents pertaining to their legal possession of the houses were also burnt. In some areas of Mangolpuri, we heard from survivors that even children were not spared. We also came across reports of gang-rape of women.

The orgy of destruction embraced a variety of property ranging from shops, factories, houses to *gurdwaras* and schools belonging to Sikhs. In all the affected spots, a calculated attempt to terrorize the people was evident in the common tendency among the assailants to burn alive the Sikhs on public roads. Even five days after the incidents, on 6 November, in the course of one of our regular visits to Mangolpuri we found that, although the ashes had been cleared, the pavement in front of the Congress Party office was still blotched with burnt patches, which the local people had earlier pointed out to us as spots where four Sikhs were burnt alive.

Throughout the carnage, Delhi's policemen were either totally absent from the scene; or they stood by while mobs freely burnt Sikhs alive; or they themselves participated in the orgy of violence against the Sikhs. But in Lajpat Nagar, on 1 November, when a group of concerned citizens tried to organize a peace march in support of Hindu–Sikh amity, a police jeep blocked the way and police officials demanded to know if the marchers had official permission.

In areas such as Trilokpuri, policemen were seen supplying diesel oil and petrol to arsonists.

In Kotla Mubarakpur, several witnesses heard a police inspector say to a group of rioters: 'We gave you thirty-six hours. Had we given the Sikhs that amount of time, they would have killed every Hindu.'

A number of Hindu residents of areas such as Mangolpuri tried to hide their Sikh neighbours from the marauding mobs.

But when two Hindus, Dharam Raj Pawar and Rajvir Pawar went to a police station at Ber Serai and asked for police protection for their Sikh friends, a policeman said to them: 'You being Hindus should have killed those Sikhs. What are you doing here? Don't you know a train has arrived from Punjab carrying bodies of massacred Hindus?'

On the evening of 31 October, Atal Behari Vajpayee, an Opposition leader, called on Home Minister P. V. Narasimha Rao to express outrage over the mounting attacks against Sikhs.

'Everything will be brought under control within a couple of hours,' Narasimha Rao told Vajpayee, a former foreign minister.

But Narasimha Rao did not impose a curfew until two days later, and he belatedly called the army in to restore law and order. Even then, however, the violence against the Sikhs continued, aided and abetted by those in power.

One eye-witness to these events was Ashwini Ray, head of the department of political science at Delhi's Jawaharlal Nehru University. This is his account: 'There was a police vehicle with four policemen parked near Bhogal market. I came out of my house and saw smoke billowing out. I heard the sound of a tyre bursting. Policemen were reading newspapers and drinking tea inside their car while arson was going on all around. I went to the police car to ask why they were not stopping the arson and was told to mind my own business. I then saw several looters carrying off radio and television sets from stores right in front of the parked police vehicles. Some of the policemen asked the people to hurry with the loot.'

None of the looters or rioters was arrested during the carnage that took place between 31 October and 5 November, but the police did take into custody several Sikhs who defended themselves and their families with weapons. The Rajiv Gandhi government dragged its feet in providing relief money to Sikh victims, authorizing the equivalent of no more than $300 per family. Few of the victims have received this money.

The report prepared by the PUDR and the PUCL makes some dramatic points in its conclusion:

The social and political consequences of the government's stance during the carnage, its deliberate inaction and its callousness towards relief and rehabilitation are far-reaching. It is indeed a matter of grave concern that the government has made no serious inquiries into the entire tragic episode which seems to be so well planned and designed.

It is curious that for the several hours the government had between the time of Mrs Gandhi's assassination and the official announcement of her death, no security arrangements were made for the victims.

The riots were well organized and were of unprecedented brutality. Several very disturbing questions arise that must be answered:

What were the government and the Delhi administration doing for several hours between the time of the assassination and the announcement of Mrs Gandhi's death? Why did the government refuse to take cognizance of the reports of the looting and murders and call in troops even after the military had been 'alerted'? Why was there no joint control-room set up, and who was responsible for not giving clear and specific instructions to the army on curbing violence and imposing a curfew?

Who was responsible for the planned and deliberate police inaction and their often active role in inciting the murders and the looting? Who was responsible for the planned and well-directed arson?

Why were highly provocative slogans (such as '*Khoon ka baadla khoon*': 'blood for blood') allowed to be broadcast by Doordarshan during the televised transmissions depicting the mourning crowds at Teen Murti Bhavan, where Mrs Gandhi's body was kept on display?

Why has the Congress Party not set up an inquiry into the role of its members in the arson and looting?'

In those hours and days of terror following the assassination of Mrs Gandhi, there were some Hindus who came to the assistance of besieged Sikhs. A number of young people got together in Delhi and formed an umbrella organization called the Nagarik Seva Manch – Citizens' Service Group. A Sikh named Tejeshwar Singh – who is a publishing executive and who also appears on the government's evening network news programme – defiantly led a procession of Hindus and Sikhs through Delhi's streets. The participants urged Indians to shun violence and renew their commitment to communal harmony.

'Hindu Sikh *bhai bhai*!' the marchers shouted. 'Hindus and Sikhs are brothers!'

But as the procession moved through low-income neighbourhoods, crowds sometimes heckled them. Stones were thrown at Tejeshwar Singh. The marchers were threatened with violence.

A number of Hindus offered shelter to their Sikh friends. My brother-in-law, Ajai Lal, and his wife, Indu, went across to the home of their Sikh neighbour, Anand Singh, and invited the former army colonel to pack up and stay with them until the trouble subsided. When Hindu friends found out that Khushwant Singh, the well-known Sikh writer and historian, had sought refuge in the Swedish embassy, they implored him to come to their homes.

Scores of Sikh men in Delhi cut their long hair, threw away their turbans and shaved their beards so that they wouldn't be singled out as Sikhs. The barber shops in Delhi's luxury hotels did roaring business.

Noni Chawla, a young executive with the ITC-Sheraton Hotel group, moved to his employer's flagship hotel, the Maurya-Sheraton, with his wife Nilima and their two children. The homes of a number of Sikhs in the Chawlas' affluent neighbourhood in the Vasant Vihar section of Delhi had been attacked by mobs who came armed with lists of voters. Several Sikhs were dragged out of their houses, stripped in the streets, beaten, then burnt alive. Some Sikh children were reportedly hanged in front of their parents, while others were castrated and their penises stuffed into the mouths of their mothers and sisters.

'What kind of a country has this become?' Noni Chawla, who refused to doff his turban or cut his hair, asked.

'I've never felt discriminated against in India,' he said, 'but clearly times are changing. Among many young Sikh professionals I now hear increased talk of emigrating to the West. We don't want our children taunted in school. A lot of us feel a sense of alienation, of separation. I think Sikhs will increasingly have a difficult time in India.'

o

At ten o'clock on the morning of Wednesday, 31 October Payal Singh and several other Sikh friends and relatives boarded a train in the eastern metropolis of Calcutta. Singh, a writer, and her group were heading for Delhi to attend a wedding.

It was not until six o'clock that evening that the Sikhs heard the All-India Radio bulletin about Mrs Gandhi's death – and about the fact that her assassins had been two Sikh security guards.

'Every passenger irrespective of his religion was in a state of shocked silence,' Singh later recalled.

At eleven o'clock the next morning, the train reached Ghaziabad. Delhi was still a hundred miles away.

'That was the beginning of two harrowing hours for us, when we were suspended between life and death,' Payal Singh said later. 'A bloodthirsty mob, almost like a pack of hungry wolves hunting for prey, went from coach to coach in search of Sikhs.

'In a frenzy of madness, the mob, armed with iron rods and knives, brutally dragged out Sikhs, burnt their turbans, hacked them to death and threw them across the tracks. Even the old and feeble were not spared. The barbaric mob, totally devoid of rationality, declared that women would be spared. But in what sense were they spared? After all, what can be more terrible for women than seeing male members of their family hacked to death in front of their eyes?

'The only *sardars* [male Sikhs] who were spared were the six with us. And all because of the concern and cooperation of the passengers in our coach. Before the train even halted at Ghaziabad, the hysterical mob had caught a glimpse of the six *sardars* with us. A fusillade of stones followed and the glass windows were smashed to bits. Shutters were hastily put down for protection. The police, we were told, could not control the wild mob and so they just turned their backs and walked away.

'We had a ladies' compartment and the other passengers in our coach, realizing there was more trouble ahead, suggested that the *sardars* in our group occupy it. At first, they were reluctant but we literally forced them to stay inside. It was ironic. *Sardars*, who were historically known for their valour now had to protect themselves by hiding in a ladies' compartment or else become victims of a hysterical horde.

'The main doors of our coach were locked from inside. And we waited with bated breath. The mob, hell-bent on destruction, was not to be deterred.

'They pounded on the heavy metal door for over fifteen minutes. The incessant pounding was accompanied by threats to set the train on fire. One non-Sikh passenger shifted uncomfortably in his seat and said he felt they would all lose their lives if the door was not opened. But he was sternly reprimanded by the others, who declared that under no circumstances would the door be opened.

'But the mob finally broke open the door. Their violent

mutilation of the train had only whetted their appetite for more destruction.

'The mob stormed into our coach. And walked past the ladies' compartment. But before we could even sigh with relief, they turned around and demanded that the door of the ladies' compartment be opened, so that they could check it.

'By now our nerves had reached breaking point. Yet we couldn't lose our composure lest they suspect that something was amiss. We tried to convince them that there were just women inside but the mob was adamant. And they began to bang on the door.

'The petrified screams of two women inside our compartment, our own pleas, and the persuasion of the other non-Sikh passengers finally seemed to convince the mob that there were no *sardars* inside. The mob retreated.'

When Payal Singh's train reached Delhi at three o'clock that afternoon, its surviving Sikh males helped carry out corpses from compartments. By then other trains were also arriving in Delhi from northern Indian cities. Scores of Sikh males lay dead in them.

'The bodies had been battered,' Payal Singh said later. 'Those Sikhs were innocent people who had done nothing – except for being Sikhs and travelling toward Delhi on that fateful day.'

In Britain, where there are said to be nearly 500,000 Sikhs, there was jubilation in the Sikh community over Indira Gandhi's death.

Jagjit Singh Chohan, the self-appointed 'president' of Khalistan, gave several television interviews when the news of the assassination broke in London.

'She was doomed to die,' Chohan, a physician with a long white beard and a gentle manner, said. 'She deserved to die.'

What about Rajiv Gandhi, an interviewer asked, would he now also be killed?

'He's definitely a target,' Chohan said, 'and he should be.'

Sikhs organized processions in Southall, the London neighbourhood that the British call 'Little India'. They distributed sweetmeats and chocolates. Sikh women danced in the streets. Non-Sikhs recoiled in horror. Hindus conducted special mourning services in temples. In New York City, too, many Sikhs were ecstatic over the event. They bought hundreds of dollars' worth of candy and distributed it to passers-by in front of the Indian grocery stores on Lexington Avenue in Manhattan. They drank cham-

pagne. They gave out roses. They tore up photographs of Indira
Gandhi and spat on the Indian flag. Like Chohan across the
Atlantic, they appeared on television programmes and said they
were delighted about Mrs Gandhi's death.

If tensions between Hindus and Sikhs had built up in India
because of the Punjab problem, these frictions had until now rarely
been mirrored in relations between the two communities in Britain.
Hindus and Sikhs had mostly lived in harmony here. They were,
after all, both strangers in a land where white people's attitudes
towards non-white immigrants were becoming guarded, even hostile. Britain, which once hired people from its former tropical
possessions in the West Indies and India for its textile and manufacturing industries, was now withdrawing this welcome. Britain's
economy was languishing; the great foundries of the Midlands were
shutting down, as British manufacturers lost out in the face of sharp
competition from Western Europe, Japan, Taiwan, even Singapore; unemployment was in excess of 12 per cent – in a country of
barely 53 million people. (Total immigration into Britain in 1983, in
fact, was 12,000, the lowest annual figure in recent years.) The
immigrants from the Indian sub-continent worked especially hard.
Sikhs, particularly, had become the single most affluent ethnic
community in Britain. Many of these wealthy Sikhs had started off
as farmers in the Punjab.

It was in Britain that the Khalistan movement gathered steam.
Men like Jagjit Singh Chohan, who became unhappy with Indira
Gandhi's stonewalling tactics concerning Sikh demands for greater
autonomy in the Punjab, decided that the time was propitious to
launch an agitation not for an autonomous state but for an independent and theocratic nation – Khalistan. Khalistan means 'Land of
the Pure' (as does the word Pakistan; perhaps it is no coincidence
that Islamic Pakistan, once part of Greater India, has tacitly
supported Chohan's Khalistan struggle). Chohan raised millions of
dollars for his cause from rich Sikhs all over the world. Khalistan
cells were created in Canada and the United States, where there are
significant Sikh enclaves. The Khalistan supporters issued their
own passports and their own currency, neither of which, of course,
was legal anywhere but in Chohan's well-appointed home in
London.

The Khalistanis feared that Sikhism was on the decline: Sikhs
were freely inter-marrying with Hindus; Sikh males were cutting off

their long hair (their religion requires males never to cut their hair) and beards; some Sikhs were returning to the folds of Hinduism – Hindus viewed Sikhism not as a separate religion but as a variation of Hinduism, much as Hindus hundreds of years ago had initially tended to regard Buddhism as a branch of their own faith.

The Khalistanis' fears were exacerbated by reports that orthodox Hindu proselytizers in the Punjab were proclaiming that Sikhs were only Hindus by another name. The Khalistanis were aware of Hinduism's great *modus operandi* – triumph not by coercion but by co-option; Hinduism assimilated and absorbed, it did not convert by the sword as Islam did. Chohan and his supporters felt that the purity of Sikhism could only be preserved in a totally independent Sikh nation. They began to solicit and receive the endorsement of many Sikh clergymen in the Punjab, who shared Chohan's apprehension that unless something dramatic was done soon – like creating a new Sikh nation – Sikhism would be completely absorbed by Hinduism in the not-too-distant future.

Supporting Chohan, too, was Sant Jarnail Singh Bhindranwale, the fiery Sikh fundamentalist. Bhindranwale, once an ally of Mrs Gandhi, took refuge in the Golden Temple in Amritsar. From there he directed a terrorist movement that would result in the deaths of hundreds of Hindus and moderate Sikhs in the Punjab who did not support him. Indian intelligence officials were convinced that Bhindranwale's terrorist activities were financed by Sikhs living abroad, including Jagjit Singh Chohan. These officials also seemed convinced that the Sikh separatists were somehow being helped by the American Central Intelligence Agency. (The widely held assumption among Mrs Gandhi's aides was that the United States wanted to keep India – which was perceived as a Soviet ally – off-balance; Indian officials noted that with the deepening military and economic ties between the Reagan Administration and Pakistan, India was forced to buy more high-tech weapons from the Soviets.)

Indira Gandhi viewed the Khalistan 'struggle' not only as a secessionist movement, but also as one that directly and immediately threatened the unity and integrity of India. If Sikhs were allowed to break away into their own nation, then would the people of another strategic border state, Kashmir, not also accelerate their simmering movement to gain independence from India? Mrs Gandhi was aware that in the cases of both Punjab and

Kashmir, neighbouring Pakistan, India's bitter foe, was providing moral support, and maybe more. Sikhs were in the majority in the Punjab; Moslems enjoyed a majority in Kashmir. If the Punjab became Khalistan and Kashmir became independent – or was annexed by Pakistan, as was possible – then, as the Indian writer M. J. Akbar said, the Indian capital of Delhi would 'end up as a border city'.

This Mrs Gandhi could never allow.

After much hesitation, she sent in her troops in June 1984 to flush out Bhindranwale's terrorists from the Golden Temple. Ralph Buultjens recalls her anguish over the military action. He had been in New Delhi the day that the prime minister gave her military commanders the green light, and to the very end Mrs Gandhi was worried about the toll that the military action would inflict. Awesome damage was done to the historic shrine during the military operation; not only Bhindranwale and his key lieutenants but also hundreds of pilgrims, including women and children, were killed. Sikhs all over the world were horrified. The Khalistan leaders swore they would take revenge.

So on this October morning in London, Chohan and his friends were beside themselves with joy when they heard that Indira Gandhi had been murdered by two of her Sikh security guards.

'In June, when we said we would kill her, no one believed it,' said a Sikh who identified himself as Baldev Singh. 'We've done it. And we will continue until Khalistan is formed.'

Later in the day, various television programmes recapped Prime Minister Gandhi's turbulent career. The BBC ran snippets from one of her last television interviews. Did she fear being killed by the Khalistanis who had vowed vengence, an interviewer asked Mrs Gandhi?

'I've lived with danger all my life,' she replied, 'and I've lived a pretty full life. And it makes no difference if I die in bed or die standing up.'

Late in the evening of Wednesday, 31 October Rajiv Gandhi appeared on Doordarshan, India's government-run television network, to address the 800 million people whose prime minister he had so suddenly become. He spoke from One Safdarjung Road, with a garlanded portrait of his mother in the background. He spoke slowly, in English first, then in Hindi, and his face was composed. He did not even look tired, although his day had begun at four o'clock in the morning in distant West Bengal, where he'd been sent by Mrs Gandhi on a political mission.

'Indira Gandhi, India's prime minister, has been assassinated,' the new prime minister said. 'She was mother not only to me but to the whole nation. She served the Indian people to the last drop of her blood. The country knows with what tireless dedication she toiled for the development of India.

'You all know how dear to her heart was the dream of a united, peaceful and prosperous India. An India in which all Indians, irrespective of their religion, language or political persuasion, live together as one big family in an atmosphere free from mutual rivalries and prejudices.

'By her untimely death, her work remains unfinished. It is for us to complete this task.

'This is a moment of profound grief. The foremost need now is to maintain our balance. We can and must face this tragic ordeal with fortitude, courage and wisdom. We should remain calm and exercise the maximum restraint. We should not let our emotions get the better of us, because passion would cloud judgement.

'Nothing would hurt the soul of our beloved Indira Gandhi more than the occurrence of violence in any part of the country. It is of prime importance at this moment that every step we take is in the correct direction.

'Indira Gandhi is no more, but her soul lives. India lives. India is immortal. The spirit of India is immortal. I know that the nation will recognize its responsibilities.

'The nation has placed a great responsibility on me by making me head the government. I shall be able to fulfil it only with your support and cooperation. I shall value your guidance in upholding the unity, integrity and honour of the country.'

If his speech seemed a bit disjointed, that was because at least half a dozen aides had been responsible for it. One draft was written by H. Y. Sharada Prasad, Mrs Gandhi's information adviser and chief speech-writer; other contributors included Rajiv Gandhi's closest friend at the time, Arun Singh, a former corporate executive and scion of a royal family. Arun Nehru, Rajiv Gandhi's third cousin and his adviser on Congress Party affairs, also made some suggestions, as did Gopi Arora, a powerful bureaucrat attached to the prime minister's secretariat. Even Sonia Gandhi pitched in.

Although the speech was broadcast close to midnight, millions of Indians – perhaps as many as 75 million, according to several estimates – were believed to have watched Rajiv Gandhi on television. Few Third World leaders had ever had such a huge audience.

He had been sworn in as prime minister barely five hours before the speech at a simple ceremony at Rashtrapati Bhavan, the residence of India's constitutional head of state, President Zail Singh. There, under a glittering chandelier in a vast chamber called the Asoka Hall, Rajiv Gandhi had become India's seventh and youngest head of government. Zail Singh, an amiable Sikh who had been selected for the job by Indira Gandhi mostly because of his total loyalty to her, fawned over the new prime minister, who didn't seem inclined for much small talk. Members of the cabinet stood around.

Zail Singh had risen that day in Sanaa, the capital of the Yemen Arab Republic. Yemen was the last stop on a two-nation official tour that had included Mauritius. It was his secretary, A. C. Bandopadhyay, who gave Singh the news of the shooting of Indira Gandhi. The president decided at once to abandon his tour and leave for India. He asked the formal guard-of-honour ceremonies at the airport to be dispensed with. His chartered Boeing 707 would normally have flown from Sanaa to Bombay for a refuelling stop, but Singh requested the pilot to fly directly, if possible, to New Delhi. The plane's crew were not happy with the request, but under the circumstances they said they would oblige.

During the five-hour plane journey, Singh's aides – who included Bandopadhyay, Special Assistant I. S. Bindhra, and a senior secretary in the external-affairs ministry – kept in touch with Delhi by radio. Singh himself declined lunch and lay in his bed for more than three hours. He reflected on the years he had served Indira Gandhi, and he reflected on his own years as chief minister of the troubled Punjab, where he was Mrs Gandhi's emissary to Sikh leaders who agitated for greater autonomy for the state. He had failed to bring about a lasting solution to the Sikh crisis, and indeed there were some critics who felt that he had contributed to escalating that crisis. And now Indira Gandhi was dead, killed by two Sikh guards, and Zail Singh wondered whether history would have changed had he and his Punjab Congress associates acted differently.

Singh was met at Delhi's Palam International Airport by Vice-

President R. Venkataraman; Rajendra Kumar Dhawan, who had been Mrs Gandhi's closest aide, Balram Jakhar, the speaker of the lower house of Parliament, the Lok Sabha; Dr P. C. Alexander, who had served as principal private secretary to Mrs Gandhi; and Arun Nehru.

During the twenty-minute ride from the airport to the All-India Institute of Medical Sciences Arun Nehru raised the question of succession.

'The Congress parliamentary board has decided that Rajivji should become PM,' Nehru, a giant of a man with a permanent scowl bolted to his face, said to Singh.

The board at that time had just four members instead of the normal nine: Home Minister P. V. Narasimha Rao, Finance Minister Pranab Mukerjee, Maragatham Chandrasekhar, and senior Congress Party aide Kamalapati Tripathy. Mrs Gandhi had been a member of this board, which served as the highest policy-making unit of the ruling Congress Party. When the assassination occurred, Narasimha Rao was in his home constituency of Warangal, Andhra Pradesh, and Mukerjee was with Rajiv Gandhi in West Bengal, his own home state. Tripathy and Chandrasekhar were also out of Delhi.

It did not, of course, matter that these men were not at their station. Arun Nehru – who had muscled his way to pre-eminent power in the Congress Party – had already resolved that his cousin, Rajiv Gandhi, would become India's next prime minister. He was supported in this by Sitaram Kesari, treasurer of the Congress Party. Nehru and Kesari met with top Congress officials in a fifth-floor conference room at the All-India Institute of Medical Sciences and declared that the party had no other choice but to name Rajiv Gandhi to succeed his mother. Concurring with this were Chief Ministers Chandrasekhar Singh of Bihar, Janaki Ballav Patnaik of Orissa, Arjun Singh of Madhya Pradesh, and Shiv Charan Mathur of Rajasthan. The Nehru–Kesari decision was conveyed to other senior Congress Party officials during the afternoon. A formal letter advising President Zail Singh of the Congress parliamentary board's 'decision' was drafted by G. K. Moopanar, general secretary of the All-India Congress Committee. The letter also formally requested Singh to appoint Rajiv Gandhi as prime minister (under India's Constitution, it is the president who must name the prime minister).

Rajiv Gandhi and Zail Singh met up with each other on the eighth-floor of the All-India Institute of Medical Sciences. Singh hugged Gandhi. Then he plucked the red rose from the buttonhole of his *achkan*, and gently placed it on Indira Gandhi's body. He asked Rajiv Gandhi to come to Rashtrapati Bhavan at 6.30 p.m. for the formal ceremony during which Indira Gandhi's son would be sworn in as independent India's prime minister.

When Gandhi turned up at the president's sprawling sandstone home – where British viceroys had once resided and ruled – most of the Congress Party's top officials had already assembled in the Asoka Hall. Gandhi wore a white *kurta* and tailored pyjama trousers. He had shaved. His eyes seemed slightly red, but otherwise he looked remarkably self-controlled.

At 6.40 p.m., nine hours after his mother was shot, former pilot Rajiv Gandhi was sworn in as prime minister of India. He had never held a cabinet portfolio before; he had been a member of Parliament only since 1982; he had entered politics only reluctantly, and that too after his mother applied much emotional pressure on him after the death of her initial heir-apparent and younger son, Sanjay. All Rajiv Gandhi had ever wanted to do was fly planes for Indian Airlines, the domestic carrier. Now he was in charge of 800 million Indians.

By a stroke of fate, the forty-year-old Gandhi had become the leader of the world's largest democracy, the most powerful nation of the 101-member bloc of countries calling themselves the Non-aligned Movement. He was now chief executive of a country with the biggest military force in the world after the United States, the Soviet Union and China. His theatre would no longer be the cockpit of the turbo-prop planes he had piloted for Indian Airlines, nor even just the great land mass of the sub-continent. From now on, it would be the whole world itself.

CHAPTER FOUR:
INDIA AFTER INDIRA

The murder of Indira Gandhi in her own garden by two trusted Sikh security guards changed for ever the political landscape of India, and arguably of the Third World as well. It touched off a holocaust in which thousands of innocent Sikhs were massacred by Hindu mobs who were blessed, if not led, by factotums of the ruling Congress Party. The very idea of secularism, ardently espoused by Mrs Gandhi's father, Jawaharlal Nehru, and so eloquently enshrined in the Indian Constitution, was suddenly threatened. Government in the capital city of Delhi was paralyzed. The question on everyone's mind was: will India, the world's biggest democracy, survive as one nation?

On the day that the prime minister was assassinated, there was no massive outpouring of grief for Mrs Gandhi in most places across this huge country. There was, of course, alarm over the brutal manner in which she had been murdered by her own security guards – and Sikhs at that – but about Indira Gandhi herself there was a noticeable ambivalence. Shops and offices shut down, and people welcomed the opportunity to go home early. Other than her friends, her Congress Party associates and the sycophants who now stood to be deprived of her patronage, most people simply did not shed tears for her.

I recalled the day when Mrs Gandhi's father, Jawaharlal Nehru, India's first prime minister, died in 1964. I was in high school then. The whole nation shook with shock and sadness; people cried openly. Nehru, the father of modern India, attracted hero worship and affection from the masses as no one before him had done –

perhaps not even Mahatma Gandhi, Nehru's mentor and the man who more than any other helped obtain for India her independence after 150 years of British colonial rule.

Nehru's daughter was far less loved by ordinary Indians, although there were periods – after the 1971 victory over Pakistan in the Bangladesh War, for instance – when Indira Gandhi enjoyed overwhelming popular support. She lacked his public warmth, his affability and his gift of laughter. She lacked his conviction that people would ultimately respond to enlightened leadership with good civic behaviour. Throughout her years of stewardship of India, Indira Gandhi came across to many people as a grim woman of unbridled ambition who would stop at nothing to gain and consolidate power.

There was more to it than that: both Nehru and Mahatma Gandhi (who was not related to Indira Gandhi) paid enough attention to the essential plurality of India; they sought consensus, they solicited advice from many people, including those politically and ideologically opposed to their own positions. These tactics obtained for Nehru, especially, widespread popular admiration. His daughter, instead, had imposed on the national scene the will of one person.

It was, of course, a matter of style, and maybe of circumstance. Rajni Kothari, one of India's most distinguished political scientists, puts in this way: 'That she wanted "national unity" and strove for it, there need be no doubt. But the politics that she pursued to achieve her goal left deep scars on the country's communal, regional and political framework. During her reign, well-established institutions began crumbling. One reason why many of her admirers, as well as some among her critics, thought that there was no alternative to Mrs Gandhi was that she had succeeded in creating a number of problems that she convinced everyone only she could handle. Now she is gone, but the problems are very much there – if anything, likely to get worse.'

What Indira Gandhi did since her swearing-in as prime minister on 24 January 1966, was to attempt a transformation of the manner in which political power was exercised in India. Rather than seek popular and secular support as Nehru had, she sought, especially in her last years, to rouse – however subtly – the chauvinistic sentiments of the country's Hindu majority (Hindus constitute nearly 80 per cent of India's population of 800 million people) whose electoral support she considered vital to her political survival. 'My father was a statesman, I am a political woman – my father was a saint, I am not,' Mrs Gandhi once said, in a rare moment of candour.

The name of her game was always political survival. She moved from her father's policy of seeking national consensus to one of confrontation. Confrontation, of course, was her way of keeping her opponents constantly off-guard. The creation of problems was a key aspect of her style – because then she could demonstrate that only she could solve those problems. So what Indians were left with were situations like the Punjab, where Mrs Gandhi refused to grant what were essentially simple demands by Sikh leaders for more economic benefits for the state that continues to be India's granary.

She refused to accept the legitimacy of an opposition government in another strategic border state, Kashmir, and actively undermined and subsequently toppled that administration. She alienated the sensitivities of southerners when she authorized a clumsy – and unsuccessful – attempt to overthrow a legitimately elected opposition government in the state of Andhra Pradesh. In short, Indira Gandhi could tolerate no opposition of any kind: she wanted to be unchallenged. It was not necessary to create these problems, and Mrs Gandhi was not able to manage them – and now they remain to haunt her son and successor, Rajiv Gandhi. She bequeathed to Rajiv the office of Prime Minister of India, but she also left him a legacy of chaos and confusion.

In the end, Indira Gandhi fell victim to the very poisons she injected into the Indian system. And so, in the days following her assassination, India mourned, but it did not cry for Mrs Gandhi.

It occurred to me that October day that the murder of Indira Gandhi in her Delhi garden nevertheless brought to an end a special era, just as Nehru's death from natural causes at the age of seventy-four had. It was an era dominated by an on-going confrontation between Mrs Gandhi and the Opposition parties, but it was also an era of a charismatic leader whose style and character had been forged in the freedom struggle against the British. Later that day, 31 October, it was announced that Mrs Gandhi's son, the forty-year-old Rajiv Gandhi, would become prime minister. His ascension opened the door for a generation of political leaders who were born or who grew up after independence in modern India, and who were likely to be more technologically oriented and receptive to modern business strategies than Mrs Gandhi and the politicians of her generation.

On 24 and 27 December of that year, nearly 300 million voters participated in elections for the national Parliament – and Rajiv Gandhi's ruling Congress Party won an unprecedented 401 out of 508 seats contested. The young Gandhi had campaigned promising change, but he provided few specifics.

When the election results were announced on the morning of 29 December, the stunning majority that Indian voters handed to Rajiv Gandhi was widely interpreted not as an endorsement of Indira Gandhi's policies, nor as a sympathy vote. Gandhi was seen as having received a mandate to institute accelerated change; he was seen as the man to fulfil the aspirations of a young population, 75 per cent of whom were born after independence. For this post-independence generation, Rajiv Gandhi, despite his political inexperience, was clearly India's hope for the future.

His triumph also reflected the widespread disenchantment of Indian voters with the national Opposition parties, which they saw as being disunited, petty-minded and aimless. It was the first time since independence in 1947 that a massive negative vote was cast by Indians not against a government in power but against an Opposition. It was not an especially heartening campaign: more than $300 million was said to have been spent by Gandhi's ruling Congress Party, among other things on an advertising campaign that stirred up voters against any public dissidence by raising the spectre of disintegration. The Opposition parties were cleverly portrayed as promoting disunity at a time of deepening national crisis over issues such as the Punjab and Kashmir; the Congress message was that the Indian nation was in danger and that Rajiv Gandhi's party alone was capable of saving India from anarchy. As Professor Kothari said to me, this was a big *coup* by a party that had brought the country to the brink of disintegration but successfully sold the line that the Opposition was actually responsible for it.

The Congress Party, with less subtlety, also appealed to the deep-rooted communal instincts of India's Hindu majority, particularly in the so-called 'Hindi-speaking belt' in the states of Uttar Pradesh, Haryana, Bihar, Madhya Pradesh and Rajasthan. It was not just that India's 14 million Sikhs felt alienated; the Moslem population of nearly 80 million – which is the largest in the world after Pakistan, Indonesia and Bangladesh – felt similarly shut out of the political process. No doubt a major factor underlying the 'Rajiv Wave' was the big communal backlash of the Hindu voter: the backlash represented a dramatic reversal of India's political culture, as also of the core of Hindu identity.

According to many Indians, a long period of pluralistic, segmented existence was leading to a slow sense of uneasiness with mainstream politics, to a sense of being cheated, a feeling that the very spirit of accommodation and tolerance on which the Hindus pride themselves was being misused, that India's 'minorities' – from Moslems and Sikhs to tribal communities in Assam – were being pampered.

Many Indians saw the heavy Hindu communal vote for Rajiv Gandhi's Congress Party as a sign of assertion by India's Hindu majority. In addition to appealing to the communal instincts of that majority Rajiv's campaign shrewdly combined his 'Mr Clean' image with the confrontational rhetoric of a nation in peril. His election rhetoric had it all: the Opposition was illegitimate, we could do without one; there were serious threats from Pakistan and China, India's traditional enemies, and from the unidentified 'foreign hand' that guided anti-national forces. It was this combination that made Rajiv the darling of both the communalists and the progressives, and that gave him his victory.

His mother's death had brought him to leadership and given him his massive mandate. Had Mrs Gandhi voluntarily retired from politics, and had the trauma of her death not gripped the nation, such a mandate would not have been possible. But the challenge Rajiv Gandhi faced was how to overcome his mother's political legacy of communal discord and regional hostilities.

Indira Gandhi was a consummate practitioner of the politics of confrontation, both along communal and regional lines, and within the country's bewilderingly complex party system. She left behind an atmosphere of anxiety and insecurity about where India was heading. Rajiv Gandhi did not possess his mother's overwhelming personality, nor her charisma, and probably not her ruthlessness. So how was he going to do it? How was he going to tackle the problem of Sikh separatism in the Punjab? Of tribal discord in Assam? Of Moslem dissatisfaction in Kashmir? How was he going to reassure India's diverse minorities that their welfare would be looked after? How was he going to arrive at some working accommodation with Pakistan and Bangladesh and Sri Lanka, neighbouring nations that had long felt that Big Sister India behaved like a bully and actively worked to destabilize their own nations under one pretext or another?

And what about the thorny business of relations between the central government and the states? India's twenty-five states were certain to demand greater devolutionary powers, and they were certain to ask for a larger share of tax revenues. These states, after years of being treated like stepchildren by Indira Gandhi, were certain to demand more equitable treatment. The only way for Rajiv Gandhi to deal effectively with such demands would be to federalize India's political system even more and to decentralize authority. But his mother, who didn't much care for states' rights, had left behind an extremely centralized system.

So in the months following Indira Gandhi's assassination, I felt that the great theme in India in the years ahead was likely to be one of the management of power in a multi-cultural nation state given to what the Indian press likes to call 'fissiparous tendencies'. Would Rajiv Gandhi be willing to devolve power when his mother had left him a heavily centralized administration? Would he interpret his huge election victory as a justification for more concentrated authority in Delhi, or as an opportunity to share power with the states? Would the Delhi-states power nexus consist of an iron chain emanating out of the prime minister's office in the capital? Or would this nexus consist of a silken thread?

During my travels across India, I repeatedly asked Indians about the effect Indira Gandhi's helmsmanship had on their individual lives. One bitterly cold evening in Delhi, the late Romesh Thapar, one of India's most incisive political and social analysts, shared tea and his thoughts with me. 'Indira Gandhi has left behind an extraordinary record of mercurial, manipulative, conspiratorial and brilliant leadership,' he said. 'Everything she did affected the entire political system.' But how did her actions touch India's ordinary people? Had she been an agent of change for the better?

There were other questions I put to people, or that rose out of conversations as I moved through the country: How did a society that set out on a particular model of integration find its secular vision collapsing? How had popular disenchantment with tra-ditional politics led to a growing belief in the value of modern managerial techniques to bail the country out of its woes? Would 'technology and science' – the new buzzwords in India – really clean up the country's socio-political mess? I looked into the economic 'liberalization' that was being instituted: would India open itself to the West? Would Rajiv Gandhi allow free enterprise to thrive?

I asked whether the enormous problems of poverty were being tackled correctly? Had 'development' failed in India? Had land reform worked? Had the emphasis on rapid heavy industrialization led to intolerable deforestation and destruction of the environment? How could such institutions as Parliament, the police and the judiciary, which were weakened during Indira Gandhi's rule, now be revitalized and strengthened? A big question: with India expected to contain more than 2 billion people within the next fifty years, what urgent steps would be taken to slow down population growth without violating human rights?

And the biggest question of all was: would India hold together?

Nations, like people, do overcome tragedies, of course, and life does go on. In late 1984 and early 1985, what I saw and heard during my travels caused me to share the excitement that my friends Vir and Malavika Sanghvi said they felt in post-Indira India. There was a definite sense in the country that a new era of rejuvenated political leadership had arrived under Rajiv Gandhi. But would it bring better times for India's tens of millions, so many of whom had been kept hoping and waiting for so long? And when would the better times arrive?

I think it is fair to say that the five years since Rajiv Gandhi took power have truly offered few solid answers to those central questions. While there have been some striking economic gains – India has become the world's tenth largest industrial nation, for example – the principal beneficiaries of Rajiv Gandhi's economic liberalization programmes have been the already privileged upper-classes. To be sure, India's middle-class, estimated to number about 150 million, is growing along with the economy; but inflation has also eaten into the purchasing power of this middle-class. Down near the bottom of the social structure, India's impoverished millions – the majority of Indians, I might add – are still waiting for lastingly better times.

I flew from Bombay to Bangalore to meet Ammu George and her husband, T. J. S. George. They had given up a flourishing publishing business in Hong Kong and resettled in India. After more than two decades abroad, the Georges were tired – and they missed the ambience of India.

George had started a magazine called *Asiaweek* in Hong Kong, which soon became so successful that it set the standard for several weekly publications covering the turbulent political scene in East and South-East Asia. But he had had his fill of success; George now wanted to return to his first love, writing books in his native language of Malayalam. He and Ammu decided to settle in Bangalore, where they had bought some land.

By the time I visited them, however, George had been once again drawn into the fray of publishing. A friend of his, the newspaper magnate Ramnath Goenka, asked him to take over the languishing Bangalore edition of the *Indian Express*. So now T. J. S. George was back in the world of deadline-meeting, headline-fitting and leader-writing – except that working conditions at the *Express* were far more primitive than at *Asiaweek*, and the type of ultra-modern technology George had been accustomed to in Hong Kong's presses was unavailable in Bangalore.

I asked George why he had accepted Goenka's offer.

'Once a newsman . . .' George replied elliptically, and with a smile.

'He must have promised you lots of money,' I said.

'Yes,' George said, with an even bigger smile. 'My salary is one rupee a year. Thank God I'm financially secure because of *Asiaweek*. I couldn't afford to work on what the *Express* pays!'

George, a chunky, balding man with a low-key manner, seemed both buoyant and cautious when I met him. He had never been a supporter of Indira Gandhi, but now he felt that her son Rajiv was displaying encouraging qualities of leadership. He thought Rajiv Gandhi had the nation's goodwill with him and that most people wanted to give him a chance.

'Journalistically speaking, I cannot think of a more exciting country to be in than India,' George said. 'But what really saddens me is that India hasn't become a great country because of unimaginative and low-grade leadership. We have ample resources. Now, if only we have truly inspired and civilized political leadership, this is going to be a great country.'

I asked George if he honestly believed that lethargic Indians could be so disciplined that they would work in unison for the national good.

'Look, I was never a supporter of Indira's Emergency, but just think about what happened during those three years,' George replied. 'One day this country was hopelessly inefficient. The next day? Well, the next day the trains started to run on time, people started to report punctually for work, and so on. So while the Emergency was a political tragedy, it also proved to Indians that they possessed the intrinsic ability to do things well.

'I think one of Indira Gandhi's great failures was that she concentrated excessively on India's external role, when she should have focused on developing the country's internal strength. But I feel that you cannot expect to have a meaningful external role unless you have solid internal strength. Whatever leverage and strength you have in foreign affairs has to be a reflection of your internal strength. I think we should have taken a lesson from the Chinese. They first attended to their internal consolidation.'

The challenges to Rajiv Gandhi?

'I worry whether communalism in India will ever be contained,' George said. 'The way it has been allowed to grow – it's become a cancer. I think the biggest question facing us is: will India be able to rise above its communalism? I really worry about this. Can the majority Hindus live in peace with Moslems? And with the Sikhs? I don't think you can solve communalism through public speeches. Will the demands of electoral politics allow the containing of religious passions? No one knows the answers. What is encouraging is that democracy has taken deep roots in India. But Rajiv must not allow those roots to be consumed by the cancer of communalism.'

We broke for lunch. Ammu, a skilled cook, had prepared a savoury fish curry, which I polished off with zest. Ammu spends her time doing social work among the poor of Bangalore. She seemed heartened by the fact that Prime Minister Rajiv Gandhi had recently done something that his mother had failed to do – he had created a new Ministry for Women and Social Welfare. Moreover, the prime minister had included five women in his cabinet, and had also elevated several more women to high positions in his ruling Congress Party. As Ammu George saw it, Rajiv Gandhi had clearly calculated the benefits of thus appealing to half the country's population of 800 million.

Her husband was not surprised by Rajiv's actions concerning opportunities for women. The young Gandhi had always impressed him as a man who was sophisticated and modern in his approach.

'If first impressions are anything to go by, then I'm optimistic about Rajiv's prospects for success – and optimistic for India,' George said.

He paused to sip coffee.

'I'm not a man given to hyperbole,' George said, presently, 'I'm cautious by nature. But I can't but help feeling that the kind of India there was at Indira Gandhi's death may have died with her – the India of political cynicism, the India where the masses had nothing to look forward to but more frustration.

'I think what we are seeing now is a completely new India. This is a rebirth.'

Rebirth or replay? I pondered the question one evening in Bombay as I watched Rajiv Gandhi address a massive rally in Shivaji Park. The same placard-waving and slogan-shouting crowds that used to turn up at his mother's public appearances around the country were again in attendance here, and they cheered Rajiv repeatedly. Pictures of Indira Gandhi were hung on bamboo poles so that her stern face was everywhere. And there seemed to be as many security personnel as ordinary citizens. The young prime minister spoke about the great dream of development, and about how India would enter the twenty-first century a proud and prosperous nation. Change the voice, and it could have been Indira Gandhi speaking.

Clichés. Already Rajiv Gandhi had become a skilled employer of them. But this much can be said for him – he spoke with conviction and compassion.

It occurred to me as I listened to the prime minister that perhaps he and his youthful coterie might just be single-minded enough to forge ahead and make a success of their clichéd plans. I recalled the words of my friend Mohan Shah, a New York businessman, who said that in India anyone with a little bit of imagination and a bit of enterprise could make himself successful in almost any field he chose because there were so many opportunities for advancement. And that evening in Shivaji Park I also recalled the words of another friend, Bradford Morse, who then headed the United Nations Development Programme, an agency which has long dispersed around a billion dollars annually for economic development projects in the Third World. Morse once said to me that the chief responsibility of national leaders was to enlarge the capacity of their people.

As I looked at the young man on the platform, his unlined face smiling and acknowledging the accolades of his people, his eyes glinting with ambition, I remembered something else, too – something that Rajiv Gandhi's grandfather, Jawaharlal Nehru, had once said. In a celebrated speech to the Indian Constituent Assembly minutes before India became independent in August 1947, Nehru said:

'Long years ago we made a tryst with destiny, and now the time comes when we shall redeem our pledge. . . . A moment comes, which comes but rarely in history, when we step out from the old to the new, when an age ends, and when the soul of a nation, long suppressed, finds utterance. . . .'

My father had been among those who heard Jawaharlal Nehru speak. Years later, he told me that as he heard Nehru utter those memorable words the sentiment that kept swirling in his mind was: 'I wish him well – for his sake and for the sake of India.'

Both Nehru and my father are gone, and it is now more than forty years since India made that first tryst with destiny. But what Nehru said then, and what my father felt at that heady time of independence were, I thought, especially appropriate as Rajiv Gandhi took over the reins of India.

In those early days after Rajiv Gandhi's resounding victory in the December 1984 parliamentary elections, India's newspapers and news magazines carried editorial after editorial about the challenges that the forty-year-old prime minister faced. Poverty, unemployment, fissiparous tendencies, ethnic turmoil, sinister Sri Lankans, aggressive Pakistanis, renegade Sikhs – it was all laid out for Gandhi. He was reported to be so preoccupied with putting together a new cabinet in those days and finding jobs for his friends that I doubt if he had the time to take in all this advice.

It struck me that with notable exceptions such as Prem Shankar Jha – then of *The Times of India* – few of these editorial writers dealt with India's urban problems. During the election campaign, it had become fashionable for some opposition party leaders to rouse rural crowds by putting down the cities. Chowdhary Charan Singh, a former prime minister and now head of the Dalit Mazdoor Kisan Party, told rally after rally in his Haryana constituency: 'The cities can go to hell. The future of India lies in its villages.' Charan Singh was to die some months later, of natural causes.

Implicit in his speeches at the time was a sense that it was perhaps too late to do anything about urban decay, both physical and spiritual. Cities like Bombay, Calcutta and Madras had already become unsalvageable in the opinion of many urban planners. They suffered from irremediable housing, transportation and power problems. They had to be left to sputter along from crisis to crisis; they would survive somehow.

Sadly enough, I found, there were very few spokesmen for India's cities, very few dedicated men and women who were willing to address themselves to and redress urban woes. But in Bombay I met a woman named Bakul Patel, a management consultant who devoted several hours of her day to voluntary social work. Her emphasis was on providing proper learning environments for poor children. She has also worked to promote literacy and employment projects for destitute women in urban areas, and raised funds to build a planetarium in Bombay for children; she has also initiated the establishment of several day-care centres.

'What really bothers me is that the deteriorating conditions of our urban children and women are simply not priority issues in policy-making circles,' Bakul Patel said. 'Child labour is rampant in our cities, even though our Constitution forbids it. Brides are burned daily because they did not fetch their husbands' families sufficient dowry. Poor widows are forced into prostitution and begging. In Bombay alone, several studies have shown that nearly 60 per cent of the city's children don't even have basic immunization. Isn't it time our leaders really moved energetically to tackle such problems? Or do there have to be urban explosions before action is taken?'

Those questions were echoed in a lengthy conversation I had some days later in Bangalore with that southern city's controversial police commissioner, P. G. Halarnkar. He had become controversial precisely because he raised those very questions in public and in his private sessions with local politicians. Urban India, Halarnkar said repeatedly to anyone who cared to listen to him, was sliding dangerously fast into a crisis that would affect the well-being of the entire nation.

I did not think that Halarnkar was sounding false alarms. Consider the growth rates of the following Indian cities over the last decade: Jaipur, 57 per cent; Delhi, 56 per cent; Pune, 48 per cent; Ahmedabad, 43 per cent; Hyderabad, 40 per cent; Nagpur, 39 per cent; Bombay, 37 per cent; Madras, 34 per cent; Kanpur, 32 per cent; Calcutta, 30 per cent; and Lucknow, 23 per cent. The government's Census Department says that the overall rate of growth during the last decade for all India's cities was 46 per cent!

Halarnkar's Bangalore has become the fastest growing city in India, and one of the ten fastest growing cities in the world. Between 1974 and 1984, its population increased by 76 per cent to 3.5 million. Ten years ago there were an estimated 70,000 cars registered with owners in Bangalore; now there are at least 300,000. Ten years ago, Bangalore was a neat little city of parks, wide boulevards and quaint bungalows. Located in south-central India at an altitude of 3,000 feet, its climate was cool and healthy all year round; people from all over the country came here for their holidays – now they come here for jobs, in the process making Bangalore even more cosmopolitan but also adding to the city's congestion. Bangalore has become the Silicon Valley of India: its electronics companies account for more than 80 per cent of the national production; there are scores of micro-chip manufacturers here; eight industrial estates have sprung up in the last ten years and these estates – such as Peenya, Veerasandra and Dyavasandra – now contain nearly 10,000 small-scale industrial units, and more than 400 large and medium-scale factories.

Such industrial growth may be good for Bangalore's economy, but it has polluted its air beyond reprieve. Even the hardy plane trees and the bougainvillea that edge the city's roads look unhealthy. Huge government-owned enterprises such as the Indian Telephone Industries, Bharat Electronics Limited and Bharat Heavy Electrical Limited contribute heavily to the deterioration of the environment. On the outskirts of the city is yet another government-run industrial giant, Hindustan Aeronautics Limited, where sophisticated fighter jets such as the Jaguar IS are assembled or produced.

'This was largely unexpected and unplanned growth,' Commissioner Halarnkar said to me as we sipped aromatic Karnataka coffee in his office. 'The authorities knew that the city would expand – but what happened was beyond anyone's imagination.'

Politicians come and go, as do planners. Police commissioners in India tend to have greater longevity, but the job is not exactly sought-after. This is another way of saying that every official in the city likes to dump his problems with Halarnkar, because his office is a handy clearing-house for complaints. If the chaotic building boom results in traffic jams in part of the city, Halarnkar is summoned by the mayor for a dressing-down; if shoddy construction results in the collapse of a factory's floor, Halarnkar is asked to explain why the police did not keep a watchful eye when the building was raised. When it was recently revealed that property owners were selling residential plots for the equivalent of more than $25,000 an acre, Commissioner Halarnkar was asked by the state's chief minister why speculators and peculators weren't being kept in check. But when Halarnkar moved against men suspected of violating zoning and building codes, the city's political establishment conveyed its displeasure to him. Why? Because the commissioner had cited friends of these politicians.

'Every now and then I hear rumours that I'm going to be transferred,' Halarnkar, a tall handsome man with an infectious smile, told me. 'Then the rumours quickly fade. I suppose no one wants this job! I'm expected to be both a good cop and a good boy.'

(Halarnkar's remarks reminded me of another conversation I'd had with a man named Arun Bhatia. The Cambridge-educated Bhatia had been a rising star in the élite Indian Administrative Service until he exposed corruption in the rural Dhulia district of Maharashtra state where he had been posted as chief administrator. Lower-level bureaucrats were routinely fudging the records of a multi-million-dollar government employment guarantee scheme for local people. Fictitious names were put on the employment rolls and the 'salaries' siphoned off to local officials and their friends. The local police, who were in league with the bureaucrats, declined to make arrests – even when Bhatia painstakingly documented evidence of wrongdoing.

(The state government transferred Bhatia to Bombay. There he again exposed large-scale corruption in the so-called floor-space-index business: wealthy builders of high-rise apartments were falsifying their applications to the local authorities, who in effect would allow these builders to raise structures bigger than the zoning regulations permitted. Money obviously changed hands. What happened to Bhatia? He was demoted and given a minor post under a senior official at whom he had pointed an accusing finger. Arun

Bhatia finally left the Administrative Service. He now works for the
United Nations in Botswana.)

'A police officer in India is also a social worker,' the commissioner continued. 'And the cop's boss, the commissioner, has to
be a sort of grand uncle. In India people come to a policeman for
everything, not just problems of law and order. We have to be not
only professional but always personable. We must deal with communal disputes. We must sometimes officiate at religious ceremonies! I even have a full-time worker who does nothing but go
out and kill snakes. He's caught more than a thousand snakes so
far.'

Halarnkar was worried that Bangalore was rapidly losing out on
three fronts: its salubrious climate was worsening because of the
pollution, its pleasant physical environment was deteriorating because of the crowds and the dreadful traffic, and crime was on the
increase. 'I'm afraid we're headed for complete confusion here,' he
said. 'Traffic is already nightmarish. The authorities have done
nothing about building flyovers, or about widening the major
arteries. The people of Bangalore laugh at the plight of Bombay –
but let me tell you, we're heading in that direction. The joke may be
on us if we go on like this.'

The police force in Bangalore has not been strengthened as much
as Halarnkar would like. Because this city is spreading out and
because its residential colonies tend to consist of bungalows rather
than more easily protected high-rise buildings, burglaries and
house break-ins are on the rise. Halarnkar wants the authorities to
increase the number of police precincts from sixty-seven to ninety
at the very least. Still, the commissioner has significantly stepped up
such things as night patrols; he has formed neighbourhood civilian
patrol groups; he has sponsored security seminars in residential
colonies. One social problem afflicting Bangalore is a form of
gambling known around here as *matka*. Men often gamble away
their property and sometimes even their wives. The *matka* dens
have been known to finance campaigns of politicians, which makes
Halarnkar's job that much tougher.

The Indian police system came under special scrutiny following
the assassination of Indira Gandhi. Many members of the 30,000-
man Delhi police force participated in the widespread looting and
ravaging of Sikh homes in the capital, and law and order collapsed
for nearly a week after the prime minister's murder. Policemen in

several northern Indian cities helped themselves to goods taken
from Sikh homes, or stood idly by as Sikhs were beaten and burned
alive. Although thousands of Sikhs died in the violence, not one
arrest was made in the capital, nor in most other northern cities.
The key question that was raised by many thoughtful observers of
the Indian scene was: does India's million-strong police force have
sufficient integrity? The national police force consists of the states'
police officers and the centrally supervised Indo-Tibetan Border
Police, Border Security Force and Central Reserve Police Force.
Police officers in India are notoriously ill-paid – even top officers
earn no more than 4,000 rupees a month, the equivalent of $300;
the ordinary constable takes home less than $50 a month. No
wonder policemen are susceptible to bribery and corruption.

One would think that in a country of 800 million, police manpower and budget would be items of special interest to the nation's
leaders. Yet the combined national and states expenditure annually
is less than $800 million. There are fewer than 26 policemen per 100
square kilometres – or just about 13.1 for every 10,000 Indians. A
government-appointed National Police Commission has recom-
mended several measures to improve the quality of police work in
India; the recommendations include such things as more modern
equipment, higher salaries, better training and greater supervision
of police constables in rural areas, where police atrocities have
often gone unpunished. The commission has given the government
eight separate sets of recommendations since 1977 – when it was
formed – but nothing has been done about improving the situation.

As Bangalore's most visible public official, Commissioner
Halarnkar accepts the fact that his performance will seldom be
applauded here. Behind his attitude is a very strong conviction that
the way in which he handles the problems of growth in India's boom
city will significantly influence its future. I think, as I suspect
Halarnkar does too, that all is not lost in Bangalore yet. It still has a
chance to make order out of chaos. But Karnataka's political
leadership will have to act more forthrightly. Bangalore's city
fathers must act on the commissioner's advice and enact tough
legislation concerning emission-control and industrial waste; they
should get the city's industrial magnates to contribute towards a
beefing-up of the police force; they should enforce building and
zoning codes more strictly. I don't think that Bangalore's current
status as India's fastest growing city is one for anyone to covet or

cherish; it is in fact one that Bangalorites are already regretting.

On the way out of Bangalore, I looked through some old newspaper cuttings about the city. I came across one that described a visit that Prime Minister Jawaharlal Nehru made to the city in 1962. This, in part, was what he said:

'Bangalore, in many ways, is unlike the other great cities of India. Most of the other cities in India remind one certainly of the present, certainly of the future but essentially of the past. But Bangalore . . . more than any other great city of India is a picture of the future.'

And now, much more so than when Nehru spoke almost thirty years ago, the future has arrived in Bangalore. The future is now.

For several years I have known a man named Ajay Mody. He is a pilot with Air India, and during my travels in Africa and the Middle East as a foreign correspondent I would sometimes find myself in planes flown by Captain Mody. Each time we met, Ajay would urge me to go and visit his wife Aruna's brother, Daleep Mukarji.

'He is a very idealistic young man,' Ajay would say to me. 'He could have been a very successful, very rich, doctor in Bombay or any of the large Indian cities. Instead, Daleep chose to go and live in one of India's most backward districts and practise his medicine there. He is a very unusual young man – there just aren't too many people like him around, and one wishes there were.'

I finally caught up with Dr Daleep S. Mukarji. He is a tall, rather plump man, with a wide forehead, grey eyes, and an engaging manner. From Captain Mody's earlier description, I had expected to meet an intense, wound-up man – for many of the 'committed' development specialists one encounters in the field are sometimes afflicted with a zealousness that to an outsider can seem absurd. But Dr Mukarji turned out to be a jolly sort of fellow, with a puckish sense of humour, a man who enjoyed his occasional scotch on the rocks.

He lives in a village called Palyakrishnapuram, in the North Arcot district of India's southern Tamil Nadu state. About a thousand people live in Palyakrishnapuram, which is part of a rural 'block' of eighty-five villages. Dr Mukarji heads a medical team that looks after 100,000 people in this 'block', which is known as Kilvayattanankuppam, often abbreviated to K.V.Kuppam. This area is about as rural a region as there is in India. There is no organized industry of any kind here. Dirt roads criss-cross the area; water must be lifted from community wells. Electricity is only now being introduced in the region. Virtually everybody lives below the poverty line, which is to say that the average villager earns less than the equivalent of $100 a year. Most people eke out a livelihood from cultivating rice, bananas, sugarcane, peanuts and mulberries, and most work as landless labourers in the agricultural sector. There are two or three small factories which produce *beedis*, the strong, foul-smelling cigarettes smoked by villagers all over India.

Most houses have thatched roofs. The walls of these homes are fashioned from mud and bricks. At first sight, the area looks somewhat parched and, for otherwise lush southern India, surprisingly bereft of trees. I learned that until a decade or so ago this area was actually renowned for its tamarind, gulmohur, drumstick and peepal trees, but the villagers foraged heavily for firewood and indiscriminately tore down trees. There are very few trees left in Kilvayattanankuppam today, and the saplings that have been planted by Dr Mukarji and his associates will take many years to mature.

Daleep Mukarji and his wife Azra – a slim, beautiful woman from Hyderabad – came here in 1977. Dr Mukarji had earlier obtained his medical degree from the Christian Medical College in Vellore, in southern India, and then received a diploma in public health from the London School of Hygiene and Tropical Medicine. While in London, where many Indians have traditionally studied because of the colonial links between India and Britain, Dr Mukarji also took a degree in rural planning. Why did he choose to spurn offers he had received to practise medicine in some of India's wealthy urban areas?

'I believe it is possible to change India,' Dr Mukarji said to me. 'Unless we work at the grassroots where people matter, unless we work for some meaningful change in rural areas where 80 per cent of India's population lives – unless we do these things urgently, I don't see a viable future for our people. Our villagers have been hearing too many official statements about what is being done for them. It is only when you come to places like Kilvayattanankuppam that you realize how little of this political rhetoric gets translated into action at the grassroots.'

'I felt I had to go beyond the textbook,' he continued. 'I felt I had to bring about measurable changes in village health care. I wanted to demonstrate that we could indeed devise low-cost, feasible medical, family-planning and development schemes that were relevant to our country.'

Dr Mukarji came to Kilvayattanankuppam under the auspices of the Rural Unit for Health and Social Affairs of the Christian Medical College in Vellore. The college receives some financial assistance from its affiliations in the United States. He brought with him seven other physicians and three veterinarians, mostly young men and women who had just graduated from medical school and who were assigned by their institutions to Kilvayattanankuppam for practical training. In addition, there were about 200 field-workers whom he assigned to the eighty-five villages of Kilvayatta-nankuppam. 'We quickly found that there were practically no health services in this area,' Dr Mukarji recalled. So clinics were set up, as were centres to train more field-workers.

Kilvayattanankuppam was a horror story, a microcosm of many isolated regions of rural India. This area was an on-going example of what many delegates at a world conference in Alma Ata, in the Soviet Union, had warned about back in 1978. They had praised the conference's initiation of a campaign to achieve 'Health for All' by the year 2000, but some of the delegates said that conditions were so bad in many rural areas around the world that unless there was a major infusion of money and medical manpower in those areas, the conference's goal of primary health care for all would almost certainly never be met. In Kilvayattanankuppam, Dr Mukarji found that the infant-mortality rate was 117 per every 1,000 live births. Malnutrition was rampant. The local people suffered from respiratory diseases, and the incidence of tuberculosis and measles was high. Children were dying from diarrhoea and dehydration. Superstitious traditions persisted.

One afternoon, a woman brought her emaciated one-year-old boy to Dr Mukarji's clinic. The child had contracted diarrhoea, and was now dying of dehydration.

'Why haven't you given the child any water?' Dr Mukarji asked.

'Why should I?' the woman said. 'He is passing so much water with his stools. If I give more water, he will only pass it out.'

Dr Mukarji patiently explained to this woman that the child needed to replace the fluids he was losing. He administered a glucose solution to the child and asked the woman to bring the child back for further examination in a day or so. He gave her packets of a special solution to be fed to the child. To no avail – the boy died. The woman's in-laws had refused to let her carry out the physician's directives.

On another occasion, a young peasant couple visited Dr Mukarji at his modest, one-storey house in Palyakrishnapuram. They were the parents of a two-year-old girl. Two previous children had died. The peasants had come to consult Dr Mukarji not about their daughter but about the family cow.

'Why haven't you brought your daughter over for the second round of inoculations, as I had asked you to?' Dr Mukarji said sternly.

'We are more concerned about our cow right now,' the peasant said, in the local Tamil language. 'Our cow is a valuable asset. She is dying. Can you send someone to look at the cow and give medicine?'

'Are you saying that the cow is more important than your own child?' Dr Mukarji asked.

The couple looked uncomfortable.

'Well, you see, if our child dies we can always produce another one – we are still young and capable of having many more children,' the father said presently. 'But if our cow dies, we will not be able to afford another animal.'

I found this exchange intriguing. Later, Dr Mukarji explained that it was not as though the Kilvayattanankuppam peasants were being callous about the welfare of their child. But the fact was that the cow, whose milk the peasants sold, was the only source of subsistence for this couple. They simply could not afford to lose the animal.

'When I first came to Kilvayattanankuppam, I found these attitudes quite shocking,' Dr Mukarji said. 'I quickly found that you cannot be effective if you use conventional health approaches. You have to be both physician and sociologist, both physician and psychologist. Health is really a behavioural matter. Being a doctor here is not good enough – you have to get people to change their lifestyle. You have to study local customs and traditions.'

In places like Kilvayattanankuppam and other backward rural areas of the Third World, one also has to take into account the fact that the high illiteracy rate creates a situation where local people often simply do not follow nor understand the directions given to them by doctors. One afternoon a woman named Laxmi came to see Dr Mukarji, complaining of a severe earache. Dr Mukarji gave her some aspirin tablets – which Laxmi immediately proceeded to insert in her ears!

This incident recalled for me another situation in Andhra Pradesh several years ago. A friend of mine – a Sri Lankan political scientist (who asked me not to name him here) – was asked by the World Health Organization (WHO) to conduct an experiment where local women were given foam contraceptive tablets. Local medical personnel told the women that if they used these tablets they wouldn't get pregnant.

After nine months, the WHO team found that there was absolutely no change in the region's fertility patterns, which remained high. The women who had agreed to use the foam contraceptive tablets had all become pregnant.

'I was astonished,' the political scientist said. 'These women all swore they used the tablets. It was inconceivable that the tablets had failed in every case.'

Then he decided to ask the women themselves what had gone wrong.

'Have you been using the foam tablet before intercourse?' the political scientist asked one woman.

'Of course,' she replied.

'Then how did you get pregnant?'

'I don't know.'

'Did you have any problems using the contraceptive tablet?'

'Well,' the woman said, somewhat uncertainly, 'you see, all was fine – but whenever I swallowed the tablets, they started foaming in my throat.'

The tablets were meant to be inserted in the vagina – but somehow the medical team carrying out the WHO experiment had forgotten to explain this to the women. The experiment was a failure, but it cost $230,000.

One of the major problems that Daleep Mukarji encountered when he came to Kilvayattanankuppam was that there was no such thing as a 'community'. All the development textbooks talk about the need to develop the 'community' and to foster a 'community spirit' – but in many Third World societies local areas are characterized by factions, castes and tribal groupings. In Kilvayattanankuppam, Dr Mukarji had to contend with the fact that neighbouring villages sometimes lived in disharmony with one another. Some of the animosity dated back dozens of years to dimly remembered altercations over cows or brides. At any event, the Mukarji medical team found itself also having to play a peacekeeping role. This was achieved by frequent visits to homes and by frequent group meetings to which villagers from all over Kilvayattanankuppam would be invited.

'We all need to join hands to improve our living conditions,' Dr Mukarji would say during a typical meeting. 'In our fight against disease, there can be no room for personal hostilities.'

An initial priority was bringing down the frightening infant-mortality rate in Kilvayattanankuppam. Over the years, there had been a perceptible shift from breast-feeding to bottle-feeding of infants. Dr Mukarji saw that because bottles were not properly sanitized, and because the water in which the milk-formula was mixed wasn't usually boiled, babies became infected. Moreover, the quality of local cows' milk was inferior, contributing to malnutrition among infants. Dr Mukarji explained to local women that because of bottle-feeding, infants lost the colostrum in the early milk produced by mothers. Colostrum transfers from mother to child a fair amount of natural immunity and resistance to disease.

'Part of the problem in Kilvayattanankuppam was that people traditionally thought of a doctor as someone who could cure anything,' Daleep Mukarji said. 'The fault also lay with doctors who had treated these people in the past. They kept giving medicines, but the local people kept returning to their normal unhealthy environment. It became a sort of game: someone would fall ill, go to a doctor, get medicine, get well, then fall ill again in the same old unhygienic environment in which that person lived. So we decided early on that we'd work to change the local environment. We started teaching people about balanced diets, and vitamins and tonics, and proper domestic and personal hygiene. And then we quietly introduced family planning as well.'

The infant-mortality rate in Kilvayattanankuppam was brought down through such measures from 117 per 1,000 live births to 47. Mortality rates for children between the ages of one and five years dropped from 24 per cent to 11 per cent.

The fall in infant and child mortality in recent years has led to a decrease in Kilvayattanankuppam's annual birth rate – from 36 per 1,000 of the population, to 24 per 1,000. The area's peasants, like their counterparts in many other rural parts of the Third World, traditionally viewed more children as assets. When children kept dying through disease, these peasants kept having more as an insurance against old age: there is no old-age social security system in Kilvayattanankuppam.

'People here don't understand such concepts as doubling of population and limitations to the area's carrying capacity,' Dr Mukarji said to me. 'You have to just go ahead and make sure that their kids live, and then start persuading them that smaller families are happier, even more productive families.'

What struck me as significant about Daleep Mukarji's efforts was his integrated approach – his attention not only to health care and family planning, but also to economic activity in Kilvayattanankuppam. He and his associates have started a dairy farm in the area; there are now workshops where villagers can learn about water-pump maintenance and bicycle repair-work. Women are being taught how to weave. The Mukarji team has also set up thirty dairy cooperatives and three sheep cooperatives; one new development is an enterprise where villagers are being instructed how to raise broilers.

The other significant thing here is that Daleep Mukarji no longer performs charity work in Kilvayattanankuppam. When he and his associates from the Christian Medical College first came here, everything they did for villagers was for free; not a rupee was charged for medical services and supplies.

'Now the area is somewhat better off economically – and our feeling is that if you charge even a nominal amount for services rendered, you actually increase the self-esteem of local people,' Dr Mukarji said. 'No one likes hand-outs, no one – however poor and however illiterate – relishes the idea of being dependent on the largesse of others. Of course we don't insist on people paying, and when someone comes along who genuinely cannot afford our modest fees for medical care we don't press them. But those who can't afford to pay cash often pay us in chickens, milk or vegetables.'

Daleep Mukarji and his wife are so committed to Kilvayatta-nankuppam that they adopted a local child; they have two other children of their own. One day, of course, the Mukarjis will move on and go somewhere else where they are also needed. I bet it will be to another destitute area. Kilvayattanankuppam will miss them, but the work that Daleep Mukarji has performed will be his lasting legacy here.

Kilvayattanankuppam is near the eastern coast of India. Kolaba District is on the western coast. In Kilvayattanankuppam, the main language is Tamil; in Kolaba, it is Marathi. In Kilvayattanankuppam, almost everybody is Hindu; in Kolaba, Hindus are in the majority, but there are also enclaves of Moslems, traditionally bitter foes of Hindus. I went to Kolaba District, which is about sixty miles away from Bombay, at the suggestion of Asha Puthli, an old friend.

Asha is a jazz singer and actress who now lives in New York. She grew up in Bombay and in Kolaba District, where her parents long ago bought a farm in a small village called Tara. It was Asha's father, Umanath Puthli, who pioneered health care and family planning in the area. He went where he was needed, and even though he has been dead for a decade, Umanath Puthli's work for the deprived of Kolaba lives on in the improved quality of their lives, in the better health care that is available for them and in the enhanced economic opportunities for the region.

To get to Kolaba from Bombay, one must drive. Once the densely populated tenements of Bombay are left behind, you would expect the scenery to change quickly, to become greener, cleaner. That doesn't happen, because of the suburban sprawl. The fumes fifty miles out of Bombay are as noxious as they are in the centre.

Tara Village, where the Puthli family has a farm, consists of about eighty huts. Next to Tara are four other villages: Barapada, Kalai, Dolghar and Bandhanwadi. The local people here are mostly Hindus, but there are also some Moslems; and there are the Adhivasis, the tribal folk who came to the coast from the nearby Karnala *ghats*, or hills. The road from Bombay to the southern Indian resort of Goa (once a Portuguese enclave) cuts right through these five villages. They are villages like any other to be found in rural India: mud-splattered children run about; peasants toil in fields; women carry buckets of water on their heads and gracefully head home from the community well; cows graze languidly; chickens flutter around; mangy dogs yelp. It is quite possible that the motorist will give this scene no more than a glance, or perhaps even fail to notice these villages at all.

But no motorist will fail to spot the Yusouf Meherally Centre, a squat structure that sits by the Bombay–Goa road, across from the Puthli farm.

The Centre was Umanath Puthli's gift to the area. It is a fully equipped health-care and family-planning clinic. There is an operating theatre in the Centre, and a maternity ward. People come here daily not only from the five-village area but from hamlets as far away as a hundred miles. Signs painted in English and the local language of Marathi welcome patients. There is a neat garden all around the Centre, which is named after a legendary figure who participated in India's independence struggle against British colonial rulers; Yusouf Meherally was a friend and contemporary of Umanath Puthli. Smartly-uniformed nurses work in the facility. Local villagers contribute *shramdhan* – or free labour – and assist in the cleaning and maintenance work.

Asha Puthli remembers the days when all Tara Village had by way of a clinic was a corner in her parents' farmhouse.

'One weekend, my father suggested that I instruct local women about birth control,' Asha said to me. 'He was concerned about the high birth rate in these villages.'

At first Asha thought of distributing contraceptives, but that would have meant first setting up some sort of para-medical system. Then she saw that a popular local gadget was the abacus, an instrument villagers used for making calculations by sliding beads along rods or grooves. Why not use the abacus to instruct women in 'natural birth control', or the rhythm method, under which a woman abstains from intercourse during her fertile period?

So Asha got together a group of local women and told them all about fertile periods and infertile periods. She told them that each evening they should slide one bead from right to left: the beads marking infertile days – and therefore days when sexual intercourse was not likely to result in pregnancy – were painted black; the beads marking fertile days were red. When each womam came to the first red bead, she should abstain from intercourse until the fertile period was over, Asha told the villagers. They all nodded and went home with their abacuses.

Some weeks later, Asha found that virtually every woman who had used the abacus had become pregnant. She began investigating the situation.

'Haven't you been using the abacus the way I showed you?' Asha asked one woman.

'Yes,' the woman said, bashfully. 'But it is difficult for me to see the colour of the beads in the darkness.'

In those days, of course, there was no electricity in Tara Village. Once it became dark, it was pitch dark – most villagers couldn't even afford kerosene for lamps.

It is very different here now. All homes have electric power. Umanath Puthli, who had made his fortune as a businessman in Bombay, made certain of that. A paper factory was set up by some of his industrialist friends and jobs were thus created. A school was started. Hybrid seeds were introduced so that rice cultivation and fruit production could be stepped up. Avabai Wadia's Family Planning Association of India helped train local people to introduce birth-control facilities. Some of Umanath Puthli's physician friends from Bombay would come and spend weekends at his farmhouse and treat patients from the villages in the surrounding area.

Virtually every couple now uses birth control of some sort. Children are no longer rickety, and tuberculosis has been eliminated. Agriculture is flourishing. All this was achieved not through any massive infusion of foreign development aid but because one man decided he would devote all his resources to being where he was needed most – at the grassroots level. Well before the development experts started talking about the need to 'integrate' economic development efforts with family planning and health care, Umanath Puthli and his friends showed that when you improve living standards – however slightly and tentatively – of poor people 'development' does indeed act as the best contraceptive.

I asked a woman named Lalitha what she thought were the most dramatic changes in Tara Village. Lalitha is a short, thin woman and the mother of three children. Her husband grows a variety of high-yield rice that Umanath Puthli introduced in the area. Lalitha helps out in the Meherally health clinic. She has also learned to read and write.

'The most important change for us has been that we now know that is is possible to improve our lives,' she said, in Marathi. 'Before, there used to be despair here. Now we have some hope.'

What about family planning, I asked. Were villagers now enthusiastic about having smaller families?

Lalitha told me that she had undergone a tubectomy and that her husband had also been sterilized. No coercion was applied by anybody, Lalitha said. They decided to have sterilization operations after careful consideration.

'No one wants big families these days,' she said. 'What use are big families?'

In Kolaba District, the talk was about smaller families and birth control. Everywhere else, in those months following the December 1984 election, there was spirited talk of a 'new technological age'. Prime Minister Gandhi's youthful aides were quoted in newspapers and magazines as averring that their forty-year-old leader would guide India towards an unprecedented era of economic growth and social justice. It was not always just political rhetoric. Gandhi's government moved swiftly to liberalize import policies for the car industry, opening up that cobweb-ridden industry for vigorous new competition that would surely result in more, better and cheaper cars for ordinary Indians. Industrialists petitioning for new licences for expansion or joint ventures with foreign firms were now finding their applications being processed with greater alacrity. There was a sense in the business community that Rajiv Gandhi wasn't merely mouthing platitudes about change: he meant to hold his administrators accountable for their actions, and seemed determined that government should be a good manager.

Still, I was troubled by what I perceived to be the excessive adulation of the young prime minister. Of course, I could understand the reasons for such adulation: here was a handsome young man who spoke well; he particularly appealed to those Indians who had been born after independence – and there were now more than 400 million of them. Still, it occurred to me that Indians had forgotten that when Rajiv Gandhi's mother, Indira, won her huge electoral victories more than a decade before, there had been similar public outpourings of enthusiasm for her; she was seen as the leader who would pull India into a new age of modernity. She fulfilled few of her promises. Were Indians now again setting themselves up for similar disappointment? Was Rajiv Gandhi simply promising too much to his eager millions?

I looked up a number of fellow Indians whose opinions and judgements I valued. How did they assess the challenge of change in post-Indira India? And what faith did they have in Indians' capacity for change? I talked to Vasant J. Sheth, a self-made industrialist and chairman of India's biggest private shipping enterprise, the Great Eastern Shipping Company. Sheth, a tall, lanky man in his fifties with bushy eyebrows and a courteous manner, invited me for a cruise on his yacht. We went out past Bombay's harbour, past a number of tankers that Sheth owned, past destroyers, frigates and an aircraft carrier of the Indian Navy, and down India's western coast. It was a brilliantly sunny Sunday morning, and the breeze was sharp. We sat on the deck of the yacht, sipped freshly squeezed orange juice, munched peanuts and talked.

'Modernization means, most of all, having a modern mind,' Vasant Sheth said. 'Rajiv Gandhi has a modern mind, but I don't know about most of his government – and I don't know if most Indians possess a modern mind. The average Indian is a low-risk-taker. He believes in a *status quo* society. And all governments are important instruments of the *status quo*. My biggest fear is that this monolith, this octopus-like government that reaches into every area of our lives, can't and won't be able to bring about the changes we vitally need in our country. Over the years, governments have tried to absorb discontent by thoughtless recruitment to the lower-echelon bureaucracy. These lowly and low-paid public servants, in turn, have fattened themselves on bribes and "speed money" – gratuities they demand to push a file along towards the decision-making official. The bloated bureaucracy curbs individual enterprise and initiative.'

I asked Sheth what change he would most like to see made, and who he saw as being the instrument of that change.

'The most cherished goal for India to my mind is how best to enter the twenty-first century with real economic freedom,' he said. 'India already has the world's largest technological pool, after the United States and the Soviet Union. India is now the eighth or ninth biggest industrial power in the world. International bankers have given India triple "A" credit ratings.

'But I really do believe that if you want to get beyond rhetoric and the illusion of progress and want to work for honest change, only the country's élite can do it. Who are the élite? Top bureaucrats, professionals, voluntary agencies, businessmen, politicians. Members of this élite have to make sacrifices themselves in the national interest. India's economic success is only possible provided we cooperate rather than confront – we have to remove the labels that separate us, and, believe me, there are plenty of such labels. The task is gigantic.'

The next day, I went to see a man who is widely perceived to be at the leading edge of India's drive to become a technological power. His name is Ratan Naval Tata, and he is chairman of India's huge business house, Tata Industries. The Tata group consists of companies that manufacture, among other things, fertilizers, steel, locomotives, textiles, cosmetics, chemicals, heavy engineering equipment and vehicles. The Tatas also own a chain of luxury hotels in India and abroad. It was the Tata family that started Air India, the country's international airline. The Tatas have long enjoyed the reputation of being socially aware employers; they have channelled millions into charities, educational foundations, and family-planning programmes. The annual turnover of the Tata companies is more than $3 billion.

Ratan Tata is a tall, handsome and amiable man, who was then forty-seven. He received a degree in architectural engineering from Cornell University, and worked for several years with the Los Angeles architectural firm of Jones and Emmons. A few days before I met him, Tata had announced that his group would be investing millions of dollars into the development of appropriate high-technology products for India. His announcement had been applauded in Delhi by another youthful leader, Rajiv Gandhi – whom Ratan Tata occasionally meets for informal chats (Gandhi subsequently appointed him chairman of Air India).

Tata received me in his fourth-floor office at Bombay House, the Victorian building that serves as the group's headquarters. He had just returned from a visit to one of his factories and was in shirt-sleeves. For a man who was heir to a huge fortune and headed a distinguished group of companies, he had a surprisingly modest office – just some beige sofas, shelves that were packed with books and files, a large picture showing the cockpit of a plane, and a modern impressionistic painting that brightened up the otherwise drab room.

I asked Ratan Tata how realistically optimistic he was about the possibility of fundamental change in India.

'Six months ago there was great frustration in India,' Tata said. 'There was the obstacle of ideology. There was the obsession with promoting the public sector at the expense of the private sector – despite the proven track record of failure of public sector enterprises. There was also the obstacle of those who were close to power and had influence and who could therefore swing things their way for purely personal reasons. You concluded that things didn't happen on merit in Delhi.

'But today I sense there's been a change in ideology. The bureaucracy seems to be goaded to produce results rather than to stop progress. The sounds are different. And not only are the sounds different – I see that governmental attitudes are already changing in Delhi. There's a new courtesy that seems to be present in government. You feel it in the air in Delhi, where all the decisions that matter concerning economic progress are made. Bureaucrats have started listening to you more carefully – you're no longer kept hanging as in the old days. What I'm saying is that if all this is sustained and expanded, then maybe we'll see a new India being fashioned from the old.'

'Challenges?' he continued. 'The challenge before Rajiv Gandhi is to mould and marshal the great store of talent that already exists in the country. The challenge really is to find the right mechanism – the tools for change are already there in the form of manpower and management skills. The challenge for Rajiv is to make the country as a whole lose its lethargy and increase productivity and growth in all economic sectors. One of his major challenges is to make far more effective use of resources. In my view, Rajiv faces the challenge of changing the fabric of a very corrupt political environment.

'Rajiv has before him the task of creating a new industrial environment. Our industries must face the rigours of international competition – for too long they have enjoyed excessive protectionism. We have to create an environment where people are result-oriented and answerable for their actions. Here at Tata's, I welcome opening up to competition. Sure there will be some bloodshedding, some pain, suffering. But in the long run the new competition will make us all healthy. Some of my colleagues obviously don't agree – but this is the way I feel.'

What were his apprehensions?

'Most of all that Indians might be expecting too much of their new young prime minister,' Tata said. 'I worry that Indians, who generally assume that the government will do everything for them, will now expect that the Golden Age will automatically arrive.'

After leaving Ratan Tata, I walked down the corridor from his office to meet Nani A. Palkhivala, the vice chairman of Tata's. He is also India's most eminent constitutional lawyer and income-tax specialist. The author of several books, and a sought-after speaker, Palkhivala also served as India's ambassador to the United States from 1977 to 1979, during the time that the opposition Janata Party was in power and Indira Gandhi was in the political wilderness.

I found Palkhivala in a relaxed mood. His strained relations with Indira Gandhi had been much publicized by the Indian press, and it was no secret that Mrs Gandhi smarted under Palkhivala's frequent criticism of the corruption and inefficiency of her government. Gandhi aides had ordered numerous – and unsuccessful – investigations into Palkhivala's finances (he is probably the most expensive lawyer in the country). But Palkhivala has always led an open and scrupulously moral life, and given away much of his wealth to charities. One reason Palkhivala is widely respected is that his personal lifestyle is a model of austerity and rectitude. I thought that he was one of the best ambassadors India had ever sent to Washington, and during his two years there he made many friends for India.

'Rajiv Gandhi should be a quite different prime minister from his mother,' Palkhivala told me. 'I think his instincts are good. We all must wish him well because this is the most crucial turning point in Indian history.'

Palkhivala's view was that Mrs Gandhi left India in a mess, that her own rule was a disaster for the country. His interpretation of the massive electoral mandate Rajiv Gandhi received in the December 1984 parliamentary election was that people were simply tired of the old leaders who represented the various Opposition parties.

'The country clearly thinks that this young man with a fresh outlook might be the answer to all our problems,' Palkhivala said. 'I have always believed that if the country gets as a leader a wise man of humility, what could we not do in India? We have the manpower, we have the scientific brains, we have the industrial expertise, we have the technology, we have all the raw materials we need for rapid economic growth. This country is just yearning for the right leader – and so I hope that Rajiv shows the requisite degree of strength and wisdom. It is not beyond a man of vision to put the country on the right track.

'A vital point which is normally missed in political histrionics in India is that while it is possible in a poor country such as ours, to have economic growth without social justice, it is impossible to have social justice without economic growth. It seems to me that

"Economic growth for social justice" would be a more rewarding slogan than Mrs Gandhi's empty *"Garibi hatao!"* ["Remove
poverty!"] slogan.'

Nani Palkhivala had spoken of his confidence about India's ability
to achieve progress. I looked up one of the country's most eminent
scientists to ask his view on the subject.

Dr M. R. Srinivasan is chairman of India's Nuclear Power Board,
which makes him the head of one of the country's most important
industries and one which Prime Minister Rajiv Gandhi himself has
paid special attention to. He is a man of medium height, bearded
and with a pleasant disposition. Srinivasan invited me for breakfast
at his apartment on Malabar Hill, from where one can command a
view of virtually the whole of Bombay. Mrs Srinivasan, a jolly
southerner like her husband, served *idlis*, the typical South Indian
rice pancakes that can fill you up without filling you out. The
Srinivasans' living-room contained several photographs of the
scientist receiving various awards from President Zail Singh and
the late Prime Minister Indira Gandhi. These photographs were
tastefully displayed alongside Indian antiques.

Srinivasan told me that in the harnessing and use of atomic
energy, India had made far more progress than most people
realized. Already, India possessed what was called in the scientific
jargon 'control of the complete nuclear cycle' – which is to say that
India could now mine uranium, produce plutonium and nuclear
fuel and properly handle and dispose of nuclear waste products.
India is the only developing country that has such a capacity. By
early 1985, India produced more than 1,000 megawatts of power
through nuclear energy, or about 2 per cent of the total power
produced in the country. (By contrast, nuclear power accounts for
about 10 per cent of the power produced in such Western countries
as the United States and Britain.) The advances in the nuclear
field, Dr Srinivasan said, were largely home-grown – and he was
justifiably proud of the achievement.

'In any discussion of the challenge of change I don't think that
"science and technology" are just buzz words,' he said. 'If we are to
dramatically improve our standard of living, then we simply must
link science and technology to everyday living. By this I mean that
we need to develop better industrial methods, better varieties of
grain, safer and cheaper consumer products. One reason Japan has

done so well is the total ability of the Japanese people to accept science and technology as an integral part of their everyday life. In India we have to cultivate the scientific temper. For this we need an accelerated education programme that emphasizes the role of science. I think where we've failed as a society is that we've not been able to transform or motivate people to incorporate scientific habits so that they live in a healthier and more hygienic way. The key to this is education.'

The day after I met Dr Srinivasan, Rajiv Gandhi announced that his government would initiate a comprehensive review of India's educational system. Of course, nothing much came of the review.

While in Bombay, I also sought out a man named Anil K. Malhotra. Like Dr Srinivasan, Malhotra worked in a field to which Rajiv Gandhi was paying special attention. Malhotra was the senior member of India's Oil and Natural Gas Commission (ONGC). He was in effect the man who supervised the country's entire off-shore and on-shore oil and gas exploration and production programme; Malhotra, forty-five years old, was also the man who decided where to drill for oil – he controlled a budget of more than $3 billion. In the last decade, the ONGC, largely under the direction provided by Malhotra, had shown not only that its six thousand employees could master the latest in world oil and gas technology; more importantly, the ONGC's work had resulted in a dramatic reduction in India's annual oil imports.

Malhotra, a stocky man with a Van Dyck beard, gave me the following figures: in 1980, India imported $5.2 billion worth of crude oil and petroleum; the foreign oil accounted for 42 per cent of all imports, and gobbled up 85 per cent of the country's export earnings. But in 1984, oil imports had tumbled to $2.9 billion, or barely 18 per cent of all of India's imports; the oil and petroleum imports consumed, in 1984, only 25 per cent of all export earnings. Why? Because the country's oil production – largely under the guidance of Dr Malhotra – rose from about 10 million metric tonnes in 1980 to nearly 30 million tonnes by the end of 1984. Malhotra was confident that if the current trends in hydrocarbon production continue, India is within sight of self-sufficiency before the end of this decade.

A remarkable situation indeed! And one that was the consequence of the extraordinary and unusual autonomy that was granted by Indira Gandhi to Malhotra's operations. Malhotra, who was skilled at cabinet presentations, persuaded Mrs Gandhi to approve a budget in 1980 that would enable him to increase the ONGC's staff from 1,500 to 6,000. Instead of recruiting from India's fusty bureaucracy, Malhotra made the deliberate decision to hire new college graduates so that he could mould their attitudes about productivity; he gave responsibility to young people, thus building up a team spirit and morale rare in Indian government organizations.

He did not hesitate to bring in foreign consultants when necessary. Malhotra also introduced the concept of bids, which resulted in better value for every dollar spent. India now has twelve off-shore rigs, and on-shore oil production and exploration in twenty of the country's twenty-five states. The ONGC drills 200 new oil wells a year, with the figure expected to rise to 1,000. (This figure is still considerably short of the 12,000 new oil wells drilled annually in the United States, and the 4,500 in China.)

Malhotra had shown that a Third World country could make rapid strides in oil production by retaining full indigenous control over its oil industry and by instituting sophisticated management techniques. Malhotra had been asked by the Vietnamese government to send in an ONGC team to search for oil in the Mekong river delta (Vietnam's political and economic patrons, the Russians, apparently do not possess the kind of sophisticated technology necessary for off-shore drilling); he saw India being able to assist other developing countries in exploring for oil.

'The challenge of change?' Malhotra said. 'Well, I see it as a call to achieve economic self-sufficiency for India. The challenge is to bring about institutional reforms so that we institute modern management practices in all our public enterprises.'

Some months after our conversation, Anil Malhotra was offered a choice job in Washington by the World Bank. He took it.

CHAPTER FIVE:
LAND OF THE FIVE RIVERS

On the evening of Saturday, 22 June 1985 Air India's Flight 182 from Toronto to Bombay via Montreal, London and New Delhi was fully booked. Most of its Indian passengers were heading home for the summer holidays, while others were bound for Britain. There were Hindus on board, and there were Sikhs and Moslems and Christians. There were lots of children. The terminal building that Air India uses at the Toronto Pearson International Airport was, as habitually happens when the weekly India-bound flights are about to depart, filled with relatives and friends who had come to say goodbye. The cavernous departure hall echoed to the sound-track of a dozen different languages.

On this particular Saturday evening the security checks of depart-ing passengers were especially strict, for the Toronto authorities had been concerned about threats against Air India in general and against Flight 182 in particular. The authorities had deployed more policemen than usual at the terminal, and every piece of luggage – hand-carried as well as checked baggage – was being X-rayed. These security precautions meant that Flight 182 would not take off, as scheduled, at 6.35 p.m.; in the event, it did not leave for Montreal, its next stop, until eight o'clock.

Tahir Sadiq, a longtime resident of Toronto, was uneasy about this delay. He had come to see his mother off, and he was struck by the unusually heavy security arrangements at the Air India counter. He knew, of course, that for the last several months there had been vague threats by Sikh separatists seeking an independent Khalistan that every imaginable tactic would be used to force the Indian government to accede to their demands. Sadiq also knew that the

Canadian authorities had been monitoring the large Sikh communities in this north American nation.

The Toronto resident also knew that Air India's offices in Canada and in New York had received anonymous calls over the last several months warning of bomb attacks. But he had no way of knowing that, some hours before Flight 182 was scheduled to take off, a specific threat had been received by Air India about this flight. Although Sadiq's mother had already boarded the plane, the 'Emperor Kanishka', he now insisted on seeing her again. He told airline officials that his younger brother had reached the airport only after their mother had entered the plane, and that he would like him to say goodbye to her. But Air India officials turned down his request.

As Sadiq and his brother left the terminal, they passed a man called Tom Soni. Soni, an electrical engineer, had just said goodbye to his wife Usha, his ten-year-old twin daughters Rina and Monica, and his three-year-old son Pankaj. The children had cried a bit, and Soni had tried to placate them with sweets. Such scenes of farewell at the airport were nothing out of the ordinary. Airports are for arrivals and departures, and tears are shed and kisses exchanged, and sweetmeats popped into mouths. These things happened at Toronto Airport on Saturday night, and they happened at Montreal's Mirabel International Airport, where Flight 182 landed at 9.10 p.m. The security precautions at Toronto had resulted in the flight being about ninety minutes late.

But barely six hours after Air India Flight 182 left Montreal, it exploded off the coast of Ireland. The 307 passengers and 22 crew members on board were killed. Debris from the seven-year-old Boeing 747 jumbo jet was scattered over a ten-mile, shark-infested area in the choppy Atlantic Ocean. Irish government helicopters and naval vessels recovered scores of bodies and transported them to a makeshift morgue at a hospital in Cork. Bereaved relatives flew to Ireland to identify the dead. Aviation experts opined that there had been a bomb on board the Air India flight. The bomb theory was given credence by an unusual coincidence: just as Flight 182 was taking off from Montreal, a Canadian Pacific Boeing 747 was landing at Narita Airport in Japan. Minutes after its arrival from Vancouver, a bomb exploded in baggage that had been unloaded from the plane. Two Japanese baggage-handlers were killed in the blast, and a dozen others injured.

The Air India accident was the third worst air disaster ever, and it at once raised disturbing questions about airline safety, about airport security and about terrorism's power to challenge governments and take innocent lives. And because at least two groups representing Sikh separatists claimed responsibility for the elimination of Flight 182, the tragedy thrust India's 'Punjab Problem' back into the international limelight. The Canadian authorities were reported to be searching for two Sikhs from the New York area who had been earlier sought by the Federal Bureau of Investigation in connection with an alleged plot to kill Prime Minister Rajiv Gandhi during his visit to the United States in June 1985. Threats had also been made against Air India in Canada, the United States and Britain. The fact that the security of Air India planes had been increasingly threatened seemed to reinforce the young prime minister's view, expressed privately during his recent visit to the United States, that an international terrorist conspiracy was actively at work to destabilize India.

The story of what happened to Flight 182 is startling not only because of the human tragedy. In the opinion of many officials and academicians, perhaps the dominant question the Air India episode pushed to the forefront was: are we drifting into a kind of global lunacy, one which makes no distinction between adults and children? The tragedy followed by a week the taking of American hostages aboard TWA Flight 847. Some of those hostages were released, but about forty of them were sequestered by Lebanese Shiite terrorists in the war-torn city of Beirut. The Shiites demanded that Israel release some 731 prisoners it had taken during its retreat from Lebanon earlier that year as an insurance against attacks from Moslem militiamen. The hijackers of TWA Flight 847 killed one of the passengers, a young American Navy diver. A few days after the TWA hostage incident, half a dozen Americans were mowed down by gunmen in El Salvador. That same week, terrorist bombs went off in Nepal, killing at least six people. In each of these instances, the victims were innocent passengers whose only crime was to have been in the wrong place at the wrong time.

What happened to Air India's Flight 182 demonstrated that India was no longer immune to global terrorist activity. Assuming that the plane was destroyed by a bomb and that the bomb had been placed on board by terrorists, one could then ask a frightening question: if this was what terrorists could do to the innocent, what would they be planning to do to those whom they perceived as the 'guilty' – such as the Gandhi family?

I heard about the fate of Flight 182 early in the morning of Sunday, 23 June. A New York friend telephoned me to say that the plane had gone down some 150 miles off the coast of Ireland. The aircraft had been cruising at 31,000 feet and had been in radio communication with the Shannon Airport control tower at 7.01 a.m., GMT. The pilot, Captain Narender Singh, had received clearance to move towards the flight's next destination, London's Heathrow Airport. Some five minutes later, the plane suddenly vanished from the air-traffic controllers' radar.

Huge aircraft such as the Boeing 747 simply do not disappear without trace from radar surveillance. The immediate explanation that sprang to the controllers' minds was that the Air India plane had exploded. The weather in the area wasn't particularly turbulent. And even if there had been structural problems or mechanical failures, the 747 was equipped with a variety of back-up systems that would have permitted continuation of the flight. Moreover, modern commercial airliners are built to withstand such things as powerful lightning strikes. Had all four engines stopped – an unlikely possibility – the plane would still have been able to glide on its cushion of air for at least thirty minutes. And no matter what the mechanical failures on board, the pilot would still have had the opportunity to send out on his radio the international Mayday distress signal. But after the 7.01 a.m. contact with Shannon Airport, the pilot of Flight 182 was not heard from again.

Experts at once asserted that if the Air India plane was brought down by a bomb, it would be the first time that a jumbo jet had crashed for that reason. Jumbos, which include such aircraft as the Lockheed L-1011, the McDonnell Douglas DC-10 and the Airbus 300, are harder to destroy than smaller planes because the larger interior allows for greater dissipation of explosive force before it can reach and severely damage vital structures and sensitive flight controls. In other words, nothing short of a well-placed, powerful bomb would have so swiftly destroyed the Air India plane.

'A 747 wouldn't break up and disappear because of an engine disintegration,' said Thomas Ashwood, first vice-president of the international Air-line Pilots' Association (ALPA) and head of the Association's anti-terrorism committee. 'It might crash, but that would be gradual. The rapidity with which the Air India plane was gone suggests that it would have been an explosion of great magnitude.'

In the days following the disaster, experts seemed to have little doubt that the plane was indeed destroyed in one massive blast. They noted that the aircraft was a normal blip on a radar scope one second and was gone the next. Experts said that on other occasions when planes have been fatally crippled in the air, the radar blip has remained on the scope for several minutes as the aircraft fell out of control. This happened, for example, when the Korean Air Lines Boeing 747 was brought down by a missile fired by a Soviet fighter plane in September 1983.

An investigation by Canadian authorities soon after the crash showed that the X-ray equipment used to examine the baggage at Toronto Airport had malfunctioned, and that not all the luggage that was stowed in the cargo holds of the Air India jumbo jet had been subjected to scrutiny. Three suitcases had been pulled out of the baggage hold at Montreal Airport, however, because police dogs seemed agitated while routinely sniffing in the area for bombs. Nothing suspicious was found in those suitcases. Nevertheless, senior Canadian authorities said later that, perhaps because the Air India flight had already been delayed by nearly two hours, Montreal officials were anxious to speed up baggage-check procedures. It is conceivable, therefore, that an explosive device was smuggled on board in Montreal.

Canadian officials did not seem anxious to acknowledge that a bomb had indeed been on board Air India Flight 182. Canada's prime minister, Brian Mulroney, told reporters in Ottawa that security at Canadian airports was among 'the most stringent in the world'. And other Canadian officials said that they had yet to find any solid evidence linking terrorists to the Air India disaster, or to the Canadian Pacific flight on which a bomb had been apparently hidden inside luggage. Because Canada has a substantial Sikh immigrant population (close to half of Canada's 200,000 Indian immigrants are said to be Sikhs), and because many Canadian Sikhs have supported the Khalistan separatist cause, there has been considerable speculation that some of these Sikhs might have backed a terrorist plan aimed at hurting the Indian government.

But Canadian prime minister Mulroney said that there was no evidence linking any terrorist group to the Air India disaster.

'Fairness and decency require that the Sikhs be given the benefit of the doubt,' he said.

Mulroney said that airport security in Canada had been raised to an 'unprecedented level'. But senior Canadian officials conceded that there had been security lapses in connection with scrutinizing baggage being loaded on Flight 182 at Toronto's International Airport on Saturday evening. Because the X-ray machines had faltered during the evening, much of the baggage was reportedly checked with handheld scanners.

The Air India incident, along with the plight of TWA Flight 847 and the case of the Canadian Pacific jet, have resulted in airline and airport officials stepping up their exploration of what might be done to inhibit potential terrorists. President Ronald Reagan was given a set of recommendations by his Transportation Department on measures to increase aviation security. Some of these proposals, if put into effect, could result in delays of two hours or more in boarding aircraft at many airports. The Transportation Department wants airlines to be more aggressive in screening hand luggage, for instance, and also to be more thorough in inspecting baggage that is checked in.

The United States also wants several nations to step up airport security. Government officials have noted with dismay the fact that many busy international airports, such as Athens, New Delhi, Cairo and Beirut, have almost primitive security procedures. The ALPA has cited these airports, among others, as hazardous to aviation. In the wake of the Air India disaster, authorities in Canada, Japan and many Western European countries reported new measures to heighten security at their airports. President Reagan dispatched George Bush (then vice-president, and now president) to Europe to intensify the international effort against terrorism.

The Air India disaster brought several other issues besides airport security to the surface. One key issue was the question of insurance – officials said that the accident could result in the largest property insurance claim in aviation history. Insurance officials in New York and London said that the so-called 'hull insurance' on the Air India Boeing 747 aircraft and equipment amounted to about $100 million. This type of insurance is called hull insurance because it originated in the shipping field and is more or less similar to collision insurance on motor vehicles. In addition to this hull insurance – which was underwritten by Lloyd's of London, with the primary insurer being the General Insurance Corporation of India – liability claims by dependants and estates of the 329 people who perished on board Flight 182 will almost certainly raise the final insurance figure considerably beyond $100 million, according to insurance officials.

The largest previous property settlement in an aircraft disaster was $85 million for a UTA plane lost in a fire on the ground in Paris a few years ago. Other large settlements have included $52 million paid for a Madrid crash of an Avianca plane in November 1983, and $45 million paid for a Saudi Arabian plane that burned on the ground in Riyadh in August 1980. But it will be a while before any insurance claims are fully settled. In the meantime, the people who lost their loved ones in the Air India crash will have to adjust to the enormity of the tragedy.

George Bush spoke for many people when he said that the Air India disaster had 'shaken the conscience of the world'.

'I would hate to think that anyone was so depraved that they would take three hundred and some innocent lives to attempt to settle some grievance,' Bush said.

It is often hard for a writer not to be personally affected by what he sees and monitors. I learned that distant relatives of some friends were on board Flight 182. I had never met them, yet the news of their deaths depressed me. But one scene stands out as a particularly poignant reminder of the fragility of life.

There was a brief shot on American and British television of an Irish naval diver retrieving the body of a boy from the sea. The boy's body seemed intact. He wore a bright red shirt and a pair of blue shorts. He looked as if he was asleep, and as the diver hauled his body from the water on to a rescue ship I almost expected the boy to wake up at any moment.

There seemed to be a slight smile on his face, as if he was deep in a sweet dream. Perhaps he was deep in such a dream when the plane exploded. I don't know who the boy was, but I do know that India's Punjab problem has escalated into such a disaster that the murder of that child won't be the last such death.

There are Sikhs in Britain, Western Europe and North America who swear that their community has always been persecuted by Hindus in the Punjab. It is almost impossible to argue intelligently with such people. The fact is, however, that the Punjab's Hindus and Sikhs lived mostly in amity for four centuries.

There was periodic agitation since the 1930s for a separate Sikh nation – which at first was called Sikhistan, later Khalistan – but a hardcore separatist movement did not get going until the late 1970s. By then, Sikh leaders had realized that the arithmetic of population in the Punjab, as elsewhere in India, increasingly favoured the country's Hindu majority, which was breeding at the rate of nearly 3 per cent a year, or twice the rate of the Sikhs. That translated into diminishing power for the Sikhs, these leaders said.

In a perceptive report prepared for the United States Congressional Research Service in August 1984, Richard P. Cronin said that the Sikh–Hindu crisis was rooted in a long-term assertion of a Sikh communal identity. Cronin, an expert on Asian affairs, said that in addition to this assertion, four specific developments helped exacerbate the 'Punjab Problem': one, the return to power of Prime Minister Indira Gandhi's Congress Party in the January 1980 national parliamentary elections and her subsequent dismissal of the Opposition Akali Dal and Janata coalition that had governed Punjab state since 1977; two, the victory of the Congress Party in the June 1980 state elections; three, growing economic discontent among Sikhs and other Punjabis over agricultural pricing and industrial licensing policies of the Gandhi government; and, finally, the emergence of Sant Jarnail Singh Bhindranwale, a militant Sikh fundamentalist, as a dominant force in the Sikh heartland.

Cronin, whose research resulted in a remarkably clear analysis of the Punjab situation, said that the accelerating tempo of the Sikh agitation for a homeland and the violence in the Punjab may be dated from the brief arrest of Bhindranwale in connection with the assassination of a Hindu Punjabi newspaper editor, Lala Jagat Narain, in September 1981. In his report, which was published two months before the murder of Mrs Gandhi, Cronin, stated that:

The government's ineffective attempts to deal with Bhindranwale led him from one political triumph after another until he met his death in the 5–6 June army attack on his headquarters in the Golden Temple in Amritsar.

Wherever blame may lie for the failure to find a peaceful settlement, an early end to the confrontation is unlikely. Although the Gandhi government had earlier conceded most of the specifically religious demands, it is still not clear whether an accommodation can be reached on the more contentious economic and territorial demands, whether Prime Minister Gandhi will deal with the 'moderate' Akali Dal [the main Sikh political party] leaders now under arrest, or whether she will seek to bargain with other representatives of the Sikhs. It is too early to tell whether the storming of the Golden Temple has been a net gain for stability by eliminating Bhindranwale and his extremist supporters, or a net loss due to the radicalization of previously uncommitted Sikhs.

It also remains to be seen what the long-term impact will be on the stability of this vital grain-producing state. Although Hindus predominate in the cities and towns, the Sikhs constitute a strong majority in most of the countryside. Punjabi Hindu traders and businessmen in rural villages are especially vulnerable to local Sikh majorities. Even before the Golden Temple incident, terror and communal killings had spread to border villages north and south of Amritsar, causing anxious Hindu Punjabis to flee. The Hindu majority in Punjab's cities and towns also resorted to violence. A continuation of this violent polarization would be a major setback for India and could presage a wider breakdown of civility between ethnic, religious and linguistic groups that live side by side in many parts of India.

Polarization. That is precisely what has characterized Sikh–Hindu relations in the Punjab in recent years.

The genesis of the Sikh–Hindu polarization of the 1980s dates back to the last century, when India's British rulers successfully sowed the seeds of mutual suspicion among members of the two communities. It was quite an achievement, and one that was the harbinger of a policy that was to be repeated again and again: divide and rule. The British proved adept at pitting community against community, region against region, rajah against rajah – thereby giving them the opportunity to settle quarrels they themselves had spawned, and thus to consolidate their own position.

The differences the British generated among Sikhs and Hindus were especially noteworthy because Sikhism was born out of Hinduism in the sixteenth century; unlike Hinduism, which evolved over the centuries out of the hymns and naturalistic beliefs of the pastoral Aryans who came to India from Central Asia, Sikhism is a revealed religion. Its founder, Guru Nanak (1469–1539), claimed to have had mystic experiences. God appeared to him and said, according to Nanak himself: 'Nanak, I am with thee. Through thee will My Name be magnified. Go into the world and teach mankind how to pray. Be not sullied by the ways of the world. Let your life be one of praise of the word (*Naam*), charity (*Daan*), ablution

(*Ishnaan*), service (*Sewa*) and prayer (*Simran*).' Nanak was a simple, gentle soul whose sensibilities were outraged by the mistreatment of the lower classes by upper-caste Hindus, and by the abuses perpetrated by the country's Moslem rulers of the time.

Khushwant Singh, the eminent Sikh historian and writer, says that it is still unclear whether Guru Nanak intended to reform Hinduism, or form a new sect, or bring Hindus and Moslems together. 'It would appear that in his early career he tried to bring the two communities closer to each other,' Singh says. 'Being himself a Hindu he was at the same time equally concerned with reforming Hinduism. But as the years went by and his message caught on among the masses, he decided to give his teachings permanency through a sect of his own.'

His disciples were called Sikhs – the word means 'disciple'. They did not chant Sanskrit hymns to stone idols, as Hindus did, but sang devotional songs that Nanak had composed himself in his native language, Punjabi. Sikhs also broke down existing caste barriers and encouraged communal dining in the guru's kitchen, a ceremony known as *Guru ka Langar*. Nanak's chief disciple, Angad, devised a new script, Gurmukhi. Several decades later, Arjun, one of Sikhism's ten main gurus, built the Golden Temple in Amritsar. It was Arjun's son, the Sixth Guru, Hargovind, who developed a militant role for the Sikhs. He urged his followers to arm themselves. He appointed himself both spiritual and temporal head of the Sikh community. The Sikhs were seen as the militant arm of Hinduism. In fact, says Khushwant Singh, Sikhism's Ninth Guru, Tegh Bahadur, appeared before the ruling Mughal court as a representative of the Hindus of northern India to resist forcible conversion to Islam. He was beheaded. Tegh Bahadur's son, the Tenth and last Guru, Gobind Singh, completed the transformation of the Sikhs into a martial community. He directed his male followers not to cut their hair and beards, to append the name 'Singh' – which means 'Lion' – to their first names, and always to carry a *kirpan*, or sword.

The Sikhs continued to be the defenders of India's Hindus against Moslem tyranny: they fought not only the Mughals but also Persian, Afghan and Pathan invaders. Sikh kings like Ranjit Singh worshipped in Hindu temples and made the slaughter of the Hindus' sacred cow a criminal offence punishable by death. But the British had arrived on the scene by then; by 1849, they had annexed the

Punjab, where Ranjit Singh had established his formidable empire. The Moslem rulers of India, the Mughals, had also by now been reduced to figureheads. It was the British who sowed the seeds of Hindu–Sikh separatism, according to Khushwant Singh. They rewarded loyal Sikh princes with land, they inducted Sikhs into the British army in large numbers and they used Sikh troops to keep rebellious Hindu chieftans under control.

While this was happening, a Hindu revivalist wave washed across northern India. Hindu leaders of the Arya Samaj proselytized against Sikhism and tried to bring Sikhs back into the Hindu fold. This raised the Sikhs' hackles. The Akali movement of the 1920s to wrest control of the Sikh *gurdwaras* from the Hindu-influenced priests who managed them also aggravated Hindu–Sikh relations. The Akali movement found expression in the creation of the Akali Dal, which was formed as the militant wing of the Shiromani Gurudwara Prabandhak Committee, the organization that eventually took over the supervision of Sikh temples. It was at a huge Sikh rally in Amritsar on 20 August 1944 that Master Tara Singh, a cagey old Sikh leader, first issued a formal call for a sovereign Sikh nation. His colleagues were amused.

By this time India's Moslems had now started agitating for their own state, Pakistan. Sikhs correctly saw the rising Moslem communalism as a threat to their own well-being, just as it was to that of the Hindus. When Partition came in 1947 and Pakistan was carved out of India, the Sikhs of the Punjab were the worst losers. The choicest farmland of the state was in its western region, which was given to Pakistan. Thirteen of the Punjab's twenty-nine districts went to India, and just 38 per cent of the land area – mostly scrubland or meadows with poor topsoil – and very little of the vast irrigation network that the British had helped build. Two million Sikhs, terrified of being locked into the new Moslem state of Pakistan, migrated eastward to India, leaving behind their hereditary homes and possessions, and also 150 Sikh shrines.

partit[Their migration, and that of another 2 million Hindus from Pakistan to India, coincided with a reverse flow of traffic of 4 million Moslems who left East Punjab and northern India for Pakistan. They clashed. A bloodbath ensued. Nearly 2.2 million men, women and children died, many of them Sikhs. This tragedy perhaps explains why Sikhs – who form 10 per cent of India's military forces of 1.2 million – fought especially ferociously in the three wars between India and Pakistan since independence in 1947. But considering the historical Sikh animosity towards Moslems, it is especially puzzling how proponents of Khalistan have proclaimed Pakistan as an ally in their 'struggle' to set up a new nation in the Punjab. (The Pakistanis may choose to ignore it, but the Khalistan proposal also calls for the inclusion of a sizeable chunk of the Pakistani portion of the Punjab; the great city of Lahore will be part of Khalistan, as will virtually every district of the flourishing farmbelt that now feeds Pakistan.)

In the two decades after independence, the Punjab's Sikhs worked especially hard to make their state India's success story. The central government in Delhi, under Prime Minister Jawaharlal Nehru, encouraged economic development and poured billions of rupees into projects for building canals and dams in the Punjab. Sikhs also prospered elsewhere in the country: they gained a virtual monopoly over the road-transportation industry, for instance, and they obtained important positions in the government bureaucracy.

Khushwant Singh says that the notion of an autonomous Sikh state started taking shape with Nehru's announcement that new Indian states would be created along linguistic lines. Nehru's decision was influenced by a lengthy and violent agitation in the Telangana region of south-central India – in the area that is now Andhra Pradesh state – for a Telugu linguistic state. Thirteen of India's fifteen major languages would thus find a formal home within the boundaries of a new state. But Punjabi was the only language not thus represented. Sikhs resented this, and the Akali Dal launched a Punjabi Suba – or 'linguistic state' – movement in April 1960. Punjab's Hindus suspected that in demanding a Punjabi-speaking state what the Sikhs were really after was a Sikh majority state. So when census commissioners came around, the Punjab's Hindus claimed that their chief language was Hindi – not Punjabi, which was actually their main *lingua franca*. 'The battle over language in effect became a confrontation between Punjabi Hindus and Punjabi Sikhs,' Khushwant Singh says.

That battle eventually led to the Indian government's decision in 1966 to split the Punjab (which soon after independence in 1947 had been converted into two administrative units that were called the Patiala and East Punjab States Union, more popularly known by their acronym, PEPSU) into three states: Haryana, with 16,835 square miles and 7.5 million people, of whom barely 5 per cent were

Sikhs; Himachal Pradesh, with 10,215 square miles and 1.2 million people, barely 2 per cent of them Sikhs; and the Punjab, with 20,254 square miles and a population of 12 million people, about 52 per cent of them Sikhs. The Sikhs got their Punjabi-speaking state, but its land area now covered just nine districts, not the Punjab's original thirteen. And the Punjab had to share its capital city of Chandigarh with neighbouring Haryana, until such time as Haryana built its own capital. (It still hasn't.) The prime minister at the time of the creation of Punjab state was Indira Gandhi.

The Punjab thrived economically, largely because of the 'green revolution'. Because of a new canal system financed by the central government and high-yield seeds that were distributed by Delhi in the 1950s, crop production in the Punjab has risen six times since 1951. More than 60 per cent of the state's population of some 12 million was engaged in agricultural production – production that accounted for more than 62 per cent of the Punjab's annual income. The high-yield grain developed at Rockefeller University in the US and at Ludhiana State University in the Punjab by Norman E. Borlaug – an American scientist who was later awarded the Nobel Prize – resulted in rice production increasing from 892 kilogrammes per hectare in 1950 to 3,000 kilogrammes by 1981; wheat production grew from 901 kilogrammes per hectare to 3,100 kilogrammes during the same period.

As the state prospered, Sikhs started to look for new ventures in which to invest their wealth, and for a better yield on their crops to pay for the rising costs of fertilizers and mechanization. Richard Cronin says in his Congressional report:

Many Sikhs came to see the Indian government's policy of controlling all industrial licensing from New Delhi and steering investment to poorer but more populous and vote-rich provinces in the Hindi heartland as an obstacle to these aspirations. Some frequently quoted figures include the claim that 70 per cent of the state's cotton and 60 per cent of its molasses are 'exported' for processing to other states due to the refusal of New Delhi to approve licences for plant construction. The Delhi government was also judged slow to create adequate price incentives for Punjabi wheat and rice.

Revolutions have a way of fizzling out, and the Punjab's 'green revolution' and the economic progress associated with it reached a plateau in the early 1970s. Punjabi farmers found themselves not as well-off as they were a decade before.

Around this time, Sikhism's elders discovered to their dismay that the religion's hold over the young was loosening as Western fashions and lifestyles were imported into the state. Indeed the 'green revolution' that Norman Borlaug and others generated in the Punjab generated many spin-offs. The number of primary schools in the state rose from 7,183 in 1967 to 12,400 by 1982; in 1967, there were just 700 high schools in the state, but by 1982 the figure had climbed beyond 2,200. In 1967, there were 71 colleges of further education in the Punjab, and by 1980 there were 200. In 1967, the Punjab had no medical colleges; by 1982, there were 9, including 2 in Amritsar. Sikhs also went abroad in increasing numbers to work, and they sent back to their relatives in the Punjab more than a billion dollars annually. This money stimulated consumerism.

But as the Punjab's schools and colleges began turning out more and more graduates, there wasn't commensurate expansion in the non-agricultural economy to provide jobs for them. Indeed, unemployment was now on the rise because, apart from agriculture, there were no major industries in the state. As families grew bigger, land holdings became smaller. The annual influx of more than 200,000 low-caste Hindu workers from Uttar Pradesh and Bihar states who were hired to work on Punjab farms also created some social tensions. Many of these migrant workers would stay on and enrol as voters – thus increasing the percentage of Hindus in the state. Sikh clergymen felt that their religion was under siege. More specifically, they felt that Sikhs and the Punjab were being Hindu-ized.

Even as the proportion of Sikhs in the Punjab was declining, Mrs Gandhi's ruling Congress Party in Delhi accelerated its interference in socio-religious politics in the state. Mrs Gandhi seemed determined to prevent the political ascendancy of the main Sikh party, the Akali Dal. The Akalis stepped up their demands for the readjustment of state boundaries to include in the Punjab the Punjabi-speaking areas of neighbouring Haryana, Rajasthan and Himachal Pradesh; the Akalis also wanted Chandigarh to be the exclusive capital of the Punjab; they demanded a fairer allocation to the Punjab of the waters of the rivers Ravi, Sutlej and Beas. On 16 October 1973, the Akali Dal approved a document, known as the Anandpur Sahib Resolution, that not only included these demands but also referred in vague language to a 'separate Sikh nation'. Actually, the word used in the resolution was *quam*, which in Punjabi means anything from a community to a nation. That resolution was interpreted by Mrs Gandhi and her advisers as a call for a separate state.

The Anandpur Sahib Resolution was passed at a meeting the Akali Dal held in the historic Punjab town of Anandpur, where the head of the Ninth Sikh Guru, Tegh Bahadur – who was decapitated by the Mughal emperor Aurangzeb on 11 November 1675 – was cremated by his son and successor, Guru Gobind Singh. Anandpur is the site of one of Sikhism's five major *gurdwaras* (the other four are the Golden Temple in Amritsar, Dam Dama Sahib in Ropar, Patna Sahib in Bihar, and Hazoor Sahib in Maharashtra's Nanded district). The Akalis said in their resolution that the central government in Delhi should restrict its functions in the Punjab to defence, foreign affairs, communications and currency. The resolution advanced the proposition that the Sikh religion was 'not safe without sovereignty'. The historian Khushwant Singh has said that this could be interpreted 'as leading to Khalistan'.

A separate state was never formally called for by the Akalis – but Punjab's Sikh fundamentalists thought it an excellent idea. The purity of Sikhism, they said, could only be preserved in an independent Sikh nation. Their fervour was fuelled and financed by wealthy Sikhs living abroad. One of these Sikhs was a London physician named Jagjit Singh Chohan, a former secretary-general of the Akali Dal and a finance minister in the Punjab, who proclaimed himself 'president' of Khalistan and even produced Khalistan passports, postage stamps and currency (which were 'recognized' only in his London home, of course).

The fundamentalists rallied around their fiery leader, Sant Jarnail Singh Bhindranwale. He had once been used by Mrs Gandhi and her Congress Party to undercut and embarrass the Akalis, but Bhindranwale soon convinced himself that he was capable of dispensing with Mrs Gandhi's patronage and that he could blaze a new career as an advocate for Khalistan. He recruited men who shared his firebrand fundamentalism, soon launched a terrorist campaign to murder Punjab's Hindus and moderate Sikhs, and became a media star.

It is disputable whether it was Bhindranwale's status as a media star rivalling Mrs Gandhi or his role as a terrorist leader that roused the prime minister's ire. After dithering for months over whether she should send her troops to flush Bhindranwale out of his sanctuary in the Golden Temple, Mrs Gandhi finally authorized the military operation of 5–6 June.

For almost three years prior to her death, Mrs Gandhi had been negotiating with the Sikhs. The Akalis had submitted a list of forty-five demands to the Delhi government in September 1981. These demands – which were virtually identical to the ones enumerated in the Anandpur Sahib Resolution – were grouped into religious, political and economic categories.

I talked to a man named Manmohan Singh, who was among those involved in the negotiations. Singh, a pleasant man of about sixty, is chairman of Frick India, a flourishing engineering company. A Sikh, he has headed such organizations as the Delhi Chamber of Commerce. The talks started in October 1981, Manmohan Singh told me, but they progressed only fitfully, floundering often over the issues of Chandigarh and the sharing of river waters.

In mid February 1983, Mrs Gandhi announced the partial acceptance of some Sikh religious demands: instead of the original Akali demand for a radio station, for example, she agreed to allow the broadcast of religious services from the Golden Temple on the government's network, All-India Radio. The government also agreed to the Akali demand that Sikhs be allowed to carry the *kirpan* – the traditional knife that male Sikhs are asked by the religion always to carry – on all internal flights of Indian Airlines: the specification was that the *kirpan* be no longer than six inches.

The Akalis, however, dismissed these concessions as being fraudulent. They stepped up their agitation against Mrs Gandhi. Manmohan Singh was one of those who urged everyone to cool down, but the prime minister was in no mood to listen to anyone. Singh told me of a conversation he had had with Dr P. C. Alexander, Mrs Gandhi's principal private secretary and her key adviser on the Punjab. (Alexander was appointed by Rajiv Gandhi as India's High Commissioner to Britain; he later became the governor of the southern state of Tamil Nadu.)

'The PM never listens – either she demands an explanation or she gives you a lecture,' Singh quoted Dr Alexander as saying. In fact, Mrs Gandhi declined to meet the Akalis personally, passing on the task instead to top aides such as Dr Alexander. Her son and heir-apparent, Rajiv Gandhi, also occasionally met the Sikhs. Manmohan Singh told me that the Akali Dal's president, the late Harchand Singh Longowal, expressed to him his dismay over Mrs Gandhi's refusal to meet him or the rest of the Akali leadership.

'She's said to oppose the Anandpur Sahib Resolution,' Longowal said to Manmohan Singh. 'But why don't you tell her from me that she can delete anything from it she wants – and we will agree!'

Singh said that when he relayed Longowal's request to Dr Alexander, the latter said: 'The Anandpur Sahib Resolution is not even an issue in all this.'

The Akalis and others familiar with the on-off negotiations suspected that Mrs Gandhi was being recalcitrant because she had an ulterior motive in mind. She let the Punjab crisis drag on, they suspected, in order to rally the state's Hindus behind her and in order to unify the Hindu majority of the north Indian states – all of whom were concerned about the growing shrillness of the Sikhs' demands. The Hindus wanted the Delhi government to deal more forcefully with the Sikhs. By stonewalling the Sikhs, Mrs Gandhi was consolidating her position with the Hindu majority of north India, whose support she deemed especially critical in the national elections that were to be held by January 1985.

As the Akalis' dealings with Mrs Gandhi faltered, the strength of the Bhindranwale extremists grew. More than five hundred Hindus and moderate Sikhs were killed by the terrorists. On 25 April 1984, a senior Punjab police official named A. S. Atwal was shot to death at the entrance of the Golden Temple. The assailants were seen running into the temple, and the widespread assumption was that they were Bhindranwale's men.

But Bhindranwale told Manmohan Singh that his group had nothing to do with the Atwal murder. 'I can prove to you that it was the Indira Congress people in Punjab who killed Atwal,' the 37-year-old preacher told Singh. 'Why do the government accuse me of being a murderer? In my whole life I haven't even killed a sparrow.'

Bhindranwale's sentiments to Manmohan Singh ran counter to his other pronouncements, however. His homilies were always fiery and filled with threats against Hindus. He promised that if the Sikhs did not get their own nation, 'rivers of blood will flow' in the Punjab. He drew crowds the like of which had never been seen before in the Golden Temple.

Manmohan Singh told me that the mobs that attacked Sikh homes in Delhi after the murder of Indira Gandhi often shouted the name of Bhindranwale – they were taking revenge for the murders Bhindranwale and his men committed.

Singh himself had to flee his home in New Friends' Colony, hidden in the trunk of his car. 'Even in the darkest days of the Partition, I walked upright across the border from Pakistan,' he told me. 'Even then I didn't have to hide. At my age, I cannot forget this humiliation. It will never be the same for me again.'

His 22-year-old son, Gurmohan Singh, had said to him: 'Dad, at your age isn't it simply better to stay at home and fight the mobs with your gun – rather than hide like this in your car?'

And Manmohan Singh had replied: 'No, at my age, discretion is the better part of valour.'

As he was being driven away from his home, Manmohan Singh thought of how, only a few weeks before, he had led a delegation of Indian businessmen to the United States. He had told Americans in speech after speech how proud he was to be an Indian.

'I would never have dreamed that in my own country I would have to run away from a mob like this,' Manmohan Singh said to me, tears in his eyes.

I went to Amritsar at the invitation of Inder Mohan Khosla, who was then the manager of the local branch of the Standard Chartered Bank. On the evening of the day I flew in from Delhi, Khosla – who I'd met through a relative of mine – took me to the home of Karuna and Satish Chander Mahajan. The Mahajans had lived in this city for several generations, and had prospered in business. Both Satish and Karuna, an elegant Hindu middle-aged couple, seemed pained at the chasm that now separated Amritsar's Sikhs and Hindus.

'There's a total divide between Sikhs and Hindus,' Karuna Mahajan said, in her book-lined living-room. 'They no longer come to our homes, and we are seldom invited to theirs.'

How long had it been since the Mahajans visited the Golden Temple?

'The temple doesn't any longer have the aura the Vatican does,' Mrs Mahajan said, with surprising acidity in her voice. 'It's become the hotbed of Sikh politics. Sikhs and Hindus are being increasingly separated – but the separation of the Sikh religion and Sikh politics is no longer there.'

The next day, I was tempted to walk into the Golden Temple by myself. After all, Hindus had been visiting it for hundreds of years. But Inder Singh Monga, a Sikh I had met at Khosla's bank, suggested that I wait a bit.

'There's a meeting on at the temple,' Monga, who worships daily at the temple, said. 'All the high priests are there today. They're deciding what to do about the killing of Sikhs that is going on in Delhi. You might want to wait until tomorrow.'

The five high priests of Sikhism ordinarily met at the Akal Takht, Sikhism's Vatican. This is a few yards away from the Golden Temple itself, and is an impressive three-storey building with marble walls, domes with gold leaves, and balconies that offer an unimpeded view of the Harimandir, the Golden Temple, which sits in the middle of a lake considered sacred by Sikhs. It is from the Akal Takht that the high priests periodically issue *hukamnamas* (encyclicals) and *tankhaiyas* (formal condemnations of irreligious conduct). The priests usually meet without fanfare and work quietly. Few of India's 14 million Sikhs have heard of these five men, fewer still know their names.

'Most of us Sikhs don't even know who these five men are,' Noni Chawla, a young man who is the marketing director of the ITC-Sheraton hotel chain, had told me in Delhi. 'Sikhism is a religion that doesn't demand too much attention to its hierarchy.'

Mrs Gandhi had jailed the political leaders of the Sikh community, however. Officials of the Akali Dal and the Shiromani Gurdwara Prabandhak Committee – the 129-member organization that oversees most of India's Sikh temples, with an annual budget of $10 million raised mainly from individual donations – had been imprisoned ever since October 1983, when the Punjab was put by Mrs Gandhi under direct control of the Delhi government. Bhindranwale, who had become a *de facto* leader of the Sikhs, was dead. A political vacuum now existed among Sikhs. So the five high priests of the Akal Takht found themselves in a unaccustomed and uneasy role as high-visibility Sikh spokesmen. This role required them to span the longstanding divide between their religion and politics.

And the high priests had quickly made a mess of things. Their spokesman, Giani Kirpal Singh, issued a statement of condolence following the murder of Mrs Gandhi. Within a day, he withdrew that statement, thus enraging the government.

'We are neither happy with her death, nor do we condemn it,' Kirpal Singh was quoted as saying.

The remarks did not please Amritsar's Hindus.

The day I turned up in Amritsar, the head priests were reported to have urged Sikh members of Mrs Gandhi's ruling Congress Party to resign immediately. The following day they rescinded that directive.

In Hindu homes, and even among some of the Sikhs I met in Amritsar, the five priests were coming under increasing criticism for not issuing a strong call for religious harmony and not asking Sikhs to refrain from retaliating for the attacks against them in Delhi and northern India. Their silence was construed as suggesting timorousness or as an implied threat that left open the possibility of a Sikh counter-assault.

Some weeks before the Gandhi assassination, the high priests had written a note to the then President Zail Singh, a Sikh and a former chief minister of the Punjab. The government, the priests said, was courting trouble. Zail Singh, who was widely and correctly perceived as a stooge of Mrs Gandhi – who had selected him to be India's Constitutional president, a position of much pomp and no authority – visited the Golden Temple on 26 September 1984, not long after the Delhi government had repaired some of the damage to the Golden Temple incurred during the military assault in June. Giani Kirpal Singh, the first among equals of the five high priests, hectored him publicly.

'If the government continues its anti-Sikh attitude and treats us like second-class citizens, it will not only endanger the unity of the country, but also cause communal disharmony,' Kirpal Singh said. He then listed the things the high priests wanted done immediately:

● The revocation of the Delhi government's ban on the All-India Sikh Students' Federation. Many members of this organization had been imprisoned on charges of terrorism.

● The unconditional release from prison of all Akali Dal leaders as well as activists of the Sikh Students' Federation. These leaders, and also top officials of the Shiromani Gurdwara Prabandhak Committee, had been locked up to prevent them from further stirring up Sikhs.

● Adequate compensation to the families of the people who were killed or injured during the army's assault on the Golden Temple. (The government hadn't released the names of the terrorists who were killed during the army operation, nor the names of pilgrims who were trapped in the Golden Temple and died in the crossfire between the troops and the terrorists.)

• An end to the random arrests of Sikh youths in the Punjab. The authorities periodically rounded up youths suspected of sympathizing with terrorists.

The hectoring and scolding were deliberate. The high priests had earlier excommunicated Zail Singh by issuing a *tankaiya* against him: he was accused of religious misconduct. Why such a strong step? Because the president of India is technically the commander-in-chief of the country's armed forces, and since the military had assaulted the Golden Temple the president should be held accountable for the action.

Zail Singh was almost reverentially subdued when he visited the high priests in Amritsar.

'I ask for sincere forgiveness from the gurus for the unfortunate incidents,' he said.

That was at once interpreted by the priests as an apology from the Gandhi government for the military assault. The *tankaiya* against Zail Singh was lifted. He was a Sikh again.

I was introduced by Inder Mohan Khosla to a man named Bhagwant Singh Ahuja, a tall, stocky Sikh who ran a profitable trading business, with shops in the Punjab, Delhi and Bombay. Ahuja said he would take me to the Golden Temple – but only after the priests' meeting had ended. Implicit in what he said was the caution that perhaps it would be inflammatory for a non-Sikh such as myself to be seen in the precincts of the temple while a religious/political meeting was going on. That meeting would last through much of the night.

'This is a very dangerous time,' Ahuja said. 'People's emotions are very raw. We now more than ever need to get across the message that Sikhs and Hindus are brothers, that we have great common links. But what's happening in Delhi now – this slaughter of innocent Sikhs – this is wrecking people's faith here in amity. The feeling among Sikhs is that a minority community is being held to ransom because of the actions of two misguided madmen.'

We were having dinner at Ahuja's home, a large bungalow with a glass wall that overlooked a neat lawn. The house itself nestled under mango and eucalyptus trees. On the mantelpiece above a fire place were porcelain figures and bronzes of various Hindu gods. There was a stone Buddha, and there was an exquisite wooden cross with the crucified Jesus.

'We need the healing touch,' Ahuja said.

There was a murmur of agreement from around the mahogany dining-table. With us were Ahuja's wife, his daughter and two sons. Also present were a local judge named Gurdial Singh and his wife, and a couple of other Sikhs from the area. The round table easily accommodated a dozen diners. In the middle of the table were enormous dishes of tandoori chicken, curried lamb, *parathas* (roasted bread) and spicy aubergines and potatoes. There was also a mound of saffron rice.

'Bhindranwale was spitting poison, he was propagating things that were not normal for the people of the Punjab,' Ahuja continued. 'The whole atmosphere was polluted here. People had lost faith in the Akali leaders as well. And Mrs Gandhi was not applying the healing touch. So what were we left with? Bitterness, anger, sorrow. The joy of life, our hopes, these were all being darkened.'

'Nothing justifies the atrocities in Delhi,' Gurdial Singh, the judge, said. 'I really question the allegations that Sikhs were distributing sweets to celebrate Mrs Gandhi's death.'

'I want to show you something,' Ahuja said, getting up suddenly.

He returned shortly with a newspaper clipping and started reading extracts from an article by Dharma Kumar, a well-known economic historian in Delhi. It appeared on the editorial page of *The Times of India*, and Mrs Kumar, a Hindu, had said:

If all the sweets in India had been distributed, that would not have justified the burning alive of one single Sikh. If burning alive were the punishment for vulgarity and folly, there would be few people left in India.

Why should every Sikh be responsible for the doings of all other Sikhs?

Earlier that evening, Ahuja and his friends had met up with some Hindu neighbours. They had decided to form citizens' groups to patrol neighbourhoods in the event of trouble. They also agreed to telephone and visit as many Sikh and Hindu families as they could to urge everyone to keep calm.

The bazaars near the Golden Temple were packed with people this Sunday morning. We parked outside one of the four main gates, in what seemed to me to be an extension of a bazaar: Ahuja's station-wagon had to be squeezed in between a vendor of oranges and a man who had set up a stall of spicy savouries. Ahuja's wife and mother went in separately. He and I checked in our shoes at a booth near the entrance, and Ahuja hired for me a *patka*, a sort of cap to cover my head – everyone must have their head covered when inside the Golden Temple. We washed our feet in a small basin and then walked down a flight of marble steps into the courtyard of the temple.

The Harimandir sparkled in the brilliant sunshine. The sacred pool in which it sat was lightly ruffled by a cool breeze. I looked around. I was the only non-Sikh male in the vast courtyard. The temple's public-address system was broadcasting hymns in the Punjabi language that were being sung inside the Harimandir by *granthis*, or acolytes. Ahuja and I walked on the marble-floored perimeter, known as the *parikrama*. We occasionally weaved through columns and under doorways. Ahuja kept very close to me physically. I thought: this is a gesture of protection, this Sikh wants to make sure that his Hindu companion comes to no harm. If I was being bold turning up inside Sikhism's holiest shrine even as Sikhs were being butchered not far away in Delhi by non-Sikhs, then Bhagwant Singh Ahuja was even more courageous in escorting a Hindu to the temple. Several Sikhs stared at us as we walked by. Ahuja would sometimes stop at the steps that led into the sacred pool and sip holy water: I repeated his actions. The water was cool, even sweet.

We bought a tray of flowers from a vendor who had parked himself not far from the Harimandir.

'The very fact that you are here must tell you how tolerant Sikhism is,' Ahuja said, as we walked on. 'You are my brother. That is why you and I are here together. Even if you were my political enemy, I would still bring you here. Why not? The temple is one place where we must all leave our politics and social differences outside.'

He paused to bow before an ancient tree in whose shadow a Sikh saint, now long ago, once lived and preached.

'But there are people who brought their politics and weapons into this temple,' Ahuja said. 'Look around you. Look carefully.'

I was startled by what I saw. Abutting the *parikrama* were mounds of rubble. Marble flooring had caved in. Bullet holes

pocked many of the buildings. The sunburst of shells marked
several walls. Even the Akal Takht, which had been restored by the
Indian government at the cost of $40 million since the June storm-
ing of the Golden Temple by the Indian army, somehow looked
hastily patched up.

Heavy tanks had been brought in during that military operation
to counter Bhindranwale and his terrorists. More than a thousand
people died, although the Delhi government insists to this day that
the figure was no more than four hundred. The man in operational
charge of the military assault was himself a Sikh – Lieutenant
General Ranjit Singh Dayal, chief of staff of the army's prestigious
Western Command. General Dayal's main adversary was not Sant
Jarnail Singh Bhindranwale, who had no formal military training,
but another highly decorated war hero like Dayal himself – Major
General Shahbeg Singh.

Shahbeg Singh had been among those who trained the Mukti
Bahini guerrillas who fought to establish the state of Bangladesh in
what was then East Pakistan, but he was later cashiered from the
Indian army on corruption charges. Singh was subsequently recruited by Bhindranwale to train his growing band of terrorists. It
was Shahbeg Singh who had planned the fortification of the Golden
Temple. It was he who had trained Bhindranwale's motley band of
militants in the use of highly sophisticated weapons such as anti-
tank cannon. Those weapons were fired by the terrorists with
deadly accuracy on 5 and 6 June. Scores of Indian soldiers died.
Officials in Delhi said that the army had been surprised to confront
sophisticated weaponry in the Golden Temple. The government's
intelligence system had clearly let it down again.

Looking at the Temple on this lovely November morning, it
seemed inconceivable to me that anyone could have dared to defile
its serenity and sanctity – whether it be Bhindranwale or Shahbeg
Singh or the Indian army. Temples are our last sanctuaries for
peace and reflection. Punjab's Sikh terrorists had infiltrated not
only the Golden Temple, but also forty-two other *gurdwaras* across
the state. Why hadn't those temples' priests protested? The lines
between the spiritual and the temporal in the Punjab had blurred.

I wept.

Inside the Harimandir, the prayers were for peace and brother-
hood this morning, as they are every day of the week. *Granthis*
played on harmoniums. Priests chanted hymns in front of the holy

Granth Sahib – the collection of sayings and songs of Guru Nanak, which serves as Sikhism's bible – which lay covered by a burgundy silk shawl. The gold-sheathed walls glistened. There was a powerful fragrance of incense. I followed Ahuja in walking round the inner shrine, then I knelt in front of the *Granth Sahib* and applied my forehead to the floor. A hand touched my head. I looked up. It was a Sikh priest, and he was blessing me. I rose, and he handed me some marigolds. He was an old man, and there was a gentle smile on his face.

Ahuja and I walked up to the balcony of the Harimandir. I looked out at the Golden Temple's courtyard, and beyond it toward an entire residential block that had been razed during the June military operation. So much history here, I thought, so much violence, and now what? Will Sikhs and Hindus ever again worship here without mutual suspicion? Will they intermarry with the same zest and enthusiasm? Will Hindu families, who had traditionally converted their eldest sons to Sikhism, continue the practice? Or will Sikhs now be a besieged minority in a country for which so many had shed their blood and perished in battle over the years? Ahuja and I looked at each other, as if the same thoughts were rushing through our minds, but we said nothing to each other. What was there to say?

We started toward the *parikrama* again. On the way, Ahuja lingered near a blackboard on which was handwritten, in chalk, the daily quotation from the *Granth Sahib*. The script was Gurumukhi, which had been devised by Guru Nanak's successor, Guru Angad. The script was one of the very first steps toward establishing a separate Sikh identity.

'This world is a transitory place,' the quotation read. 'Some of our compatriots have already gone, and some day the rest of us also have to go. This world is only a temporary abode.'

It was an astonishing quotation to have put up at a time of such crisis, I thought. It was weighted with humility and fatalism. I wished I could have broadcast it to those Hindus in Delhi: the quotation would have put them to shame.

We climbed the stairs that led away from the *parikrama*. A fresh hymn was being broadcast now, sung in Punjabi by a *granthi*. He sang softly at first, then his voice rose clear and sharp.

'If God is with me,' came the *granthi*'s words, 'what do we have to fear? Nothing.'

I returned to the Punjab in December, more than a month after my
first trip, to see for myself what changes had taken place in the state.
Although the assassination of Indira Gandhi had taken place less
than two months before, it was no longer the main item for
discussion in most people's homes. One of her assassins, Beant
Singh, had died within an hour of shooting the prime minister: he
was killed by troops of the Indo-Tibetan Border Force in a guardhouse just yards from where Mrs Gandhi was shot. The other assassin, Satwant Singh, had also been shot by his captors, but he survived and was now being questioned by the authorities. Officials
were soon to arrest another alleged conspirator, Kehar Singh. In the
event, Satwant and Kehar – who once worked as a minor official in
the government's supply office in New Delhi – were found guilty
after a long trial; both men were sentenced to be executed,
although their lawyers began what appeared to be an uphill campaign for clemency. (Meanwhile, Ram Saran and T. S. Jambhal,
two of the guards who had allegedly shot Mrs Gandhi's assassins,
were also being tried in a Delhi court.)

All sorts of theories were being advanced about conspiracies.
The American Central Intelligence Agency – always a convenient
scapegoat in most of the Third World, but particularly in India –
was said to be behind the assassination of Mrs Gandhi, whose
political alignment with the Soviet Union had long been resented by
Washington. Pakistan, which was said to support the separatists
who wanted to establish Khalistan, was also believed to have been
behind the plot. Relatives of Beant and Satwant were arrested in
their Punjab villages, then freed, then re-arrested, and let go again.
The investigators appeared to be making little progress.

Many Indians were coming around to the view that, rather than
being a major international conspiracy, the murder of Indira
Gandhi had been a case of vengeance by a handful of Sikhs who
were maddened by the invasion of the Golden Temple. Beant and
Satwant were reported to have taken vows of revenge at the Bangla
Sahib Gurdwara in Delhi. By mid-December, few Indians I encountered bothered to speculate much about conspiracies and the
motives of the killers. Their attention, instead, seemed focused on
the political future of India.

A national election campaign was in full swing in India – but the
Punjab had been excluded from the parliamentary poll because of
the political instability here. The army was still out in force around

the state, but places like Amritsar were no longer under curfew. Rajiv Gandhi, the new prime minister, was going around the country saying that Sikhs would have no reason to fear for their safety under his administration – but few Sikhs had been compensated for the extensive loss of property during the riots after Mrs Gandhi's assassination. And not one rioter had been arrested and brought to justice.

The Hindus and Sikhs of the Punjab continued their dangerous drift away from one another. Few civic leaders in this troubled state dared to call openly for rapprochement. No one issued calls for national unity – there were already two countries within this one state. More than 8,000 men and women suspected of being terrorists or of sympathizing with Sikh terrorists were in the Punjab's jails; few of them had been allowed to see lawyers. Among those behind bars were said to be boys and girls under eleven years of age.

'It is very difficult now to go to the Punjab and talk to the masses about any reconciliation,' Manmohan Singh told me. 'There are thousands of Sikh students now in jail on what are at best vague charges. Their parents won't even hear of reconciliation. So what does one do? You bide your time.'

I found that Hindus were even more angry that Sikhs hadn't, as a community, formally condemned the assassination of Indira Gandhi. And Sikhs were bitter that not one of those who had murdered their brethren across north India, and looted their homes, had been arrested or punished.

'This is justice?' asked Mickey Singh, Bhagwant Singh Ahuja's son. 'You call this a free, civilized society?'

He was echoing the outrage that was being expressed around the country by people who were shocked at the breakdown of law and order in the wake of the Gandhi murder. I asked Mickey, a tall, sturdy Sikh who is only twenty-three but who appears much older, what he thought Mrs Gandhi's legacy was for the Punjab.

'Legacy?' Mickey Singh said. 'You ask about legacy? Just look around you. Look at the army, and the unhappiness. You want to find out about her legacy?'

On the plane to Amritsar, I had read an extraordinary essay by Pritish Nandy, editor of the *Illustrated Weekly of India*. Nandy, a Bengali Hindu, had this to say:

The assassination of Prime Minister Indira Gandhi was a brutal and reprehensible act, condemned by everyone. An act of murder that laid to rest all our pretensions to civilized politics.

What the assassination brought in its wake was equally brutal. A retaliation quite unthinkable. Rampaging mobs went berserk. Particularly in Delhi, where they took upon themselves the divine right to avenge the prime minister's murder.

Just because those who killed her owed allegiance to the frenzied fringe of the Sikh community, who were seeking vengeance against those whom they saw as responsible for the sacrilegious act of sending the army into the Golden Temple in Amritsar, the entire community became the victims of organized violence and sheer butchery.

Marauding gangs went around, reportedly with voters' lists in their hands, burning down Sikh homes, looting, maiming, killing and setting them ablaze. Even defence personnel were not spared. Trains reached stations with people lying dead inside. Trucks and lorries lay charred on the highway. People were beaten to death and burnt as torches, doused in kerosene.

Thousands fled, leaving behind their homes, their families. But where could they go? The lumpen mobs ruled the streets, led by men in power. The police, as always, quietly stood by and watched. As homes went up in flames. As dead bodies littered the streets. As train after train rolled in, with unidentified corpses.

It was incredible. A shocked and bereaved nation watched with dismay the collapse of the entire law and order machinery in the face of such savagery.

The riots are now over. But who will put out the fires that still burn? Thousands lie dead. Many more are alive, but destroyed for ever. We all see the victims. And we all know who the people responsible are. And why they did it.

But what are we going to do about it? Let it pass again into books of history and old newspapers as yet another tragic episode to be quickly forgotten, healed with easy charity – so that we can get back to our comfortable clichés?

Can a stupid and barbaric act committed by a few people owing allegiance to a lunatic fringe destroy our faith in our own ability to live together as a single nation, irrespective of religion, caste and community? For the faults of a minuscule minority, who may or may not have celebrated the prime minister's death, shall we humiliate an entire community whose loyalty to the nation has never been in question before?

Is this the way we, as Indians, ought to behave with each other? Is this the secularism we preach and pretend to practise?

In the weeks since my first visit to Amritsar, the arithmetic of population in the Punjab had started to change.

More than 75,000 Sikhs emigrated to the state from other parts of India. They came here from Himachal Pradesh and Uttar Pradesh and Haryana, even from as far away as Bihar and Orissa. They fled their homes to escape further harassment. Many of the emigrés are widows and orphaned children. There are still some 7 million Sikhs spread across states other than the Punjab – but the 75,000 men, women and children who poured into this already troubled state brought with them tales of horror.

These tales were narrated every day, and the narrations exacerbated tensions.

One evening near Amritsar, I listened to Amrik Singh, a young carpenter who had moved from his home in Delhi. He spoke before a small gathering of friends and relatives in a *dhaaba*, a roadside restaurant. People squatted on the floor, huddled in blankets to keep out the December cold. Singh was a tall, thin man, with a moustache and narrow eyes that looked at you with pain. His voice was so low that the slightest rustling of someone's blanket would smother a sentence, but everyone's attention was riveted on him.

He said that he lost his father, five brothers and two sons during the riots following Indira Gandhi's assassination. They were hacked to death, he said. His wife was gang-raped while he was forced to watch; his seven-year-old daughter was molested. He himself was repeatedly stabbed, almost castrated and left for dead. Now he and his wife must start all over again in the Punjab.

His audience seemed stunned as he spoke. It is not often that a Sikh male will volunteer information that his wife's honour has been violated. Women started weeping. Men began to shout in anger.

I thought: these tales will be told and retold until they become part of the Punjab's mythology. How many young men like Amrik Singh will swear revenge? How can Sikhs ever forgive Hindus? How will the bitterness and anguish ever disappear from this land? We need the healing touch, Bhagwant Singh Ahuja had said to me that November evening not long after the murder of Mrs Gandhi. But who will bring a healing hand to these proud and wounded people of the Punjab?

Rajiv Gandhi? Will he be able to forget – and forgive – the fact that his mother was murdered by two Sikhs? His December election campaign was not especially heroic: his ruling Congress Party appealed shamelessly to the sentiments of India's overwhelming Hindu majority by accusing the Sikh leadership of balking at resolving the Punjab problem. He accused Opposition leaders of being in collusion with anti-national elements in the Punjab. A 'foreign hand' was working actively to destabilize the Punjab, Gandhi said. He did not elaborate. This was not the sort of rhetoric that would reassure the Punjab's Sikhs. But then, the Punjab wasn't voting in the 1984 election (as it was under the direct rule of the central government – President's Rule.)

In Delhi I came across posters put up by Congress Party candidates that said: 'Would you trust a taxi driver from another state? For better security, vote Congress.' Since a large number of Delhi's taxi drivers were Sikh, the message was clear.

Even clearer, and more sickening, were hoardings commissioned by Congress candidates in states like Andhra Pradesh and Kerala. These depicted a slain Indira Gandhi, blood gushing from her body, being held by her son Rajiv. Two Sikhs crouched at one side, their guns smoking. Indians rewarded Rajiv Gandhi's Congress Party with 401 out of 508 seats contested for the national parliament.

Healing hand?

During my travels around India, I was astonished at how many non-Sikhs, particularly educated and affluent Indians, voiced the view that the Sikhs 'had it coming' to them.

One very cold January evening in Delhi, I sat in the drawing-room of my brother-in-law, Ajai Lal, a successful producer of audio-visuals and television commercials. The mood in Lal's home was one of general jubilation over Rajiv Gandhi's unprecedented victory in the December national elections. Gandhi and some of his top aides, such as Arun Singh, had studied at the exclusive Doon School in north India – and most of the males present this evening were also Doon graduates (they called themselves Doscoes). In fact, thirty-two newly elected members of Parliament had attended the Doon School in Dehra Doon.

One particular guest did not, however, dwell too much on the old-boy angle. He was a young local businessman, and he consumed several glasses of whisky and kept up a harangue about the Punjab. He himself was a Punjabi Hindu.

'We will fix them now,' he said. 'They thought they were God's gift to India, eh? They thought they were the only strong, virile ones around, eh? Well, they sure showed themselves to be cowards recently, didn't they? How many faced the mobs with courage, eh?'

'Would you have faced a mob like that?' I asked.

The businessman shrugged. He helped himself to another whisky.

'Those bastards,' he said, presently, 'those Sikh bastards. If I had my way, I would rip their bowels out. I would slaughter every last one of them. I would decimate them. Those arrogant, filthy bastards. Who do they think they are? They have destroyed India.'

I shivered, and it was not because of the cold.

Just two months short of the first anniversary of Indira Gandhi's assassination, there was another murder of another well-known Indian. It, too, rocked India. The victim this time was Sant Harchand Singh Longowal, president of the Akali Dal, who had signed a pact with Prime Minister Rajiv Gandhi on 24 July 1985 that appeared to offer effective solutions to the Punjab crisis.

Under the terms of that accord, Gandhi had agreed to local elections in the Punjab. More significantly, the Gandhi administration conceded a number of long-standing Sikh demands concerning regional autonomy. Chandigarh, which doubled as a capital for both Haryana and the Punjab, would be the sole capital of the latter (Haryana would have its own new capital). The Punjab would get a greater share of the waters of the 'Land of the Five Rivers'. Gandhi also agreed to step up the promotion of industrialization in the beleaguered state. In return, Longowal committed himself to finding a peaceful solution to the Punjab's problems within the framework of the Indian Constitution.

The Gandhi–Longowal accord was widely hailed in India, especially by moderate Sikhs. The very fact that Gandhi and Longowal had sat across the negotiating table and worked long and hard to accommodate each other was seen as a historic development indeed. It was the first political settlement which Sikhs had agreed to sign publicly; morever, they agreed to police the enforcement of the pact – particularly the anti-terrorism component – themselves.

Not everyone, of course, thought highly of the accord. Barely had the accord been signed when rumours started swirling that Khalistan terrorists had vowed to kill Longowal. The terrorists put out the word that Longowal had caved in to pressure from Gandhi, that he had sold out. The Sikh leader, a cheerful man whose optimism about the Punjab now seemed increased because of the accord, didn't seem perturbed by the criticism; he shrugged away rumours about his being the number one target of the terrorists. He had a fatalistic view of life, and if his time was up, Longowal told associates, then, notwithstanding the heavy security around him, there was nothing that he could do.

Late in the afternoon of Tuesday, 20 August Longowal walked into a *gurdwara* near Sangrur, his home village in the heart of the Punjab, to offer prayers for peace. He had spent the earlier part of the day in Chandigarh, where he conferred with party colleagues on how to contest state and parliamentary elections that had been set for September. The elections were intended to restore political normalcy in the Punjab, which had long been under direct rule from Delhi. Gandhi also seemed keen on transferring to local authorities in the Punjab the responsibility for tackling the escalating terrorism. The prime minister was aware, of course, that it was by no means certain that his Congress Party would win the Punjab elections; in fact, the strong likelihood was that the Akalis would be swept into power.

In the *gurdwara*, Longowal, a fifty-four-year-old man with a long beard and a gentle face, bowed before the *Granth Sahib* and then began speaking to the mostly Sikh congregation, urging reconciliation between Sikhs and Hindus.

Suddenly, a Sikh youth seated in front of Longowal pulled out a pistol and started firing. The assailant was grabbed by a teenage boy next to him, and the bullets intended for Longowal tore into the boy, killing him on the spot. In the confusion, another Sikh man – who many took to be one of Longowal's bodyguards – rushed towards the Sikh leader, shouting for order and urging the congregation to remain calm. But this man then spun around towards Longowal, produced a pistol from his jacket, and pumped several shots into him at pointblank range. Longowal was taken to a nearby hospital, where he died within minutes of arrival.

The cause of peace in the Punjab was dealt a devastating blow by the tragedy. Many Indians feared that, by removing the one moderate leader courageous enough to conclude an agreement of reconciliation with the Indian government, Longowal's assassination would provoke a still deeper crisis for the trouble-torn Punjab. The Akali leader had begun to create a middle ground where Sikhs could indeed reconcile their own internecine political differences and also begin to deal collectively with an Indian government that many of them felt continued to be insensitive to their community. Even more important, perhaps, Longowal had attempted to reach beyond politics alone to urge broader reconciliation between Hindus and Sikhs. For that reason, his death was not only a blow to peace in the Punjab, but also a setback to a deeper healing of communal differences throughout the country. The carefully planned assassination was also seen widely as a warning to other Sikh moderates who may have wished to speak out against terrorism and find a peaceful solution to the worsening crisis.

A month after the Longowal assassination, the Akali Dal won an overwhelming majority in the elections for the Punjab's 117-seat legislative assembly. The Akalis named Surjit Singh Barnala to head the Punjab cabinet, and there was much expectation – perhaps too much expectation – that the Akalis would be able to curb, if not entirely eliminate, terrorism in the state. The Barnala government was to last only eighteen months, however, before Rajiv Gandhi once again imposed President's Rule in the Punjab. Why? Because, said Gandhi, law and order had deteriorated hopelessly under Barnala. The state government was incapable of combating terrorism – an assertion that was vigorously but vainly challenged by the Akalis.

In October 1988, Governor S. S. Ray – the man who administered the Punjab on behalf of the central government – announced with a flourish that during the first sixteen months of President's Rule, 469 terrorists had been killed, compared to 118 killed during the eighteen-month tenure of the Barnala Administration. Ray also said that during this period there had been a sharp increase in the seizure of terrorists' weapons, and that there had been 580 encounters between the Punjab police and terrorists, compared with 192 such encounters in Barnala's time.

Of course, statistics can be misleading. Notwithstanding the figures supplied by Governor Ray, terrorism had hardly abated in the Punjab. Indeed, during the same sixteen-month period of President's Rule cited by Ray, more than 3,000 civilians were killed by Khalistani terrorists, compared with about 850 during the Barnala Administration. Prime Minister Gandhi, in October 1988, toured a couple of rural communities in the Punjab in a show of courage and governmental resolve not to be intimidated by the terrorists – but he was shielded by such heavy security that this

underscored the continuing tenuity of life in the Punjab. The
Khalistanis continued to demonstrate that they could strike at will
anywhere.

When I visited the Punjab a third time, I was struck by how
gloomy the overall situation seemed. The most powerful impressions that an outsider has these days of the Punjab are not of its
prosperity, as spelled out by the shiny tractors and the television
antennae and sleek motor cycles and the Japanese cars and trucks.
It is not the greenness that dazzles the visitor, but the tens of
thousands of bright saffron turbans worn by Sikh men, young and
old alike. Saffron has become the colour of protest against what
many Sikhs believe is needlessly authoritarian rule in their Sikh-
majority state by the central government. The saffron turbans and
the saffron *duppattas*, the long garments worn by Sikh women, are
meant to convey how terribly hurt and humiliated Sikhs feel at their
alienation from India's majority Hindus.

A senior Indian army official who I met in Chandigarh felt,
however, that many Sikhs and their leaders had simply abandoned
reason. 'They have closed their shutters,' he said, wearily. 'They
have imaginary fears and their total distrust of the Indian government is often based on wild rumours. They seem to have transferred
guilt to the "other side". Which is to say that nothing in Punjab is
ever their own fault. That it is always us, the outsiders or Hindus,
who are to be blamed. And Sikhs abroad get excited by such wild
charges. The Sikhs abroad have seen how tiny territories obtained
independence – like Djibouti and Bangladesh – so now they feel
that they, too, have a chance.'

This official, who requested anonymity, said that what really
worried him was the fact that more and more young Sikhs seemed
to be attracted to the terrorist cause – into a state of fanaticism
about their religion. He said that while 'Khalistan' was still a
knee-jerk concept for many young people, one espoused mostly to
annoy the authorities, an expression of frustration not unlike
teenagers' tantrums, there now appeared to be a growing hardcore
of rabid terrorists in the Punjab. Little wonder, then, that the
districts of Ludhiana, Patiala and Ropar, which were considered
quite peaceful when Surjit Singh Barnala was the state's chief
minister, were now plagued with murders and bomb blasts.

The army official, one of India's most decorated soldiers, told
me that the terrorists found it easy to slip into neighbouring

Pakistan because the 375-kilometre border with the Punjab was inadequately patrolled. He said he had no doubt that these Sikhs received training in Pakistan, and once back in India the terrorists were sheltered by relatives in their villages. The aim of these terrorists was not only to disrupt government activity, indeed even to make the Punjab impossible to govern, but also to drive a wedge between Sikhs and Hindus. In time, as the situation deteriorated beyond repair, New Delhi would have no choice but to yield to the creation of an independent Khalistan. I was convinced that it was unlikely that any central government would let this happen, but I was astonished at how many Sikhs believed in this scenario.

As I travelled through the Punjab this time, I thought of how aspects of life in the Punjab increasingly fitted into a vicious cycle: terrorism begat rigorous anti-terrorist campaigns by the authorities, which in turn alienated Sikh youths even more. Many Sikh moderates now felt that all Sikhs were, implicitly at least, under suspicion. Parkash Singh Badal, a former chief minister of the state and a top Akali leader, told me: 'All ordinary Sikhs are having to pay the price of the government's dispute with the terrorists.'

One evening in Chandigarh, I saw for myself what Badal was talking about. I had been invited to dinner at the home of a businessman named Shivinder Singh. At one point before the food was served the doorbell rang, and Shivinder, who happened to be near the door, opened it.

A group of policemen were at the door.

'We have come to impound your jeep,' one of the policemen said to Singh.

'Why?'

'Because its colour is olive-green – and it can be easily mistaken for a military jeep,' the policeman said.

Shivinder argued unsuccessfully that he only used his jeep to hunt partridges in the bush, but the policemen were adamant, producing documents that authorized the seizure. They took the keys of Shivinder's jeep and drove it away. Afterwards, Shivinder's two small children kept asking why the cops had come to their home.

Later, Shivinder said to me: 'You see what has happened here – the Punjab situation is already affecting the minds of our children.'

A couple of days after that, I was introduced to Sukhinder Singh, another young businessman, and his wife, Kunal. They spoke with despondency about how a great social divide had already occurred in the Punjab between Sikhs and Hindus.

What also especially bothered Kunal was the constant security searches. Whenever her children saw security checkpoints, they now reflexively opened the glove compartment of their car, switched on the interior lights, and raised their hands.

'What sort of a place has this become?' Kunal said ruefully. 'I used to be the greatest ambassador for India. But now we Sikhs are being suspected at every turn. I want my kids to grow up in a place where they feel proud of belonging. But it's become really frightening these days. I see no future in India for my children.'

Her husband added: 'We used to laugh at the notion of Khalistan. But today it may very well become a reality.'

I listened to Sukhinder Singh – and I hoped fervently that he was wrong. I would like to think that, despite all his travails and those of other decent Sikhs like him, Sukhinder would still like to live in the entity that is known as India – and not in Khalistan. For some people, particularly misguided Sikh expatriates who don't have to contend with the consequences of their folly, Khalistan may be a legitimate political dream. In truth, that dream is a dangerous illusion that can only harm Sikhs and Sikhism.

Dreams. Illusions. Terrorism. Will the 'Land of the Five Rivers' ever again see peaceful times? On 6 January 1989, Satwant Singh and Kehar Singh went to the gallows in Delhi. Predictably, there was fresh violence in the Punjab and elsewhere following the hangings of the two Sikhs. Some Indians felt that Rajiv Gandhi should have persuaded the Indian president, R. Venkataraman, to commute their sentences to life imprisonment. Others felt that in jail Satwant and Kehar would have been living symbols of strength for the Khalistan cause. Still other Indians felt that it did not matter what Rajiv did: the condemned, along with the late Beant Singh, had already become martyrs for many Sikhs.

The questions will continue to be debated. Should they have gone to the gallows? Should Rajiv have interceded? Like so much about the tragic situation in the Punjab, these are short, hard questions – with no easy answers. Only when Sikhs begin to look forward to a more secular vision and genuinely work for it – a prospect that seems unlikely right now – will separatism based on religious fervour begin to decline.

CHAPTER SIX:
'FISSIPAROUS TENDENCIES'

The Punjab's problems seem especially dramatic because of the continuing terrorism. But virtually every region in India seems to have its fires: Kashmir in the north, another strategic border state like the Punjab, where local Moslems were believed to be 'soft' on Pakistan and desirous of independence from India; Assam in the east, were local tribes massacred Moslem refugees: Andhra Pradesh in the south, where a regional ethnic party is clamouring for greater state rights; Tamil Nadu, whose local leaders had supported the Tamil insurgency in Sri Lanka; and Maharashtra in the west, where Hindus and Moslems had murdered one another. And, of course, Madhya Pradesh in central India, where poisonous gas from a Union Carbide plant in Bhopal had resulted in the deaths of more than 4,000 men, women and children and in the permanent blinding of thousands more in December 1984. Was modern India afflicted by some ancient curse?

I recall something that a distinguished Indian once said: 'India today presents a very mixed picture of hope and anguish, of remarkable advances and at the same time of inertia, of a new spirit and also of the dead hand of the past and of privilege, of an overall and growing unity and many disruptive tendencies. Withal there is a great vitality and a ferment in people's minds and activities. Perhaps we who live in the middle of this ever-changing scene do not always realize the full significance of all that is happening. What will emerge from the labour and the tumults of the present generation?'

The author of these words was Jawaharlal Nehru, and he said them in 1959, a year of much communal strife. As I recalled Nehru's words, it seemed to me that they were so appropriate to the India of late 1984, for this was as dark a time, if not darker. And Nehru's words seem to me to be even more appropriate in 1989.

Not long after my visit to the Punjab in 1984, I went to see a man named Romesh Thapar in Delhi. He was a tall, silver-haired man, with a rich, resonant voice and the assured ease of an aristocrat. Thapar was one of India's best political analysts. He and his wife, Raj, published a magazine called *Seminar*, which for nearly three decades had been the country's most important intellectual monthly. Along with their friend Professor Rajni Kothari, of the Centre for the Study of Developing Societies, the Thapars had become Delhi's most sought-after sources for local writers and visiting journalists. They were very congenial, and seekers of insight were rarely turned away by them, no matter what the hour or the visitor's ideology. Because they rarely hesitated to question the Delhi government's policies and express their reservations about many of Mrs Gandhi's actions, the Thapars and Professor Kothari hadn't endeared themselves to the prime minister's aides and associates.

Romesh Thapar received me in his art-filled house on Kautilya Marg, and Raj promptly offered tea and toast. The collation warmed me up; the Delhi winter had frozen my blood.

The conversation quickly turned to Indira Gandhi's legacy. What had she left behind, I asked?

'When she died, she left nothing behind,' Romesh Thapar said. 'She left nothing behind of any redeeming value. She tried to destroy our Parliament, our judiciary, our press, and she tried to undermine the states – particularly states that were governed by opposition parties. Look how she tried to destabilize the Punjab. And look what she did in Kashmir.'

'Those who maintain that an India without Indira is a land without a leader should think again,' Thapar said. 'Indira Gandhi left behind a sterile political landscape. The infrastructure, designed by her father to buttress healthy federal functioning and to cultivate those autonomies without which no democratic system can be sensitive and effective, civilized and respected – that infrastructure had been made impotent. The basis of a genuine secular policy is not to integrate various ethnic communities but to create mutual respect between the majority and the minorities – this was lacking under Indira.

'Assam and the tribes of the north-east took the first onslaught of
"imperial" Delhi's aberrations.'

(In the eastern state of Assam, which produces much of the crude
oil that is making India almost self-sufficient in petroleum, local
tribes were angry about the influx of Moslem refugees from neighbouring Bangladesh, whose increasing presence they feared would
confer on indigenous tribes the status of minority groups. Bloodshed occurred periodically, with the biggest massacre taking place
in May 1983, when thousands of tribespeople, armed with bows and
arrows and spears, killed thousands more of the Moslem emigrés.
Mrs Gandhi's government was astonishingly tardy in clamping
down on the tribespeople, whose electoral support her ruling
Congress Party had sought; she pushed through local elections that
were blatantly rigged by her Congress Party. The situation deteriorated so rapidly that Assam, along with the Punjab, were the only
two Indian states where the December 1984 national parliamentary
poll wasn't held: in both cases, the political situation was deemed
too unstable, with a high potential for violence.)

'The Punjab was massively mishandled,' Thapar continued, 'and
even the monster of terrorism was nurtured to divide and rule the
assertive but stupidly advised and led Sikh community. Kashmir
followed, a crude example of authoritarian intervention, endangering another strategic area. And then, Andhra. Only a popular
revolt in that state, from village to village, revived Chief Minister
N. T. Rama Rao, who had been illegally unseated, and made
Indira Gandhi retreat.

'These events, punctuated by the storming of the Golden
Temple, which had been fortified almost as if with the blessing of
Indira Gandhi's minions, and the incredible partisan handling of
the traumatic aftermath, took on the dimensions of a classical
tragedy as she was gunned down in vengeance by her own security
guards. And what happened then? The lumpen leaders she had
cultivated in her Congress Party sparked a holocaust against the
Sikh community stretching from Delhi to Bengal. The corrupt
police system looked on. The government sat paralyzed.'

I told the Thapars that I planned to travel around India to see for
myself what impact Mrs Gandhi's politics and policies had had on
the lives of everyday people. I thought that India seemed to be in
chaos. Were there any signs of a new social order? Or was India
falling apart?

'If you looked at the scene even before the assassination, you could see that Indian states were highly disturbed over the concentration of power in Delhi,' Thapar said. 'But then came 31 October and the assassination. The public was terrified. There was a total breakdown of law and order. There was a shockwave across the country, and Rajiv Gandhi capitalized on it. He raised the spectre of disintegration. People thought, "Let's support and strengthen the national government at this time of crisis."

'But well before Indira's death, the crisis of political and economic management in India had already expressed itself in many parts of the country – in the Punjab and Kashmir, for instance. As the states were alienated, you saw the Congress base becoming restricted to the Hindi-speaking heartland in the north. Thus, Rajiv and his Congress had to mobilize Hindu opinion, rather than fashion the kind of national secular consensus that his grandfather, Nehru, put together. He won the election largely because of this undisguised appeal to the majority Hindus, because of nationwide sympathy over the murder of his mother, and because of the 500 crores of rupees [the equivalent of $500 million] that the Congress Party spent on slick advertising and electioneering.'

I knew I was keeping Romesh and Raj Thapar from their dinner engagement. But even as I looked at my watch, Romesh Thapar signalled me to stay on.

'The question now is: will the trauma of 1984 continue into 1985?' Thapar said. 'How will Rajiv Gandhi manage relations between the centre and the states? If there is to be a new social order, it will have to emerge at the level of our states. The corrective measures in our sub-continent have to come from the states – because it is in the states that you implement policy and affect the everyday life of people. Any alternatives to the current national political mess, any new social order, must come at the state level. So if you are travelling through India's states, I wish you God-speed!'

That was the last time I saw Raj Thapar: she died a few months later after a long battle with cancer. Romesh Thapar died of a heart attack not long afterwards.

India's history and political development constitute a remarkable story. The entity that is India today consists of twenty-five states and nine 'union' territories, or areas directly controlled by the Delhi government, which everyone calls 'The Centre'; some states, like Madhya Pradesh, are larger than France. When the British left in 1947 after ruling the Indian sub-continent for 150 years, there were 565 princely states in the territory that was then partitioned into India and Pakistan. These states were given the option of joining either India or Pakistan; virtually all chose to be part of India, whose leaders vowed at the very outset to establish a secular state (as opposed to Pakistan, which was set up as an Islamic nation).

The departure of the British in 1947 was the culmination of a long and sometimes turbulent 'freedom struggle' during which leaders such as Mahatma Gandhi, Jawaharlal Nehru and Nehru's daughter Indira Gandhi were frequently arrested and jailed by their colonial rulers. It was during this freedom movement that Mahatma Gandhi fashioned his philosophy of *ahimsa*, or non-violence. He urged his followers to counter the brute strength of the British Empire with passive resistance. It was a philosophy that decades later would influence the Rev. Martin Luther King, Jr, who adopted it for his civil rights struggle in the deep south of the United States.

Independence brought India into the modern comity of nations, but Indian civilization had been around continuously since at least 2900 BC. Inhabitants of the Indus river valley developed an urban culture based mostly on commerce and trade. Around 1500 BC, Aryan tribes rode in from central Asia and drove the Indus inhabitants – known as the Dravidians – southward. During the next several centuries, various indigenous Hindu and Buddhist kingdoms flourished in India; the land also attracted waves of invaders from Persia and Moslem Asia, marauders whose greed was stirred by accounts of travellers such as Marco Polo and Vasco da Gama about fabulous wealth in India's temples and royal courts.

Most of these invaders foraged, pillaged, raped and then left. But some stayed on, the most prominent of these being the Mughals. They established a dynasty that ruled most of India until the British conquered the sub-continent in the nineteenth century. It was the Mughals who accelerated the conversion of millions of Indians to Islam, which was often accompanied by great cruelty towards those who resisted such conversion. But the Mughals also left behind extraordinary architectural achievements – the Taj Mahal in Agra, the Shalimar Garden in Kashmir, the sandstone city of Fatehpur Sikri, the Red Fort in Delhi. And it was the Mughals who established ateliers where miniature paintings were produced – paintings that survive to this day and which can command hundreds of thousands of dollars at international auctions.

The British did not enter India as the Mughals did, which is to say that they did not come with swords unsheathed and war-cries on their lips. They came instead as traders and established a warehouse in Surat in 1619. They came under the auspices of the East India Company, which had been formed in London to promote trade in spices. Various native rulers, flattered by gifts given to them by the foreigners and perhaps intrigued by the sight of white skins, offered the traders 'protection'. Christian missionaries arrived in force, too, to introduce British-style education and to 'convert the heathens'. The traders steadily expanded their influence by subterfuge sometimes, and sometimes by outright conquest. Local kingdoms, already beset with internecine succession problems and family squabbles, fell like ninepins. By the 1850s, the British East India Company controlled most of the land area that today covers India, Pakistan and Bangladesh.

But in 1857, much of northern India revolted against the British. *1857* The revolt, known as the Great Mutiny, was largely the work of Indian foot-soldiers, or sepoys. Most of them were Hindus who revered the cow, or Moslems who abhorred pork, and they were angered by the fact that animal fat was used to grease cartridges which had to be bitten open when loading the new Enfield rifle. Their mutiny sparked riots in cities such as Lucknow, Meerut and Cawnpore, and there was considerable savagery against the British. But in the end there were simply too many poorly led and disorganized groups in too many places, and the mutiny was put down by the better equipped British troops, who were ably assisted by Sikh regiments.

The Great Mutiny resulted in the formal takeover of Indian territories by the British Crown. India was now part of Britain's Empire.

There is a particularly eloquent passage in Welsh writer James Morris's *Heaven's Command*, which forms part of his trilogy on the British Empire:

Swept away with the carnage of the Indian Mutiny were the last dilettante deposits of England's eighteenth-century empire. There had been a pagan, or at least agnostic charm to that old sovereignty – short on convictions, rich in gusto and a sense of fun – but there would be little that was airy or entertaining to the new empire emerging from the shambles of Lucknow and Cawnpore.

It knew its values now, stern, efficient and improving, and it recognized as its principal duty the imposition of British standards upon the black, brown and yellow peoples. The Mutiny had demonstrated indeed that not all the coloured peoples were capable of spiritual redemption, as had earlier been supposed, but at worst the British could always concentrate on material regeneration – the enforcement of law and order, the distribution of scientific progress and the lubrication of trade.

That is exactly what Queen Victoria's minions proceeded to do. They created regional police forces, they whipped into shape an impressive national army, they introduced telegraph communications, they built more than 25,000 miles of railway tracks, they established a nation-wide postal service, they built schools and churches, they constructed roads through thick jungles and tall mountain ranges, they started the élite Indian Civil Service to which educated Indians eventually began to be admitted.

But the British also bled India dry. India's fine cotton fed the looms of Lancashire; the indigenous textile industry was crushed by the import of British fabrics made from Indian cotton and silk. Indian iron ore went to Britain's steel mills, only to reappear in India in the form of locomotives and vehicles and machinery. The British barred industrial development in India because it would compete with their own factories and furnaces. Poverty widened in India. Joblessness increased.

In 1885, an Englishman named Allan Octavian Hume started an organization he called the Indian National Congress. Hume was a liberal-minded man who had served in India for many years as a British bureaucrat, and it was his feeling that the country's colonial rulers were dangerously out of touch with ordinary people's feelings. Hume was keen that his new organization should serve as a vehicle of communication between the rulers and the ruled. Unlike the overwhelming majority of Britons of his time, Hume did not subscribe to the theory that India's white rulers were racially superior to its brown masses.

The Indian National Congress quickly became a forum not only for ideas concerning relations between the British and their subjects but also a platform from which India's struggle for independence was launched. Starting in 1920, Mohandas Karamchand Gandhi – later to be known as the Mahatma, or 'saintly soul' –

transformed the Congress into a mass movement. He used it to mount a popular campaign against the British.

The British finally left in 1947, but not before they had carved out from Greater India a homeland for many of the sub-continent's Moslems. The division of India into India and Pakistan was known as the Partition, which to this day evokes memories among many Hindus, Sikhs and Moslems of widespread bloodshed and rioting. Although India became independent in 1947, it did not formally become a sovereign republic until 26 January 1950, when its Constitution was promulgated. Jawaharlal Nehru, who had become prime minister in 1947, continued in that post until his death from natural causes in 1964.

The Nehru years saw India make important progress in industrialization. These were also the years when the country was divided up into linguistic states. Nehru was succeeded by Lal Bahadur Shastri, a veteran of the freedom struggle. Shastri died in January 1966, soon after India had defeated Pakistan in the second of three wars between the two states since independence. Shastri's successor as prime minister was Indira Gandhi. She was to serve in that office almost exactly as long as her father had.

'Nehru, Shastri, Indira – there evolved over the years a gradual suspicion among ordinary people about the Indian state itself. During the latter part of Indira's reign, the state dropped all notions of benevolence. And people's suspicion about the state, which kept accumulating wide-ranging police powers, was coupled with the disgust people felt over the growing corruption and criminalization in public life. Then you had situations like Punjab and Kashmir, where she constantly employed cost-calculating approaches instead of instituting measures that would lead to lasting solutions of thorny problems. She let thorny problems become thornier.'

The speaker was Ashish Nandy, an associate of Delhi's Centre for the Study of Developing Societies. Professor Nandy and I were talking in his musty, book-filled and generally untidy office at the centre's building on Rajpur Road in Old Delhi. Squirrels played on the well-kept lawn outside his office. Bougainvillea and magnolia trees added colour to the scene. Nandy, a prolific writer and academic, was urging me to start my fresh round of travels in Kashmir. By the time I met Nandy I had already been to the Punjab, where I had seen for myself the impact of Indira Gandhi's handling of a sensitive communal issue in a strategic border state. Now I was eager to go to Kashmir, where Mrs Gandhi had won the last political battle of her life: she had conspired to topple the legitimately elected government of an opposition party and replace it with a government that supported her.

I found it useful to meet people like Romesh Thapar and Rajni Kothari and Ashish Nandy. They gave me their valuable time, asking nothing in exchange except my attention; they offered insights into the Indian scene; they provided pointers to what was happening in different parts of the country; and, without unduly imposing their own assumptions and opinions, they helped me make the connections between what I saw and heard and felt and the broader currents that coursed through India at this particular point in time.

As I flew to Kashmir, I thought about what Ashish Nandy had said about Indira Gandhi's 'cost-calculating' approach to the management of power. She had, in fact, gone home again to Kashmir to whip it into line.

For Mrs Gandhi was a Kashmiri Brahman, a descendant of the scholarly, shrewd and sturdy Hindus who flourished in a mountainous state that was overwhelmingly Moslem. The Nehrus – her father's family – had of course left Kashmir long before her birth to settle in Allahabad, a city on the banks of the river Ganges. Still, in Indira Gandhi's heart home was always Kashmir. The few people she was close to in her adult life were almost all Kashmiris. (Of course, she married a Parsi, whom her father hadn't particularly approved of; the marriage faltered and failed. Nehru once wondered to a friend whether Indira would have been happier had she married a Kashmiri.)

I looked out of the window of the Indian Airlines airbus – and I gasped at the view. The plane was cruising over the snow-helmeted Pir Panjal Range. The crenellated peaks shimmered in the clear winter sunlight. To the west were the rich, alluvial plains of Pakistan; to the east lay the mountainous wastelands of Tibet and, beyond Tibet, China. Soon we were over the mighty Banihal Pass, through which invaders over the centuries had entered Kashmir. It was ironic, I thought, that the most recent invader had been a hometown girl.

Kashmir. The Switzerland of India, with 85,000 square miles of choice land, over which India and Pakistan fought three costly wars to establish proprietorship. Kashmir, more than 80 per cent

Moslem, but ruled traditionally by a Hindu clan whose scions squandered their fortune on sex and soft living, while their subjects starved. Jawaharlal Nehru once said of this state: 'Kashmir, even more than the rest of India, is a land of contrasts. In this land, overladen with natural beauty and rich nature's gifts, stark poverty reigns and humanity is continually struggling for the barest of subsistences. The men and women of Kashmir are good to look at and pleasant to talk to. They are intelligent and clever with their hands. They have a rich and lovely country to live in. Why then should they be so terribly poor?'

Poverty in the midst of great natural beauty is a characteristic of many Third World countries. The beauty of Kashmir is especially breathtaking, with the green and fertile valley surrounded on all sides by tall sentinels of snow – which is why the scenes of deprivation are so dismaying. On the road from the airport, I passed massive camouflaged military bunkers in the shadow of which nestled knots of wooden houses. At first sight, they resembled those marvellous toy homes one comes across in the Swiss countryside, with A-shaped roofs and long beams supporting the ceilings. But instead of neat gardens and well-turfed yards, there were open sewers and dusty spaces in front of these houses. Men and women walked forlornly, with *kangris* (coal stoves) under their robes; the *kangris* made everyone look heavily pregnant, men and women, but in a state where sub-zero temperatures aren't unusual during the winter and where there is no such thing as central heating, the *kangris* serve as portable heaters – just as hand-carried air-conditioners cool American astronauts' space-suits as they walk from bunker to spacecraft before the launch. During political rallies, *kangris* serve as deadly weapons: the very day I arrived in Kashmir, more than thirty people had been hurt in a *kangri* free-for-all that erupted at a rally sponsored by Rajiv Gandhi's Congress Party.

The road from the airport was edged with poplar, walnut and chinar trees. I passed apple and cherry orchards and saffron fields. The road rolled over many culverts and streams; attractive children frolicked by these streams, but their clothes were frayed and often torn. There was a rundown appearance to these houses, an impression that was sustained all the way into Srinagar. There was nothing beckoning, or even welcoming, about this capital city of 2 million people.

I checked in at the Hotel Broadway, a modern Scandinavian-type building with comfortable rooms and a polite staff. In the lobby were several electric stoves. Large men wearing thick sweaters and peaked, lamb's-wool caps lounged on sofas, drinking spirits. I was immediately beset by carpet salesmen and purveyors of shawls. To decline such offers was to offend, and the salesmen sulked away. But I wanted to read up on the tourist literature which I'd picked up at Srinagar's airport. I was also waiting for my friend Rahul Singh, who was driving up to Srinagar from the state's winter capital of Jammu, which lay south of the massif I had flown over on the way to Kashmir's elevated valley. Rahul Singh was then editor of the Chandigarh edition of the *Indian Express*, and he was coming to Kashmir to get a view of the election campaign that was on in full fury here. We had agreed to meet up in Srinagar, a place neither of us had visited for years.

The tourist brochures were shabby, the photographs poorly reproduced. Kashmir did not seem inviting in this literature. And, indeed, tourism – the mainstay of the state's economy – was sharply falling off. I had been told in Delhi that in the first eleven months of 1984, Kashmir attracted 275,000 domestic tourists and about 45,000 foreigners; the previous year, the figures had been 400,000 Indians and 44,000 foreigners; and in 1982, more than 600,000 Indian tourists and 50,000 foreigners were estimated by the authorities to have skiied, toured, trekked, played golf and tennis, fished, hiked, camped or climbed mountains in Kashmir. State officials attributed the decline in tourism to poor publicity about Kashmir, and the poor publicity to the fact that since 1983 the state had been experiencing a political upheaval. Moreover, tourists who travelled by land seemed deterred by the fact that virtually all major roads into Kashmir led up from a troubled neighbouring state, the Punjab.

Tourists were also deterred by reports of growing unemployment in Kashmir. This, to be sure, was a classic case of the chicken-or-egg theory, because with fewer tourists coming to Kashmir, the state's tourism industries and such tourist-predicated businesses as carpet-manufacturing and shawl-making slid into the doldrums. About 75 per cent of Kashmir's 6 million people lived in the Srinagar Valley, the rest in Jammu. In the valley alone, there were said to be more than 200,000 unemployed adults by December 1984. (Those who do visit Kashmir can wind up with unexpected bargains: I was able to buy an intricately knotted and designed Kashmiri silk carpet at Ali Shah's shop outside Srinagar for the equivalent of $600 – a 50 per cent discount; in New York I was subsequently offered six times that amount for my new acquisition!)

Kashmiris have long felt that the Delhi government has neglected their economic development, despite the strategic importance of the state, which has borders with Pakistan and China. This sentiment was highlighted by Sonam Gyalsan, a lean, compact lawyer from the remote Kashmiri province of Ladakh. I was introduced to Gyalsan by a jolly local character named C. B. Kaul, who is Srinagar correspondent for the *Indian Express*. Kaul had brought Gyalsan to my hotel so that he could meet Rahul Singh, but since Singh was late in getting here from Jammu I served as a stand-in. Gyalsan, whose family members in Ladakh are still pastoral tribesmen, is a member of the Kashmir state assembly, and he invited Singh and me for breakfast the next morning. He cooked a Ladakhi breakfast for us in his small suite in Srinagar's hostel for legislators.

There was no heat in the suite, nor gas, nor electricity. Gyalsan lit up a kerosene stove and swiftly concocted a thick soup called *snamthuk*. In it were chunks of mutton, bits of goat's cheese, barley, flour, ginger and rich local butter. The *snamthuk* was very filling, yet it was followed by boiled eggs, outsize apricots that Gyalsan had brought from Leh (Ladakh's capital), boiled cauliflower and milky tea that was so sweet that my teeth vibrated as I consumed it. The meal made me drowsy, but I perked up when Gyalsan started to talk.

'We are at the brink of extinction in Ladakh,' he said, in crisp English.

Extinction?

'Absolutely,' Gyalsan said. 'We tribespeople are the modern-day 'untouchables' of Kashmir. There are still 140,000 of us in Ladakh's two districts, Leh and Khargol. But look how we are forced to live – in caravans, in shacks made out of sheepskin, in degrading poverty. I have tried to impress on the powers-that-be in Delhi and in Srinagar that Ladakh should be developed in the national interest. After all, we, more than any other Indians, directly face two enemies – Pakistan and China. We are in the frontline. Ours is the first blood to be shed whenever there are wars, or even minor skirmishes. And what do we get in return? Nothing. No jobs, little investment in economic development. Even the Indian army people are sometimes arrogant in their dealings with us. Indira Gandhi said she cared for all of India's border peoples. Not much evidence of her caring in our area. I hope Rajiv Gandhi is more attentive.'

Sonam Gyalsan's life story is a sort of Indian Horatio Alger tale. He was born forty-nine years ago in a caravan near Nurla Village in Ladakh, the youngest of five brothers and a sister. His parents were nomadic traders in wool, and they frequently wandered into neighbouring Tibet. Gyalsan travelled with them as they traversed mountain roads that rose as high as 18,000 feet. Winters were harsh, but at these heights it was bitterly cold even during the summers. His parents would stop at tiny hamlets to bargain for Shartush shawls, made out of the fine hair that grows under the necks of the spiral-horned wild mountain goats known as Tsos. (These shawls can now cost the equivalent of $7,000.) When he was sixteen years old, his parents arranged his marriage to Tsering Dolkar, a fourteen-year-old girl. (They now have four children.) As Gyalsan learned to read and write in his parents's caravan, it struck him that there were not many people he had encountered who were literate. And the people of Ladakh, whose native language was Tibetan, simply could not communicate with traders and visiting politicians from the Kashmir Valley; the outsiders spoke Kashmiri and Hindi and Urdu, but seldom Tibetan.

'As a child I was inspired by biographies of Nehru and Mahatma Gandhi,' Gyalsan said. 'These books instilled in me a strong drive to uplift myself. I studied very hard and obtained admission to a high school in Srinagar, and then won a scholarship to Ram Jas College in Delhi. It was on a visit home one day that I learned there wasn't a single lawyer in Leh. Feuds and disputes were still being settled the old-fashioned way – with fists, or knives, or abusive language! I decided to become a lawyer.'

He received a law degree from Delhi University and returned home to Ladakh to set up his practice. He started civic organizations to inculcate in Ladakhis notions of hygiene; he coaxed friends in Delhi to underwrite visits by physicians to attend to Ladakhi children's illnesses – the infant mortality rate in this remote northeast province of Kashmir was well over 300 per every live 1,000 births; he persuaded the Srinagar administration to build several primary schools; Gyalsan even founded a chapter of the Lion's

Club in Leh – at 12,000 feet above sea level, the Leh chapter is believed to be the highest Lion's Club in the world.

It was only a matter of time before he entered politics. Gyalsan headed several delegations that went to Delhi to ask Mrs Gandhi formally to declare Ladakh a backward area so that it could receive special development funds from the central government. The prime minister wasn't particularly receptive to the idea. No special funds were allocated for the development of Ladakh, although vacation bungalows for government officials were erected near Leh. A hydro-electric project called Stakna was delayed so much by the government that the initial budget of $5 million now ballooned five times, with Delhi giving the money only grudgingly. Kashmir state officials in Srinagar didn't seem particularly inclined to assist the 140,000 people of Ladakh, most of whom were Buddhists.

So Sonam Gyalsan ran for the state assembly elections and won a seat. In the legislature, he has been vocal and insistent about obtaining a better deal for Ladakh.

'I see myself as a link between my backward society and the rapidly progressing modern-day India,' Gyalsan said to me. 'I'm a Buddhist – and Buddhism asks each of us to go outside ourselves and look for the larger good. I don't especially subscribe to political rhetoric. I say to the big shots in Delhi: "Don't just tell us how much Ladakh means for the security of the nation – show us." Delhi has been allowed by people like us to get away with neglect and inattention. Well, our time has come. We won't stay silent any longer. We want everything that other Indians want – better schools, better homes, better health care, more jobs, cheaper food, good roads. We want to be part of the Indian dream, and not just dream that dream.'

I thought that Sonam Gyalsan was exceptionally articulate about his objectives for the people of Ladakh, a people who have not profited by their association with India. But they are not alone. In states like West Bengal, Bihar, Orissa, Andhra Pradesh and Maharashtra you often come across backward tribes whose life has not improved in the four decades since independence. Such tribal communities as the Adhivasis and Bhils still live in primitive conditions, foraging through forests for food, occasionally slaughtering a goat, sometimes raiding farms in the stealth of the night. At least Gyalsan's Ladakhis are represented in a legislature, at least Sonam

Gyalsan can relay their yearnings and longings to a wider audience. The aborigines of most of India have little such repesentation, few special allowances.

Gyalsan had spoken about his people's dreams. Different people dream different things. The mostly Buddhist people of Ladakh are, after all, a minority community in a state whose population is overwhelmingly Moslem. Indira Gandhi had long suspected – as did a few of her father's key advisers – that some of these Moslems did not want to continue to be a part of India, that they either preferred to join Pakistan, which was an Islamic state, or that they wanted their own separate nation.

That suspicion continues, and it lies at the heart of India's 'Kashmir Crisis'.

KASHMIR To understand the crisis, one must go back to the nineteenth century. Kashmir until then had been ruled by a succession of Moslem rulers, mostly descendants of the Mughals or of various invaders who came from Afghanistan and central Asia. In the early part of the last century, Kashmir was absorbed into the empire of Ranjit Singh, the Sikh maharaja who had braved the British and built a kingdom whose power was unchallenged at the time. One of his ablest generals was a man named Gulab Singh Dogra, a Hindu of the western Indian Rajput clan. Gulab Singh had performed well in battle, and Ranjit Singh rewarded him with suzerainty over Jammu, a territory that was situated south of Kashmir. Ranjit Singh died on 27 June 1839, and almost immediately the British again began plotting to seize the Sikh empire.

They began secret negotiations with Gulab Singh Dogra. He gave British troops 'safe passage' through Jammu on their way to fight the First Afghan War in 1841. They were trounced in that war's critical battle, at the Khyber Pass in January 1842, but Gulab Singh was seen as a friend because of his assistance. Four years later, Gulab Singh displayed his friendship again, this time by refusing to assist his patrons, the Sikhs, in the First Anglo-Sikh War which began on 10 February 1846. The Sikhs lost that war, and Gulab Singh was widely accused of being a traitor. But he came out ahead. A month after the Anglo–Sikh War, the British 'allowed' him to buy from them the territories of Jammu and Kashmir, which they had seized as a result of their victory over the Sikhs. Gulab Singh Dogra paid a nominal sum of 75 lakh rupees, or the equivalent of $75,000.

Gulab Singh and his heirs were for ever indebted to the British after the 'purchase' of Kashmir. They showed gratitude by sending Kashmiri troops to help the British further defeat the Sikhs, then sent troops again to overwhelm the Afghan tribes, and helped in British military campaigns in the two great wars of this century. The Dogras were not benevolent rulers of their mostly Moslem subjects. They were profligate, they were corrupt, they were depraved. Maharaja Hari Singh, who was Kashmir's ruler when India became independent in 1947, paid a heavy price for his licentiousness: blackmailers took photographs of him in the nude with a British prostitute in a London hotel room, and Hari Singh was made to cough up $6 million.

At the time of independence, the rulers of the 565 princely territories of India were given the choice of joining India or Pakistan. Pakistan's leaders cast covetous looks at Kashmir. The understanding was that states with heavily Moslem populations would associate themselves with the new Islamic nation of Pakistan, particularly if they were contiguous to it. Kashmir met both criteria, but Hari Singh dithered. And local Moslems, led by the extremely popular Sheikh Mohammed Abdullah – widely known as Sher-E-Kashmir, or 'The Lion of Kashmir' – did not seem very keen on the idea of being part of Pakistan. Sheikh Abdullah, who had started a political party known as the National Conference, was a great secularist and was influenced in his beliefs by his close friend, Jawaharlal Nehru. Abdullah insisted that Hari Singh had no right to make any decision concerning the status of Kashmir – only the people could decide this, he said at rally after rally across the state, and not some degenerate feudal ruler.

The degenerate maharaja finally did accede his state to India, but only after Pakistani-sponsored tribesmen had launched an attack on Kashmir. Sheikh Abdullah and other Moslem leaders sought India's military help. Nehru, who had become prime minister of independent India, wanted to make sure that he could legally send his troops to counter the Pakistani-inspired attack on Kashmir. He first wanted Hari Singh to agree to let Kashmir join India. Hari Singh, however, had packed up his jewels, Persian rugs and paintings, gathered his family and his concubines, and fled to Jammu. He was traced there by Nehru's trusted aide, V. P. Menon, who got the maharaja to sign a document of accession. Kashmir was now formally part of India.

Accession to India was thus achieved under pressure, even though there was no opposition to it at the time from Kashmir's leading politicians, such as Sheikh Abdullah. Nehru pledged that the accession would be validated by a popular referendum under international auspices, perhaps the United Nations. Sheikh Abdullah himself said: 'Kashmir has linked itself to India, not because it has been lured by any material gain but because it is at one with her in the Gandhian ideals of justice, equality and humanity. A progressive state could join hands only with another progressive one and not with a feudal state like Pakistan. Our decision to accede to India is based on the fact that our programme and policy are akin to those followed by India. New Kashmir and Pakistan can never meet. Pakistan is a haven of exploiters. India is pledged to the principle of secular democracy in her policy and we are in pursuit of the same objective.'

The Lion of Kashmir became the state's chief executive. Throughout his life and until his death on 8 September 1982, he always publicly swore allegiance to India. But some of Nehru's key aides in Delhi whispered in his ears that the Sheikh was secretly 'soft' on Pakistan or that, worse, he wished to break away from India. The Sheikh early on insisted that India should hold a referendum, as indeed Nehru had promised; there was little doubt in the years immediately after independence that Kashmiris would have voted overwhelmingly to stay with India.

However, Sheikh Abdullah and Jawaharlal Nehru fell out over the referendum issue – which Nehru aides saw as a code for Kashmiri secession from India – and over the next twenty years the Sheikh spent more time inside Indian jails than outside them. No referendum was ever held in Kashmir. India and Pakistan went to war three times. Countless debates were held at the United Nations over Kashmir. Pakistan continued holding on to a bite-sized bit of Kashmiri territory in the north-west of the state, and in the north-east China illegally held on to a sliver of mountainous wasteland.

Even though Sheikh Abdullah was imprisoned for a long time by the Indian government under the National Security Act, his supporters continued to agitate for a referendum, or a 'plebiscite'. It was only on 24 February 1975 that the Sheikh and his supporters agreed to disband their movement for a plebiscite. Their agreement was formalized in the six-point 'Kashmir Accord', which was drawn up by Prime Minister Indira Gandhi's trusted foreign-policy adviser, G. Parthasarathy.

The accord resulted not only in the abandonment of the plebiscite movement; it pledged Sheikh Abdullah to honour Article 370 of the Indian Constitution, which gave Kashmir special status within the Indian union. And the accord specifically emphasized that Kashmir was a constituent unit of India. The accord cleared the way for a triumphant return to power by the Sheikh, who was duly made Kashmir's chief minister on 25 February 1975. He was to serve in that office until his death of a heart attack seven years later, at the age of seventy-seven. Whatever his political appeal, the Sheikh's administrative helmsmanship had not been especially distinguished (corruption rocketed under the Sheikh, the state's development plans went astray, and the budget ran out of control.)

Dynastic politics is perhaps a special characteristic of Kashmiris. Jawaharlal Nehru was followed as India's prime minister by his daughter, Indira Gandhi (after the two-year interregnum of Lal Bahadur Shastri, of course). And now Sheikh Mohammed Abdullah's anointed heir-apparent, his flamboyant son Farooq, was sworn in as Kashmir's chief minister.

Farooq Abdullah had trained to be a physician and, indeed, had practised medicine for several years in Britain. He married an Irishwoman; he loved fast cars and motorbikes; he was so fond of Mrs Gandhi that he called her 'Mummy'.

But 'Mummy' was less than appreciative of two things: firstly, the fact that however supportive Farooq Abdullah was of her as a national leader, Kashmir was still governed not by her Congress Party but by the National Conference, which was technically at least an Opposition party. And secondly, the fact that Farooq Abdullah had joined with chief ministers of other opposition-ruled states in starting a forum to reform centre-state relations. Mrs Gandhi felt that implicit in the formation of this forum was the hope that India's squabbling opposition parties would form a common front against her ruling Congress Party in the next parliamentary elections, which were widely expected to be held by January 1985. (They were, of course, held in December 1984.)

Farooq Abdullah, perhaps out of political naïvety and inexperience, may not have realized that his very presence on a public platform with Opposition politicians would be viewed extremely dimly by Indira Gandhi. 'Mummy' set in motion a plan to unseat him, initiating first a sinister whispering campaign against the physician-turned-politician. Suggestions were floated that Farooq Abdullah was sympathetic towards Sikh separatists. Then a rumour circulated in Delhi that Abdullah had made a secret deal with Pakistan's military dictator, Mohammed Zia ul-Haq, under which the National Conference would act as a fifth column in India on behalf of Pakistan. Some Gandhi associates openly joked about Abdullah's sexual preferences and questioned his loyalty to his wife.

The eminent Indian writer M. J. Akbar, in his best-selling book, *India: The Siege Within*, wrote a particularly astute passage that assesses this period in Farooq Abdullah's star-crossed career as Kashmir's chief minister:

The Abdullahs were always conscious that, no matter how many times they protested otherwise, they would for ever be vulnerable to the charge of being 'soft' towards Pakistan, and in quiet league with secessionists. They knew that each time Delhi wanted them to kneel, it would always resurrect this allegation and, if necessary, even use such an excuse to dismiss the government. Sheikh Abdullah had spent his life listening to accusations of treachery; his only answer lay in his personal faith and self-confidence, and in the end he was vindicated. Farooq Abdullah now knew that it was only a matter of time before the many hostile forces started such a smear campaign against him.

He decided to meet the problem head-on. One of the mistakes which the Sheikh had made, in his son's view, was that he had kept himself confined, by and large, to his own state. Farooq Abdullah decided that he would build personal and political bridges across the country. He would convince India, and not just Mrs Gandhi, about his commitment to the country. If he could clear the minds of the people and the political parties in the rest of the country, he would be much less dependent on the goodwill of just one party, the Congress. If, therefore, he was ever called secessionist, he hoped that there would be more than one powerful voice in India saying that the accusation was a partisan fraud designed to cover up an unethical power game.

The game was much more unethical than Farooq Abdullah had bargained for. Mrs Gandhi coaxed his brother-in-law, G. M. Shah, who hated his wife's brother with a passion, to form a cabinet with the help of 'defectors' from Abdullah's National Conference. The men and women who now affiliated themselves with Shah were all promised – and subsequently given – cabinet positions. Farooq

Abdullah seemed unaware that these moves were being plotted in his own backyard. On the afternoon of the evening he was deposed, the tall, handsome chief minister was with Shabana Azmi, the film actress, who had turned up in Kashmir to shoot a Hindi movie.

Srinagar's masses rioted when they heard the news of Abdullah's overthrow. Mrs Gandhi sent in troops to restore law and order. Opposition leaders around the country roared their disapproval.

No amount of protests helped. Farooq Abdullah was out, G. M. Shah was there to stay, and Indira Gandhi had won in July 1984 what would be her last political victory.

Indira Gandhi may have succeeded in dethroning Farooq Abdullah in July 1984, but by the end of the year he had humiliated her Congress Party in the Kashmir Valley. (And, indeed, by 1987 Abdullah – having made his peace with Rajiv Gandhi – was back in the saddle.)

Not long after the assassination of the prime minister, it was announced by her son and successor that national parliamentary elections would be held across India on 24 and 27 December. Astrologers consulted by Congress Party chieftains said that those were the most auspicious dates for a poll, and so it was decided that the election would be held in some states on the first date and in the rest of the country on the latter date.

In the event, Rajiv Gandhi's Congress won an unprecedented 401 out of 508 seats contested in all of India's twenty-five states other than Assam and Punjab (where the poll was postponed on account of unstable political conditions). The 107 seats the Congress did not win included all 3 in Kashmir. Farooq Abdullah's National Conference steamrollered the candidates put up by Abdullah's brother-in-law, Chief Minister G. M. Shah. The losers, who were backed by the Gandhi Congress, included Shah's own son. The winners included Farooq's mother, Begum Akbar Jehan Abdullah.

But the election was some days away when Rahul Singh and I arrived at Farooq Abdullah's National Conference campaign office. It occupied a basement of the modern Nawa-I-Subh Building near a Srinagar landmark, the Zero Bridge. Party workers scurried about, carrying posters that featured Farooq Abdullah's smiling face. The party's flags – red, with a plough in the centre – were being distributed, as were banners that carried slogans criticizing G. M. Shah and the Congress Party. C. B. Kaul, the local correspondent of the *Indian Express*, was our escort, and he seemed to know everybody. We lost him at one stage in a knot of people, and when I went looking for him I traced him not visually but through his high-pitched laugh.

'Good fellow, this Kaul,' someone said to me. 'Has a sense of humour. Now why can't all press chaps be like that?'

I had hoped to meet Farooq Abdullah, but he was not in Kashmir. There were a number of similarities between him and Rajiv Gandhi, and I thought that some day these two men would be sure to collide in the political arena – it was probably written in the stars, I thought. Each was of Kashmiri extraction; each had a foreign-born wife (Abdullah's wife was Irish, Gandhi's wife was Italian), and each had met his wife in Britain; each had two children; each was tall and handsome and personable; each loved machines (Farooq, motorcycles and fast cars; Rajiv, planes); each was a scion of an illustrious family; each had been brought up in a politically active family; and each had a powerful, even overbearing, mother.

It was Farooq Abdullah's mother, the formidable Begum Akbar Jehan, whom we got to see that morning. Her husband, the late Sheikh, was notorious for possessing a roving eye, but the Abdullahs enjoyed a more or less solid married life for forty-nine years. She bore the Sheikh five children: a daughter named Khalida, who married G. M. Shah; Farooq; another son, Tariq; another daughter, Suraiya; and Mustafa Kamal, a son. The Begum Abdullah ('Begum' is an honorary title given to women of stature in the Moslem culture) herself came from a wealthy family: her father, Harry Nedou, was a Christian who converted to Islam; he owned Nedou's Hotel in Srinagar. Akbar Jehan was not brought up behind the purdah, nor was she kept behind it by her husband – as so many Moslem women still are in Kashmir. The Sheikh sought her assistance in his political party, the National Conference, and she quickly gained a wide following in her own right. There were people who even thought her the best politician in the family.

On this morning, the Begum was at the local television station. She was taping an appeal for votes that would be broadcast that evening; it was not a paid political broadcast but a free one, given to her party under a national agreement by which all major political parties received some free time on India's government-managed airwaves to take their case directly to the people. Television had come to India with a vengeance, I thought: this one broadcast alone would be heard by more people than the Begum had addressed in all her fifty years in politics. Rajiv Gandhi's speech, broadcast to the nation on the night his mother was murdered, was estimated to have been seen or heard by more than 450 million people, or nearly twice the population of the United States!

The Begum was herself a candidate for Parliament in the Anantnag constituency outside Srinagar. (She would win by a sizeable majority.) We waited more than two hours for her. Various National Conference functionaries kept pouring hot coffee for us; we were fed with tales of alleged improprieties on the part of G. M. Shah's henchmen. A pink-faced man named Wali Mohammed Itoo parked himself next to me. His elegant Kashmiri silk shawl had been sprayed with cologne.

'Shah's men have murdered democracy in Kashmir,' he said. 'And Indira Gandhi put them up to it. Now we are concerned that they will commit massive fraud to win Kashmir's three parliamentary seats.' (His fears did not materialize: Abdullah's party captured all three seats in the election.)

Itoo had been speaker of the seventy-six-member State Assembly when Farooq Abdullah was Kashmir's chief minister. When Abdullah was toppled, his friend Itoo was unceremoniously pulled out of the speaker's gilded chair and pushed out of the Assembly chamber by Shah's musclemen. Now Itoo is suing Shah in the state's high court.

An elderly Sikh named Sant Singh Teg came up to us. He gripped both my hands.

'You must tell this to the world: Farooq Abdullah is a protector of the Sikhs,' he said, in Hindi. 'There are 200,000 of us in Kashmir. Only Farooq stands between us and the blood-thirsty people down in Jammu who want to kill us. Tell this to the world.' (Sant Singh Teg was alluding to Hindu militants who had burned Sikh homes and shops in Uddampur, a town not far from Jammu, a few days before I arrived in Kashmir. Only the intervention of the Indian army prevented what would undoubtedly have been a massacre of the small Sikh community there.)

I remembered that Indira Gandhi had insinuated that Farooq Abdullah had given shelter and help to Sikh terrorists in Kashmir. I mentioned this to Sant Singh Teg, who is the leader of Kashmir's Sikh community.

'Do I look like a terrorist to you?' he said. 'The Congress has spread vicious rumours just to discredit Farooq. We have nothing to do with the Khalistan people. We are Indians first and foremost. Sheikhsahib had said that thousands of times, Farooqsahib says it all the time. What has Farooqsahib done that shows otherwise? Tell the world that.'

There was a flurry of activity in the hallway outside. Begum Abdullah had arrived. Everyone stood up. She was very short – from her photographs I had expected her to be much taller; her face was unlined, although she must have been pushing seventy (Kashmiri women are known for their great beauty, which many manage to preserve – as the Begum obviously had done – well past their chronological youth). She wore a brown kaftan, and her head was covered with the same silky wool material: Kashmiris call the outfit *fheran*. She inquired after our welfare and offered us more coffee. I thought she seemed a bit agitated, and I said so.

'You are correct,' the Begum said. 'These policemen and soldiers here bother me. Do you know that after my son was unconstitutionally overthrown back in July, Indira sent more than 30,000 paramilitary troops into Kashmir. What did they come here for? To give protection to the undemocratic government that Indira had installed. These troops are still here.'

But wasn't Kashmir always heavily guarded by federal security forces? Wasn't the threat of a raid by Pakistani-sponsored marauders always present?

'But these new forces here are meant to squash public protests against Shah's illegal regime,' Begum Abdullah said.

Had Chief Minister Shah and his wife Khalida – who was the Begum's eldest daughter – met Begum Abdullah recently?

The Begum sighed and looked at her manicured hands.

'My son-in-law has parted ways with us and has taken to the Congress,' she said, softly. 'We count him as a traitor. He is a traitor to the Kashmiri people, to the country, to our party and to the democratic ways we have always adopted. He has created chaos, he has done a lot of harm. I haven't been in touch with my daughter Khalida. It's a great sacrifice for a mother when she sees that her own child has parted ways with her in order to head towards the camp of enemies.'

But hadn't Rajiv Gandhi praised Shah for having re-instituted law and order in Kashmir?

'What law and order? Now you find killings, injustice. Nobody seems to feel secure. With Rajiv's ascendancy we had hoped for the better. But he has kept a lot of his mother's advisers, which is a sad reflection on him. Those very advisers, like Alexander, gave Indira so much wrong advice, which made her take so many wrong steps.' (The adviser Begum Abdullah referred to was Dr P. C. Alexander, who served as principal private secretary to both Indira and Rajiv Gandhi. Dr Alexander resigned in late January 1985 after disclosures that several of his staff members allegedly spied for American and French intelligence agencies.)

'The problem with Indira Gandhi was that she could never trust the states – particularly if those states were administered by parties other than the Congress,' the Begum said. 'So power was increasingly concentrated in Delhi. State chief ministers had to go begging to Delhi for permission each time they wanted to sneeze. How can you run a huge federal system like India this way? Her style brought India to the edge of the precipice. What a legacy for Rajiv to overcome!'

What about her son's alleged association with the Punjab's Sikh separatists?

'It was absolutely baseless that Farooq had anything to do with people like Bhindranwale,' the Begum said. 'Farooq had in fact warned Indira that she needed to solve the Punjab's problems as soon as possible. He told her that the Sikhs did not feel they were being treated as equals. He told her that the Punjab was Kashmir's lifeline because of the road traffic that transports grain to us and that takes our fruit produce to be sold elsewhere in India. Farooq told her that the situation in Punjab, if allowed to deteriorate, would affect the well-being of Kashmir. And that has now happened. Our tourism revenues used to be a 100 crore rupees a year [the equivalent of $100 million]. Now what are we left with? Barely a fraction of those revenues.

'Farooq told Indira that it was in the national interest that she should solve amicably the Punjab problem. But Indira said that she didn't feel it was time for her to talk with the Punjab's leaders. Then she accused Farooq of being an extremist. I wouldn't like to say anything more that would hurt her departed soul – but she has left us all in quite a mess.'

Begum Abdullah asked for another cup of coffee.

'Anyway, we hope for the best,' she said. 'We hope good sense prevails.'

She got up to leave for a rally in Anantnag. We accompanied her to her car. Just before she drove off in a procession of jeeps and trucks whose speakers blared out slogans and other campaign propaganda, Akbar Jehan Abdullah leaned out of her window and said:

'Tell me, haven't Kashmiris got the right to live with dignity? That's what we've always fought for. That's what we are still fighting for.'

It is not only Kashmir's indigenous politicians, such as the Abdullahs, who have long been suspected by Delhi of harbouring secessionist, or pro-Pakistan, sentiments. The Abdullahs have had to prove themselves as being more 'Indian' than political leaders in other Indian states, but even ordinary Kashmiris are generally perceived by ordinary Indians elsewhere as not quite emotionally 'with' India. The feeling among many top government officials in Delhi is that the Kashmiri Moslem has yet to completely reconcile his state's formal affiliation with India, and that among these Moslems India is still viewed as an alien country. These officials point to surveys that have shown that the most popular radio and television programmes in the Kashmir Valley are not those broadcast by India's government networks but by those of Pakistan. (That may well be because Pakistan's broadcasts, although heavily religious in nature, are generally much better produced than the Indian ones.)

What Kashmiris call 'Delhi's handiwork' has involved a continuing effort to discredit the state's political leaders, especially those not belonging to the Congress Party. For example, Mrs Gandhi's henchmen spread the word that Farooq Abdullah accumulated a personal fortune of $50 million during his twenty-two months as Kashmir's chief minister, and that among other things he maintained a fleet of twenty expensive foreign-made cars. His father, Sheikh Mohammed Abdullah, amassed even greater wealth, according to the propaganda spread by the Abdullahs' opponents. But whenever Farooq Abdullah referred to reports that some of Indira Gandhi's factotums were charging million of rupees in fees just to provide access to her or to ensure that a valued industrial licence was approved, he was at once accused of being unpatriotic, or of lying.

The whispering campaign concerning Kashmiris' 'patriotism' had also been extended to the state's Moslem religious leaders and organizations.

Here the critics and questioners have probably been on firmer ground – for the theological leaders of this overwhelmingly Moslem state have frequently changed their allegiance. The Jamaat-E-Islami, a religious organization with considerable support among peasants, had been openly pro-Pakistan. It was only when neighbouring Pakistan's military dictatorship started establishing a cruel, intolerant theocracy that the popularity of the Jamaat-E-Islami began to wane in Kashmir. The Moslems of Kashmir may be religious, but they have never been known to be Hindu-haters or Hindu-baiters; Kashmiri Moslems like the idea of free speech and their leaders have seldom advocated clamping down on political or even theological dissent. I think General Zia ul-Haq did India a great service: he showed Kashmiri Moslems how intolerant and intolerable life could be in his Islamic state – and this in turn seems to have convinced many Kashmiri Moslems that they would be guaranteed far more liberties under Delhi's continued Raj than under Islamabad's iron rule.

For many years, the chief religious priest of Kashmir, a man named Maulana Yusouf Shah, advocated affiliation between Kashmir and Pakistan. Shah's heir, Moulvi Mohammed Farooq, endorsed his predecessor's position concerning Kashmir; but Moulvi Farooq then suddenly abandoned his pro-Pakistan stand and declared himself a supporter of Farooq Abdullah, who frequently advertised his own pro-India position. There are those who suggest that much money changed hands before Moulvi Farooq altered his political views; certainly, the Moulvi's backing of Abdullah was a major political plus for the son of Sheikh Mohammed Abdullah, who had been bitterly opposed for decades by the Moulvi's predecessor, Maulana Yusouf Shah.

I wanted to meet Moulvi Farooq. C. B. Kaul, the *Indian Express* correspondent, arranged an appointment for Rahul Singh and myself. There was nothing that Kaul didn't seem able to do: he had extensive contacts; he spoke the local language because he himself was a Kashmiri; he knew wonderful restaurants where Srinagar's political gadflies gathered for hearty repasts and hectic repartee; he

knew shops where Rahul Singh and I bought choice but cheap
walnuts, almonds and dried apricots; he took us to boutiques where
we purchased silk scarves for the women in our lives. We set off for
the Moulvi's home, which was several miles north of Srinagar
('Moulvi' means head priest; Farooq is also known as 'Mirwaiz',
which means the same thing).

Srinagar seemed grey and bleak; thick clouds hid the serrated
mountain wall that rose beyond the city. The roads were rutted. We
drove by the Hari Parbat, a hillock crowned by a fort built in the
sixteenth century by the Mughal Emperor Akbar. At the foot of the
fort were Moslem, Hindu and Sikh shrines – a lasting tribute to
Akbar, who was a champion of secularism. We passed several lakes
on which were berthed Kashmir's famous 'houseboats'. These
serve as hotels during the tourist season, and guests are transported
to their quarters from the shore by gondola-type canoes. Debris and
excrement floated on the lakes of Srinagar. This was India's star
tourist attraction?

Moulvi Farooq lived in a heavily guarded house made of red
brick, glass and concrete. Chinar trees – whose leaves are almost
heart-shaped – graced the front and back yards. The doors were
made of solid teak, as were the window frames; the furniture was
walnut-wood. The curtains were of thick wool, with chinar-leaf
patterns embroidered on them. We were requested to remove our
shoes, as is the custom in orthodox Sunni Moslem homes. We were
first taken through an inner courtyard to a waiting-room, and the
floor in this unheated area was so cold that shivers scrambled up my
spine. There were three video machines in the waiting-room, where
the Moulvi often shows religious documentaries to his visitors.

We were spared these films. The Moulvi was prepared to see us
immediately. We trekked through the cold courtyard again, and we
were shown into a bedroom-cum-office. The Moulvi rose to greet
us.

He was tall, hirsute, fit-looking. He wore pink-tinted glasses, a
typical Kashmiri lambs'-wool peaked cap, and a *sherwani*, a long
jacket that is buttoned up from knees to neck; *sherwanis* are
normally tightly fitted, but the Moulvi wore one that looked like a
loose smock: it was made of white wool, and there were intricate
green patterns on the sleeves and collar.

The Moulvi sat down in a high-backed chair, behind which was a
picture window. He then signalled us to sit on the floor in front of

him, on a thick Kashmir rug. An old manual typewriter rested in a corner of the room; the bedstead was covered by a magnificent silk spread. One wall held bookshelves. The Moulvi's aides brought blankets and covered our feet and thighs. They also placed *kangris* in front of us. It was so comfortable that I felt like taking a nap.

But refreshments arrived. Hot coffee was served, then pastries and biscuits. The Moulvi ate nothing, although his aides feasted. Outside, the sun had broken through the clouds, and now the Moulvi's head was framed by a halo. It occurred to me that his seating arrangement was deliberate. It was difficult for us, huddled on the floor, to gaze up at him and make out his facial expression, for we were staring directly towards the window and the dazzling sunlight outside. But although seated in a chair, it was almost as if the Moulvi was in a pulpit, looking down at his audience. This was theatre.

And the Moulvi was theatrical in his speech and gestures. He spoke in cadence-filled Urdu and Kashmiri – which Kaul translated for us – and sometimes he employed English phrases.

'I am a simple man who preaches a simple message,' the Moulvi, who was born in 1944, began. 'I believe in democracy, and I desire that morality should be practiced in politics.'

He rose from his chair and raised his hands towards the heavens.

'There should be nation-building,' he roared. 'Nation-building is important to build people's character. In Kashmir, I want all the rights that are guaranteed under the Indian Constitution. I want Kashmir to be an ideal democratic and secular model state. There should be no religious or communal or political intolerance. There should be room for all in India, and a modern secular state must respect the fact that a province can be heavily Moslem by faith and yet totally secular in practice. I want bonds of the heart, not chains that are held in place by the police and the army. I want silken threads, not iron chains.'

Had he not long ago called for a merger of Kashmir with Pakistan, I asked?

The Moulvi sat down.

'There is a campaign against me because I preach tolerance and Indo-Pakistani amity,' he said, in a less strident tone. 'The campaign is on because I head a certain religion whose followers are in a minority in India. But because I am a religious leader doesn't mean that I cannot be secular-minded. The feeling in Delhi seems to be that if I'm not a member of the Congress, then I must be anti-nationalistic. Delhi is pushing people here up against the wall. Temperamentally, I am a democratic person: I value India's democratic efforts, its rich cultural traditions. I see Kashmir belonging to this tradition. Kashmir hasn't acceded to the Congress Party but to an India of certain principles, democratic principles. But when I say that I'm a Kashmiri, that doesn't mean I'm anti-India.'

That last sentence seemed significant. Successive leaders in Delhi have interpreted Kashmiri aspirations for greater autonomy as being coded calls for establishing a separate state, or for politically linking up with Islamic Pakistan. Instead of encouraging genuinely popular Kashmiri leaders like Farooq Abdullah who were in a position to consolidate pro-Indian sentiments in the state, Congress officials in Delhi worked hard to overthrow them because these leaders did not belong to the Congress Party. Delhi repeatedly neglected to take into account a fundamental fact of life in ethnically varied India – that every state occasionally needs to assert its special regional identity. Despite his theatrics, I believed the Moulvi when he said that his being a Kashmiri did not mean he was anti-India.

The Moulvi has succeeded in combining his spiritual duties with temporal functions, something that few religious leaders in India have been able to do. He has succeeded because there is no competition for him in Kashmir – the Moulvi, or Mirwaiz, is traditionally the Sunni Moslems' undisputed leader. Moulvi Mohammed Farooq has shrewdly fashioned an able cadre of workers who not only proselytize at the hundreds of mosques around the state but also work with officials of political parties, which themselves are heavily Moslem in composition.

'I don't see a contradiction between religion and politics,' Moulvi Farooq said. 'While I don't support demagoguery, I feel it is the responsibility of theological leaders to pay attention to the political health of their community. My pulpit is my platform.'

From his pulpit he has called for a new political dialogue between India and Pakistan, something that Prime Minister Rajiv Gandhi is said to want as well. He has called for a fresh re-assessment of centre–state relations, which Rajiv Gandhi may be more reluctant to undertake. And the Moulvi has called for a complete revision of Delhi's attitudes towards Kashmir; he wants new guarantees of autonomy, of political non-interference, of new infusions of federal funds for economic development.

And yet I found something vaguely disturbing in the Moulvi's combining of the spiritual and the temporal. It challenged the very essence of India's secular system, I thought – no matter that Moulvi Farooq has protested his own commitment to secularism. He seemed to have mobilized the support and sentiments of many of Kashmir's Moslems, who apparently thought it quite all right that a spiritual leader should dabble in politics as well; moreover, the Moulvi was wooed by Kashmir's political establishment – Farooq Abdullah had thought it important enough to seek the Moulvi's endorsement.

I thought: what if the Moulvi expanded his influence to the rest of India's 80 million Moslems? What if these masses were politicized in the manner approved by the Moulvi? How vulnerable would they be to theological rhetoric? How would India's Hindu majority, already suspicious that the country's Moslems represented a fifth column on behalf of Pakistan, react and retaliate? There was no comparable Hindu religio-political leader in India. And a chilling question: if, at some later date, a Moslem preacher emerged who called for a new commitment by India's Moslems to Pakistan, or who called for a new Islamic state within India (India's Moslem population was almost the size of that of Pakistan), would there be a bloodbath reminiscent of the 1947 Partition?

These were probably all academic questions, and maybe even irrelevant, but they eddied through my mind as I flew from Kashmir to the south-central state of Andhra Pradesh. It was in Andhra that the seeds of India's linguistic states were sown three decades ago, and it was in Andhra, too, that some very bloody riots between Hindus and Moslems had taken place in recent months. And it was in Andhra that the renewed regional assertiveness of the country was to be seen. Andhra's leaders were saying that India's states must be allowed greater political autonomy, that the time had come for the central government to allow the floodgates of grassroots creativity to be opened more fully.

CHAPTER SEVEN:
LIFE IS A MOVIE STUDIO

The capital of Andhra Pradesh is a 400-year-old city called Hyder-abad. It has one of the most modern airports in India, and one that works remarkably well in spite of the heavy traffic. The city is situated some 1,800 feet above sea level on what is called the Deccan plateau. Hyderabad and its twin city, the much younger Secunderabad, together have a population of nearly 6 million. Hyderabad, with its crumbling forts, old monuments, its silver bazaars and its filigree markets has long been a tourist attraction. The climate is agreeable through most of the year. A number of the nation's top military officials have built retirement homes in the area; Hyderabad and Secunderabad have large cantonments, and retired military personnel presumably find the atmosphere congenial.

Hyderabad used to be the seat of the old Deccani Moslem *nawabs*, or noblemen, and also of the Nizam of Hyderabad state, once believed to be the wealthiest man in the world. (The Nizam, in fact, was so rich that whenever he hosted huge banquets, which was almost every evening, he would bury gold nuggets in the mounds of steaming rice he served to his guests: those who found the nuggets could keep them!) The noblemen of Hyderabad developed a highly literate and sophisticated culture. The 'old world' manners and graciousness of the *nawabs* still survive in some measure in Hyder-abad. Old Hyderabadi families still serve up heavenly meals in high style. But the grand old palaces and mansions of Hyderabad are being torn down at an alarming rate, to make way for modern high-rise apartment blocks or commercial buildings. Progress has come to Hyderabad in a big way. The old farmsteads around the city have been gobbled up by electronic factories and textile mills and glass industries. The air here, once considered the most salubrious of all India's medium-sized cities, is steadily becoming sour. The plane trees are dying, and the meadows get browner every year.

In his highly readable *A New History of India*, Stanley Wolpert notes that at the time of independence, the Nizam of Hyderabad dithered over joining India – even though his state had a majority Hindu population. The Nizam wanted nationhood for Hyderabad; he was said to have hired Pakistani fighter planes to 'attack' India in order to achieve his goal. But the Nizam was tamed by the strong-willed Sardar Vallabhbhai Patel, then India's home minister: Patel despatched two divisions of the army's Southern Command to 'convince' the Nizam that joining India was in his best interests. Hyderabad acceded to India.

Within a few years, this region was again in the news. As Professor Wolpert says: 'The first vigorous agitation for a "linguistic province" emerged in the Telugu-speaking region of northern Madras, which wanted a state of its own, to be called Andhra, after the ancient Deccan Empire. Nehru was less supportive of the linguistic-provinces movement than Gandhi had been, and he succumbed to its popular pressure only after Potti Sriramalu, the saintly father of the Andhra movement, fasted to death in December 1952, leading to the creation of Andhra on 1 October 1953.' The princely state of Hyderabad was integrated into the new Andhra, as were the Telangana region that was part of the Madras Presidency, a section of the Bombay Presidency, and parts of the state called Madhya Pradesh.

The moment it was announced that a new state was being created along linguistic lines, scores of provincial leaders all across India began clamouring for states that would reflect their own language and ethnicity. Riots broke out. Property damage amounted to hundreds of millions of dollars. Prime Minister Nehru did what heads of government do when they don't want to make a snap decision – he appointed a commission to study the nationwide agitation for linguistic states. That body was called the States Reorganization Commission, and it included three highly respected Indians: Saiyid Fazl Ali, H. N. Kunzru, and K. M. Panikkar. The commission members spent two years reviewing mountains of memoranda, interviewing thousands of individuals all over India, and reflecting on the possible repercussions of slicing up India into linguistic units. They were not at all sure that such linguistic division would be good for the country, but pressures for linguistic states were building up dramatically and in December 1955 the commission made the recommendations on which India's twenty-five states eventually came into being.

The basis for creating linguistic states was not just the demand for establishing formally the supremacy of various languages in their respective regions. The creation of these states was also an acknowledgement of a basic fact of life in an ethnically diverse democracy: that politics in such a state is always the politics of the majority. Thus, the Telugu-speaking minority in the old Madras Presidency – where Tamil was the language of the majority community – felt that it was being left out of the political process and therefore out of economic progress. When Kerala state was created in 1956, to cite another example, the Malabar region – which was part of the Madras Presidency as well – was grouped together with the princely territories of Travancore and Cochin because, like them, it too was heavily Malayalam-speaking. Regional culture in India is strongly linked to language: indeed, language, more than ideology or religion or even caste, is the main unifying factor in the country.

Whether the creation of linguistic states has been beneficial or not is a topic still under discussion in India. And people talk as much about how Nehru mollified various state renegades as about the granting of their demands. The chief example always cited in such discussions is that of Madras. In that southern region, well-organized Tamils had banded together in a political party called the Dravida Munnetra Kazhagam, widely known as the DMK. The DMK was overtly secessionist, much more so than any Sikh political group in the Punjab has been in recent years. Its leaders, such as C. N. Annadurai, asserted that the Tamils of the south needed their own nation to realize their potential fully; the message was that the Tamils resented efforts by the Delhi government to impose Hindi – a language spoken by 42 per cent of the country's population, but mainly in the northern states – throughout the country.

The DMK, because it was secessionist, was barred from contesting state elections in Madras – not because Nehru said so, but because Article 19 of the Indian Constitution prohibited any secessionist party from participating in an election. In 1962, while the Tamils' agitation was in full swing, Chinese armies invaded northeast India. The DMK's leaders, although in jail then, issued public statements supporting the Indian military's resistance to Chinese claims to the barren, mountainous wastelands. After the cease-fire, Prime Minister Nehru did not forget the DMK's gesture. He quietly authorized his law minister to present in Parliament an amendment that eased the strictures of Article 19. The DMK could now contest state elections in Madras. It did so and won the majority of the seats. As the ruling party, it could hardly now agitate for secession. In more than two decades of DMK-dominated rule in Madras (whose name was changed to Tamil Nadu, or Land of the Tamils) no call for secession has been heard.

Nehru could have been obstinate, he could have kept the DMK leaders in jail, and he could have kept Madras state indefinitely under army rule. But he was convinced that when regional leaders shrieked for secession, they did not necessarily mean it – it was often an expression of regional frustrations, a desire to assert their local cultural identity. Nehru increasingly felt that the extraordinary ethnic and cultural diversity of India's regions must be allowed to bloom and blossom. He was aware that few regions in India – including the Punjab – could survive as independent countries; few Indian states were totally self-reliant in food and industrial requirements.

In short, hardly any region could break away from the Indian Union and expect to thrive economically. Nehru knew that a concession here and there might be construed as a giveaway on his part, but that interpretation would be far outweighed by the good his action would do in the longer term for the country. Indira Gandhi never learned from her father such worthy lessons in political accommodation and calibration. One wonders how the Punjab situation might have turned out had she studied her father's methods more closely and replicated them.

In the three decades since Potti Sriramalu fasted to death, Andhra Pradesh had become a key Congress Party stronghold in southern India. Its politicians prospered, its bureaucrats became corrupt. Indira Gandhi would decide in Delhi who served as Andhra's chief minister, and ministerial selections appeared to be based solely on one criterion: loyalty to the prime minister. She picked a succession of clowns to head Andhra's state administration. None of these men was likely to pose a challenge to Mrs Gandhi, regionally or nationally. The state's economy languished. Law and order broke down. Even the police would riot for salary increases. But the Congress flourished because no Opposition party could raise the money needed to develop a strong grassroots organization in this overwhelmingly rural state of 60 million people. Salvation, as it were, came in the form of a wealthy movie star who had specialized in roles depicting mythological Hindu gods.

The actor's name was Nandamuri Taraka Rama Rao – known popularly as NTR – and he decided to switch from the world of make-believe to make-belief. He had starred in 300 films over thirty-five years in the business, and had become the most popular star in the history of Telugu movies. Now NTR wanted to shape the political beliefs of his people. He formed a new party, called the Telugu Desam, or the Telugu State Party.

His ambition was simple: to gain power. But few leaders can afford an open declaration of such ambition. So NTR made the corrupt local Congress chieftains his main targets. More importantly, he said that regional creativity and aspirations were being stifled because Andhra was being ruled not from Hyderabad but from Delhi. He touched a raw nerve among ordinary people, whose living conditions had been daily deteriorating. He capitalized on his stardom by appearing at public rallies in saffron robes, which recalled the roles of mythological gods and holy men that he often played in Telugu movies. The simple rural folk on the countryside showered him with rose petals; the city folk lavished rupees on the Telugu Desam party.

When the January 1983 election results were announced, NTR had won power. His Telugu Desam obtained nearly 150 seats in the 295-member Andhra Pradesh Assembly, with about 30 independently elected legislators pledging support to the party. As chief minister, the former film star moved quickly to establish his style. Road signs and bulletins in government offices were now required to be written not only in English but also in Telugu. NTR also made virtually all his public addresses in Telugu. He started a free midday meal service in state schools. He authorized state subsidies for rice, an Andhra staple. The government's Anti-Corruption Bureau doubled its annual investigations to 2,000 during NTR's first year in office. Shrewd leaders make use of their popularity by sometimes ramming through unpopular measures while they can – and NTR trimmed the state government's bloated bureaucracy by 30,000 employees, by lowering the retirement age from fifty-eight to fifty-five years. The state budget was streamlined, but more money was channelled into promoting cultural activities such as the Kuchipuri dance native to Andhra, and the theatre, and into assisting local poets, essayists and novelists.

Back in Delhi, Indira Gandhi was alarmed. NTR had become a media star: foreign journalists and television crews started paying him a great deal of attention. Her aides warned Mrs Gandhi that he would soon export his political and cultural revolution to other parts of the country. And if he became a national figure, NTR would be a direct threat to Mrs Gandhi, whose own nationwide popularity was declining.

So Prime Minister Indira Gandhi set into motion a plan to get rid of Nandamuri Taraka Rama Rao. Rajiv Gandhi, who by now had been made a general secretary of the Congress Party, was persuaded to become a party to the plot. (Of course, all top Congress officials, including Mrs Gandhi, later denied any complicity.) The Gandhis were still heady from the recent 'victories' in Kashmir, where Chief Minister Farooq Abdullah had been toppled in July 1984, and in the border state of Sikkim, where a majority Opposition government had been peremptorily dismissed.

In Andhra, as in Kashmir and Sikkim, the instrument of Mrs Gandhi's machinations was the Delhi-appointed state governor. The Andhra governor was a man named Ram Lal, a former chief minister of Himachal Pradesh, against whom were still pending charges of misuse of power in that northern state. He suddenly announced that NTR had lost his majority. (In India, governors are appointed by the president upon the recommendation of the prime minister. Governorships are very comfortable sinecures; governors do exactly as they are told by Delhi.)

NTR had only been back a day from the United States when the governor's announcement was made. He had just been through triple coronary bypass surgery in America. He learned that he was being replaced by a man he had appointed to his own Telugu Desam cabinet, Nadendla Bhaskara Rao. Governor Lal had dispensed with normal procedures in announcing the new government: ordinarily, no chief minister can be dismissed and someone else asked to form a new government unless there is a show of strength on the floor of the state legislature. Bhaskara Rao never had to prove that he now commanded a majority in the assembly through defections that he had engineered from NTR's party.

NTR was appalled. So were most Andhra-ites. So was the nation. NTR claimed that he had documented evidence of the allegiance of 161 of the assembly's 295 members – enough to ensure a comfortable majority. He now did something so dramatic that the media were beside themselves with joy at the opportunity afforded them by NTR's actions for a strong, continuing story: NTR rented a train and escorted the 161 legislators to meet President Zail Singh in Delhi.

There was simply no question that NTR had ever lost his majority. The 161 legislators happily posed for photographs on the steps of Rashtrapati Bhavan, the Indian president's sandstone palace. They waved affidavits of allegiance to NTR. Accompanied by NTR – who was so weak he had to be propped up in a wheel-chair – the legislators spoke at rallies in Delhi. But even after that Bhaskara Rao continued in office in Hyderabad. NTR now sequestered his legislators in hotel rooms in two neighbouring states to make certain that none of them was bribed into defecting to Bhaskara Rao's party. Legislators were being offered the equivalent of $300,000 each to leave NTR's fold. Popular protests against Mrs Gandhi mounted all over Andhra, and there was violence.

Finally, in a face-saving gesture, she removed Ram Lal as governor (Congress Party officials quietly spread the word that it was all Ram Lal's fault, that the governor, and not Mrs Gandhi, had illegally deposed NTR!) and replaced him with Shankar Dayal Sharma, another Congress Party hack.

Sharma's arithmetic was better than that of his predecessor. He could count how many Andhra legislators supported Nandamuri Taraka Rama Rao. NTR was eventually reinstated. He was now more popular than ever before. Indira Gandhi had fought what was to be the last political battle of her life, and she had lost.

I had wanted to meet NTR, but I was told by his aides that the chief minister was too busy. I had arrived in Hyderabad with two London friends, Tim Llewelyn of the BBC and Leslie Plummer, his girlfriend and a writer for Canadian newspapers. Like me, they had wanted to get a sense of India after Indira Gandhi. It was my father-in-law, Anand Mohan Lal of Secunderabad – no relation to ex-Governor Ram Lal – who suggested to us that the way to a VIP's door was usually via his friends.

And so it was that we went to meet a man named Ramoji Rao.

Rao was the owner and editor of Andhra's biggest and richest Telugu-language newspaper, *Ennadu*. He had also started another daily newspaper, the English-language *Newstime*. Rao received us in his office. I was accustomed to editors' offices being busy and messy. Ramoji Rao's office was clean, quiet and bare. The furniture consisted of a red-vinyl couch and some wooden chairs. There weren't even copies of his own newspapers. The news-room outside was deserted; it was lunch-time.

Rao was a plump man who smiled easily and seemed keen to talk about the prospects for an India without Indira Gandhi.

'She was, of course, ruinous for India,' he said. 'But let's look at the son, Rajiv. Now just because he wears the *kurta*-pyjama and the Gandhian cap, does that qualify him to become a politician? Just because he was his mother's son, does that entitle him to become prime minister of India? Let's see what the young man is going to do. He'll soon find, though, that the sympathy "wave" over his mother's death will ebb – and then he'll be on his own.'

Ramoji Rao had vigorously opposed Mrs Gandhi's intrigues in Andhra Pradesh. During the short time that Bhaskara Rao was chief minister, efforts were made to shut down both *Ennadu* and *Newstime*. Tax officials raided the homes of Ramoji Rao and his top executives. Every time Ramoji Rao drove his car, he would be given traffic-violation tickets. Finally he decided to move into the newspaper's office.

'Under Indira Gandhi this country came very, very close to becoming a fascist Raj,' Ramoji Rao said, with sudden passion. 'She showed us all that with money and muscle you could control the country. Well, NTR showed her that we would not go under without a fight.'

'I don't know why these people in Delhi keep raising the bogey of regionalism,' he continued. 'They know very well that Indian states cannot afford to secede. In Andhra, we don't want to be a separate country. We want to be an everlasting part of the Indian Union. The feeling of Mrs Gandhi's people that if you let regional parties assert themselves then the country will one day break up – this feeling is totally erroneous. I think the Congress bosses used "regionalism" as an excuse to help Indira centralize power in Delhi. NTR has shown that regional parties can be very good for their regions: they're in touch with the grassroots, they care about ordinary people.'

He rang a bell and ordered coffee for us. It came within seconds, as if Rao's peons had only been awaiting his summons.

'You really must meet NTR,' Ramoji Rao said.

Tim Llewelyn, Leslie Plummer, Anand Lal and I exchanged conspiratorial smiles.

'Could you arrange an appointment for us?' I said. 'We'd be very grateful.'

Ramoji Rao dialled a number. He spoke quickly and quietly in Telugu. I suspected that he had reached the chief minister on a private line.

'He's waiting for you,' Rao said. 'My driver will take you to the chief minister's home. Let me know if there's anything else I can do for you. Consider this building your home always.'

Ramoji Rao's driver took us through the densest sections of Hyderabad. There were more bicycles than pedestrians in the streets and the tinkling of their bells was an unsettling soundtrack to our journey; we couldn't hear one another speak in Rao's car. Hundreds of cycle-rickshaws squeezed past us; I recalled that soon after he was reinstated, NTR made available more than a million dollars in low or no-interest loans to poor people wishing to buy these rickshaws. As a result, public transportation was amply available in this city, although the traffic had thickened intolerably. But the rickshaw-owners would surely not abandon NTR when it was time to vote again.

I reflected on NTR's popularity. He had convinced the masses that he truly cared for the common man. But perhaps as importantly, he had shown that a state leader could confront the national political establishment in modern-day India and could win if he was in the right. All along, NTR maintained that nearly three decades of centralized planning and decision-making had not benefited India's states but instead had only widened regional disparities. NTR held that the main excuse for concentrating power and resources at the Centre had been the existence of mass poverty. NTR said that it was not enough for the Delhi government to encourage village councils and to sponsor provincial elections. The state governments themselves had to be endowed with sufficient power and resources.

We had arrived at NTR's home, passing along the way several huge statues of historical and mythological figures he had commissioned from local sculptors. He did not live in the chief minister's official residence, a huge bungalow with long, rolling lawns and a view of a lake. NTR preferred his family's house, which was a three-storey building in the heart of the city. Tall steel gates and a high wall shielded the house from the view of passers-by, and several sentries had been posted at the entrance. Ramoji Rao's car was allowed in without any question; obviously, both car and driver had been to this place many times.

Aides greeted us with smiles. We were led up a flight of steep stairs. I wondered how NTR, a heart patient, climbed these stairs; no lift was in sight. Maybe he was carried up in the time-honoured palanquin. We were led into a second-floor waiting area, which was the size of a ballroom. Chairs were placed against the walls; a floral-patterned rug stretched from end to end. Files were stacked on top of desks. We had hardly entered this area when the aides beckoned us. We were taken to another room.

I was hit by an overpowering blast of incense. The room was small and smoky. There were more mountains of files on desks. Two bulbs on the ceiling spread a weak light.

'Come in, come in,' a deep voice said. 'Do come right in.'

In one corner of this room, clad in a saffron robe, with holy ash smeared across his forehead and a wooden cane in his hand, sat Nandamuri Taraka Rama Rao.

The voice had sounded friendly, but NTR looked grim and in pain. Behind him, high on a green wall, was a black-and-white framed photograph showing him receiving a large glittering trophy at some function. The person who was handing him the award was Indira Gandhi. NTR looked much younger in that picture, as did Mrs Gandhi, so it must have been taken many years ago when NTR was still in the movie business. Still, it seemed an odd picture to put up in his own home, considering the bad blood between the two.

'One national leader is gone, and now we look to see what the next one will do,' NTR began.

'Mrs Gandhi tried very hard to do you in,' I said. 'But she lost, and you won. Now she is dead. Do you forgive her?'

'In our Hindu tradition, we think only of the goodness of the departed one's soul,' NTR said, vaguely waving his hands. The thin light from the ceiling bulbs bounced off his heavily studded diamond and emerald rings. 'But my policies concerning the Congress will remain unchanged,' he continued. 'I will make clear my opposition to the Congress.'

He spoke in English. He did not look sixty-six years old, which he was said to be; much less a man who had been through major heart surgery a few months ago. The combination of his saffron robes and the weak lighting in the room could, of course, have created the illusion of youth. And why not? This man had been an accomplished illusionist all his life.

'Why do you wear saffron robes?' Tim Llewelyn asked. 'For the effect?'

'Because they are comfortable,' NTR replied, with a smile, not seeming to mind the lack of credulity in Llewelyn's tone.

The chief minister wanted to talk about his campaign to develop federalism in India.

'Federalism is not a new concept,' he said. 'Our Constitution clearly intended India to be a federal union, with a strong state system. You see, once you accept the linguistic principle as the basis for creating states, then states must be given the freedom to develop themselves within their own cultural framework. The states should not be made beggars, beggars who are made to wait with outstretched hands at Delhi's durbar.'

NTR had met Prime Minister Rajiv Gandhi quite recently. He had requested that the Delhi government make available $40 million in addition to the $350 million it had already approved for drought relief in Andhra Pradesh. From the way NTR said this, it seemed to me that Gandhi's answer had been in the negative. NTR had also raised with the new prime minister the question of increased participation by states in policies concerning the growth of industries, trade and commerce, and production. At present, more than 95 per cent of all industrial output in India is directly controlled and monitored by the central government – even small items like razor blades, gum, matchsticks, soap, zip fasteners and domestic appliances cannot be produced without formal clearance from Delhi.

'My message to the people in Delhi is this: if the limbs are strong, then the body will be strong,' NTR said. 'So let the limbs get strong.'

He would be broadcasting this message not only from Hyderabad, NTR said. Each one of India's twenty-five states was an
appropriate platform from which to address Delhi.

I recalled a conversation I had had in Bombay with Nani A.
Palkhivala, one of India's leading constitutional lawyers and a
former ambassador to the United States. 'The day is bound to come
when India's states will repudiate the wrongful subjection by the
Union and will awaken to claim their legitimate status under the
Constitution,' Palkhivala had said. 'A national consensus should
clearly remind the centre that it has not inherited the Viceroy's
mantle of paramountcy. What is needed at the centre today is not
an authoritarian government but the moral authority to govern.
And the centre would have no moral authority to govern unless it
displays a sense of constitutional morality – particularly a sense of
justice and fairness toward the states.'

'We do need a strong Union,' he had continued. 'But a strong
Union is in no way inconsistent with strong states. On the contrary,
by definition a strong Union can only be a union of strong states.'

Not long after my meeting with NTR, his Telugu Desam Party
won twenty-eight seats in Andhra in the late-December parliamentary elections. In the previous Lok Sabha, or lower house of the
national Parliament, the party had only 2 seats. Now Telugu Desam
had become the biggest Opposition party, followed by the Communist Party of India (Marxist Wing) with 22 seats. Rajiv Gandhi's
ruling Congress Party won 401 seats out of the 508 seats contested
nationwide. NTR announced that he was creating a nation-wide
umbrella organization called the Bharat Desam.

'It has been thrust upon us to play the role of the Opposition at
the national level,' he said.

The gods had provided yet another role for Nandamuri Taraka
Rama Rao. All India, not merely Andhra Pradesh, was his film set
now: NTR was now making a movie not just for Andhra-ites but for
all Indians. The question in my mind was: will it play in Patna? Or
Benares? Or Jaipur? Or Kanpur?

That evening I went to meet an old friend, Lessel H. David. He and
his wife, Pramila, were both physicians; both had done acclaimed
research in family planning, and Mrs David operated a service in
Hyderabad where poor people were given low-cost health care and
vocational training. Lessel David no longer practised medicine; he

taught social medicine and organized seminars on development strategies at the Administrative Staff College in Hyderabad, where top corporate executives from all over India enrol for refresher courses.

The Davids had invited me to their new rented home, a spacious house perched atop Jubilee Hills, the city's newest residential area. It was dusk when I reached the house, and the lights of Hyderabad were spread out on all sides of Jubilee Hills, like diamonds and sapphires strewn on a jeweller's tray. It was cool up here. Pramila David offered me thick, milky tea, which had been flavoured with *elaichi*, or cardamom; it was delicious. I told the Davids about my visit with Nandamuri Taraka Rama Rao.

'The movement for greater decentralization and for more autonomy for India's states will gather steam,' Lessel David said, settling his large frame on an ottoman. 'It will gather steam not because NTR is spearheading it – but because there is a deeply felt demand in villages and small towns. This business of referring to Delhi for every little thing is absurd.'

He cited one absurdity. The curriculum for training midwives all over the country is devised by the Ministry of Health in Delhi. If any health facility wants to make changes in this curriculum, or adapt it to suit local conditions, clearance must be obtained from Delhi – a process that can take months.

Another example: the United States Agency for International Development had allocated $16 million for non-governmental organizations involved in promoting family-planning activies in states such as Andhra Pradesh, Bihar and Uttar Pradesh where the birth rate was particularly high. But the Delhi government, which controls the disbursement of all foreign aid, had channelled only a million dollars to the states. Why? Because of bureaucratic delays and red tape. One would think, David said, that with India's population still growing alarmingly rapidly (there will be a billion people in India by the end of the century, if not earlier) the central government would act more expeditiously to ensure that foreign aid is distributed where it is needed the most.

'The centre's hold over the states is very considerable,' Lessel David said. 'It has to be loosened in order to make things work better at the grassroots. If power doesn't devolve, then you'll have more Assams and Punjabs.'

I asked him how he thought NTR might be received in other parts of India.

'Very well, I should think,' Lessel David said. 'Indians don't hate one another that much, you know. The class struggle in India is between the haves and the have-nots – not between the states. Besides, think of how spread-out the country's religious shrines are. Benares, Hinduism's holy city, is in the north. The great Hindu temple of Tirupathi is in the south. Another great Hindu temple, Somnath, is in the west. Moslems from all over the country go to pray at the Jama Masjid in Delhi. Christians go to shrines in Goa and Malabar. In other words, Indians travel more than we suppose. There is a built-in network for tolerance. NTR can turn up in Bombay or Calcutta, and he won't be seen as a stranger. A novelty, perhaps, but not a stranger.'

By 1988, NTR had accelerated his nationwide appearances. The Opposition parties had banded together in an effort to oust Rajiv Gandhi, forming the Janata Dal – the seven-party National Front – and NTR constituted part of the leading edge of this campaign. Whether the Opposition would continue to stay together and win the next election was arguable; perhaps NTR could invoke his mantras to ensure that the coalition didn't come unglued, as Opposition alliances had in the past.

He continued to wear his saffron robes in public. In private, however, and especially at night, he reportedly wore sarees. There were whispers that an astrologer had warned him that his life and political career were in danger unless he garbed himself in such female attire. Danger? It didn't take an astrologer to know that NTR had made powerful enemies in Andhra Pradesh. They revealed to local newspapers that, despite all his talk of rectitude, NTR hadn't been beyond looking the other way when close relatives made millions in questionable deals.

There were other problems, too. His administration was finding it difficult to sustain its rice-subsidy programme, under which 9.6 million Andhra Pradesh families received rice at 2 rupees a kilogram. (The families, in order to qualify, had to have a monthly income of no more than 500 rupees.) When the programme was launched, amidst much fanfare, these low-income families were eligible to receive 25 kilogrammes of rice per month, but now that figure was lowered to 15 kilogrammes. Why? Well, said NTR, because Rajiv Gandhi's government wasn't allocating enough rice to the state. Gandhi's Congress Party, NTR said, 'has mortgaged the interests of the people'.

Some NTR critics saw things differently. They suggested that bureaucratic mismanagement in NTR's state administration had brought about the rice crisis. Indeed, one of the banes of the Third World has long been the inability of local governments to ensure proper distribution of foodgrains. When drought struck Africa's Sahel region, local leaders implored the West to provide emergency food relief; Mother Nature was vilified as being the cause of the famine. These politicians were unwilling to admit that, as much as the drought, it was their own bureaucratic ineptitude that ensured poor distribution of existing food supplies.

In Andhra Pradesh, I thought, one thing was certain. NTR would surely exploit this crisis to his political advantage – even if, in the short run, the situation highlighted his own administration's management failures. After all, the rice-poverty programme was essentially an anti-poverty programme, and such programmes are always the staple of politicians' rhetoric in India – especially during elections. I was convinced that, as the national election approached, NTR would miraculously – in the manner of his movie roles – produce additional rice for the poor of Andhra Pradesh. Rice has a way of metamorphosing into votes.

NTR's political career owes much, if not all, to his movie background. Well before NTR descended on Andhra's political scene in the manner of one of the Hindu gods he portrayed in his films, another movie star, the late M. G. Ramachandran, had become the chief minister of another populous southern state. The state was Tamil Nadu, and MGR – as he was widely known – lost no time in translating the antics and heroics of the silver screen into political theatre. Even in death, he is revered by Tamils.

The fact is that films play an enormously important role in the daily life of India. Television is now usurping films as the public's favourite entertainment medium, but cinemas continue to draw big crowds in a country where the majority of the population simply cannot afford expensive entertainment.

India turns out a thousand feature films each year, and at least as many documentaries, in a dozen languages. It is very big business indeed, with top stars such as Amitabh Bachchan demanding and receiving from producers the equivalent of a million dollars per film. Producers can afford to cough up such sums because the inclusion of superstars can virtually guarantee box-office success. Some stars ask producers to pay part of their fees in foreign currency.

Most Indian films, but especially the Hindustani ones manufactured in the Bombay film factories, are made to a formula: two or three stars; lots of pathos; several violent scenes; suggestions of rape; a car chase or two; a few deaths, preferably of a doting father or a devoted mother, at the hands of a villain; and at least a half-dozen shrill songs (virtually every Hindustani film is a musical). Recently, India's film censors have allowed kissing scenes to be shown in Hindustani movies, scenes that were previously permitted only in foreign films. Nudity is still banned.

The critic Amita Malik has remarked that when the Lumière brothers held their first bioscope show at the Elphinstone Theatre in Bombay in 1896, they could scarcely have anticipated that they were helping plant the seeds of today's massive Indian cinema industry. The Frenchmen showed two films, *Arrival and Departure of a Train*, and *Bathers in the Sea*, which were really quite elementary works showing people and objects in movement. Malik says that the arrival of the cinema in India couldn't have been better timed: it was the turn of the century, and urban audiences were clamouring for mass entertainment. For these mass audiences, Malik says, the cinema with its direct visual impact, its easy accessibility and its relatively straightforward themes seemed 'the natural answer'.

The commercial possibility of the film medium wasn't lost on a young Indian who had been studying engineering in Europe in those early days of the century. His name was Dadasaheb Phalke, and he was so moved by a film he saw in London on the life of Christ that he immediately returned to India, sold his wife's jewels and produced *Raja Harishchandra*, India's first feature film. It dealt with the life of a mythological king who renounces worldly life and seeks solace in the wilderness. Phalke's script embodied the age-old 'good over evil' theme, to which illiterate audiences responded enthusiastically. In those days, male actors played female roles as well as those of men because it was considered socially unacceptable for women to perform on stage or on the movie set. As Amita Malik has written, Phalke lived long enough to see that the safest box-office guarantees in India came from the mythological film. Phalke is still known as the father of the Indian cinema.

The Golden Age of the Indian film is widely agreed to have been the 1930s, when several large studios flourished not only in Bombay but also in places such as Calcutta. Besides mythological themes, directors tackled such social topics as untouchability, child labour and the abuse of women. After the Second World War, however, the studio system collapsed in India; the financial stringency of the war, and the generally rigorous wartime conditions, had ensured the decline of these studios. Men who made fortunes in the wartime black market now fancied themselves as big-time producers *à la* Hollywood; they pumped millions of rupees into the film business, setting up the star system and devising the box-office formula. Their movies were drivel, but that was what moviegoers seemed to want.

'Most Indian films are pure fantasy,' says Bhaichand Patel, who writes frequently about Indian culture. 'They are fairy tales. They depict splendour and wealth that are beyond the grasp of most Indians. If you are an ordinary Indian who lives in a *chawl*, an urban tenement, or in some dilapidated village, then going to a film is an escape – an escape from the drudgery and terror of daily life. Indian films are mostly pure escapism – which, in an overwhelmingly poor country like India, explains why they are so popular with the masses.'

These films continue to be highly popular with Indians abroad as well, and with people in the Middle East. I have been surprised during my journalistic travels by the sight of Indian film posters in such cities as Amman, Baghdad, Cairo, Damascus and Marrakech. How often have I come across Arab taxi-drivers humming some top Hindi film tune – and then asking me about such Indian film greats as Raj Kapoor. I was in Morocco not long ago, and when I told a taxi-driver that Kapoor, one of India's most flamboyant actors and producers – who made such memorable hits as *Awaara* and *Sangam* – had recently died, the Arab burst into tears.

If Raj Kapoor is still the idol of millions of filmgoers in the Middle East and India who seek song-soaked and romance-ridden entertainment, Satyajit Ray remains the hero of the more serious movie-lovers. The films of this Bengali director possess a lyricism and poetic quality that Hindustani movies rarely have. His works, such as *The Chess Players* (which featured Sir Richard Attenborough), are masterful and carefully constructed morality plays whose themes are enacted at a leisurely pace. Ray's films are much too leisurely, in fact, for mass audiences in India, who prefer the pounding, pulverizing pace of the Bombay-made film fare.

Satyajit Ray has influenced an entire generation of filmmakers who view their medium as a powerful instrument of social inquiry – although Ray himself is by no means a fiery crusader for social causes. The work of these filmmakers has given rise to what is known in India as the 'parallel cinema'. Call it if you will *cinéma vérité*, or docudrama, but the productions of these men and women are sophisticated; they focus powerfully on such ongoing problems as bride-burning, child prostitution, gambling, dowries, the exploitation of women, alcoholism and oppression by landlords in rural areas. Perhaps more than any political rhetoric, these films have not only drawn attention to India's social inequities but also led to corrective legislation.

Some of the earliest exponents of the 'parallel cinema' were Mrinal Sen, Sayeed Mirza, Girish Karnad, and Mani Kaul (who once infuriated colleagues by declaring that he made films for his own satisfaction and that he did not care if people saw them or not!). Now there is yet another generation of 'parallel cinema' directors: Gautam Ghosh, Govind Nihalani, Ketan Mehta, and Gopalkrishnan. Their films tend to be more politicized than those of their predecessors, and the new purveyors of the 'parallel cinema' see themselves shaping audiences' social awareness and sensibilities, and also, of course, providing people with entertainment. (I should like to point out here that although the cinema is India's most popular source of entertainment in cities and villages alike, it has brought about the death of an ancient source of entertainment in rural areas – puppetry. Ironically, the world's biggest collection of Indian puppets is no longer in India but at the American Museum of Natural History in New York City.)

One of the newest and most celebrated filmmakers from India is Mira Nair. This petite 31-year-old Harvard graduate recently made *Salaam Bombay!* a poignant feature about street children in India's commercial capital. Nair's film has been a box-office smash in Europe and the United States, and has drawn universal critical acclaim. I think it is safe to say that she will be a major force in the international film world; some critics are already hailing her as the female equivalent of Satyajit Ray, while others are saying that because Nair sees her primary audiences as being in the West, she is likely to make more money than Ray ever did.

Another director who can be said to be a true inheritor of Satyajit Ray's mantle is Shyam Benegal of Bombay.

I went to see Benegal in his office on Tardeo Road in Bombay, a bustling commercial thoroughfare within sight of the Arabian Sea. The building was modern, but his suite was not – I thought for a moment that I was in some bus depot, so packed with supplicants, petitioners and technicians were the three rooms used by the director. In one room, a film crew was shooting footage for titles; in another room, an editor was splicing film. The spicy odour of curry suffused the suite. The walls were festooned with posters from Benegal's dozen films.

Benegal is a man of medium height with a cheerful manner and a bearded, high-crowned face that makes him look much older than fifty. He had just returned from a filming trip to Goa, and he was plainly tired. The last ten years have involved constant film production for him – not only his dozen feature films but also scores of documentaries and advertising shorts, which generate for Benegal the wherewithal for his 'parallel cinema' work. Benegal has also been producing training films for farming communities in different parts of India; the films employ a story line and their characters deal with such topics as peanut cultivation, animal husbandry and pest control. Although most of these short films are made in Hindi, they are dubbed into nine languages. Benegal sees these films as not only offering instruction to peasants and farmers but as starting points for serious discussions on improving the quality of life in rural areas.

Benegal shot to fame when he made a feature film called *Ankur*, which was about the exploitation of women in rural India; it won several Indian awards and received critical acclaim here as well as abroad. He subsequently made *Manthaan*, in which he depicted the lives of dairy farmers in the western state of Gujarat. No major stars were used in the film, only real-life farmers. The film won several major Indian and Western awards for Benegal; perhaps more importantly, it consolidated his status as an innovative filmmaker. The critical and financial successes of *Ankur* and *Manthaan* enabled him to continue exploring controversial subjects such as the failure of land reform and the cruelties of the caste system in subsequent films. Benegal went into India's villages to portray the everyday realities of the rural poor. For him it was important to understand and tell the story of the great divide that exists between urban and rural life in contemporary India. Benegal was interested in the kinds of social arrangements that exist between people in deprived communities; he investigated the codes of caste; he studied beliefs and attitudes. Throughout, his central question was: am I getting the intangible essence of a situation?

'I like to think of myself as a chronicler of my times,' Benegal told me, over successive cups of tea. 'I am very interested in the forces, often unseen, that have shaped societies and individuals. In making my films, I set out to discover what are the reference points for individuals or social groups that make them what they are or that make them turn.'

Benegal is fascinated by what he calls the 'balance of life' in today's India – how people manage to retain perspective and hope even in the midst of soul-crushing poverty. He is excited by the political changes taking place, and he shares many of Rajiv Gandhi's goals of economic development, but he doesn't see himself as a political filmmaker. His role is that of someone who undertakes social inquiry.

'To help ourselves understand what this extraordinary mosaic called India is all about – that is how I see my role as a filmmaker,' Benegal said. 'We live in exciting and excitable times, and the responsibility of a filmmaker such as myself is now even greater to be rational, to be reflective, to never stop asking questions about where we are headed.'

In asking his questions, Benegal worries that his films might get too simplistic. His obligation to his art, he says, is to strike a 'balance' himself: the plots must not be complex, but the characters must be, for people are filled with complexities. His are not the kinds of films that video-owners in the expatriate Indian communities of the Middle East, London and New York City necessarily rush out to acquire, of course. There are those critics who have expressed reservations over Benegal's cerebral approach to filmmaking – but his response is that films, especially those involving social inquiry, must make audiences both feel and think.

Such an approach has also attracted one of Benegal's great friends, Shashi Kapoor, to the 'parallel cinema'. Kapoor is a product of India's dazzling commercial film world, a man who has probably starred in more Indian films than anyone else. Kapoor, the younger brother of veteran filmmaker Raj Kapoor, was trained at the Royal Academy of Dramatic Art in London and for many years was part of a Shakespearean touring company led by the famed Kendall family of Britain (Kapoor in fact married the boss's daughter, Jennifer Kendall, who died of cancer in 1984). When he found his personal finances languishing, Kapoor followed the lead of his father, Prithviraj, and his two older brothers, Raj and Shammi, and entered the world of the commercial cinema. His fresh, boyish face, his shy smile and his youthful build helped catapult Shashi Kapoor to the top within a short space of time. Shashi Kapoor has also acted in and financially supported several art films made by James Ivory and Ismail Merchant of New York, including the critically acclaimed *Heat and Dust*. In a more recent Merchant/Ivory film, *The Deceivers*, Kapoor played the role of a prince who secretly supported the dreaded *thuggees* – highwaymen who killed travellers, usually for money and jewels, but sometimes for the sheer love of murder.

Kapoor, of course, continues to retain one foot in the commercial-cinema camp: that is where he makes his millions, which enable him to support such 'parallel cinema' ventures as *Utsav*, a historical film with a contemporary theme. But Kapoor is finding that India's major film distributors are so commercially minded that no one is willing to buy the rights to this film. In an industry dominated by stars whose education, literacy and perhaps even intelligence are limited, Shashi Kapoor comes across as a remarkably sophisticated man, and one who is unafraid to challenge verbally the titans of Bombay's film world. Kapoor invited me one morning to accompany him to Bombay's Mehboob Studios, where he was to attend the *mahuraat*, inaugural rituals, for a new film.

As we drove to the studios, Kapoor complained bitterly about how films that lacked 'commercial sex appeal' simply stood no chance with the country's 'fatcat' distributors. But India needed to encourage filmmakers of all sorts, Kapoor said. He didn't think that the government's agency for financially backing struggling filmmakers, the National Film Development Corporation, was as yet sufficiently tuned in to the growing needs of such producers. Kapoor, who spoke in a mix of English and Hindi, continued in this vein even as we reached the studios, where a mob awaited the star. After a frenetic session of dispensing his autographs, we were led into a cavernous studio, where the set of a nightclub had been constructed. Winsome starlets clustered about, casting provocative glances at Kapoor; servants went around offering steaming tea in tiny glasses; a Brahman priest stood in one corner before portraits of various Hindu gods, whose blessings would soon be invoked to make this film a success. Production on Indian films rarely starts without such a *mahuraat* ceremony.

Kapoor later told me that he was dismayed that the outside world, and especially Western audiences, did not sufficiently understand the realities of everyday India. One of the chief culprits in this, he said, was the Indian commercial filmmaker, whose work rarely reflected the wondrous ethnic and regional diversity of India and who simply did not bother to reach out to foreign audiences because his money-making was assured by tapping the mother-lode in India and among Indian emigrants in selective states abroad. 'The Indian social scene needs to be projected more effectively to foreign audiences,' Kapoor said. 'Here is the world's biggest democracy, a real-life alive-and-kicking democracy – and how many Westerners really know how we live?'

Some days later, I mentioned my conversation with Shashi Kapoor to Tina Khote, an acclaimed producer of documentaries in Bombay. She agreed with Kapoor's assessment. 'The commercial film industry in India has lost touch completely with contemporary reality,' she said, as we lunched at the United Services Club one balmy afternoon. The club was a relic from the Raj: liveried waiters, well-kept lawns smooth enough to skate on, frangipani and magnolia, bougainvillea, Victorian-style bungalows, and palms that swayed gently in the salty breeze from the Arabian Sea. 'Those who cannot make the time-honoured commercial formula work regress into sexploitation. Do you know what packs audiences in these days? Rape scenes. After all, with a thousand feature films being made each year, with competition so great, producers need a new gimmick to attract audiences. Except that these Indian producers are now engaged in exploiting the problems of women.'

I had sought a meeting with Tina Khote because she had acquired a formidable reputation as a producer of socially relevant documentaries. One of her films, a work on bonded labour, recently won the top award at the Delhi International Film Festival. Khote, a Polish-Canadian by birth and a resident of India for more than thirty years, is married to Bakul Khote, a top executive with one of India's leading industrial concerns and the son of Durga

Khote, a veteran actress of the Indian stage and screen. Her financial security thus assured, Khote has been able to devote much time and energy to exploring social issues. Her documentaries have focused, among other things, on the rural and agricultural scene, and on the problems of the environment and mental health. She specializes in twenty- and thirty-minute mini-features. Khote's innovative strength lies in the fact that her films always depict women in a non-subservient manner: she always shows girls attending school, she shows equality in relations between men and women, and she shows small families – never more than two children to a couple. Thus, all these messages – female emancipation, family planning, female literacy – are continually fed to her audiences in a manner that is not grating or proselytizing.

Like Shashi Kapoor, Tina Khote feels that the 'real' India – the India of ethnic and social diversity, the India of industrial progress, the India of democracy – is not adequately projected before foreign audiences. Film can be an ideal vehicle for such projection, Khote told me. What was needed was the participation of commercial sponsors to enable dedicated filmmakers to make socially relevant films that could be promoted abroad.

'This is a country that is humming with action,' Khote said. 'Look around you. You've been travelling through India. Are the people lethargic? Isn't there a new excitement in the air? Don't you think the story of this India should be told with pride?'

Tina Khote – blonde, blue-eyed, exceptionally fit for someone who was already a grandmother, passionate in her speech and reflective in her thoughts, and deeply caring about her adopted country – could certainly induce her guest to nod in agreement.

I had seen for myself how film stars reigned as India's modern-day gods. The sight of scores of studio hands and fans gawking at Shashi Kapoor that day at Mehboob Studios was unforgettable. But what was it really like to work in the modern Indian film industry? And even though Hindustani films dealt so much with fantasy and escapism, how did their purveyors relate to the currents and crosscurrents of contemporary India?

I posed these questions to a long-time friend called Madhur Jaffrey. She had made a name for herself in the United States and in Britain as the author of several best-selling books on Indian cuisine. In Britain, Jaffrey had hosted a widely watched television series on

Indian cooking, and she had acted in such acclaimed Western-made films as *Heat and Dust*, *Autobiography of an Indian Princess*, and *Shakespearewallah*. But she had never been in an Indian commercial film.

One day in London, the well-known Indian director, Ramesh Sippy, happened to see Jaffrey in *Heat and Dust*. She played the role of a dowager, the mother of an Indian *nawab*. So impressed was Sippy that he decided to cast Jaffrey in his next big-budget film, *Saagar*. Jaffrey had many friends in the Indian film world but she had never been exposed to the methodical madness of Indian studios. She told me that she was struck by three things: the mix of technological sophistication and strange working methods; the extraordinary status enjoyed by the director and his stars; and the fact that, although modern Indian films were all glamour and glitter, they represented a continuity of ethos from the days of the village bard – good won over evil, heroes prevailed over villains. Indian films were in effect morality plays.

Jaffrey was astonished by the long hours put in by Indian stars, many of whom worked two eight-hour shifts daily in different films! And in moving from shift to shift, often in different studios, these stars would also move from character to character – sometimes from hero to villain, from saint to sinner. 'For me the hardest thing was to get a proper script,' Jaffrey recalled; frequently, the scripts would be given to the actors minutes before the start of a new scene. And she was surprised by the widespread use of dubbing. Virtually every Hindustani film's soundtrack is re-recorded in a studio after the movie has been completed. That is because the noise level in most Indian film studios is high, and the hum of the crowds waiting outside the studios to gain a glimpse of the stars almost always filters into the sets. Thus, says Jaffrey, she found that her fellow performers often acted with their bodies but not fully with their voices – knowing that they would have a second chance to make good in the dubbing studios!

Madhur Jaffrey, no stranger to celebrity status, was nevertheless bewildered by the pampering of film stars and directors in India. Everything would be laid on for them – luxury hotels, fine meals, exquisite wines, unlimited alcohol of all kinds, all sorts of entertainment. The stars not only played the roles of gods on the screen; they were gods in real life – they could and did command devotion from their fans and their producers.

But why limit such exalted, even divine status only to the film business? Now some stars have parlayed their screen reputations into political careers. India's superstar, Amitabh Bachchan, had long billed himself as one of Rajiv Gandhi's closest friends. During Indira Gandhi's funeral, Bachchan seemed to be more constantly at his side even than Rajiv's own wife, Sonia. He was endlessly quoted by television and print journalists about how much he had admired the murdered prime minister, how she had been a true mother to him. This sort of loyalty was rewarded by Rajiv Gandhi, who asked Bachchan to run for Parliament on a Congress ticket. Bachchan took on the formidable H. N. Bahuguna, a veteran Opposition member of Parliament, in the Allahabad constituency in Uttar Pradesh. Gandhi came to campaign for Bachchan, and Bachchan won by a considerable majority. Still, I wondered why Amitabh Bachchan really decided to go into politics: was it really because of his desire to serve people, or was it because his recent films had been flops? Politics, after all, had traditionally been a means to achieve power and pelf, and a seat in Parliament would assure Bachchan of continued exposure to the masses.

In the event, Bachchan resigned from Parliament over the Bofors scandal (see page 342): it seemed that he preferred his privacy not to be invaded during 'question time' in the Lok Sabha. As a private citizen, Bachchan could hardly be hauled up before Parliament to explain his alleged role in the weapons scandal, or the role reportedly played by his Switzerland-based brother, Ajitabh. His resignation from Parliament did not result in the end of his friendship with Rajiv Gandhi, however. The Gandhis and Bachchans continue to be close; not long ago, the two families holidayed together in the Andaman Islands, situated in the Bay of Bengal. That vacation drew much criticism in the Indian media: to protect the holiday-makers, the Indian Navy assigned an aircraft carrier and, it was also reported, submarines as well!

In addition to Amitabh Bachchan, two other movie stars were asked by Rajiv Gandhi to run for Parliament in the December 1984 election. In Madras, the actress Vyjayantimala defeated a senior local politician named Era Sezhian; and in Bombay, Sunil Dutt defeated one of India's most prominent lawyers and a long-time parliamentarian, Ram Jethmalani. Admittedly, these election campaigns were colourful; the star-candidates were assisted on the hustings by their glamorous colleagues from the film world. But many thoughtful people around the country asked the following questions: were the stars really sincere in their claims that they were entering politics to serve the people? What was their record in public service? Had these stars really served the people by frequently appearing before them in films filled with lurid sexual scenes and disgusting violence? Hadn't the stars encouraged, however indirectly, by their flamboyant roles crimes like rape, murder and gangsterism?

One afternoon in Bombay, I put these very questions to Sunil Dutt. We met at the home of Murli Deora, the local Congress Party boss and another recently successful candidate for Parliament. Dutt, a tall, big-boned man, has been compared to Gary Cooper; he has graced the Indian screen for more than two decades and has also produced films with nationalist themes. He has raised money for India's defence fund. And after his wife, Nargis – herself once a movie star – died of cancer, Sunil Dutt set up a foundation for cancer research and gave millions to establish a special cancer ward in a Bombay hospital. If Indians can spend fortunes building temples, they can surely raise more hospitals, which are perhaps needed even more these days, Dutt believes.

'In recent years, I have been affected deeply by two events – the death of my wife and the murder of Indira Gandhi,' Dutt told me. 'When I took my wife for cancer treatment in New York, she said she felt so privileged to be able to afford such expensive care – and she said, what about the unfortunate millions back home who would never be able to afford even a fraction of such medical care? That was when I vowed to devote myself to raising funds for cancer work in India.

'The violence that followed Mrs Gandhi's death shook me. How could we have done those things to other Indians in a civilized country? I felt that people who are sincere about healing our communal wounds should come forward and serve the nation. I know all this sounds very grand, but I really believe in our secular principles. And I consider myself fortunate to have gained a reputation because of my films. So why not exploit that reputation in the service of ordinary people? For me politics is not a passport to glory. I have already achieved all the glory a man might want in his lifetime.'

I asked Sunil Dutt how it felt when he was sworn in as a member of Parliament.

'When I walked into the Lok Sabha, at first it was just another large hall with lots of people,' Dutt said. 'But then my name was called to take the oath of office. As I walked towards the speaker's dais, it suddenly struck me that down these same aisles had once walked such people as Nehru and Indira Gandhi and Vallabhbhai Patel. That's when it all hit me – that I was so privileged to be here, that this was a historical trust that I should never abuse. This was no movie studio – it was real life, and I was part of the drama.'

CHAPTER EIGHT:
THE COMMUNAL CAULDRON

Hyderabad is one of India's leading centres of Moslem culture. Of
the area's 6 million people, about 600,000 are Moslems. The
percentage of Moslems, in fact, is about the same as the national
figure: there are an estimated 80 million Moslems in India today, or
10 per cent of the country's overall population.

The Moslems of Hyderabad, with a few exceptions, are not a
happy people. Here too, their sentiments mirror the national scene.
Moslems are a troubled, unhappy minority in India. Trevor Fishlock, formerly the London *Times*'s Delhi correspondent, wrote an
insightful book called *India File* in which he characterized the
country's Moslems as follows: 'They are the rather unhappy rem-
nant of a once powerful and conquering people whose forts,
mosques and domes dot the landscape and remain among the most
distinctive of Indian images.' Historical animosities between Moslems and Hindus have survived in the country, but particularly here
in Hyderabad. No less a person than Chief Minister Nandamuri
Taraka Rama Rao told me: 'We have to have special protection for
our Moslem minorities here.' Some protection. Each year, majority Hindus start riots against Moslems in Hyderabad. Shops are
burned and property is looted.

Sikhs may have become the most recent villains for many Hindus
because of the murder of Indira Gandhi by two of her Sikh security
guards and because of the continuing tensions in the Punjab
between the two communities. But for an overwhelming number of
India's majority Hindus, Moslems remain the ancient enemy.
There is little forgiveness shown towards Moslems – because

of real or perceived historical wrongs – much less trust and tolerance.

If all this sounds exaggerated, consider the following: of the 4,000 officers of the élite Indian Administrative Service, only 120 are Moslems. In the 2,000-member Indian Police Service, there are only 50 Moslems. India has about 5,000 judges, but only 300 of them are Moslems. There are nearly 120,000 officers in the country's fourteen nationalized banks, but only 2,500 of them are Moslems. M. J. Akbar, in his *India: The Siege Within*, refers to a survey made of some of India's top private-sector companies. The survey found, for example, that in Pond's India Limited, only 1 of the corporation's 115 senior executives was a Moslem; at DCM, the figure was 2 out of 987; at Brooke Bond, 14 out of 673; at ITC, 17 out of 966; at J. K. Synthetics, 5 out of 536; at Ambalal Sarabhai, 5 out of 628.

When I visited Aligarh, once a flourishing city of Islamic culture and still the seat of the Aligarh Moslem University, I was told that the city's renowned locksmith industry had collapsed. Once the products of individual locksmiths from this Uttar Pradesh city used to be exported to the Middle East and to Europe. But these Moslem locksmiths could not overcome competition from the big lock factories that mushroomed in the 1950s and 1960s. Now there are few independent locksmiths left in Aligarh, and the government has made no efforts to assist those whose businesses collapsed when the machine age arrived: few of the old locksmiths were hired by the new factories.

'The ordinary Moslem has been left out of India's economic and political mainstream,' George Fernandes, one of India's leading labour leaders and a former member of the cabinet, told me. 'And he faces a bleak future. Moslems don't get ordinary jobs so easily. The Moslem is not wanted in the armed forces because he is always suspect – whether we want to admit it or not, most Indians consider Moslems as a fifth column for Pakistan. The private sector distrusts him. A situation has been created in which the Moslem, for all practical purposes, is India's new untouchable.'

The economic plight of India's Moslems has been dramatically exacerbated since independence, but it did not begin when British rule ended in 1947. Jawaharlal Nehru, in his *The Discovery of India*, said that historical causes blocked avenues of development and prevented the release of talent. He identified these causes as the delay in the development of a new industrial middle class, and the 'excessively feudal background' of the Moslems. Indeed, it can be argued that the Moslem ethos in India started shredding when the Mughal Empire collapsed in the late eighteenth century.

I met people in India who contended that the country's 'Moslem question' would never be resolved until the 'Pakistan question' was settled once and for all. Since independence in 1947, India's relationship with Pakistan has been disturbed and distrusting. Pakistan, after all, was an invented country, carved out of India's body at the insistence of Hindu-haters like Mohammed Ali Jinnah. Jinnah was a British-educated lawyer who felt that Moslems would never enjoy first-class citizenship in a Hindu-dominated independent India. He was proved right – even though two of India's constitutional presidents have been Moslems, and Moslems have served in the national cabinet. A number of national organizations, but particularly the Hindu-based Rashtriya Swayamsevak Sangh (which is more popularly known by its acronym, RSS) have engaged in Moslem-baiting over the years. Their virulent propaganda is that the Moslem may be an Indian citizen, but his sympathies lie with Pakistan.

When India was divided up in 1947, there was murderous rioting between Hindus and Moslems. Hundreds of thousands of people were killed. India and Pakistan went to war over the disputed territory of Kashmir in 1947 and 1965, and in 1971 the two countries again fought a war – which resulted in the transformation of East Pakistan into the independent nation of Bangladesh. Many Pakistanis still hold a grudge against India for having encouraged and supported the guerrilla movement that helped create Bangladesh.

These military conflicts – all of which were won by India – have resulted in a situation where India and Pakistan pump huge sums of money into defence: Pakistan spends nearly $3 billion a year on defence (its gross national product is roughly $31 billion); India, whose GNP is nearly $200 billion, is estimated by the London-based International Institute for Strategic Studies to spend $10 billion on defence. Neither country can afford such expenditures. Two-thirds of Pakistan's 500,000-man military force is positioned along the border with India. India has stationed several crack divisions of its 1.2 million-strong armed forces on its side of the border.

Since 1958, Pakistan has been almost continuously under military rule. An elected democratic administration was brutally squashed in 1977 by General Mohammed Zia ul-Haq, who took over as head of government. General Zia instigated the 'trial' and subsequent execution of his civilian predecessor, Zulfikar Ali Bhutto. Not that Bhutto was ever a friend of India, but it was generally felt by Indian policy-makers that a civilian leader in Pakistan was more likely to arrive at a political accommodation with India than a military figure. Indian leaders, to be sure, like to portray Pakistan as the continuing villain in the great drama of the sub-continent. But it might be recalled that when the then military dictator Marshal Ayub Khan proposed a no-war pact with India in the late 1950s, Nehru's aides ridiculed him. Similarly, when Zia brought up the subject again during Mrs Gandhi's last years, the Pakistanis were again ridiculed. And Zia continued to be regarded with suspicion by Prime Minister Rajiv Gandhi until the Pakistani leader's death in a mysterious air crash in August 1988.

Indian leaders point to the current re-armament of Pakistan by its main Western ally, the United States. Washington is reported to give Islamabad more than a billion dollars of arms each year, allegedly to strengthen Pakistan against expansionism by the Soviet Union, which had invaded and occupied Afghanistan, Pakistan's north-western neighbour, in December 1979. But policy-makers in Delhi have no doubts that these arms will eventually be used by Pakistan against India. India, for its part, is also accelerating the arms race by buying more weapons not only from its traditional supplier, the Soviet Union, but also from France, West Germany, Britain and Sweden.

Both India and Pakistan are developing nuclear weapons as well, although the leaders of both countries strenuously deny this.

'The fact remains that militarily Pakistan is no match for India,' George Fernandes, the Indian labour leader, told me. 'But Pakistan serves as a convenient scapegoat, an excuse for more arms deals which produce massive commissions for Congress Party agents who negotiate the deals with foreign suppliers.'

George Fernandes's words echoed in my mind when I went to meet Mehboob Khan, a scion of an old *nawabi* family. His ancestors were Moslem noblemen who were given property and prominence by Hyderabad's early *nizams* some three hundred years ago. Khan's father, Shah Alam Khan, owned a large tobacco company. The family, consisting of Khan's parents and his six brothers and their wives and children, along with his own wife and five children, lived in a sprawling mansion. The house and its lawns were an oasis of sorts, for outside the high walls was one of the most congested sections of Hyderabad.

Khan had invited me for what Indians call 'high tea'. Laid out on a long mahogany table was a spread so immense that I could have feasted for a week. There were a dozen varieties of sandwiches; there were kebabs, grilled rolls of minced lamb; there were mutton chops; there were fried turnovers filled with curried shrimps; there were custard pastries; there were assorted biscuits; there were mangoes, oranges, grapes, apples and bananas. And there was tea — rich, aromatic, sweet, milky tea. It was, Mehboob Khan said, only an ordinary 'high tea', and could I please forgive him.

For a moment I thought Khan was joking, but he was being perfectly serious. The exquisite rituals of hospitality among Hyderabad's Moslem nobility require such apologies. I had been introduced to Khan by my father-in-law, Anand Mohan Lal, who had cautioned me to be patient with such rituals. Khan explained how each item on his table was prepared, and he did not eat anything until I had finished. I thanked him profusely for the wonderful meal.

'It was nothing,' Khan said, softly, 'it was nothing at all.'

He was a huge man, so huge that when he stood up he had to be careful not to bang his head against the chandelier that was fixed to the high ceiling of his living-room. I had come to see him because of his connections in Hyderabad's Moslem community. Soon after I'd finished the 'high tea', a group of men walked in. Each wore a long *sherwani*, a gold-brocaded jacket that reached to the knees, and the typical Moslem peaked cap of lambswool. Each man also wore traditional loose white trousers. They bowed to Khan, then quietly sat down.

Mehboob Khan had invited them to tell me about how Hyderabad's Moslems felt about their condition in modern-day India. Hyderabad, Khan told me, was an ethnic microcosm. What I would hear and learn here would be mirrored elsewhere in India, too.

His guests were apprehensive about what might happen to Moslems after the death of Indira Gandhi. They were alarmed at the riots against the Sikhs in northern India, where Hindu mobs marshalled by Congress Party chieftains had attacked Sikh homes, shops and places of worship. (There hadn't been such attacks against Sikhs in southern India, whose states were controlled by Opposition parties.)

'We are apprehensive because when one minority is subjected to this kind of brutality, how can other minority communities feel safe?' said Sulaiman Sikander, a local Moslem civic leader. 'We thought for a long time that the Congress was a protector of the minorities, but in recent years we became disillusioned. And this episode concerning the Sikhs does not reassure us at all.'

'Such riots aren't communal,' Mehboob Khan said. 'They are political. That's what is so troubling. Minorities are being made a hostage for political considerations – to get votes from the majority.'

A man named Abdul Aziz spoke about the September 1984 Hindu–Moslem riots in Hyderabad. More than 150 Moslems died then, he said, and dozens of shops owned by Moslems along Abid Road were burned down. Mrs Gandhi flew to Hyderabad for a political function, but she did not visit the affected areas. Despite an estimated property loss of more than $10 million, the Delhi government sanctioned only $10,000 in damage reparation payments.

'And worse, no one was arrested, no one was punished for the attacks against us Moslems,' Aziz said, in Urdu. 'How can you create confidence among minorities with a situation like this? There have been riots against Moslems in Ahmedabad, Meerut, Assam and Muradabad – and no arrests there either, and very little by way of compensation to those who lost so much.'

It occurred to me that Abdul Aziz could well have been speaking on behalf of the Sikhs who had been attacked in northern India. No one had been arrested for rioting against them, either.

I reminded the group that the Nehru family had always been known for its commitment to secularism. Shouldn't Rajiv Gandhi, India's new prime minister and grandson of Jawaharlal Nehru, be given a chance to demonstrate his own commitment?

'Of course,' said Mehboob Khan. 'But the question is: will Rajiv be able to break away from the communalist hold over the Congress Party? We used to vote for the Congress because we felt that the other political parties had become polluted with communalism. Now look what has happened.'

I asked the group if they considered themselves Indians.

They seemed stunned.

Mehboob Khan finally said: 'This continuing suspicion of Moslems in India must stop. What have we done that is anti-national? How many Moslems have been involved in espionage? Is there really a basis for suspicion? Did we not fully support the government when there were wars? Did we not contribute to the national defence fund? Did we not send our men to fight for our homeland? So why are we still suspect? What more do we need to do to establish our bona fides?'

The birth rate among Hyderabad's Moslems is high; Islam permits a man to have up to four wives at the same time, and many Moslems exercise this option. The average Moslem family in Hyderabad is said to have eight children. (The average Hindu family has four children.) Hindu chauvinists have long expressed public alarm over the Moslems' proclivity for procreation. Their argument is that Moslem hordes could again overrun India – as they did in the tenth century, when Moslem invaders came pouring in over the Khyber Pass and defeated squabbling Hindu rulers.

The Hindu's racial memory is long and strong, and these days it is constantly pricked by irresponsible communalist organizations that have sprung up in many parts of the country. The leaders of these groups tell the Hindu that he must neither forget nor forgive the butchery and bloodshed that the Moslem conquerors brought wherever they went. In the western Indian state of Gujarat, for example, they tell horror stories of Mahmud of Ghazni, a Moslem tyrant who plundered the fabulous Hindu temple of Somnath, and also destroyed 10,000 other Hindu shrines in the province of Kanauj. Mahmud's armies swept through the area in 1025 AD. So passive and pacific were the Hindus that they simply stood by while Mahmud's men ravaged the temples, slaughtered Hindu males, and raped and carried away Hindu women.

The pillage of Hindu temples was especially popular with Moslem invaders because these temples were rich with the offerings of their devotees; and the rape of Hindu women was an attractive proposition, too, because they were beautiful and submissive. The Moslem plundering of India continued vigorously through much of the next six hundred years. Nearly six centuries after Mahmud of Ghazni's raid of Somnath and Kanauj, the Mughal emperor

Aurangzeb would ruthlessly put to the sword Hindus who refused
to be converted to Islam.

During my travels through India, I came across many fellow
Hindus who said that such historical wrongs had to be corrected.

'But what fault is it of today's Moslems – the majority of whom
were born after independence?' I said one afternoon in Hyderabad
to a local Hindu civic leader. 'Why should majority Hindus now
hold Moslems accountable for this terrible past? The Moslems of
today want to live in peace.'

'I agree it's not their fault,' he said. 'But sons have to pay for the
sins of their fathers.'

These are attitudes you cannot easily hope to overcome. Organizations such as the RSS and the Shiv Sena in Bombay flourish
because of strong anti-Moslem ideology. Now the ruling Congress
Party seems to have come around to embracing naked communalism. The votes, after all, are with the majority Hindus – this was
quite clear in the December 1984 national elections.

As economic opportunities declined for ordinary Moslems, they
were faced with three choices: to emigrate to Pakistan; to join the
underworld in India; or to take up jobs in the oil-rich states of the
Arabian Peninsula. Aziz Rahim did the first, Haji Mastaan did
the second, and Syed Abdullah Barabood did the third. Each
became affluent in the process.

Aziz Rahim was born and brought up in free India, but he found
that his career in banking in Bombay was increasingly being
stymied. He moved with his aging parents to Pakistan, married
a Karachi debutante named Zubeda Mawjee, and soon obtained a
job with a subsidiary of Citibank, the American multinational
corporation. He did well with Citibank in Karachi. The bank then
posted him to Bahrain, Beirut and Nairobi. Aziz and Zubeda
Rahim now live with their three children in Haworth, New Jersey.
Rahim is a senior executive with Citibank in New York and visits
Pakistan frequently. He and Zubeda often travel to India, too. It is
a nice place to go as tourists, the Rahims say, and the shopping is
still reasonable. But it is unlikely that Aziz Rahim would have done
as well as he did professionally had he stayed on in Bombay.

Haji Mastaan prospered by staying on and becoming an underworld king. His life story inspired a film producer to make a film of
his life which became a box-office hit. Mastaan lived as a boy in a
packing crate on the Bombay docks. He joined a street gang,

following the example of many Moslem youths from destitute families; he quickly rose to become its leader, then entered the lucrative world of gold smuggling. In the movie there is a scene based on a real-life confrontation Mastaan had with a top government official who had threatened to have him arrested. The rising young gangster says to the official: 'For the record, I don't know what smuggling is. Between you and me, I've always been a smuggler. I am a smuggler. And I will always be a smuggler. Let's see what you can do about it, big shot! Do you think you can put me in jail? Do you think you can have me hanged? Let's see if you can find the proof. The only way you can stop me is if three or four of you guys get together and decide to pump a few bullets into my body. But you won't, will you? You guys don't have the guts.'

Mastaan eventually gave up his life of crime – but only after he had made millions. He now devotes his time to philanthropy and social work in Bombay, but there are those who suspect that 'once a smuggler, always a smuggler'.

Syed Abdullah Barabood of Hyderabad found that he was simply unable to support his three wives and eleven children on his 400 rupees monthly salary (the equivalent of $40) as an elevator operator in a government office. He had heard that job recruiters from Kuwait were coming to Hyderabad; while anybody could apply for these manual jobs, Islamic Kuwait especially welcomed Moslem workers; the oil-producing Persian Gulf state had ambitious development plans but a shortage of indigenous labour.

So Barabood wound up in Kuwait. He worked there for five years as an elevator mechanic. He earned about $3,000 a month – or 30,000 Indian rupees. By the time he returned to Hyderabad, he had become a wealthy man in Indian terms. Now he sits at home all day, smokes his hookah, visits friends, plays with his children and lets his money accumulate interest in the bank.

I went to see Barabood in an area of Hyderabad known as Barkas. It consists of low brick buildings, most with neat courtyards. Ten years ago Barkas was a Moslem slum, with open sewers and muddy roads. Its residents tended guava orchards and sold their produce to Hindu middlemen, who then marketed the fruit for a profit throughout Andhra Pradesh. Then came opportunities to travel to the Gulf, and the men of Barkas who went overseas started sending money home. It is estimated that in the Hyderabad area alone, more than $600 million was sent home by Moslems in the last decade.

The guava orchards of Barkas are mostly gone now, replaced by playing fields and new houses. The roads have been paved. Several mosques have been built. I was brought here by a man named Mir Asad Ali, a local insurance agent. He wanted me to see how a poor Moslem neighbourhood had prospered because its males went away to work abroad. On the way to Barkas, we had driven through several other predominantly Moslem communities. Ali would excitedly point out men who he said had returned from the Gulf.

'How can you tell them apart?' I asked.

'Easy, just look closely,' Ali said. 'You can tell from the way they're dressed.'

Sure enough, I spotted droves of men wearing T-shirts that said 'I love New York', or 'Kiss me, I'm cute'. They sported fancy Ray-Ban sunglasses, or solid gold Rolex watches. Virtually all wore jeans, in contrast with the other men, who presumably hadn't had the opportunity to travel overseas and therefore hadn't graduated beyond the traditional Hyderabadi sarongs and smocks. From time to time I saw men in Arab headgear and gowns. Were they Arabs visiting Hyderabad, or only local men who had taken a liking to the costumes of the lands they had visited? Ali told me that Hyderabad attracted a lot of Arabs who came here to buy brides. They would marry pretty local girls, give handsome presents to their parents, then whisk away the women and force them to work as maids in the bridegrooms' countries.

'But isn't there resentment here over such practices?' I asked.

'No, not at all,' Ali said. 'Because economically these women are still better off working as maids abroad. A girl who's never even seen a string of beads now suddenly finds herself possessing a gold necklace.'

Ali was taking me to the home of a man known in the Barkas neighbourhood as 'Ustad'. Not even Ali, who'd known him for years, knew his real name. As I was to discover, Ustad – which translates from Urdu as 'The Clever One' – was Barkas's chief of commerce. We parked in front of a grocery store whose glass cases contained stacks of Kraft Australian Processed Cheese, a particularly popular brand in the Middle East. Little boys played with toy cars that looked foreign-made; some of the boys wore smart safari suits. Every house seemed to have television aerials. We walked past a parking lot in which were rows of shiny Indian-made Ambassador cars. Ali explained that these were actually airconditioned private taxis.

'Why aren't they out on the road?' I asked.

'They only go from here to Hyderabad's airport and back whenever the Bombay flights arrive and depart,' Ali said. 'You see, these taxis take passengers who leave for the Gulf, and they bring back those who've returned. No need for them to work at any other time. They charge 200 rupees per person [the equivalent of $20] and each vehicle nets the owner 2–3,000 rupees a day. That's a fortune.'

Ali had wanted me to meet Ustad because Ustad, he explained, was in the business of obtaining anything for anyone – for a price. He was, Ali said, the Harrods and Macy's of Hyderabad: you could buy anything from a pin to a plane from Ustad. The fact that Ustad had prospered in Barkas indicated how prosperous its residents had become – they now had a continuing need for fancy appliances and textiles from abroad. Moreover, said Ali, Ustad's customers came from all over Hyderabad. For example, when a rich man on Jubilee Hills or Banjara Hills wanted to give his adolescent son a Japanese video set or a German camera, he could come to Ustad and obtain one on the spot. Ali, a short man who wore a crisp white shirt and a dark blue suit, marched briskly. He exuded energy; he was a self-made man who had put himself through college in Hyderabad and went on to do extremely well in the insurance business.

We walked through a maze of narrow alleys and at last came to the pseudonymous Ustad's home. He wasn't there, but his friends and factotums were. We were received warmly in a small room, whose carpeted floor was strewn with fabrics.

'What can we offer you?' a man who identified himself as Saleem, said. 'Video? Watch? Gold? Diamonds? Camera? Motorcycle?'

Ali explained hastily that I had come merely as an observer.

'Then at least let me offer you tea,' Saleem said.

The tea was served in little glasses, just as it is in the Middle East. In India, tea is almost always offered in cups. And, as it is in the Middle East, the tea was heavily sweet and black; in India, tea is seldom served without milk. Middle Eastern habits die hard, Ali said.

As we sipped the tea, Syed Abdullah Barabood walked in. He joined us on the floor, neatly tucking his heels behind his haunches. I marvelled at the flexibility of his bones: Barabood seemed to be at least fifty years old. He wore a white skull cap, a transparent linen shirt, and a checked sarong which local Moslems call the *lungi*.

'Why did you return home?' I asked him, after he had told me about his experiences in Kuwait.

'What's the use of making all that money and not being able to see your family?' Barabood said. 'I never saw them once in the long years that I was away. Now I can enjoy my wives and children, and they can enjoy the money I made for them.'

Ali and I got up to leave.

'I am sorry I cannot invite you to my own home,' Barabood said, with some embarrassment. 'But you see, I am re-doing everything. Everything is in a mess. We just got the replacement dishwashers yesterday, and later this morning the new airconditioners will be installed. The house is in a mess, you see. We haven't finished building the new floor yet.'

As Ali and I stepped out of Ustad's home, Barabood said: 'The next time you will be welcome guests in my home. I will personally cook a mutton biryani for you. I have just got a new microwave oven.'

Pakistan was the bitter fruit of the British Raj. Its national ethos was shaped by the Hindu–Moslem fratricide in India that was the basis for its being. Pakistan was to be the first Islamic state of the post-war, post-colonial era – but the jubilation over independence was quickly cancelled out by the cataclysmic violence of displacement. Fourteen million refugees moved between India and Pakistan in the most painful two-way migration of this century, crossing into what was suddenly a new home in an alien nation.

So there wasn't any allowance, nor any time, for political growing pains, no luxury of developing national mechanisms that would expedite entry into the modern world. Pakistan came of age as a nation instantly and bloodily, an entity superimposed on a sub-continent where religious tensions had long been subsumed by the dream of driving out colonialism. And as if communal bloodshed weren't baptism enough, Pakistan's political adulthood was branded by a border war with India in 1947, the first of three conflicts that widened the chasm between two nations that sprang from the same womb – two nations with the same culture, the same cuisine, some of the same languages, the same racial memories and the same history.

That common background, however, did not yield the same economic development strategies for the two nations that had simultaneously won their 'freedom at midnight'. India, from the very beginning, seemed to know what social, political and economic goals it wanted to pursue. Its leaders, proclaiming secularism and socialism, had an expansive vision of the future: the alleviation of poverty, the promotion of democracy and nonalignment, the dismantling of a debilitating caste system. Because of India's sheer size, of course, and because of its ethnic diversity, administering the country would always be a messy, untidy and disputatious affair. But there was never an ongoing search for identity, no constant asking: 'What are we?'

India's leaders were homespun – 'sons of the soil' – and after independence they stayed home to shape the national agenda. But Pakistan's post-independence leaders were transplants – born mostly in British India and infused with secular instincts and a Western sensibility rather than the Islamic ethic they formally embraced. Unlike Jawaharlal Nehru and his associates, who were the fountainheads of virtually all political activity in India, they had no master plan for development. It was as if, having achieved their once improbable ideal of nationhood, the Pakistanis were at a loss for a new goal. Moreover, the new nation's leaders were widely resented by indigenous landowners and segments of the middle classes whom they were suddenly governing. During their political lifetimes, they would always be known as *muhajirs* – refugees.

'That legacy has continued to haunt Pakistan to this day,' says Shahid Javed Burki, a well-known Pakistani author and economist. Instead of being able to get down to the task of building a new, independent nation, Pakistan tried to relive the past and justify its existence. And because of this, the country has not been able to develop the political institutions that are essential for robust social and economic development. The country has followed different and often contradictory paths in trying to achieve national objectives that were also being constantly redefined. 'No matter who its leaders have been, Pakistan has been in the throes of a continual identity crisis,' says Burki.

Nations, like people, must finally come to terms with themselves. Pakistan is no longer a young nation; it was born more than forty years ago. If its fundamental problem remains its undefined identity, then its curse has been militarism. And that curse has captured

Pakistan's political system and stoked the politics of repression. Pakistan's leaders – national and local alike – have been largely indigenous for at least two decades. But with their special brand of cynicism, they have often used Islam as an overriding ideology to reinforce the ethos of authoritarianism. This has created what Professor Ralph Buultjens calls 'an artificial leadership which draws its sanctions from God and the gun'.

How Pakistan deals with the question of developing democratic leadership and viable political institutions will be the most fundamental long-term test for the country – a test made all the more serious because of the continuing violence inside the country, the continued friction with India, the continued turbulence on its western border with Afghanistan and the simmering tensions of regionalism. This means that the common people must be assured the chance to choose their leaders freely. This means democracy, however homebred and divergent from the Westminster or Washington models.

'People must be allowed to take power on the basis of the imperatives of statecraft,' says Shahid Javed Burki. And what are the imperatives of statecraft? Internal stability, accommodation with neighbours, and economic development. In other words, a new national ethos.

Mohammed Ali Jinnah, Pakistan's founding father, said to his countrymen: 'You may belong to any religion or caste or creed – that has nothing to do with the business of state. . . . We start with the fundamental principle that we are all citizens, and equal citizens of one state. We should keep that as our ideal. And in the course of time we would cease to be Hindus and Moslems – not in the religious sense, because that is the personal faith of each individual – but in the political sense as citizens of the state.'

Jinnah is long gone, and he spoke at a time when Pakistan was young and raw and impressionable. But his message, broadcast more than four tumultuous decades ago, is still very valid. A more open and tolerant system need not imply abandoning Islam as the state philosophy. For ordinary Pakistanis, hope lies in the notion that nations are always capable of self-renewal. Hope lies in the possibility of change.

On 17 August 1988, a momentous event occurred that shook Pakistan to its foundations.

At 3.47 p.m. an American-made C-130 Hercules transport plane of the Pakistan Air Force took off from a small military airport at Bahawalpur. It was a bright, sunny afternoon, with barely a cloud in the sky. On board were nearly twenty senior Pakistani military officers. Also on board was President Zia ul-Haq of Pakistan; Arnold L. Raphel, the United States Ambassador to Pakistan; and Brigadier General Herbert M. Wassom, an American military adviser.

They were headed for Islamabad, Pakistan's capital city, a 330-mile flight that would ordinarily have taken less than an hour. In Bahawalpur, Zia and his top brass had watched a demonstration of the prowess of the M1A1 Abrams, one of the most sophisticated tanks in the world. The manufacturer of the tank, General Dynamics Inc., was so keen to make a sale that the American company had trimmed the overall price of a package deal by $500,000 to $3 million per tank. Indeed, Zia seemed so impressed by the tank's awesome capabilities that the General Dynamics executives at the scene were certain that the deal would be clinched.

Zia left the demonstration in his usual cheerful mood, pausing to chat with several local security personnel and others before he boarded the C-130. The plane took off with a roar, but in less than four minutes, while it was at an altitude of 4,000 feet and still climbing, the aircraft lost radio contact with the control tower. The plane crashed at 3.51 p.m. There were no survivors.

Pakistanis were stunned. They immediately suspected sabotage. At the top of their list of suspects were the Soviet Union and Afghanistan. Indeed, many Pakistanis recalled that just two weeks before the crash, their foreign minister, Sahabzada Yaqub Khan, had talked in Moscow to his Soviet counterpart, Eduard Shevardnadze. During their meeting, the Soviet minister had warned the Pakistani that Pakistan's support of the Afghan mujahedeen guerrillas would 'not go unpunished'. There had lately been several Afghan and Soviet raids across the Pakistan border.

India also came under suspicion. Naturally so. But Indian commentators were quick to point out that it did not make sense for their country to get rid of Zia. He had, after all, attempted a rapprochement with India in recent times – despite the occasional sabre-rattling that he engaged in to satisfy the more extreme segments of his domestic constituency. To be sure, Prime Minister

Rajiv Gandhi and his key associates suspected Zia of sponsoring terrorism in the Punjab. But by and large, relations between the two countries had not deteriorated to a point where yet another war was inevitable. Moreover, Gandhi was privately known to be respectful of Zia's skill in holding together his ethnically diverse nation and in resisting the clamorous calls of Baluchis, Pathans and others for more regional autonomy, if not independence. There was a growing realization in Delhi that Zia was probably the least thorny leader that India could expect in Pakistan at the present time.

Exactly two months after the crash, Pakistani investigators issued a 365-page report that attributed the accident to sabotage. It ruled out mechanical failure as a cause. An earlier report, prepared by a team of American experts, had suggested that mechanical malfunction had probably been the cause of the crash, although the investigators also said that the malfunction could have been the result of sabotage. The Pakistani report said that phosphorous had been found on mango seeds in the wreckage. A crate of mangoes had apparently been loaded on to Zia's plane as a gift for the dictator. The implication of the phosphorus discovery was that a bomb had been planted in the mango crate.

The truth will perhaps never be known. At any rate, Zia's death left a huge political vacuum in Pakistan because no other military figure had the stature to take his place; in fact, all the important military men who might immediately have taken power also perished. Soon afterwards, Acting President Ghulam Ishaq Khan, a civilian, announced that in November 1988 elections would be held for 217 members of the 237-seat Pakistan National Assembly (the remaining twenty seats are reserved for women and minorities, who are elected indirectly by National Assembly members). Zia had dissolved the Assembly in May 1988, ostensibly because he claimed it had grown corrupt. The real reason, his critics suggested, was that he became alarmed over the Assembly's growing assertiveness; some key legislators had begun to challenge Zia's personal authoritarianism and his style of administration. A few legislators even hinted that his associates had permitted and participated in a flourishing heroin trade.

Zia also sacked in the same month Prime Minister Mohammed Khan Junejo on the grounds that he had become ineffective. Junejo, installed as a puppet executive by Zia, had begun to acquire stature and nascent popularity that suggested a possible political alternative to Zia in the future.

President Khan announced that in November 1988 elections would also be held for Pakistan's four provincial assemblies. The new National Assembly and these regional legislative bodies would then together choose a president. The president, in turn, would name a prime minister, who constitutionally runs the government but whose power doesn't exceed that of the president. The Pakistani president appoints the chiefs of the armed forces and the judiciary, thus giving him an authority which enables him to impose his will on the body politic and control virtually all centres of political power.

The main political groupings vying for power in Pakistan were Benazir Bhutto's Pakistan People's Party, whose inspiration remains the memory and the policies of the late Prime Minister Zulfikar Ali Bhutto – Benazir's father, whom Zia overthrew in 1977 and hanged in 1979 following a kangaroo-court verdict of malfeasance and abuse of office. Another grouping was called the Islamic Democratic Alliance, a mélange of right-wing and religious factions with a lot of support in the Punjab province. And there was the Pakistani Awami Itehad, which consisted of parties spearheaded by former Prime Minister Junejo. The latter two groupings contained remnants of the once all-powerful Moslem League – the political arm of Zia's system. Finally, there were smaller groups of regional forces concentrated in specific cities or areas.

As the elections approached, the political scene in Pakistan was clouded by clashes in major cities between *muhajirs* – the refugees who had crossed over from India during the Partition to resettle in such places as Karachi – and older local residents. Their disputes weren't just political. In fact, at the core of their confrontations was a basic mutual distrust: the indigenous elements had long resented the assertiveness and commercial enterprise of the 'newcomers'. The *muhajirs*, in turn, felt that their vigorous contributions to economic development in Pakistan had not been sufficiently recognized. These tensions illustrated once again the fragility of Pakistan's social fabric and the ease with which this could be torn apart over long simmering antagonisms that percolated just below Pakistani society's surface.

The election campaign was also marred by confrontations between Miss Bhutto's followers and her opponents. The violence raised some key questions. Had Pakistan achieved sufficient political maturity to elect a woman to its national leadership? If elected would she be able to govern effectively in a system so heavily weighted against the active political participation of women? And would the slightest perceived civilian lapse in governance provoke the intervention of the military?

The fundamental reality of Pakistan was unlikely to be changed in the short run – demonstrating an old political truth: those who use authoritarian methods as a self-proclaimed argument for stability leave a legacy far more volatile than the condition they seek to cure. After all, the military would still be waiting and watching in the wings, and there would always be lingering doubts as to whether modern Pakistan could be effectively governed by any other authority. The sad legacy of Zia was that in holding his contentious nation together by the strength of his personality and the sinews of militarism, he ensured that civilian institutions which could lay the foundations of genuine grassroots democracy never fully developed.

And there was another aspect to his legacy that I am not so sure will serve Pakistan well in the long term. For reasons of political expediency – having to satisfy domestic fundamentalists and also foreign donors such as the fanatically Moslem Saudis – Zia took Pakistan so far down the road of Islamization that it may well be irreversible. He introduced the Islamic *shariat* law, which restricts many personal freedoms and institutes brutal punishments. Zia initiated the barbaric practices of lashing and chopping limbs for criminals, and he presided over an era that witnessed the dramatic deterioration of women's rights.

All these measures upset and undermined Pakistan's growing middle classes. In the emerging countries of the Third World, it is the middle classes that are most often the wellsprings of national development and, indeed, of a nation's moral and political fibre. In imposing social and political restrictions of this nature, Zia further eroded a potential source of stability in nation-building. Where he could have engendered invaluable alliances, he ignited unnecessary alienation.

The November election certainly established Benazir Bhutto as the single most important political figure in Pakistan – at the politically tender age of 35. (Several political stalwarts, including former Prime Minister Junejo, lost in the election.) Benazir acquired the mantle of national leadership, and was named prime minister on 1 December 1988, but the political inheritance that she and her generation will have to assume is a difficult one, compounded by the unclear mandate which the election provided.

The violent death of President Mohammed Zia ul-Haq dramatically changed the political landscape of his native Pakistan. To his friends abroad, especially in Britain and the United States, it seemed that Zia shrewdly maintained stability in his turbulent Moslem state of 103 million people. But it was the stability of the gun rather than the stability that flows from the establishment of democratic institutions. As Professor Ralph Buultjens puts it, 'Zia's internal legacy, for all his accent on order, is ultimately one of confusion and uncertainty in Pakistan's political system.'

This legacy will doubtless have profound implications as the struggle for political supremacy continues in Pakistan (notwithstanding Benazir Bhutto and her Pakistan People's Party). But the political scene in the whole of South Asia has also been profoundly affected by Zia's death in the still unexplained plane explosion. Policymakers in Western chancelleries now have a unique opportunity to rethink conventional wisdom about the area. On the chessboard of global politics, South Asia occupies an important corner, a strategic niche where the diplomatic, economic and geopolitical interests of the world's great powers intersect. For Washington, the stakes are especially high because of Soviet troop withdrawal from Afghanistan. Several new political openings and economic opportunities could be developed out of the general uncertainty in this part of the world.

The nine nations of the region – Afghanistan, Bangladesh, Bhutan, Burma, India, Maldives, Nepal, Pakistan and Sri Lanka – possess a fifth of the world's 5 billion people. They are undergoing an unprecedented period of demographic transformation and political transition. More than 50 per cent of people in this region are below twenty years of age. This cohort is now coming of political age. Western policymakers must recognize that the economic and political aspirations of these young people, if not met adequately and with alacrity, might well produce a new surge of radicalism. Such radicalism has already been foreshadowed by riots in Burma and by accelerated agitation in Sri Lanka by the Marxist Janatha

Vimukhti Peramuna (JVP) and the Soviet-supported Tamil Tigers who have fought for a separate ethnic state.

In the region's behemoth, India, there is a discernible weakening of the long-dominant Congress Party. There are growing doubts as to whether militarism as a political force can last not only in Pakistan but also in its former province, Bangladesh. There are also questions about the viability of the feudal monarchies of Nepal and Bhutan. Burma is undergoing political unrest and no one knows how this is going to play itself out.

And in Sri Lanka, long considered by the West as a model of democracy and development, Tamil separatists still haven't accepted the peace treaty signed in July 1987 between India and the administration of President Junius Richard Jayewardene. The octogenarian Jayewardene has retired. There is considerable doubt about the policies of his successor, Ranasinghe Premadasa, from Jayewardene's own pro-Washington party. Sirimavo Bandaranaike, an unreconstructed Marxist who in her earlier avatar as prime minister had brought economic blight to her country, opposed Premadasa in the December 1988 presidential poll.

Washington's attitude towards South Asia has generally been inconsistent. Traditionally, Turkey was considered as far more central to American concerns over the southern flank of the Soviet Union, and strategically, Turkey was viewed as being more significant than Pakistan. Over the years, in fact, Washington's support of Pakistan was generally guarded. In the 1965 and 1971 wars between India and Pakistan, US administrations failed to give Pakistan the full military support it demanded, and this resulted in a general decline in US–Pakistan relations through the late 1970s. It was only with the Soviet invasion of Afghanistan in 1979 that Washington re-assessed its relations with Pakistan and found reasons to reverse the trend of a lukewarm relationship. Suddenly, Pakistan became a 'frontline state' against Soviet expansionism, receiving $3 billion in military and economic aid since 1980, with another $4 billion package currently planned.

The basic premises of US policy in South Asia have centred on the notion that this region was generally prone to socialist economic thrusts (such as those articulated by the late Jawaharlal Nehru, a Fabian socialist); that, until the Soviet invasion of Afghanistan, Pakistan represented some sort of barrier against Soviet expansion in Asia but was strategically of secondary value to American defence interests; that India, whose political and military ties with Moscow have long been warm and strong, was virtually adverse to American security interests; that the Indian Ocean could be freely used by American naval forces and that the flag could be shown when necessary; that the perceived growing Soviet influence in the area had to be blocked through economic and military aid to receptive nations.

But the rapidly changing political, economic and social contexts of the region are now eroding many of these premises. The erosion has already resulted in a re-assessment of Washington's relations with India; indeed, the long-held notion of India being a Soviet satellite state seems to have given way to the view that there could well be a relationship here that would satisfy American strategic interests. Such a relationship would be predicated on a mutual understanding of each other's problems – or at least a recognition that Indian leaders, for domestic political reasons, would need to maintain India's 'nonalignment', however leftward-leaning.

The emphasis in this new relationship would be on what President Reagan has called 'the pragmatic' – substantial commercial and technological transfers. (Already, the US buys $3 billion worth of Indian goods annually, making it India's biggest trading partner. That would also mean encouraging American investment in joint ventures. Prime Minister Rajiv Gandhi, like President Jayewardene in Sri Lanka and President H. M. Ershad of Bangladesh, has already undertaken economic reforms that are conducive to foreign investment. With rising literacy and the spread of mass communication – especially television – the people of South Asia are increasingly aware of the benefits of the market economy. They are not going to blindly accept the old and discredited shibboleths of socialism as a panacea for economic ills or a prescription for economic progress.

The most immediate – and fundamental – contribution that Washington and its Western allies could make in the region, however, is through the promotion of democracy. Unless more genuine democracy is developed, the longer-term political stability that is required for meaningful development is unlikely to be sustained. The culture of militarism that is a creeping menace in many Third World countries could be superficially attractive in the short term but, as in Pakistan, leaves major problems in its wake. The authoritarian military caudillo is an attractive bet for the superpowers; but these dictators are really short-term political animals – they are sprinters, rather than long-distance runners who could sustain the long-term dynamic of development. The concentration of power in one person is far more dangerous than the messy, diffused and untidy processes of an open political system.

Western policy-makers must be mindful that the countries of South Asia have never been so internally fissiparous. All sorts of regional forces are being strengthened at the expense of the centre. Since these nations began achieving independence some forty years ago, the often artificially constructed central government held sway for the most part. Now, with provincialism ascending in such countries as India, Burma and Pakistan, it is unlikely that these countries can continue to be governed in the old centralist way.

And it is precisely here that they could draw lessons in governance and administration from the American federal system. The US historical experience may have considerable validity as a model for government in South Asia. (Indeed, Sri Lanka's constitution draws heavily from the American model.)

The West must also look anew at the area's new grouping, the South Asian Association for Regional Cooperation (SAARC). The very formation of this organization, which was modelled on the Association of South-East Asian Nations (ASEAN), are slithering towards some sort of regional Common Market. While their markets may currently be largely closed to foreign goods (because of these countries' foreign-exchange shortages and their import-substitution policies), the opportunities surely exist for Western companies to participate in developing the consumer-goods sector through the joint ventures that are being sought. Moreover, countries like India, Nepal and Sri Lanka are extremely anxious to crack down on the drug traffic that is worsening in the region. They urgently need help from Western – specifically British and American – law-enforcement agencies. Such help could be channelled through SAARC.

Finally, Western policy-makers (and their counterparts in South Asian countries) must be mindful of one very important point: this may well be the last generation in the Third World on whom repression can be used as an instrument of government policy – because of the rise in educational standards, increased awareness of foreign societies through global mass communications, and the growing assertiveness of young people. More and more, local governments will have to cajole, persuade and negotiate with their domestic opponents. And this is where the British and American system of discourse and debate could serve Western policy-makers well in dealing with the resurgent nations of South Asia. Although Third World leaders and citizens may not often openly acknowledge it because of domestic political constraints, the time-tested values of democracy and dissent inherent in the British and American systems have always elicited their admiration.

The promotion of multi-party democracy and development – however different from the Westminster or Washington models – will be the West's greatest gift to South Asia, the wakening giant of the Third World. The price of neglect – benign or otherwise – is today higher than ever before.

CHAPTER NINE:
THE ALCHEMY OF CULTURE

The casual visitor to India seldom gets to see how and where the majority of Indians live. Hyderabad and Bombay and Calcutta may seem crowded and overwhelming, but the country's cities and towns hold barely 30 per cent of India's 800 million people. The rest of the population lives in 576,000 villages, fewer than half of which are electrified. Nearly 400 million Indians, or fully half the country's population, live below the poverty line – which is to say that the average annual income of these people is less than $125 per person. Some of these Indians earn less than 20 cents a day.

In Hyderabad, I was urged by N. P. 'Potla' Sen, a former chairman of Indian Airlines and of the Food Corporation of India, not to neglect travelling through India's countryside. Sen informed me that India had a cultivated land area of nearly 150 million hectares, roughly the same as the United States. But while only 4 million American families depended on agriculture for their livelihood, in India the figure was 70 million families! There had been projected in the Western world an erroneous image of an India constantly hit by famine, Sen said. In reality, one of the most spectacular achievements of post-independence India had been in agriculture, he said. (Indeed, during the African famine of 1985–6, India was the biggest donor of grain to the drought-ravaged continent, after the United States.)

When the British left the sub-continent in 1947, annual food production in India was about 50 million tonnes. By December 1984, the figure had increased three-fold. The only serious famine since independence occurred in the eastern state of Bihar in 1965 as a result of drought: that year, the national grain production fell to 76 million tonnes, a drop of 12 million tonnes from the previous year. President Lyndon B. Johnson complied with a request from Prime Minister Indira Gandhi to make up this shortfall with an emergency shipment of 12 million tonnes of wheat. Widespread famine was averted, although hundreds of Biharis perished before the grain could reach them. By 1984 India maintained a buffer stock of 22 million tonnes, 7 million tonnes more than the minimum level established by the government, Sen said. The danger to Indian grain production is less and less from drought, because of new irrigation techniques; the danger is increasingly from rodents, who often overrun warehouses. It is estimated that more than 15 per cent of India's annual grain production is destroyed by these rodents.

And the danger now is that more and more of India's farmers are being driven towards the 'poverty line' because of sharply increasing fertilizer costs and lagging grain prices. (A government-appointed Agricultural Prices Commission sets these prices on the basis of a complex and highly disputed formula.) The leading spokesman for Indian farmers, Sharad Joshi, claims that despite impressive strides in agriculture, the Indian farmer is not a prosperous individual. He says that more than 25 per cent of the farmers in the Punjab – considered India's showcase of agricultural development – now live below the poverty line. A study carried out by the Agricultural Prices Commission in 1979 showed that farmers owning up to 7.5 acres of land had 'negative household savings' each year; those owning between 7.5 acres and 15 acres saved up to $250 annually; and those farmers owning between 25 acres and the national land ceiling of 80 acres per individual saved at the most $2,000 a year.

Since 1979, fertilizer prices have risen by nearly 35 per cent, so that the Indian farmer now pays the equivalent of almost 75 cents for a kilogramme of nitrogenous fertilizer. Sharad Joshi says that while such costs have escalated, the wheat procurement price is now only $1.50 a kilogramme – representing only a doubling since 1967. Farmers in India's most productive agricultural zone, the Punjab, have been especially hard hit. In the Punjab, which produces 60 per cent of India's grain, the use of fertilizers is particularly high – 134 kilogrammes per acre, compared with the national average of 36 kilogrammes. Farmers are finding that they are no longer getting remunerative prices for their production. This has fuelled a great deal of resentment. Joshi has asked farmers to switch to non-grain production where they might obtain better revenues: to horticulture, and timber and oilseed production. As a last resort, Joshi has said, farmers could even leave some of their land fallow.

I found during my travels across India that farmers were increasingly being organized politically, a new development in post-independence India. Their cry: we want a fairer deal. The farmers were first formally banded together in early 1984 in the southern state of Tamil Nadu under the aegis of the Bharatiya Kisan Union (BKU). So popular did the organization become (its name translates as the Union of Indian Farmers) that soon branches were started in other states. But it was not until Sharad Joshi emerged on the scene that Indian farmers found a truly national spokesman.

Joshi, a slim, intense man, used to work for the United Nations. He had a brilliant academic career and joined India's élite civil service before being deputed to the United Nations. He decided, however, that he would rather be an activist than a paper-pusher. He had always been concerned about such things as better health care for rural families and better economic development in the countryside. So he started a lobbying group called the Shetkari Sanghatana (which means Fraternity of Farmers). It was his nation-wide agitation on behalf of farmers that forced the government to set up, recently, a commission to investigate farmers' grievances.

However, remuneration for grain production and the rising cost of fertilizers are not the only issues that affected India's country-side. Almost forty years after independence, the question of land reform continues to be controversial. As the British consolidated their colonial rule, India's traditionally self-sufficient village system began to disintegrate. In 1830, Sir Charles Metcalfe, one of the ablest British civil administrators of his time, wrote:

The village communities are little republics having nearly everything they want within themselves; and almost independent of foreign relations. They seem to last where nothing else lasts. This union of the village communities, each one forming a separate little state in itself, is in a high degree conducive to their happiness, and to the enjoyment of a great portion of freedom and independence.

Within a few years, the village system about which Sir Charles wrote so astutely had changed dramatically. In *The Discovery of*

India – probably the best literary work of history about India –
Jawaharlal Nehru wrote:

The destruction of village industries was a powerful blow to these communities. The balance between industry and agriculture was upset, the traditional division of labour was broken up, and numerous stray individuals
could not be easily fitted into any group activity. A more direct blow came
from the introduction of the landlord system, changing the whole conception of ownership of land.
   This conception had been one of communal ownership, not so much of
the land as of the produce of the land. Possibly not fully appreciating this,
but more probably taking the step deliberately for reasons of their own, the
British governors – who themselves represented the English landlord class –
introduced something resembling the English system in India.

   The British at first appointed agents, known as revenue-farmers,
who collected land-tax from peasants and delivered it to the
government. These agents developed into landlords. The village
community was now deprived of all control over the land and its
produce, Nehru says, and 'this led to the breakdown of the joint life
and corporate character of the community; the co-operative system
of services and functions began to disappear gradually'. Large
landowners were created by the British after their own English
pattern, according to Nehru, chiefly because it was far easier to deal
with a few individuals than with a vast peasantry. 'The objective
was to collect as much money in the shape of revenue, and as
speedily, as possible,' he wrote. 'It was also considered necessary to
create a class whose interests were identified with the British.'
   That class, the landlords, steadily gained in power and prestige.
In Bengal they were called *zamindars*; elsewhere the word for
them was *malik*. They exploited the peasantry. They accumulated
vast fortunes. They were often cruel. But they were loyal to the
British, and that was what mattered. During the British Raj, feudal-
ism became a solid institution. The landlords did not wholeheated-
ly support the freedom movement – not the least because its
leaders, such as Mahatma Gandhi and Nehru, were committed to
instituting land reform once independence was achieved. The
Congress Party had pledged to abolish absentee landlordism; the
Party's leaders assured peasants that they would secure for them
permanency of tenureship and a fair share of the crop.
   The late Krishan Bhatia noted in *The Ordeal of Nationhood* that

in Nehru's home state of Uttar Pradesh, during the years that the Congress held limited local power before independence, it had enacted legislation for the abolition of the *zamindari* system. Bhatia, a former editor of the *Hindustan Times* and that Delhi newspaper's Washington correspondent for many years, wrote that the law protected the cultivator from the landlord's high-handedness by assuring him permanence of tenure as long as he paid a reasonable rent for the holding. The farmer was also given the option to own the land he worked on by paying moderate compensation to the absentee owner.

Independence came – but years went by before there was any significant land and tenancy reform or meaningful land-ceiling legislation. In countries where there has been noteworthy land reform – such as Sri Lanka, Malaysia and Thailand – the farmer was always given ownership so that he put in his best effort. It has been widely recognized that to maximize production you must make the farmer the owner of his land. But in India, the farmer has traditionally depended for his livelihood not just on the quality and quantity of his production but, more importantly, on the whims of local rulers. Moreover, antiquated social customs among India's peasants have resulted in fragmentation of land holdings where farmers have possession of property: fathers would bequeath land to their sons, who would divide up the property into small and uneconomic plots.

In the early years after independence, no sweeping land reforms were possible for a variety of reasons: land records were poorly maintained, deeds were vague, and it was difficult to establish ownership accurately; there was considerable absentee land-lordship; there were fraudulent practices such as 'donating' land to peasants who were in truth the landlords' serfs. Landlords developed cosy relationships with India's new rulers; they started contributing heavily to the ruling Congress Party. Krishan Bhatia writes: 'Before 1947 the Congress Party was a mass movement and not the Establishment. Its sense of social justice was strong and its concern for the underprivileged in the rural areas genuine. The landlords then stood by the British Government.' The dividing line disappeared after independence, when the landlords joined hands with the Congress chieftains.

For almost a decade after independence, there was not even a new land-ceiling law in many Indian states. Land reform was always a subject to be handled by the state governments, unlike foreign affairs, defence or telecommunications, which were the prerogative of the central government. It was only in 1957 that relevant legislation came into being in these states – but it was so lenient towards landlords that tenants and farmers actually suffered under its terms. Landlords were now allowed to select between 30 acres in some states and 200 acres in other states for personal cultivation; landlords could also parcel out property to family members. As a result, what was meant to be reforming legislation resulted in a situation where landlords could actually legalize large holdings in their own names and in the names of relatives; the landlord was also permitted to throw out existing tenants from the portions of his property he had chosen for 'self-cultivation'.

'Instead of bringing greater security to the real cultivators of land, the reforms only added to the numbers of landless peasants and sharecroppers,' Krishan Bhatia said in his highly praised book. 'Most state governments conveniently looked the other way while this process was occurring.'

By 1971, nationwide concern mounted over the question of land reform. In many states, absentee landlords controlled large chunks of land; their tenant-farmers languished. Regional newspapers – particularly those published in vernacular languages – highlighted abuses in areas such as eastern Uttar Pradesh and Bihar. Even Mrs Gandhi, who seldom believed anything that appeared in the media, was forced to acknowledge that landlords were exploiting the peasantry in some parts of India.

Mrs Gandhi had, by 1971, consolidated her personal authority within the Congress Party. She had broken away from the old party chieftains who had installed her as prime minister in January 1966. She was aware that there was little a national government could do to push through land reforms; but since her Congress Party also controlled many of India's states, the prime minister could apply pressure on her local representatives. She did so in an imaginative manner.

She issued a new rallying cry for Indians: '*Garibi Hatao!*' or 'Get Rid of Poverty!' The prime minister's public relations campaign glossed over the fact that the Congress Party's economic policies had exacerbated poverty since independence; these policies had promoted the development of heavy industries at the expense of light and consumer-oriented industries, which create more jobs.

With the exception of a much-publicized dam or hydro-electric project here and there, or some irrigation scheme, the Congress Party had also generally neglected rural economic development. Mrs Gandhi's '*Garibi Hatao!*' call could be seen as an indictment of her own policies, and, indeed, some of the prime minister's political opponents as well as some figures in the intellectual community were sceptical. But it wasn't taken that way by ordinary Indians. They were thrilled at this new theme the prime minister was expounding.

Implicit in the '*Garibi Hatao!*' call was a promise of further land reform. With a great fanfare, Mrs Gandhi launched in 1974 India's Fifth Five-Year Plan. It envisaged the expenditure of $10 billion by 1979 on agriculture projects. The assumption seemed to be that if agriculture was formally highlighted in the government's economic programme, then things like land reform would follow. (India's five-year plans set production targets; they are also a statement of the government's broad economic and social policies. The documents are mostly unreadable.) Some states acted on land reform; some states ignored the subject altogether. You can still visit regions like Bihar and come across landlords who control 200-acre properties.

I decided to see for myself the impact of Indira Gandhi's agricultural and rural policies. I went to Medhak, a traditionally backward area in Andhra Pradesh. Medhak had been Mrs Gandhi's last constituency. She was elected from there in 1980. For years she had contested parliamentary polls from the northern Indian state of Uttar Pradesh, but she had moved to Medhak not only because it was considered a 'safe seat' for her. She wanted to demonstrate that she was truly a national leader, that she could be elected from all parts of the country – that Indians anywhere would respond favourably to her.

I was driven to Medhak by Pramila David. She was gracious enough to take time off from the Shilpa Clinic in Hyderabad, where she ran innovative family-planning programmes for the poor. People who come to the clinic can also sign up for free vocational-training projects. Dr David is a legendary figure in Andhra Pradesh because she has helped thousands of destitute men and women in cities, towns and villages to find jobs and thus gain self-respect. She has particularly assisted Harijans, or India's long-suffering 'untouchable' community.

There are more than 100 million of these Harijans in India *Harijans*
today, an overwhelming number of them in southern states like
Andhra Pradesh. The origins of untouchability lie in Hinduism's
rigid and unrelenting caste system, according to historians like
Romila Thapar. This institutionalized intolerance, she has said,
was a result of the early Aryans' prejudice against the darker races
they encountered during their conquest of northern India. The
Chinese traveller Fa-Hsien, who came to India in the fifth century
AD, wrote that the people who removed human excrement were
considered untouchable by India's majority Hindus.

The Hindu caste system was essentially four-tiered: at the very
top were the Brahmans, the priestly class who studied and interpreted the religion and its scriptures; then came the Kshatriyas, or
the rulers and administrators; next were the Vaishyas, or the
merchant community; finally, there were the Shudras, who performed manual labour. The 'untouchables' were outside this four-
tier system: they did all the scavenging and cleaning work. They
were required to live and eat separately. If a Brahman as much as
spotted an untouchable on the street, he would at once return home
to bathe his 'pollution' away; even the mere shadow of an untouchable polluted his high-caste soul, the Brahman believed. Untouchables could marry only other untouchables. They had few rights,
only duties. Educational opportunities were denied them, as were
jobs in anything but sanitation, tanning and shoe-making. They
were not allowed to own property.

It was Mahatma Gandhi who started calling the untouchables
'Harijans', or 'Children of God'. 'The moment untouchability goes,
the caste system itself will be purified,' the Mahatma said.

He invited hundreds of Harijans to accompany him during his
travels around India. He ate with them. He took them along to
political rallies, to temples, to the homes of Brahmans. And in the
southern princely state of Travancore, Gandhi ran into resistance
from the royal family and its Brahman allies in virtually the whole of
the Kerala region, of which Travancore was a part. So roughly did
Travancore's royalty and Brahman hierarchy treat untouchables
that they were required to carry bells to warn other pedestrians that
they were coming! Whenever Hindus heard these bells, they scattered for cover.

Since late 1923, a campaign had been under way in Vaikom,
a community in Travancore. The campaign was led by a Tamil

from the neighbouring Madras Presidency, a man named E. V. Ramaswamy Naicker. Naicker, or EVR as he was widely known, campaigned for better living conditions for the untouchables of Vaikom. Specifically, he wanted untouchables to be allowed to cross the road in front of Vaikom's great Hindu temple. EVR's friend, the Maharaja of Travancore, became so upset over the campaign that he imprisoned Naicker. Mahatma Gandhi arrived in Vaikom to protest on behalf of the local untouchables. The maharaja's police put up barricades on the roads in front of the Hindu temple. Even Gandhi was not allowed access to the temple.

'My agitation here is nothing less than to rid Hinduism of its greatest blot,' the Mahatma declared. 'The curse of untouchability has disfigured Hinduism.'

He negotiated for months with the maharaja, who finally relented. Travancore's authorities now agreed to open up the roads on three sides of the temple to all people, including untouchables; the fourth side was barred to untouchables. It took another decade of agitation on Gandhi's part to ensure that Harijans could not only walk on the roads outside temples but also worship inside if they wished to.

If Gandhi's efforts led to increased social acceptance of Harijans, it was the work of a man named Bhimrao Ramji Ambedkar that eventually resulted in positive economic and political gains for them. Ambedkar was a lawyer who had received his doctorate from Columbia University. He helped draft India's Constitution in 1949, which formally outlawed untouchability. He was also an untouchable. Ambedkar organized civic associations for the welfare of India's Harijans. He influenced newspaper publishers to write editorials urging the end of discrimination against untouchables. Ambedkar rejected Hinduism, embraced Buddhism, and persuaded hundreds of thousands of Harijans to convert. He even formed the Republican Party of India to ensure that Harijans joined independent India's political mainstream.

Largely because of Ambedkar's work, the national government decreed that affirmative action be undertaken on behalf of Harijans. Special job slots were set aside for them in public sector industries. Air India, the government-owned airline, was ordered to step up its hiring of Harijan stewards and stewardesses, a directive that caused considerable grumbling among the upper-class people who had traditionally joined the airline because of the glamour involved: many of these non-Harijans felt that the new employees simply weren't bright or beautiful enough.

Resistance to the emancipation of Harijans continued in many quarters. When Acharya Vinobha Bhave, a respected social activist and disciple of Mahatma Gandhi, tried to lead a group of Harijans into a Hindu temple in Deogarh, in Bihar state, Brahman priests physically attacked the frail Bhave. The incident shocked the nation. Prime Minister Nehru's administration immediately drafted a bill that made the practice of untouchability a criminal offence.

But discrimination against Harijans persists in India. Once in a while the newspapers carry gory accounts of Harijans being beheaded in remote areas by high-caste Hindus; or there are articles about the disfiguring of Harijan women. In Tamil Nadu and Andhra Pradesh, there have been incidents where entire rural areas of Harijans were set upon by Hindu hordes, who burned down homes and killed residents. In some parts of the south, Harijans joined Moslem mullahs for conversion – out of frustration with the existing social order and on the assumption that the egalitarianism of Islam would somehow ensure a better economic life for them. I don't know, however, whether changing one's faith in itself can bring about a change in one's social and economic status, or in the way one might be perceived by others.

It would be a very long time before the spirit of corrective legislation would be mirrored in broad social attitudes towards Harijans, Pramila David said to me as we drove towards Medhak. The countryside seemed dry; it hadn't rained for months. Indeed, drought had affected twelve of Andhra's twenty-three districts, and the state's food production was expected to fall substantially short of the 1984–5 target of 1.25 million tonnes. Groundnut, rice, sorghum and millet yields were not expected to equal the previous year's harvest. Many villages were running out of drinkable water. In the Telangana region of the state, villagers traditionally held an annual festival of flowers in honour of Batakamma, the local Goddess of Life. But, Dr David told me, this year there hadn't even been enough water for the ritual bath given by priests to the goddess, who is supposed to usher in a year of abundant harvests. The lack of water was viewed by villagers as a bad omen.

We arrived in a village called Brahmanpalli. We went to the home of a man named Krishna Reddy, whose family had once owned hundreds of acres of land here but whose property had now shrunk to eighty acres because of Andhra's land-ceiling regulations. Reddy wasn't home, but his Australian-born wife, Joan, welcomed us to their ranch-style house. A group of local peasants had already assembled in anticipation of our visit (Pramila David had telephoned the Reddys the previous day). They sat on the stone floor of Joan Reddy's verandah, not exchanging a word with one another. The women sat separately from the men, at some distance.

I talked with Gajam Balaram, who belonged to the weaver community. He was a tall, thin man who wore a white *dhoti* (sarong), a long white shirt and thonged sandals. He had a cadaverous face, which appeared rather ghoulish because of the white holy ash he had daubed on his forehead.

He was extremely worried, Balaram said. The crops on his two-acre plot were failing because of the drought. Villagers did not have enough cash to spend on themselves, so his family's textile retail shop simply had no business these days. He had had to abandon weaving because of competition from Hyderabad's textile mills.

'Our life is no better than when I was a child,' Balaram said in Telugu, which Pramila David translated for me. 'In fact, my childhood was happier than the life I am able to give to my own children.'

But hadn't this been Indira Gandhi's constituency, I said, surely she must have helped people here?

'Politicians!' Balaram said. 'We can never believe any of their promises. They say so much during election time, then they vanish.'

The acute need in the Brahmanpalli area, he said, was for a better drinking-water supply, for sewage pipes and for a hospital. The 10,000 residents of the area had been clamouring for these for many years, Balaram said, but to no avail.

'What good is it to us even if our representative was the prime minister of India?' said a man named Nandi Narasingrao. He had completed high school but could only find a job on a rice farm. He had recently got married, he said, but now he was finding it difficult to feed his new bride. 'What face do I have to show before my in-laws?' he said.

I asked a woman named Mutuah if Mrs Gandhi was going to be missed in this area.

'Why should we miss her?' Mutuah, a Harijan, said. 'Her death makes no difference to our daily lives. Our struggle to survive goes on regardless. Did Indira Gandhi truly care for us here?'

And it went on that way from village to village in Medhak. In Islampur, Paddalpalli, Topran – in community after community of mud and brick homes, dusty roads and dry, brown fields, I heard the same sentiments. The need was not only for improved health-care facilities and better schools; it was also for bank loans to develop farms and local businesses. The need was for jobs. The need was for someone to come and listen to these villagers, but Mrs Gandhi hadn't been here for many months and now, of course, she was gone. Medhak wasn't her son's constituency, so it would be unlikely that this area would figure in Rajiv Gandhi's travel plans.

The men and women of Medhak were concerned with health care, better sanitation, more employment and schools. These concerns are replicated in virtually all rural areas of India's states. National politicians always pay lip-service to the 'needs of the peasant'. But the life of the ordinary peasant hasn't improved much since independence: there are now more people than ever before who live below the poverty line – who can't adequately feed, clothe or house their families.

As Pramila David and I headed back towards Hyderabad, it occurred to me that there were actually more people in India living below the poverty line than made up the entire population of the country at independence. In another fifteen years' time, there will be at least a billion people in India; half of them will certainly be born into crushing poverty, if current trends hold.

I suddenly remembered a sobering conversation I'd had in Delhi with Hugo Corvalan, the Indian representative of the United Nations Fund for Population Activities. I had first met Corvalan, a Chilean physician, when he was stationed in Ecuador some years ago for the United Nations. He had impressed me then as a man who passionately cared for the poor and who was deeply worried that the population growth rate in many of the world's poorest countries was galloping out of control.

I found Corvalan even more troubled when I went to see him at the United Nations office in Delhi's fashionable Lodi Estate. He had asked for the Indian assignment because of its challenges. India, after all, had been the first Third World country to have formally made family planning a matter of national policy. It had launched with much publicity a nationwide sterilization drive. It had persuaded the United States and other Western donors to pump more than 3 billion dollars over the last two decades into population-control programmes.

And still, the population was growing each year at a rate of more than 2.1 per cent. The largest number of babies were born in areas where there were already the most number of people – the rural countryside, where 70 per cent of India's population lived. Moreover, improved health care had lowered the death rate in many parts of the country; killer diseases like smallpox had been eradicated. Infant mortality had been brought down. The life expectancy of the average Indian had increased from 32 years at independence in 1947 to more than 54 by 1984.

Corvalan told me that at present the average married Indian woman produced five children. If the Indian government's efforts to reduce average family size to two children was successful by, say, the year 2040, India would still have a population of 2.5 billion.

I wasn't sure I'd heard Corvalan correctly.

'Did you say 2.5 billion?' I said.

'Yes,' Corvalan said.

And he now went on to give me more gloomy information. Fewer than 35 per cent of the country's 122 million married people used any form of contraception. In order to ensure that India's population does not surge beyond a billion by the year 2000, the use of contraception must be extended to at least 60 per cent of these married people.

Were the Indian authorities capable of extending family planning so dramatically?

Corvalan declined to say anything because of his official position. But he didn't have to say anything more. The answer to my question was obvious.

The plain truth is, the Indian government bungled population control from the very start. Nehru was a relatively late convert to the idea of family planning, even though his government instituted a formal population policy in the early 1950s. The resources that could and should have been channelled into population control measures right from independence were never forthcoming. Nehru's first minister of health and family planning was a spinster of great rectitude who privately endorsed Mahatma Gandhi's oft-quoted view that celibacy was the best contraceptive. Massive grants that were later given by Western donors were misrouted – which is to say, a lot of the money went into the pockets of politicians and top bureaucrats.

Mrs Gandhi dithered over the issue of family planning. It was not until the 'Emergency' of 1975–7 that the government acted decisively. The actions, of course, proved highly unpopular because the prime minister's son, Sanjay, pushed through draconian sterilization measures. He meant well, but he was a young man in a hurry; Sanjay Gandhi, Indira Gandhi's heir-apparent, wanted to bring down India's birth rate overnight. Truckloads of pre-adolescent boys were sterilized by over-zealous functionaries in order to meet quotas. Mrs Gandhi's defeat in the 1977 election was at least partly attributable to public revulsion over the family-planning excesses of the Emergency period.

After Mrs Gandhi returned to power in 1980, little was heard from her on population. She was not about to risk talking about that subject again! As a result, family-planning programmes continued at a low pitch – when what was really called for was a renewed and rigorous commitment to reducing the population growth rate. Despite the fact that the national government had a budget of more than $250 million for distribution to the states for family planning, much of the money went unspent. The United Nations kept pouring funds into India for population projects – and the money languished in Delhi.

Even during the December 1984 election campaign, Rajiv Gandhi did not utter a word about what many people think is India's biggest problem. Perhaps he did not wish to antagonize the majority Hindu population, particularly in the rampantly-breeding northern Hindi-speaking states, whose electoral support he sought. Later, as prime minister, Gandhi talked about doubling the family-planning budget to nearly $500 million a year. I don't think the question of how much more he spends really matters: already, Indian states have more money than they know what to do with. What is really required is better management of existing programmes.

A few days after my visit to Medhak, I found myself in Bangalore, the capital city of Karnataka state. Pramila David had suggested that I look up a man named Palli Hanumantha Reddy. He was the head of the Population Centre, which had been set up in the early

1970s with the help of money from the World Bank. The centre was intended to conduct research into family-reproduction trends in Karnataka, a prosperous state of 38 million people. Now Dr Reddy's centre functions as an arm of the state government.

The centre consists of a long, low building set in front of a playing field; it is situated in Malleswaram, one of the most congested parts of Bangalore. The playing field was like a green lung for the area: in one corner boys were battling it out at cricket; in another corner, young men were flirting with young women; in still another corner, elderly citizens were taking their evening constitutional. Dr Reddy was a middle-aged man with a shock of greying hair, spectacles and an affable manner. He made it clear at the very outset that he didn't think that the field of family planning in his state and throughout the country suffered from an overabundance of good leadership.

'In fact, I would even say that there is much negligence in this field,' Dr Reddy said.

The Karnataka government set aside more than $90 million a year for family planning, he said, yet much of the money wasn't spent. State governments generally just did not have the imagination to spend money properly on family planning programmes.

What was needed, he said, was a system of financial incentives so that small clinics all over the country could induce more people to sign up for family-planning measures of their choice. Since state governments already had funds lying around, why not give certificates or savings bonds for participants in family-planning programmes? And why not equip family-planning centres with vocational-training courses for the poor, as Pramila David had done in Hyderabad? Most state governments unwisely concentrated on promoting sterilization; they ought to encourage a range of other contraceptive measures that were not so final and terminal as sterilization. More attention needed to be paid to child-care services; it had been proven in rural areas particularly that mothers listened to midwives and nurses. So why not train more nurses to spread the message of family planning? Why not train agricultural extension workers to inject a family-planning component into their daily dealings with peasants?

Palli Hanumantha Reddy made a lot of sense. So why wasn't the Karnataka government listening to him? Or Rajiv Gandhi's administration?

He shrugged, then raised his hands to the heavens.

I flew from Karnataka to Kerala, India's southernmost state. It is a gem of a place, emerald green, deeply lush, scored with lagoons and canals and inlets, festooned with miles of coconut groves. The Indian Airlines airbus from Bangalore cruised over Kerala's inland mountains, which were carpeted with rubber, tea and coffee plantations. A Keralite stewardess informed me that alongside these plantations were acres of pepper and cardamom and cashew-nut fields. As the plane descended toward Cochin, an ancient coastal city where I planned to meet friends, I had to pull my eyes away from the window because of the violent glare from the vegetation down below. When I looked out again, we were just over the city itself. There seemed to be miles and miles of dwellings closely packed under swaying palm trees. The stewardess, who said she had recently finished college in Trivandrum, told me that Kerala had the highest population density in India – some 1,000 people to the square kilometre, or almost five times the national figure. Despite a falling birth rate, she said, the state's population was now more than 30 million.

In the Third World, Kerala long ago became a by-word for literacy and excellent health care. By 1955, when most states of the Third World were still backward, miserable places – and still under their colonial yoke – Kerala had already achieved the highest literacy rate of any region in the developing world, an astonishing 95 per cent.

The Christian missionaries who arrived in the eighteenth and nineteenth centuries established English-language schools. Kerala's two princely states, Travancore and Cochin, were traditionally governed by rulers who promoted literacy, especially among women. Hindu communities such as the Nayyars and the Namboodiripads also vigorously campaigned for education. Because Kerala had no industries until well into the 1960s government service was the most sought-after career for the young, so they studied hard for the competitive entrance examinations – and the competition among Kerala's people (who were 50 per cent Hindus, 25 per cent Moslems and 25 per cent Christians) in turn helped push ever upwards the quality of education. The state decreed that all education through high school would be free; moreover, even the salaries of many teachers in private schools were paid by the state from tax revenues. In addition, health services were free. The first public clinics for administering the smallpox vaccine were established in Travancore and Cochin.

Kerala was unusual in other ways, too. In the rest of India, women were largely confined to home and hearth; but in this state they were encouraged to study and to get jobs. The high status of women was mainly a result of the fact that much of Kerala's majority Hindu society was matriarchal.

Kerala also became a metaphor for something besides high literacy and good health care. It was the first state in the world where the Communist Party obtained power through legitimately held elections. This occurred in 1957. As literacy spread, Keralites started to harbour higher and higher economic expectations, but the system could not deliver. Because of the nature of the terrain, virtually all economic activity was confined to land cultivation or fishing. Yet each year the schools and colleges were turning out thousands of graduates. Unemployment rose beyond 15 per cent, and soon there were violent demonstrations against the ruling Congress Party of Jawaharlal Nehru. A local Communist leader named E. M. S. Namboodiripad accused the Congress of 'class exploitation'. At rally after rally, he equated the Congress rule with British imperialism. Namboodiripad's rhetoric, combined with the growing unemployment and the rising expectations of Keralites, helped put the Communists into power. Namboodiripad's government was the first constitutionally elected Communist administration in history.

Prime Minister Nehru actually seemed to be proud of the development. He told Krishan Bhatia of the *Hindustan Times* that perhaps now Communists all over the world would realize that they could attain power through the ballot box and become more tolerant of democratic political processes. Dom Moraes, in his biography of Indira Gandhi, *Mrs Gandhi*, recalls that the Fabian Socialist in Nehru even seemed delighted that a leftist government had come into being through democratic means; Nehru, according to Moraes, hoped that Kerala could be the precursor of other democratically elected Communist governments all over the world.

Mrs Gandhi had become president of the Congress Party by now. She wanted to revitalize the aging organization. She did not subscribe to her father's live-and-let-live attitude towards Opposition parties, much less applaud the takeover, however democratic, of an Indian state by the Communist Party. She advised the Kerala unit of the Congress Party to prepare for a nasty battle with Namboodiripad's government. The Congress threw in its lot with the Nayyars and the Christians of the state, who had felt discriminated against by the Communist government; Namboodiripad's party had instituted radical land reforms, pushed out many influential and established Nayyars and Christians from the bureaucracy, and tried to bring about structural changes in the educational system over which the Nayyars and Christians had long held sway. The Communist government even tried to take over the parochial schools operated by the Christians and Nayyars.

Rioting now occurred. There were Congress-sponsored demonstrations all over Kerala. Police fired tear-gas shells at mobs. Then orders were given to shoot demonstrators who had become uncontrollably violent, and several civilians died. It was clear to many observers at the time that Mrs Gandhi was calibrating the demonstrations from Delhi in order to ensure that the law-and-order situation deteriorated rapidly. She could then persuade her father, the prime minister, to dismiss the Kerala state government on the grounds that it was unable to check the spreading lawlessness.

That is exactly what Mrs Gandhi did, and Prime Minister Nehru accepted her recommendation. On 31 July 1959, the Namboodiripad government was deposed under a presidential order. The lawlessness continued, however, this time fuelled by the disaffected Communists. The Nehru–Gandhi axis ordered elections six months later, but in order to win the poll Mrs Gandhi had to make alliances with the Socialists and with the Moslem League. This was the same Moslem League that less than two decades ago had agitated so fiercely for the partition of Greater India into India and Pakistan. Mrs Gandhi's political marriage of convenience with the Moslem League distressed many of her supporters within and without the Congress Party. The Congress formed a coalition government with the League and the Socialists.

The Communist Party subsequently split into one wing favouring the Maoist version of Marxism and another wing that leaned towards Moscow. (The split had more to do with the estrangement between Moscow and Beijing, rather than developments in Kerala, but it further weakened the previously monolithic Communist movement in Kerala.) Over the next twenty years, both Communist wings held power as members of various coalition governments – but the supremacy that Namboodiripad enjoyed between 1957 and

1959 was never quite repeated again. It would not be incorrect to say that Indira Gandhi ushered in an era of coalition governments in Kerala; since 1960, in fact, the Congress and the Marxists have had to woo smaller regional and communal parties in order to form coalition governments. Tenuity, not stability, has usually been the main characteristic of these administrations.

I reached Kerala a couple of days after the December 1984 national parliamentary election. The leading newspapers, such as the *Malayalam Manorama*, were asking in their editorials whether the Communists were a spent force. Of the twenty parliamentary seats in Kerala, Rajiv Gandhi's Congress Party won an unprecedented thirteen. Namboodiripad's Communist Party, known as the CPI(M) (the (M) stands for Marxist) won only one seat; the other wing of the Communist Party, known as the CPI, was completely shut out. 'We never expected an Indira Wave in Kerala,' said one of Namboodiripad's key lieutenants and a former chief minister of the state, P. K. Vasudevan Nair.

Even in death, Mrs Gandhi had defeated and demoralized Namboodiripad.

Kerala may have looked green and inviting from the air, but Cochin was hot, sticky and dusty. I waited for almost an hour for my baggage to appear; the delay, I was told, was on account of several large crates that had arrived by another plane from the Middle East.

'These days there is nothing but crates from the Gulf that come here,' an airport official said, wearily. 'Big crates, too. We don't have the machinery to haul them. How much pushing and pulling can my men do with their bare hands?'

The crates, containing such things as television sets, dishwashers and stereo sets, had been arriving from Middle East countries where, in the last ten years, more than 500,000 men and women from Kerala had found lucrative work. Not only Moslems – known here as *moplahs* – travelled abroad; so did tens of thousands of Kerala Christians and Hindus. Their El Dorado was the Arabian Peninsula, whose oil-rich states were in need of manpower. Carpenters went from Kerala, and so did plumbers, technicians, school-teachers, professors, physicians, nurses, drivers – even maids. The traffic from Kerala was so heavy that Air India started special thrice-weekly flights from Trivandrum to the Gulf. The emigration, however temporary, eased the unemployment problem in Kerala, and it showered upon the state a financial windfall – the Keralites who went abroad have sent home more than $4 billion since the mid-1970s. The money has resulted in new homes and a spree of spending on such things as cars and scooters.

I had trouble finding a taxi outside Cochin Airport. I was told that many taxi drivers had moved to the Middle East! The drive to the Grand Hotel, where I had booked a room, took an hour because the road ran over a number of bridges that could accommodate only one traffic lane. Had traffic moved at this pace in most other Indian states, there would have been mayhem, and probably a murder or two. But Keralites seemed quiet, peaceful people – at least on their roads. My taxi driver, a reedy man named Bala, did not even curse or mutter under his breath.

I couldn't stand his silence and stoicism any longer.

'Is traffic always like this?' I asked.

'Always, sir,' Bala said.

'Is anything being done about it?'

'No.'

'Isn't it frustrating to be on such roads?'

'Yes, sir.'

We drove past a large naval yard. Cochin is the headquarters of the Indian Navy's southern fleet. There seemed to be more churches inside the yard than sailors. Christianity was said to have arrived in Kerala even before it was identified with Rome. John Keay, in *Into India*, writes that a mysterious Thomas founded what is called the Syrian Church of South India. The *Cambridge History of India* quotes from the 'Apocryphal Acts of the Apostles II' an anecdote relating to Thomas, the doubting one of Jesus's twelve apostles. 'Whithersoever thou wilt Lord, send me,' Thomas says. 'But to India I will not go.' He is eventually said to have been sold as a servant to an Indian who wanted to take home a carpenter, John Keay writes. Was the Thomas who came to Kerala the Thomas of the Apostles? Theologians in India and elsewhere still debate that one.

The early Christians of Kerala recognized the authority of the Nestorian Patriarchs of Babylon rather than the Bishop of Rome. When Vasco da Gama and his Portuguese fleet arrived in Kerala in 1502, they were angered by the Kerala Christians' rejection of the Bishop of Rome, so they began a programme of conversion. The

Keralites who resisted the Portuguese formed what is now known as the Chaldean Church of India. But those who were 'persuaded' by the Portuguese to switch their affiliation to Rome are the present-day members of the Syrian rite of the Roman Catholic Church of India. There was further fragmentation of the Christian community over the years. In addition to the Catholic and Syrian churches, there are many other Christian denominations: Jehovah's Witnesses, Lutherans, Baptists, Methodists, Anglicans and Seventh-Day Adventists, to name a few.

I had come to Kerala because my friends Kutty and Bhavani Narayan had suggested a meeting with members of India's most rapidly dwindling community, the Jews of Cochin. The Jews are said to have come to India in 72 AD. They established themselves mainly as traders and teachers in Cochin and Bombay. Before 1948, which is to say before the State of Israel was created, there were nearly 50,000 Jews in India, most of them in Bombay; in Cochin there were some 3,000 families. The Cochin Jewish community was divided into 'White Jews', who were the more affluent ones, and 'Black Jews', who weren't so well off. After 1948, the Jews of Bombay and Cochin started migrating to Israel. Now there are barely 7,000 Jews left in Bombay, and just about 100 in Cochin.

Shabdar and Gladys Koder have refused to leave their ancestral home here. For one thing, they own a chain of grocery stores in Kerala; for another, they are well into their seventies and do not fancy the prospect of making a fresh start in an alien land. There is still another reason why they have not migrated to Israel: the Koders see themselves as Indians. Their roots are here. (Shabdar Koder's great-great-grandfather came here 300 years ago from Baghdad via Burma to set up a trading business, which is still thriving.) They think that exciting times lie ahead for India and they want to be around to see Rajiv Gandhi succeed.

I went to see the Koders in their 100-year-old house in an area known as Fort Cochin. The house had three storeys and it over-looked a bay. Coconut trees rose behind the Koders' home, and in front there was a large park. Most of Cochin's 100 remaining Jews live in this area. It was the bewitching hour of sunset when I showed up. The thin light made the pink walls of the house glow softly. There was an enormous, ornate wooden door that a saree-clad maid opened. I was led up a wooden stairway to the second floor where Shabdar Samuel Koder was waiting for me in a huge sitting room.

He was a tall man, balding, with a strong handshake and a friendly face. His wife, Gladys, immediately brought out a tray of savouries and sweetmeats. The tray seemed bigger than she was. The food, she said, was all home-made. Then she insisted on showing me the Koders' collection of antique Chinese porcelain. They possessed dozens of early Ming Dynasty vases, Ching Dynasty plates, and Tang horses. It was a museum that they had there. I told them that I was impressed indeed.

'Ah, so was Rajiv,' Koder said.

'He was here?'

'Yes. And he brought along his wife Sonia.'

The Gandhis had come to Cochin several years ago as tourists. Rajiv Gandhi was still a pilot for Indian Airlines then. They visited the synagogues in the area in the company of the Koders. Sonia Gandhi, a collector of antiques, stopped off in a curio shop not far from the Koder home. She fancied a Chinese porcelain plate, but Shabdar Koder thought the store-keeper was asking too much for it. He tried to bring the price down, but the seller would not budge.

'Why don't you come and see our collection?' Gladys Koder said to Sonia Gandhi.

The Gandhis stayed for tea. Sonia Gandhi liked a particular porcelain item, and the Koders said they gave it to her. Was it from the Ming period, or the Tang period, or even the later Ching period, I asked, for porcelain items from any of these eras – but particularly the first two – would ordinarily be extremely expensive. The Koders smiled and declined to answer my question.

'Charming couple they were,' Shabdar Koder said. 'I remember clearly Rajiv telling me he wasn't interested in politics at all. Of course, in those days his younger brother Sanjay was still alive and everybody thought that he would succeed Mrs Gandhi. Who could have predicted this bizarre turn of events?'

'We think that Rajiv has a really good future ahead of him – but he must act fast to get rid of corruption in government,' Mrs Koder said. 'What a mandate! What a golden opportunity!'

I asked the Koders what future they saw for Cochin's Jews.

'What future?' Mrs Koder said, slowly and so softly that I had to edge closer to her on the damask sofa we shared. 'The Jews here have no future. We are a dying community. We can hardly even call ourselves a community any more. You know, I really miss our numbers. There used to be so much laughter here, and joy and good living. Then one by one the families started leaving. Now we feel so alone. Those of us who have remained here are old and lonely.'

Soon their married daughter might leave for Israel, the Koders said. Then what?

They told me that one reason why emigration from Cochin accelerated was that families couldn't find husbands for their daughters here. There was a fourteen-year period when, strangely enough, only girls were born into Cochin's Jewish community. Emigration did not occur because of any anti-Semitism in Cochin. In fact, the Koders said, India was probably one of the few places in the world where Jews lived in complete harmony with non-Jews.

I asked about the synagogues in Cochin. Who supported them? Shabdar Koder said that the synagogues were maintained through income generated from rental properties around Kerala that they owned; but there hadn't been rabbis at these synagogues for many, many years, he said. The community couldn't afford them. Any theological or social disputes that arose in the community were referred to rabbinical authorities in Jerusalem or Britain.

'Our synagogue services have been hit very badly,' Shabdar Koder said. Jewish custom calls for a quorum at religious services of at least ten men above the age of seventeen. It was often difficult to raise such a quorum, Koder said.

'We are a people of the past here,' he said. 'It is ironic, isn't it, that we Jews prospered in India, we were always a part of the society here, we were never ill-treated – and now we are disappearing from the one country where we were always secure.'

CHAPTER TEN:
THE NEW INDIA

A whole new generation of professionals has sprouted and succeeded in India since I first left Bombay to study at an American university. Whenever I visit Delhi or Bombay or Madras or Hyderabad or Calcutta these days, I sense the electricity in the air, the crackling of creative tension generated by the ambitions and efforts of the young men and women who came of age professionally in the last twenty years.

During my travels through India, I found that a new generation of highly motivated, achieving Indians was making its presence felt in the country. Many of these men and women received their higher education abroad, and then resolved to return home and take on the system and work in India. They could have readily found a slot in Western professional society, but for various reasons they did not want to be part of that society. A prominent example is a 42-year-old man named Sam Pitroda. He left India to seek his fortune in the United States, made his millions there as a businessman, then decided that he would return to India to create what he calls a 'technology revolution'. He gave up his US citizenship and re-settled in Delhi. Pitroda's plans, among other things, called for the introduction of computerized technology at every level of government in the country, and using modern marketing methods to expand such programmes as child immunization. He so impressed Rajiv Gandhi that the prime minister made him his technology adviser.

People such as Sam Pitroda represent a reversal of the much-publicized 'brain drain' that has resulted in thousands of bright Indians settling abroad because they could make more money overseas and work in jobs they would never be able to get back home. The political aspirations of the post-independence generation have certainly found expression in the ascendency of Rajiv

Gandhi to the prime ministership of India. Most of Gandhi's closest friends went to college in either Britain or the United States, and they are now in a position to influence the country for many years to come. Even if Gandhi were to lose the election in 1989, I think that the impact of this generation in politics, commerce and culture will continue to be felt in the country.

Still, examples like that of Sam Pitroda do not constitute a tide. Indian expatriates aren't yet returning to resettle in their homeland in very large numbers. The West still lures thousands of young, ambitious Indians who feel that the environment for achieving personal success abroad is generally far more open and lucrative than in India. The 'brain drain' still continues.

If there is a high priest of this so-called 'brain drain', it is an American by the name of Allen E. Kaye. I have known him for many years, and this time I ran into him in Bombay. He had come to India on a business trip, his fifteenth in ten years. Kaye is an immigration lawyer who specializes in assisting Indians, of whom more than 20,000 emigrate to the United States each year. In addition to these men and women, at least 100,000 others travel to America annually for holidays or short business trips. The visa applications of another 100,000 Indians are turned down every year by the American Embassy, among other things on the grounds that once in the United States they would stay there permanently.

(The United States permits no more than 270,000 'immigrants' from all over the world to enter the country each year; there are six so-called 'preference' categories for these immigrants. No country can send more than 20,000 immigrants annually. There is, however, no overall numerical limit on close relatives that American citizens may bring in every year as immigrants to the United States. And each year, too, several hundreds of thousands of people are allowed in as refugees. For the past decade, more than 750,000 people in all these categories have been coming into the United States every year. The highest number of immigrants to the United States each year is from Mexico, followed by the Philippines, China and then India.)

Each time he is in India, Kaye gives lectures on American immigration. It would be no exaggeration to say that he is the most popular foreign lecturer in India today. Kaye concentrates on cities such as Bombay, Delhi, Calcutta, Madras and Ahmedabad, from where his clients mostly hail. These cities have large pools of

unemployed, or underemployed, educated men and women who
are frustrated because there seem to be so few good jobs to go
round. Tickets to his lectures cost the equivalent of $2.50. The
lectures, of course, help widen Kaye's clientèle; he charges the
equivalent of $12.50 for brief consultations (in Indian terms, this is
a tidy sum – 175 rupees, or more than many Indians make in a
month).

Kaye finds himself working sixteen-hour days when he is in India.
His Indian work helps him in New York, and vice versa. The
Indians who seek his help here invariably seek his professional
assistance there. Moreover, one Indian talks to another, and so,
with the possible exception of Rajiv Gandhi and maybe the film star
Amitabh Bachchan. Allen Kaye is the most popular man in the
600,000-man Indian community in America today. His column for a
weekly newspaper called *India Abroad*, which is published in New
York by an enterprising Indian expatriate named Gopal Raju, is
probably the publication's most read feature. I introduced Raju to
Kaye; they subsequently started an association that has proved
mutually profitable. Kaye's column results in considerable business
for him, and other immigration lawyers envy him for it.

Kaye holds his consultations in the lobbies of the luxury hotels he
likes to stay in. People sometimes knock on his door in the middle
of the night to ask questions. He is surprisingly good-natured about
such intrusions, and so is his wife, Agneta Palmblad, who usually
accompanies him to India. When I saw Kaye in the marble lobby of
the Taj Mahal Hotel in Bombay one afternoon, he was holding a
durbar! At least a dozen people had lined up in one corner awaiting
their turn to meet him; the hotel receptionists occasionally looked
at Kaye, no doubt wanting to obtain some advice themselves. Kaye
did not dispense much good news: the United States government,
he told his callers, was making it harder each year for foreigners to
come and work in America. Even doctors and nurses, once welcomed with few reservations, were now finding the 'green card'
(a permanent visa-cum-employment document) more and more
elusive. His listeners, ever optimistic, did not seem fazed. The lure
of America is very strong indeed.

I asked Allen Kaye whether his work was in effect damaging to
India's well-being in the long run.

'I don't see this flow of people as a brain drain,' Kaye said. 'It is
not that India is being deprived of skilled services. There are more

engineers and doctors and scientists than are actually needed in India today. The people who want to leave are those who often cannot get decent employment here because of the competition. Or they are people who can get more challenging and more financially rewarding work in the United States. In some cases, they are far too overtrained for Indian conditions. Some who go to the United States as students often stay there because they acquire skills that cannot be easily used in a still-developing society like India.

'But no one forces people to leave India, or to stay abroad,' he added. 'Besides, they can always return if they want to.'

Sudha Messerly Pennathur is a woman who falls into both of Allen Kaye's categories – she has 'left' India, and she keeps returning to her motherland.

A little less than five years ago, having just turned forty, Pennathur decided that she wanted more from life than shipping jeans. She was making $150,000 a year as manager of the women's merchandise division of Levi Strauss, and was already the most senior woman in the $3 billion West Coast company. Despite her impressive record in boosting sales, however, she had her suspicions about being able to rise higher in a male-dominated hierarchy.

More to Pennathur meant realizing her dream of consummating a marriage between the mass-merchandising techniques she had excelled in at Levi Strauss and the exquisite artisanship of her native India and other Third World countries. Not for her those oh-so-cute items created by tribal weavers or silversmiths that are displayed in small, high-rent boutiques. What Pennathur had in mind was hard commerce catering to the general public.

Coincidentally, the 'Festival of India' – which was sponsored in some 200 American cities during 1985 by the Indian government – proved that the market existed for a stylized adaptation of traditional jewellery and handicrafts. Ordinary Americans had become enthusiastic about that ancient country's art and artisanship. That festival had followed a successful year-long celebration in Britain of Indian culture – an extravaganza of exhibitions, fairs, department-store sales, and media colloquia. Pennathur knew she was uniquely positioned to exploit the scene because her twenty years as a marketing specialist with Levi Strauss and other companies, such as Carter Hawley Hale and Allied Stores, had engendered a comprehensive understanding of American tastes and how to cater to them.

So she sold one of her two Californian homes and ploughed the tidy profit of $250,000 into her nascent business. She had already established an excellent network of contacts in the American retail world, sources she did not hesitate to tap. She combed the country to assess her potential market, and then travelled to India to find artisans capable of producing her interpretations of American consumers' requirements.

And the result? Orders worth $350,000 in her first six weeks.

Pennathur hasn't looked back. Sales for 1988 were more than $1.5 million – or almost a third of the total value of jewellery exported by India to the United States annually – and next year's volume may be double that figure. Pennathur's business, which is wholly owned by her, has no debts, and she realizes a profit of as much as 60 or 70 per cent of sales. The high profit margin is the result of low overheads; warehousing and freight costs are relatively minimal because her goods are seldom imported in great bulk. Pennathur admits that in a more volatile business such as textiles, for example, she would have to do six times as much business to make the money she does from her current sales. Her inventories are financed from her profits.

Pennathur's distinctive, handcrafted Indian-made jewellery, scarves, handbags, artifacts and home furnishings are not only featured in such fashionable stores as Saks Fifth Avenue and Neiman-Marcus. Some of the 600 items that Pennathur turns out – especially those created from antiques – are exhibited at the Metropolitan Museum of Art in New York, the Los Angeles County Art Museum, the Smithsonian and the M. H. de Young Museum in San Francisco. Seven departments at Seattle's fabulous megastore, The Bon, sell her products, and several stores in Britain stock her products, including Selfridge's. Pennathur's markets will soon include other European countries, Australia, and Japan.

Her big customers cannot stop raving about her. Says Richard Marcus, former chairman and chief executive officer of Neiman-Marcus: 'Sudha is a creative wizard. She is able to take traditional products, give them her special twist, and adapt them appropriately for the world's biggest market – America. She not only has ideas, but also the ability to deliver on time. And dealing with her means greater efficiency for our operations, because she is her own buyer and puts together her own collection. All we do is to place orders and edit.' Indeed, the chain recently opened yet another boutique featuring her brand called 'Designs by Sudha', this one in its Chicago store. The Asia Society has highlighted a collection of Pennathur's designs in New York. Not bad for a woman with no design background. 'It's how creative you are in marketing that is much more important than how creative you are in design,' says she.

But her commercial success is only one part of the Sudha Pennathur story. Pennathur understands the importance of theatre in what she does. She had prodded India's lethargic government bureaucracy into being a partner in her ventures. The Indian government transports master craftsmen across to the United States to give live demonstrations of their art – such as jewellery-making – at department stores where Pennathur's goods are displayed. This costs Pennathur nothing, since the Indians pay for the air fare and the stores pick up local expenses, but the events generate a great deal of attention for her. And what does the government get out of this? Nothing immediately, of course, but the expectation is that the master craftsmen's appearances will stimulate sales that in turn will fetch India valuable foreign currency.

As notable an achievement is the employment and encouragement she has given to scores of languishing master craftsmen in India's villages. (There are more than 16 million artisans and weavers in India, according to Rajeev Sethi, director-general of the Festival of India agency in Delhi.) She has taught them a new philosophy – to create their art for more than art's sake. Pennathur has persuaded them through her imaginative designs and sales that craftsmanship, however ancient, need not be constrained by tradition. Her blunt but practical message to artisans is: 'Export, export, export!'

A Marxist would look at Pennathur and denounce her as a clever merchant capitalist ripping off Indian peasants – which is why development economists in droves are throwing out *Das Kapital* and returning to *The Wealth of Nations*. The money she pays these underemployed artisans does more to raise their standard of living and enhance their self-respect than all the programmes ever devised by Delhi bureaucrats and politicians.

Pennathur prefers dealing directly with artisans themselves. The problem in dealing with established Indian jewellers and handicraft suppliers is often that the high domestic demand dampens their enthusiasm for adapting to overseas markets, says Pennathur. Merchants who are unwilling to change design styles for the Western market frequently take the easy way out and export loose cut-and-polished coloured stones, for instance – nearly $165 million worth last year. Thus, the Indian craftsmen have what amounts to a foreign-exchange override on Pennathur's success. Less tangibly, but more importantly, links – knowledge, contacts, information – are being established between a developing country's producers and a developed economy's consumers. Were it not for Pennathur, how would the craftsmen of Jaipur know what appeals to the women of Park Avenue and Russian Hill?

To sustain her network of artisans and suppliers overseas involves travelling from her luxurious San Francisco home to the remote reaches of India, Morocco, Mexico, South America, China and the Far East. It means forever being on the lookout for new sources. It means ensuring that artisans continue to manufacture artistic wares, but those that are in accordance with the standards of shoppers at the luxury stores she caters for. In other words, they should be exotic but not too exotic or impractical for everyday use. 'Just a touch of colour, a delicately drawn, clean outline, gemstones perfectly interspersed – these things can transform ancient artisanship into high fashion jewellery for the American woman, or into furnishings for her home,' says Pennathur.

Thus, the traditional fancy brocade-and-silk sarees of south India were reincarnated as shower curtains in Pennathur's collection. Intricately inlaid designs from Moroccan leather chairs were integrated into American-style dining-room furniture. She used lapis lazuli, black onyx and pink quartz from China, Taiwan and Hong Kong for pendants and large brooches made out of beaten silver in Bombay. The floral patterns of Moslem craftsmen from the Middle East and central India were used to decorate pill- and card-boxes. The colourful geometric patterns of *shamianas*, or wedding tents, were adapted for dainty handbags, big beach bags, bedspreads and tablecloths.

'I translate very elaborate ethnic designs into the very bold and contemporary looks that the Western world is looking for,' Pennathur says. 'But I do this by using existing artisan skills in India. At first I encountered resistance from many artisans. They were simply unfamiliar with meeting Western-style deadlines, or they couldn't understand why I chose a colour that wasn't used traditionally. Often, Indian artisans think that the more the detail on a piece of jewellery, the more beautiful the product. And so the piece is sometimes overdone – and therefore unsaleable in the West. I try and combine beauty with utilitarian function, so that my products have commercial value. I always say to my artisans, "Trust my judgement." We haven't gone wrong yet.'

A case in point was when she came up with a new design for a *meenakari* necklace, consisting of enamelwork on silver and an overlay of 24-carat gold. A grizzled old artisan in a Rajasthan village in western India insisted that the garnets and cubic zirconian stones be set in enamel of traditional green, turquoise and beige. Pennathur said that a necklace with so many colours would look too busy for American tastes and that, in any case, many American women didn't like green in their jewellery because it made their pale skin look yellow. Pennathur wanted the enamelwork done entirely in maroon. The artisan finally gave in and made the mould. More than 500 of those *meenakari* necklaces have since been sold at $250 each.

Such necklaces, and other jewellery and household items, are made painstakingly, one at a time, by the craftsmen. Most of Pennathur's jewellery, for example, is made in Jaipur by such well-known craftsmen as Sardar Kudrat Singh, a Rajasthani Sikh. The intricate silver inlay work is done by another renowned artisan, Yaqoub, who lives in Hyderabad. Mohan Lal Soni, a Jaipur painter, does miniature paintings for her, which Pennathur sells in shops at the Metropolitan Museum of Art, among other places. Artisans are paid on a contract basis by her, and they earn the equivalent of between $500 and $1,000 a month each – which, at the current exchange rate of Rs. 14.75 to the American dollar, is a formidable income in India.

Pennathur's success, of course, is premised on the fact that Americans and Westerners are willing to spend more on jewellery and accessories which come from the Third World. And increasingly, large American department-store chains are willing to spend heavily on promoting this premise. For example, J. C. Penney, the big US retail chain, launched a three-week $35 million promotion in 1988 of Indian-made jewellery, household effects and personal accessories. More than 900 of Penney's 1,400 nationwide stores –

including 500 of its biggest ones – hosted the India event. Under Penney's policy, foreign promotions are usually decided upon by headquarters, which then 'sells' the concept to the chain's outlets. Buyers from company headquarters – which enjoyed 1986 sales of $14.7 billion – select items and then pitch the merchandise to local outlets, which then decide what to buy from headquarters. Penney brings in $30 million in retail goods from India through importers, and expects to increase the figure to $70 million.

To be sure, imports of hard-crafted jewellery and handicrafts from the Third World are not a recent phenomenon – although never has the volume and commerce been so high. Back in the 1950s, Jim Thompson, a burly American adventurer, travelled to Thailand and started exporting Thai silk and hand-made brass statues, woodcrafts and other goods to the US and elsewhere. Today, the Thais send more than $25 million worth of such goods annually to the United States. The Philippines is another popular source for American stores. A New York- and Massachusetts-based company called Peabody International imports more than $1 million in furniture made from rattan and other natural fibres. These goods are made by Filipino craftsmen in rural areas, and are popular not only in America but also in Britain and Western Europe.

One of the most recent entrants into the artisan-export business is Honduras, whose craftsmen now sell more than $150,000 in earthenware, terracotta plantpots, mahogany and corn-husk goods to American stores. Credit for this goes to a Farmington, Connecticut organization called Aid to Artisans Inc. Clare Brett Smith, president of the ten-year-old non-profit-making company, says that it received a $500,000 grant from the United States Agency for International Development to develop the crafts industry in Honduras – which Washington sees as a geopolitically strategic country in Central America, and one whose domestic economy needed to be revived.

Mrs Smith's group first identified 200 products that Honduran villagers could make, then set up a privately run export company to despatch these to the United States. The organization also enlisted the help of a private group in Elizabeth, North Carolina to promote the sale of the Honduran artisan-made goods in this country. Aid to Artisans, which Mrs Smith says believes 'in a totally market-oriented approach to selling Third World artisan-made goods', ensures that 71 per cent of the revenues from sales in the United States goes back to the Honduran artisans. The organization is currently working with artisans in Indonesia, Somalia and Belize to create specific items to meet the requirements of the American consumer.

'The important lesson in promoting Third World artisan exports is that no one can go it alone,' says Mrs Smith, who imported handicrafts herself for many years before selling her business to join Aid to Artisans. 'The Third World artisan can never make it in the Western market without someone there helping.'

Aid to Artisans concentrates on helping these artisans to sell to gift stores. Sudha Pennathur has been successful on a bigger scale and in a different market. The key thing for both is, as Pennathur puts it, 'to keep our fingers and ears on the pulse of the market-place. The trick lies in finding new uses for old techniques and products. There is nothing, no matter how ancient, that you cannot keep re-interpreting – and selling.'

Sudha Pennathur belongs to the 'New India' – she is an Indian who has recognized the export potential of the country's awesome ancient heritage. In the modern world of hi-tech and hard market-ing techniques, she has ably and amply demonstrated that resource-fulness can always be the key to commercial success, especially if you have a unique resource to begin with. 'For me that resource is India,' Pennathur says.

More than fourteen years ago, a young man with an engaging smile and a British degree in accounting returned to his home in Delhi from London. He was the son of rich parents, and it was taken for granted that he would join the family business. His father was a distributor of films and also owned a printing plant.

The young man decided instead that he was going to revolution-ize Indian journalism. It was quite a leap from the world of figures to the world of words. But just as Sudha Messerly Pennathur figured that the Western jewellery market was ripe for raiding, this young man thought that Indian journalism was poised for plucking. The country's big newspapers were like aging dinosaurs, and the leading news magazines, once fiery and enterprising, had become toothless tigers. Journalism did not pay well, it no longer attracted the energetic and enthusiastic, and some practitioners – among them editors whose writings 'influenced' the masses – seemed to have been seduced by their political patrons.

So the young man, with no journalistic experience, started a bi-weekly news magazine called _India Today_. What Aroon Purie /970 has done since is the success story of Third World journalism.

'We were there at the right time,' he says.

The initial print-run of his magazine was 5,000 copies. Now it sells more than 475,000 copies per issue, and has an estimated readership of 4.5 million. There is a Hindi-language edition of _India Today_ that is equally successful. These two editions make _India Today_ one of the most widely read journals in the world. (The circulation of India's daily newspapers, and there are some 5,000 of them, is estimated to exceed 50 million. Most people don't know this, but more English-language books are published in India each year than in any country except the United States. The indigenous press is flourishing as never before, a sign of increased literacy.)

Purie's magazine has colour pages, is stylishly slick and is characterized by punch-packed prose and tight editing. It looks, in fact, like a clone of _Time_ magazine, a description that must irritate Purie, who says: 'My main criterion is readability.' The contrast with the country's English-language newspapers couldn't be greater: these papers, rooted in the staid style of the British press of the 1930s, are dull and grey for the most part. There are few feature articles; the emphasis is on pronouncements by politicians. Editorials are mostly ponderous; opinion pieces are loaded with jargon. Few newspapers are brightly laid out – the idea is to pack as much type in as possible, with little regard to style and visual appeal.

India Today has spawned a crowd of imitators in India, where people genuinely believe that imitation is the best praise. Indeed, even daily newspapers have started to introduce better graphics, catchier headlines and punchier prose. The magazine's belief is that, irrespective of the efforts by Third World leaders to force Western news organizations to portray their states more positively – efforts that have assumed sinister dimensions in such international forums as Unesco, which has advocated a 'New Information Order' – journalists in developing countries have a special obligation.

This obligation involves better coverage of their culture and societies by their own media – coverage that is disinterested yet compassionate, pithy but professional, comprehensive and, yes, objective. These are criteria that Purie acknowledges do not generally characterize publications in developing countries, where journalists are often inhibited by the heavy hand of government. *India Today* reports on the colour, clangour and confusion of India. It reports on the political shenanigans, the sophistry of policy-makers and planners, police brutalities in remote villages, the growing awareness of peasants about the inequities of India's caste and class structures, the mounting aspirations of the burgeoning middle classes. And it reports on the men and women in this land of 800 million people who are working quietly to bring about economic and social change.

The magazine's attitude toward the country's politicians is iconoclastic, but both Purie and his associates say their publication has rarely been subjected to government harassment. Not long after Indira Gandhi's assassination in October 1984, Purie wrote in his magazine about what it was like to cover the prime minister:

Mrs Gandhi never made it an easy job for the Indian media. For one thing, she was distrustful of most Indian publications and treated the domestic press with a certain disdain. For another, her tremendous energy made it difficult to keep up with her. What she, a lone woman, could achieve in a working day, a clutch of coordinated reporters couldn't effectively cover.

She may have had her difficulties with the media, but it is to her eternal credit that after her return to office in 1980 it was her stated and practised policy not to interfere with the free functioning of the press. *India Today* carried several stories extremely critical of her policies and governance, but not once was any pressure, direct or indirect, official or unofficial, brought to bear on the magazine to toe the line or desist from publishing anything. True, she declined to meet representatives of the magazine either for formal interviews or informally. But on the few occasions on which her government took exception to what *India Today* had published, the criticism was public, not covert.

There are those who suggest that one way the magazine was able to flourish despite its often critical coverage of the Gandhi administration was by rarely attacking Mrs Gandhi herself. Indeed, in the fourteen years since *India Today* was launched, the prime minister was featured on the magazine's cover no fewer than thirty-five times – often enough to raise some charges of partisanship. (Sanjay Gandhi turned up six times on the cover, and now Rajiv Gandhi has appeared more than a dozen times as well.) Purie responds that Mrs Gandhi was, after all, India's leading politician and generated more news than anyone else; topicality demanded the attention given to her. I think that implicit in what Purie says is admiration, however grudging, for Indira Gandhi.

'It is said that the American presidency is the most powerful job in the world – the most difficult must be to rule the world's largest democracy,' Purie says. 'It was a job that Prime Minister Indira Gandhi did at considerable personal sacrifice with seemingly effortless grace, style, stamina and, above all, with guts. For more than fifteen years, she was a living symbol of India. In spite of its differences with her, the magazine held her in high esteem – not just as the country's prime minister but also as a politician of accomplishment, a leader of unmatched stature and on the whole a remarkable human being.'

Topicality has demanded that Purie and his staff of sixty men and women pay close attention to world issues – specifically those that affect developing countries. Issues such as the transfer of technology, Western aid, and the North–South dialogue are written about far more regularly in *India Today* than in most Third World publications. Special correspondents in Washington, London, Bonn and Paris report on topics involving Indian and Third World interests. There are few sacred cows at *India Today*. Corruption in developing countries, autocratic and abusive rule, the self-indulgence of those in power – these topics are tackled with the same enthusiasm Purie displays in sending his small staff of writers to investigate charges of torture or extortion by some local political chieftain. Not long ago, a young reporter named Shekhar Gupta uncovered the presence of camps in the southern Indian state of Tamil Nadu where Sri Lankan Tamils agitating for a separate state were being trained by Indians in guerrilla warfare. Gupta's story received worldwide attention.

'I am generally surprised by our success,' Purie says with a smile. 'I'm surprised at the way our magazine took off the way it did. We did things differently – we were younger and not rooted in the often-stifling traditions of Indian journalism. Our growth therefore was attributable to the fact that we were in the right medium, we did things differently – and to the special circumstances around us when we started.' He says this slowly, patiently, as if to ensure that his interviewer gets it just right.

Aroon Purie's sister, Madhu Trehan, endorses this assessment. She was the one who prepared the original layout of the magazine, and it was she who helped to recruit the young staff. 'The joke used to be that we ran a kindergarten at *India Today* – so young was our staff in those days,' Mrs Trehan says. Every word had to be cleared with the government censors in those days because of the Emergency that Indira Gandhi had imposed on the nation. This meant huge delays in production. One day, Trehan waited several hours for her layout artist to turn up and then decided to go to his house to find out why he was so late; the artist had no phone at home. When she got to his house, she found it locked. A guard explained that the artist, Pinaki Dasgupta, had left that morning for Calcutta: he was to be married the next day.

'I don't know how we put out the magazine in those days,' Madhu Trehan recalls. 'But it seemed to come out as if by magic.'

In fact, at one point problems seemed so awesome that her brother said, half jokingly and half in despair: 'There's no way this can make any money, mate!' But make money the magazine did, and now both Aroon Purie and Madhu Trehan are very wealthy in their own right. Madhu Trehan feels that *India Today* reflects the new, aggressive mood of India. The magazine is nicely positioned to explore and explain the 'new' India of Rajiv Gandhi, she says.

Perhaps in recognition of this, the prime minister granted his first formal press interview to *India Today* soon after he took office. Of course, Rajiv Gandhi couldn't have been very pleased with a number of other articles that have since appeared in Purie's magazine. Some of these stories questioned Gandhi's judgement, and indeed even his grasp of politics and understanding of world affairs. Some Gandhi aides have privately chafed at the fact that *India Today* has given disproportionately prominent coverage to the prime minister's opponents, such as V. P. Singh of Uttar Pradesh. These aides complain that while *India Today* is quick to point to allegations of wrongdoing involving those around Rajiv Gandhi, the colourful and often financially suspect lives of some Opposition leaders haven't been subjected to the same sort of scrutiny.

There is general agreement, however, that what helped establish the magazine was its reporting on the alleged excesses of the Indira Gandhi government during the 1975–7 Emergency period. That was when Mrs Gandhi, citing a national breakdown of law and order, suspended the Constitution and jailed scores of political opponents and journalists. Following the 1977 elections, which Mrs Gandhi lost, the Janata Party government appointed judicial commissions that turned up evidence of excesses, and *India Today* thrived on the material.

'Our real contribution lies in the kind of magazine *India Today* is – it is not obliged for its existence to anybody.' Purie says. In short, Purie is independent, his magazine is independent. He does not buckle under political pressure, nor under commercial strain. His independence has made him rich, and his wealth has strengthened his independence. To my mind, Purie has been one of this last decade's most extraordinary achievers in Indian society.

Characteristically, he rarely talks about his own drive and single-mindedness. When *India Today* was started, Purie's family owned one of the most modern printing plants in the country. His father had established himself as one of Delhi's most successful business-men and film distributors, but it was Aroon Purie's ambition that has accounted for the phenomenal growth of *India Today* – that, and the efforts of the young acolytes that he attracted to his magazine, men and women with a flair for writing and a keenness to examine the social issues of the day. His sister Madhu Trehan is now branching out into TV journalism with the production every month of a two-hour video cassette news programme, which is proving very popular.

I had gone to see Purie at his office above a warren of shops in Delhi's Connaught Place. The office had a bank of four phones, which kept ringing merrily, a red carpet, a mustard-coloured sofa, three chairs, a circular table in lieu of a formal desk, a high-backed chair for the publisher, and a globe. There was also an enormous panel painting. His office had a sun terrace, which was edged with plants. Purie had been visiting his printing plant in suburban Faridabad and the late-afternoon traffic had held him up, but when he arrived he seemed none the worse for the drive. He wore a tweed jacket, a blue shirt and blue tie, dark blue trousers and well-polished brown shoes. He looked fit.

It had already been a remarkable week for him. A poll that *India Today* had commissioned came divinely close to predicting the exact number of seats that Rajiv Gandhi's ruling Congress Party would win in the December 1984 election to the national Parlia-ment (the Congress won an unprecedented 401 out of 508 seats contested). Envious competitors had sniped at him, and some particularly ill-informed writers of a national newspaper criticized his magazine's poll and political reporting. Ordinarily, Purie

[handwritten margin note: 1989 CONG (I) wins ~ 200]

ignores attacks on *India Today*; but in this instance he felt that his publication had been so smeared by this newspaper that he responded with a strongly worded letter to the editor, which the newspaper published.

'We do what we do well, and we do it on a regular basis – we are not a flash in the pan,' Purie told me. 'We display consistent quality in terms of talking about what's happening in the country. This has created a certain heightened awareness in decision-making circles. Part of our constituency is the government élite – and they are affected by how we interpret events. Ours is a magazine they can trust and rely on to be consistent in its reporting and judgements.'

Aroon Purie does not, however, see himself as a campaigning journalist. 'Our job is to reflect what is happening in society and in the world around us, to clarify issues and developments,' he told me. 'We hold a mirror up to society. If you concentrate just on crusading, you tend to lose your edge – you then tend to dilute your basic function, which is to inform. Journalism is only an indirect instrument of social change.'

It seemed to me that *India Today* had demonstrated a unique ability to interpret and perhaps even influence the vast changes occurring in Indian society. The most dramatic recent change, of course, was the overwhelming victory of Rajiv Gandhi and his ruling Congress Party.

'No question that his election represented a tremendous change in our country,' Purie said. 'It was a psychological change as much as a political one – the change represented by a leader who is of post-freedom-movement vintage. So I feel positive about that. I think Rajiv Gandhi can set the tone, the direction, for government – he is in a position to do some streamlining. If he does that, just that and nothing else, he'd have achieved something remarkable. But I don't think he can turn the economy upside down, or root out corruption.'

Supposing Prime Minister Rajiv Gandhi asked Aroon Purie to write him a memorandum, a word or two of advice concerning the press and government, what would he say, I asked?

Purie smiled, and paused to wipe his glasses.

'I would urge him to run an open government – a government that is open to the press and is not anti-press,' he said, presently. 'Rajiv doesn't have to like the press, but I think there should be a certain respect towards the media. This hasn't happened in our government. Either you're with them or totally against them – that's how our leaders perceive the press. This must change. I would emphasize to Rajiv that a free press is an essential part of democracy – so let it flourish. In India, government can make life difficult for anyone owning or running the press through the control of newsprint, the wage boards, accreditation of correspondents covering government, approval of government advertisements – there are lots of measures in the hands of the Indian government which serve as handles for harassment.

'And I hope Rajiv improves access to government departments, and to the prime minister's office itself. The entire government machinery needs to be opened up to the press. It would lead to a much better functioning of our system.'

Supposing, I said, Rajiv Gandhi were to ask him to ghost-write a speech that the prime minister wanted to deliver before a gathering of the high and mighty of the Indian media. What would the publisher of *India Today* say in his draft?

Again a pause, again a slight smile.

'I think the press in India to a large degree exercises power without responsibility,' Purie said. 'The press should be more aware of their responsibilities. Their performance has affected their credibility. The general newspaper coverage of this recent election was not the papers' finest hour. I also think that there must be a greater degree of professionalism in the press. There must be better pay, there must be more professional norms and standards, there must be a self-policing system.

'If Rajiv Gandhi were to address the press, I would expect him to urge the press to be socially responsible. I don't think that the press can or should be a vehicle for change – but its primary responsibility must be to tell as fairly and fully as possible what's going on in our society. Of course, the press should encourage the writing of stories that are positive. But for journalists the prime objective must be to be good journalists and not social activists. The moment they see themselves as agents of change, that leads to role confusion and to political identification.'

He had lived through an extraordinary time in India, a decade of tumult and great anxiety and so much turbulence. What was the one thing about India – and about being an Indian – that really moved Aroon Purie?

There was no hesitation, no pause for thought this time.

'What really impresses me is that India is a working democracy,' he said. 'That is a remarkable achievement, especially in a Third World country. I am a free man, I have choice, I have options. I really believe that the roots of democracy are quite deep in our country. I don't think that anybody can rule India by dictatorship. Democracy is the only way to rule this country – democracy is deeply imbedded in our consciousness.

'You know, that really thrills me. I have been travelling a great deal around India, and I see that in spite of so much poverty, in spite of the fact that there hasn't been great improvement in the lives of most people – in spite of all this, there is the determination to vote, to exercise their options, there is the clear feeling that their vote would make a difference. The feeling that the ordinary individual matters has filtered down to the grassroots, to the remotest village. I find this heart-warming. I think this is priceless.'

Aroon Purie, in a sense, represents both the old and the new in India. His initiative and imagination resulted in an extraordinarily successful product, *India Today*. He pioneered a hard-hitting and highly readable kind of magazine journalism. But his own education reflected the traditions of upper-crust Indian families: he attended the Doon School, an exclusive prep school that was started in 1935 by an Anglophile Indian who modelled it on the English public school system. Purie's contemporaries included Rajiv Gandhi. Then he did what sons and daughters of the wealthy generally did – he went abroad for higher education; specifically, he went to the country that was long favoured by India's élite because of the old colonial ties, Britain.

The two universities in Britain most popular with Indians were Oxford and Cambridge – what in the salons of Bombay and Delhi and Calcutta and Madras is called the 'Oxbridge connection'. The 'connection' has resulted in an extraordinary old-boy network in India. If you went to Oxbridge, it is reasonable to assume that you are doing well in contemporary India: Rajiv Gandhi attended Trinity College, Cambridge; he worked at a bakery during his leisure hours to make extra cash, for even though most Indian students got handsome allowances from their families, Britain was becoming increasingly expensive. Gandhi's close friends from Cambridge days remain his close friends: among them is Suman Dubey, the former editor of Purie's *India Today*. Oxbridge alumni include captains of industry, top journalists, powerful bureaucrats, filmmakers, and now the inner circle around Prime Minister Rajiv Gandhi.

'We were a privileged lot,' says Rahul Singh, now editor of the *Sunday Observer*, based in Bombay, and a Cambridge graduate. 'The fact that we went to Oxbridge in the first place meant that we were privileged. Virtually all of us came from highly affluent families, and affluence meant influence. It helped that we came from this privileged background – and it helped that we went to study abroad.'

The sons and daughters of the privileged still go abroad, but they do not only go to schools and colleges in Britain. Increasingly, they are enrolling in American universities. There are an estimated 50,000 Indian students currently in the United States, and their numbers are increasing. Not all receive scholarships, especially with many educational institutions in America desperately short of cash these days; but they seem to manage all right. Wealthy parents in India have a way of converting non-convertible Indian rupees into hard foreign currency.

In recent years, as India's political and military ties with the Soviet Union have deepened, more and more scholarships have been given by Eastern bloc countries to Indian students. Thousands of Indians have received graduate degrees from the Patrice Lumumba University in Moscow. These Indians travel to Eastern Europe mainly to study engineering and technical subjects; and once their education has been completed, they return to India – there is no such thing as emigrating to Communist countries! There are thousands of such students who return to India every year, and I wonder how they will influence Indian professional life in years ahead. While it is fashionable to talk about Western values and sensibilities that Oxbridge graduates bring home with them, the number of Indians who have studied in Eastern bloc states and who return home is getting larger each year. Will we soon hear about the 'Lumumba connection'?

I met a young man in Bombay whose parents weren't wealthy enough to finance a foreign education for him. Some Indians want to grow up and become pilots; Mahendra Jain always wanted to become a doctor. His parents were thrilled with his ambition. There were no doctors in Jain's family, who were conservative Gujaratis, members of the merchant community. His father and grandfather had run a small trading business, but it was clear that the family wouldn't be able to send Jain to a foreign medical school as he had hoped. Jain did well in high school and fared well, too, at the K. C. College in Bombay. When he applied to medical school in Bombay, he was turned down time after time.

'Weren't your grades good enough?' I asked Jain.

'They were superb,' he said. 'But that wasn't the problem.'

The problem was that virtually every medical school demanded 'donations' of up to five lakh rupees, or the equivalent of $50,000, merely to grant admission. There were four major medical schools in Bombay, and each year they took in 560 new students between them. But each year more than 70,000 applicants competed for these seats. Because it is considered very prestigious to have a doctor in the family, many parents manage to raise such incredible sums just to assure their progeny of admission to medical school. By the time graduation comes around five years later, a medical education will have cost the equivalent of another $100,000 per student.

Mahendra Jain decided that he was not going to subject his parents to the humiliation of even trying to raise the bribe money. He applied to the A. M. Sheikh Medical College in neighbouring Karnataka state, where no 'donations' were required for admission. He worked during his time off at the college's laboratory, and graduated with honours.

'All right, so I don't have a degree from a prestige university,' Jain, a lanky, earnest-mannered man, said to me. 'But so what? At least I have a medical degree. I am qualified to be a doctor. I have the power to shape my future with my abilities. Experience is the main thing.'

He served a gruelling internship at a hospital in Bombay. The hours were continuous; there was no such thing as weekends off. Mahendra Jain had no time for recreation. He lived in a spartan dormitory within the hospital's compound. Hard work may not kill a twenty-four-year-old medical graduate, but it certainly gave him deep dark circles under the eyes and a sickly pallor.

'I knew what I was in for when I made the decision to become a doctor,' Jain told me. 'All this hard work may tire me out, but it doesn't faze me. I know very well what this experience is worth – I know that the pain I suffer today is going to reap me rewards tomorrow. India could dispense with politicians, it can even do without Indira Gandhi – but a country of 800 million people will always need doctors. And good doctors, too.'

The grind yielded gold. Jain met a wealthy patient who was so impressed by the young physician that he offered to help him set up a private clinic. His benefactor asked Mahendra Jain specifically to set aside time every day to attend to poor people who couldn't afford medical care. Now Dr Jain is nicely settled, with a new wife and a flourishing practice.

I mentioned my encounter with Mahendra Jain to another Bombay physician, Rusi H. Dastur. I told Dastur that I was horrified to hear about the extent of bribery that was allegedly involved in the field of medical education.

'Things were very different in my younger days,' Dastur, who is about sixty years old, said. 'There wasn't this kind of money around in those days. Who had five lakh rupees available? In those days if you wanted to become a doctor, and your grades were good, you secured admission to medical school. It was as simple as that. None of this "donation" business. But in today's India we seem to have lost our basic sense of honesty, we have lost our values. There is a price for everything. Corruption is everywhere. There is a growing need for doctors, but no one thinks of starting more medical schools. Why? Because when you artificially create an economy of shortages, you create more opportunities to line your pockets. Corruption in modern-day India does not grow at the grassroots – it filters down from above.'

Rusi Dastur is one of the best-known physicians in India. His fame is attributable to the fact that he has written several best-selling books on stress; he also contributes a column on health matters to *The Times of India*. He has stimulated public aware-ness about health issues; his books, newspaper columns and lectures have influenced policy-makers in government to draft major reforms in India's public health-care system. Dastur has pioneered the practice of social medicine in India. One of his on-going themes is that in Third World countries social ailments like poverty, squalor and unemployment are the main causes of medical illnesses. Stress isn't the monopoly of corporate executives, Dastur says; it is increasingly to be found among India's urban and rural poor – only, most doctors don't consider it fashionable enough to recognize this.

Over the years, Dastur has pressurized state governments to pay more attention to the environment. He has persuaded authorities in Bombay, for example, to institute adult-education courses in public hygiene. He has led campaigns for safer drinking water. He has personally led teams of medical students to clean up slum areas. He has visited the offices of cabinet ministers and important health officials to warn them that India's traditional governmental emphasis on curative medicine must change to greater focusing on preventive medicine.

I visited Dastur in his office on Marine Drive. It was late in the evening, and through his window I could see the setting sun streak the Bombay sky with ochre. Dastur, a tall, lean man with an ever-ready joke or aphorism, seemed fresh despite the fact that his first appointment with a patient had been at seven o'clock that morning. An article he had recently written on the need to eliminate corrupt practices in the country's medical schools attracted so much attention that strangers kept telephoning him to volunteer their views.

'I've reached an age where I can afford to dispense some advice,' Dastur said, after I'd asked him what he would suggest to Prime Minister Rajiv Gandhi concerning a new health policy for India. I had been told by someone who knew Gandhi well that he followed Dastur's health columns regularly. Until he became a professional politician in 1980, Rajiv Gandhi had been a professional pilot – and in that job he'd had to cope with stress. Now, of course, there were even more stresses in Gandhi's life.

He would advise the new prime minister, Dastur said, to concentrate on promoting health education around the country. Why not a sophisticated nationwide advertising campaign?

'Such a campaign could focus on the need to change some of our everyday habits,' Dastur said. 'I mean, spitting on the road is a favourite national pastime of Indians. How many people are conscious of how unhygienic a habit that is? Or this business of coughing without covering one's mouth. How many people realize that this is the best way to transmit disease-causing germs? We are a nation of spitters and coughers – 800 million coughers and spitters. I'm calling for heightened public awareness concerning health and hygiene.'

Dastur believes that the Western nations have by and large conquered infections not because of antibiotics but because of better nutrition, improved water supply and sanitation. The medical problems of these Western societies now are largely such problems as heart attacks, strokes, and cancer – which is why there is a growing need for sophisticated gadgets such as scanners and sonograms for diagnosis and treatment.

'But in India we are still grappling with infections,' Dastur said to me. 'We have not solved the problems of nutrition, clean water and improved sanitation. There is therefore no place for the instituting of sophisticated and costly allopathic medical care uniformly throughout our country. Besides, the problems in our cities and in our villages are entirely different. People who live in rural India still rely on ancient systems of medicine for the cure of their simple ailments – allopathy is alien to them.'

Dastur points out that 80 per cent of India's physicians are urban-based, while nearly 80 per cent of the country's population lives in rural areas. Because these urban-trained doctors have become accustomed to sophisticated equipment such as scanners and sonograms, many of them are reluctant to relocate to the villages. But Dastur believes that in India's villages the need is not so much for more doctors as it is for social workers. He advocates the establishment of a system of 'barefoot doctors', or paramedics, ← Garwal just as neighbouring China has done. These barefoot doctors are picked from the village community and trained to handle minor ailments common to rural life. Such personnel, Dastur feels, will be able to communicate effectively with fellow villagers.

He also advocates tackling on a war footing the pressing problems of nutrition, safe drinking water and sanitation. Dastur told me that more than 200,000 children under the age of five become blind each year because of the lack of a proper diet. It is also estimated by Unicef that more than 75 million Indian children go to bed hungry each night. Better nutrition from an early age will produce a better race of Indians, Dastur asserts, instead of the sickly millions who populate the country. He feels that India can ill-afford lavishing expenditure on high-tech medicine.

'The problems which India faces today are overpopulation, malnutrition, high infant mortality, pulmonary tuberculosis, hepatitis and diarrhoea,' he said. 'The basic need therefore is not for advanced technology but an appropriate one suited to the indigenous ethos. It is not intensive care that is the need of the hour but extensive care that can fan out across the length and breadth of the country. Instead of a hundred new body-scanners, why not establish a thousand new family-planning and family-health centres?'

Rusi Dastur is among a growing number of Indians urging Rajiv Gandhi to pay greater attention to issues concerning the quality of life for ordinary citizens. Not long ago, thousands of farmers from several states descended on Delhi to petition the prime minister. Their demands were not only about such matters as price incentives and more water for their crops; some of the farmers also expressed alarm over environmental deterioration, soil erosion and the depletion of forest cover.

I met a farmer called Shivram Ghate one afternoon outside Lonavla, a town about ninety miles from Bombay. Lonavla is situated in the hills of the Sahyadri Range that hug the western coast of India; many affluent Bombayites have weekend homes here. The train ride to Lonavla is quite pleasant, with the route taking the traveller through two dozen tunnels and over scores of bridges and embankments. It is also a delightful journey for the motorist because the two-lane highway from the coast winds through forests and valleys.

My parents had long ago bought a small bungalow here, and as a child I enjoyed spending holidays in the cool heights of Lonavlā. My memories of the place were of country roads cutting through verdant fields, and of hills across which ran thick woods that seemed inviting, not intimidating. I was never much of an explorer of woods, but my father often took me for long walks. We would stop and talk to peasants who chopped firewood, and we would occasionally visit local farms where maize and rice were cultivated. They were happy days.

When I visited Lonavla this time, it was an altogether different place. I hadn't been here for more than a decade, largely because my trips to India from New York were always hurried. I was truly startled by the changes that had occurred in the intervening period. Gone were the quiet streets of a small town; modern Lonavla was an urban metropolis, a chaotic city of mushrooming housing developments and roads through which lurched fume-belching trucks and cars. There were rivers of people everywhere. Beggars thronged street corners; even the quaint railway station was filled with urchins who clutched at travellers' sleeves and demanded money.

Perhaps the most startling change was how denuded of forests and greenery the whole place now seemed. Beyond the edge of the urban sprawl, during a walk through what remained of the countryside, I encountered Shivram Ghate, the farmer. He was furrowing the soil on a tractor. Ghate was a small, sinewy man of about fifty; his skin was tanned deeply; his face was lean and his teeth stained from a lifetime of chewing tobacco and *paan*, the betel leaf popular with Indians. Ghate wore a *dhoti*, the Indian sarong, and a loose shirt; Hindi music played from a small cassette-recorder that he had placed in a compartment below the dashboard of the tractor.

Ghate seemed like a typical farmer from the area. He told me that his income was about 10,000 rupees a year – about $700 – and that he had inherited his acre of land from his father. I said that his income appeared much higher than that of most local farmers – but Ghate pointed out that the amount was considerably less than the average annual income of a clerical worker in the area. Because of rising costs of fertilizers, seeds and farm equipment, he was getting to keep less and less of his income each year, Ghate said. Fortunately, he added, his three sons were grown up and worked as factory hands in Lonavla; they supplemented his income.

What was his most pressing worry other than inflation?

'Water,' Ghate said in Marathi, the local language. 'What farmers could once use freely is now channelled to these new houses that are rising here.'

It was a complaint one hears from farmers all over India. Because of the seasonal nature of India's rainfall, even areas of high rainfall have problems of water supply. Although the country has abundant resources in its river systems and groundwater supplies, these resources are likely to remain constant while demand increases with population growth, industrial expansion and continued urbanization. The World Bank estimates that 80 per cent of India's 576,000 villages are without safe and clean water supply, and only 50 per cent of the country's urban population has ready access to drinkable water.

Up until recently, the Bank notes, Indian water development has involved a disjointed, uncoordinated pursuit of several different goals by the central and state governments: development of industrial and municipal water-supply systems; hydro-electric power, flood control, irrigation and water-quality control. Pollution of water resources continues to be a major problem as well: several

British television documentaries in recent months have shown how the mighty Ganges river has been polluted heavily with industrial and other wastes dumped into it in places such as the holy city of Benares. (A massive clean-up programme of the Ganges has been initiated, involving local and international agencies, but this is certainly going to be a daunting and long-term task.) Indeed, almost 80 per cent of India's rivers are said to be polluted by sewage and industrial and agricultural wastes.

In recognition of all this, Rajiv Gandhi's administration announced in September 1987 that it was initiating a 'National Water Policy' to harmonize central and state governments' pro- grammes. Already, however, various experts are voicing doubts about the capacity of the national government to implement the policy.

When farmers such as Shivram Ghate talk about water problems, they usually also allude to wider problems concerning land-use and soil erosion. India is about two-fifths the size of the continental United States; about 70 per cent of the country either has short crop-growing seasons – less than 179 days – or inadequate growing seasons, or dry spells that generally last almost twelve months. Poor biomass cover, caused by long dry seasons that are followed by intense monsoon rains lasting two to four months often cause severe soil erosion. This is exacerbated by poor farming practices. Moreover, says the Hyderabad-based Centre for Energy, Environ- ment and Technology, about a quarter of the 65 million hectares under irrigation suffer from waterlogging or salinization.

World Bank officials say that 'wastelands' in India are increasing at an alarming rate. 'Wastelands' are defined as unproductive land or areas producing crops substantially below their potential. More than 45 per cent of India's potentially productive land area of 266 million hectares is now categorized as wastelands – with the figure edging upward. Why this increase in wastelands? Because of the burgeoning demand for fodder and fuelwood, overgrazing, lack of natural regeneration of land, soil erosion, salinity and desertifi- cation. Indians often point to the wastelands of the Middle East or the Sahara as dramatic examples of how nature and man combine to alter the environment, transforming more and more areas into desert. But the process has intensified in India as well.

I mentioned to Shivram Ghate the changes I had seen in the local natural scenery. Lonavla was no longer bucolic.

'What can I tell you?' he said, shrugging. 'Everybody wants to chop away our trees for fuel. Our local government people say we must use efficient electric stoves for cooking – but then the power supply here is unreliable. So people prefer to rely on their fuel-wood.'

It is not just in Lonavla that India's forest cover is being depleted at an alarming rate. This is happening virtually everywhere in the country – even in the foothills of the great Himalayas. The reasons? Rapid population growth, lack of fuel for domestic cooking needs and intensive cattle-grazing in forests. India has only about 0.33 per cent of the world's forests – but it has 16 per cent of the world's population, 19 per cent of the global cattle population, 50 per cent of the buffalo population, and 20 per cent of the world's goats.

While government statistics assert that India's total forest cover is more than 74 million hectares, surveys by international authorities suggest that the actual figure is half that amount. The World Bank says that most of the fuelwood extraction in rural areas is illegal or unrecorded. And the problem with illegal chopping of trees is that no trees are planted to replace those that are destroyed. Such activity results in loss of wildlife habitat, and in soil erosion, siltation, floods and droughts.

I asked Ghate about the government's much touted 'social forestry' projects. He wasn't familiar with them, he said. I explained that in these projects – supported by various international donors such as Britain, Canada and Sweden – farmers are encouraged to plant trees on their own land, and villagers are urged to develop community woodlands and also to rehabilitate denuded forests. Ghate asked me how this programme was working out, and I said that I did not know. It was perhaps too early to tell, I said.

'But at least a beginning seems to have been made,' the farmer said, smiling, as he restarted his tractor. 'In India, however, we start a lot of things and often never carry on.'

As I left him, it occurred to me that he could have been speaking about Rajiv Gandhi's own oft-declared commitment to preserving the environment and protecting India's natural resources. The prime minister heads India's Ministry of Environment and Forest, and has pushed through several pieces of legislation calling for tough action against those who damage the environment. But India is a vast country and its governmental machinery simply cannot be the sole taskmaster. In the final analysis, the cause of environmental protection must be sustained by the grassroots efforts of community leaders, businessmen and peasants themselves. The cause calls for massive national cooperation, not from the top down but from the bottom up. And I am not so sure that Indians are often inclined to galvanize themselves to work for causes whose rewards aren't easily forthcoming.

CHAPTER ELEVEN:
OPENING THE DOORS

Mindful of the mistakes of his socialist predecessors – who included his mother and grandfather – Rajiv Gandhi has increasingly opened up India to foreign investment. At the same time, he has urged greater competitiveness within India's private sector, offering a wide array of tax incentives. And finally, the youthful prime minister has tried to eliminate a licence system that has seriously hampered industrial productivity.

Now, you would think that such moves would be heartily welcomed by Indian businessmen who have long grumbled about bureaucratic red tape. Well, not quite, Ashok Birla told me one day.

He is the head of one of the five major branches of the Birla Group, India's richest industrialist group. He is a slim man, so trim in fact that he looks almost boyish even though he is fifty years old. 'India's businessmen hate the idea of fierce competition,' he said. 'They may complain about the endless regulations, but the fact is that our big business houses have done quite well despite the red tape. They have carved neat niches for themselves. They have mastered the art of making bureaucracy work for them.'

Birla should know. No one has been more adept at co-opting the bureaucracy and overcoming India's Licence Raj than the Birlas. There are more than 200 Birla companies in India, Britain, the United States, Malaysia, Indonesia, the Philippines, Kenya and Nigeria – producing, among other things, cars, synthetic fabrics, textiles, steel, paper and edible oil. In each of these enterprises, the Birlas traditionally own between 25 per cent and 45 per cent of the shares. The net assets of the five major interlocking Birla family branches exceeded $4 billion.

That figure may well be on the low side. Why? Because in a high-taxation Third World country such as India, true family wealth – measured not only in identifiable corporate assets, cash, foreign holdings and property, but also in jewellery – is usually a closely guarded secret. Few industrialists disclose their true worth; the last thing they want is to pay more under India's prohibitive tax system. According to the Indian government, annual sales of the 200-plus companies owned and run by the group in India are around $3.5 billion.

When her colonial rulers left forty years ago, India's British Raj was quickly replaced by the Licence Raj – a bewildering maze of government decrees, directives and regulations affecting what and how much industries could produce. The system spawned widespread corruption as bureaucrats and cabinet officials demanded hefty bribes to approve permits. India nevertheless became the world's tenth largest industrial power – a tribute to the resourcefulness of its entrepreneurs.

No entrepreneurial group has been more successful than the Marwaris, a small, closely-knit community originally from the western state of Rajasthan. And the most prominent members of this community have been the Birlas.

Long before independence, they dominated the Indian industrial scene. Indeed, the group's founding patriarch, G. D. Birla, made his first million as a textile manufacturer by the time he was thirty. He turned down a knighthood because of his friendship with Mahatma Gandhi, India's spiritual leader, and joined forces with Gandhi and Jawaharlal Nehru in their campaign to oust the British. Birla donated tens of millions of dollars to the independence movement. (Some say it would be no exaggeration to put the figure at $500 million in Birla contributions to the Congress Party from the time of the Raj to Rajiv's era.) The revolutionaries who later became Free India's powerful élite would reward the Birla family with lucrative production contracts.

After the British left in 1947, the Birlas' power and wealth grew rapidly – not least because of their proximity to those in power, their continuing contributions to the ruling Congress Party whose socialist creed did not get in the way of cosy relations with selected capitalists, and their mastery of the ways of the labyrinthine Indian bureaucracy. So accomplished are the Birlas in manipulating the bureaucracy, and so vast is their network of industrial intelligence, that they frequently obtain pre-emptive licences, which enable them to get approvals for new ventures that may not even be on the drawing-board, or increased production quotas that consolidate the Birlas' grip on a particular industrial sector. Result? Competitors are seriously crippled.

Although the late G.D. Birla made his fortune in textiles, his successors have greatly diversified the family's business interests. There are five major Birla branches today: Bombay-based Aditya Birla, G.D.'s grandson and heir, heads the most powerful group, including such huge concerns as Hindustan Aluminium (which Kaiser Aluminium originally helped to set up); Calcutta-based G. P. Birla runs Hindustan Motors, which has long enjoyed a near-monopoly in the car industry and whose hardy Ambassador sedan's chassis and engine designs have remained virtually un-changed since the 1950s) K. K. Birla owns the powerful *Hindustan Times* in the capital city of Delhi; S. K. Birla recently bought Chloride India, a battery-making enterprise, from a British cor-poration, and also purchased an edible-oil refinery near Chicago; and Ashok Birla, also Bombay-based like Aditya and S. K. Birla, owns, among other businesses, steel mills in India, and textile and paper-making enterprises in Thailand, Indonesia, Nigeria and East Africa.

The Birlas' growing foreign holdings are said to be worth nearly $1 billion (the Indian government's calculation of the Birlas' net assets does not reflect the group's international enterprises). Birla employees total some 125,000, and 600,000 Indians depend directly for their livelihood on the Birlas' industries. Like most Marwaris and unlike many Indian industrialists, the Birlas do not lead flamboyant lives. They are strong on family values, are often abstemious, and rarely marry outside the Marwari community. The Birlas traditionally spend millions of dollars each year on building Hindu temples, often ones where the presiding deity is Laxmi, the goddess of wealth.

Their piety does not preclude ruthlessness in business. The Birlas have evolved a unique indigenous management style known as *partha*, which roughly translates as 'costing'. Under this system, the top executives of all Birla companies are required to construct a profit-and-loss statement at the end of each working day. What for?

To enable the Birlas to monitor closely their companies' performance and thus exercise family control. 'There are no pretentions to corporate democracy in Birla companies,' says Dilip Thakore, editor of *Debonair* magazine and one of India's most respected business writers. 'The Birlas' management style is patriarchal and authoritarian. The boss is a godlike figure. The Birlas value loyalty and high performance, above all, and they generously reward their best performers.'

Some rewards. More than a hundred of their top managers – most of whom come from outside the Birla family – have become millionaires in their own right. A lot of the financial rewards are reported to be under-the-table cash payments.

How are the Birlas viewed by their fellow Marwaris? Mohan Shah, a New York-based textile importer, has this to say: 'They are India's strongest champions of free enterprise. The Birlas have shown that their uniquely indigenous, non-Harvard-Business-School management style works in their homeland and even abroad. Their success has not diluted their traditional orthodox family values, and in today's fast-changing India that's saying a lot.'

It was Mohan Shah who had introduced me to Ashok Birla some years ago. Unlike his publicity-shy cousins and uncles, Ashok is a prominent fixture on the social map of Bombay, Delhi, London and New York. He admits that he enjoys spending money as much as he enjoys making it. Both come easily to him. Indeed, Ashok has dazzled many a disco-goer with his footwork.

Birla says he is fully supportive of Rajiv's Gandhi's liberalization moves. And why not? He has done as well by the evolving economic liberalization as he has by the Licence Raj. In January 1988, Birla entered into an agreement with Minnesota Mining and Manufacturing to produce electronic components and tapes in India. The new company is being called 3M Birla Limited; one of Ashok's India-based units, Zenith Limited, will hold 40 per cent of the equity, 3M another 40 per cent, and 20 per cent is being offered to the public. He recently made a deal with S. G. Warburg, the investment bankers in London, to start a new investment fund called Mercury India. Its objective will be to induce expatriate Indians to invest in India's economic expansion.

Other Birlas have been similarly active. Aditya Birla, Ashok's cousin, recently announced that his part of the Birla Group would invest some $2 billion in petrochemical plants. But Prime Minister

Gandhi's push towards greater competitiveness in Indian industry has meant that at least one Birla enterprise, Hindustan Motors, is being rapidly challenged by rivals.

'My belief is that greater competition will energize India,' Ashok Birla says. 'If that means that some industrialists must take a harder look at their practices and prepare to face greater challenges to their power – so be it. In the long run, India can only benefit from such things.'

I fully support Birla's beliefs about the need for greater competition. The problem with India's economic policy, however, is that it has seldom been consistent. Even Rajiv Gandhi has occasionally sent out mixed signals about 'liberalization'. He sometimes talks about strongly promoting the private sector; at other times he resurrects talk of India's 'commitment to socialism'.

The unfortunate fact is that in a developing country such as India, few politicians can politically afford to be openly pro-business and pro-free-enterprise. In the political metaphor of India, 'rightist' policies have come to be labelled as 'right-wing' – and 'right-wing' means an unsavoury association with the CIA. I realize that this is specious logic; but it is quite amazing how the left has exploited this. Of course, 'socialist' politicians rarely acknowledge the massive corruption and management inefficiencies that their policies have encouraged – when vast resources are controlled by government administrators who aren't accountable to the marketplace, abuses proliferate.

People like Ashok Birla know the weaknesses of the system. They can work around them. They also know that no matter what nice noises Rajiv Gandhi and some of his pro-private-sector people might make about free enterprise, the political reality of India is unlikely to change much. Which is to say, national economic policy will sputter along, much in the manner of everything else.

The Birlas are popular with the Indian government not only because of their contributions to the ruling Congress Party but also because of the foreign exchange they generate through their exports. Rajiv Gandhi often emphasizes the fact that enhanced export-promotion will strengthen world perception of India as a country capable of competing with the very best rivals in the global bazaar. He truly believes that Indians are capable of producing first-rate goods in any enterprise – whether it be textiles, jewellery, computer software or shoes – and that those goods must be marketed more aggressively and imaginatively in the world's markets.

Those markets are getting increasingly tough to crack. Many Western nations are raising protectionist barriers: the efforts of certain members of the United States Congress to push through protectionist legislation are well known by now. Other countries are discriminating more subtly against Third World producers; still others are openly sceptical of the ability of countries such as India to turn out goods of internationally acceptable quality.

And there is criticism, sometimes veiled and sometimes loud, that Indians often do not deliver what they promise. Indeed, there have been some cases where Indian manufacturers set out to capitalize on highly lucrative 'one-shot' deals without concern for the consequences. This meant that foreign buyers of Indian goods, dissatisfied with their particular experience with such sellers, then chose to look elsewhere. In other words, the sins of a few get-rich-quick entrepreneurs have unfairly tarnished the reputation of many conscientious and diligent producers.

The fact is, however, that Indian exporters are overwhelmingly scrupulous in their dealings with foreign clients. The fact also is that they can match anybody in the world in their manufacturing skills and in the quality of their goods. And the fact is that they can meet delivery deadlines and legal obligations.

Without meaning to be boastful or bumptious, let me cite just one field – diamonds. India now exports $2 billion worth of small cut-and-polished diamonds each year. Indian exporters have displaced Belgian and Israeli suppliers to become the biggest source of such stones in the US market. Indians are also expanding India's clientèle in Europe and the Far East. Why? Because they deliver the best products, they deliver them faster, and they deliver them at prices that no one can match. There are currently some 2,500 diamond exporters in India, and business has never been better.

The realities of international trade are essentially simple, and they remain constant: whether the buyer is an American or a Briton or a Frenchman or a Russian, he is looking for quality, he is looking for affordable prices, and he is looking for speedy delivery.

From the supplier's perspective, this means that production conditions at home must facilitate the meeting of those demands of foreign clients. Indians must give customers not what they want to give them but what they wish to have. The domestic environment in India must lend itself to enabling its entrepreneurs to compete vigorously – and on equal terms – with exporters from other countries. To put it another way, the Indian producer must be able to match his foreign competitor in price, quality and delivery.

It has often been remarked, for example, that while India's annual exports are about $12 billion, the figure for much smaller nations such as Taiwan or Singapore is two or three times higher. The plain fact is that India has a larger labour pool, and a bigger reservoir of human and natural resources; Indians also have a remarkable ability to adapt themselves to producing whatever the market desires. Indians have the capacity to leave Taiwan and Singapore and Hong Kong and even South Korea far behind. If these countries are the 'tigers' of Asia, then India can become the 'lion' of the region. Indeed, India also has the means and the manpower to become a dominant exporting power. India is already the world's tenth biggest industrial power; it can, with the proper promotion, push its way more dynamically into the world's rich markets. With the proper mix of incentives and environment, India's exports can double or even triple in two years. Is that being over-ambitious? I don't think so.

The recent measures undertaken by Prime Minister Gandhi to liberalize India's economy are obviously very encouraging. The business community in India, and non-resident Indian businessmen all over the world, welcome and applaud the young prime minister's determination to free the economy from the maze of controls that have often impeded – and inhibited – industrial growth. Indians laud him for his dedication to improving the lot of ordinary people, and they are strongly behind him in his efforts to eradicate poverty. The important thing is going to be the sustaining of these efforts.

From the exporters' point of view, however, 'liberalization' does not mean only a lifting of constricting controls. A free-enterprise economic framework, in order to properly co-exist with a productive public sector, must be assured of the appropriate transportation network, adequate power and water supply, and relevant import allowances. Many export-conscious entrepreneurs rightly complain about the high cost of financing the import of raw materials. They say that domestic rates of such financing are frequently higher than the international financing rate. This means that at the very root, their production costs per unit are already above those of foreign competitors. Similarly, power is sometimes prohibitively expensive in India, and its continuous supply is far from assured; water supply, too, is often unreliable. Cargo facilities are so woefully inadequate in major commercial areas that bottle-necks are the rule rather than the exception. No wonder then that almost 15 per cent of India's manufacturing capacity lies unused every day.

In the competitive world of international trade, as in most other fields, perceptions often play a major role in determining success or assuring failure. In more than two decades of living abroad, my own experience has been that foreign customers overwhelmingly see India as a difficult place in which to do business.

It is not just a matter of power and water shortages. It isn't even a matter of bureaucratic hegemony. The logistics of doing business in most Third World countries, of course, are almost always formid-able and frequently capricious. Foreign – meaning Western – businessmen recognize this. What dismays them more, however, is the lack of consistency in a nation's economic policies and political pronouncements.

They are often disheartened by the time it takes for official business authorizations to arrive from Delhi, and by the inability of Indian representatives abroad to provide proper and quick re-sponses to foreigners' queries concerning the Indian business scene.

Many of these potential customers wonder why India doesn't mount a more aggressive public-relations campaign to woo more foreign business. Those of us Indians living abroad are more than willing to participate in such a campaign. Indeed, we are anxious to be part of a renewed drive to proclaim India's products and help generate new business for India in Western and other markets.

I must also emphasize the need for an on-going dialogue between the non-resident Indian community and Indian government of-ficials concerning the changing requirements of the world market. Such two-way traffic in communications would not only anticipate shifting global business trends, it would also enable Indian ex-porters to calibrate speedily their production skills and schedules to satisfy market demands.

Over the years, my foreign business friends – and also many of my fellow non-resident Indian associates – have raised troubling questions concerning the confidentiality of their proposals for economic projects in India. The gist of their complaints is this: when a new proposal is presented to an official Indian representative overseas, it frequently winds up on the desk of a competing Indian entrepreneur. Needless to say, this entrepreneur then takes it up. Of course, there can be a certain degree of exaggeration to some of these complaints. But aside from exaggeration and natural anxiety over an unborn project, this is the sort of complaint that the Indian authorities must be mindful of; and they must act with fairness and judiciousness where warranted.

Many of India's potential customers have asked why the Indian government doesn't allow fuller ownership of equity and property by foreigners. After all, they say, land isn't moveable: foreign investors are hardly likely to abscond with a piece of Bombay, or Baroda or Bhubaneshwar! But greater participation in land-ownership could well be one means by which India might attract greater investment in such favoured government projects as export zones. Similarly, foreign investors in export-promotion projects frequently express their dismay over India's foreign-exchange repatriation policies. Isn't there some way, these current and potential investors ask, by which fuller repatriation of honestly earned profits can be undertaken?

Domestic exporters could certainly use a break. For example, a recently announced scheme to permit nine new sites near Bombay for jewellery exporters was billed as innovative. But exporters need far more than just nine sites – even a hundred wouldn't be sufficient. The willingness and energy of these exporters to expand their operations mustn't be frustrated. Some of them could use land subsidies in order to compete better and to compensate for their own investment in the export zones. I have frequently been told by fellow non-resident Indians that they would be willing to invest in creating labour-intensive industries in India's economically backward and geographically remote areas. Such investment must be encouraged through active governmental consideration of the entrepreneurs' requirements concerning tax breaks, better infrastructure facilities and freight-factor alleviation.

Exporters are also anxious to see that trade and industrial disputes are quickly resolved. For instance, most exporters – and foreign importers as well – have occasional grievances concerning the quality of goods. Should there not be some sort of mechanism that would expedite the settlement of such disputes? After all, prolonging disputes translates into shortfall of revenues. Disputes are deterimental to everybody.

When we talk about accelerating India's exports, we are, in the final analysis, really talking about increasing employment in the domestic economy. Given India's population growth, and taking into account the surge in India's labour force (given the fact that more and more educated young people are coming of age politically), it is now more important than ever before to lay the proper foundations to accommodate the rising expectations of the work force. The best way to do so would be through economic expansion.

And it is precisely here that export-promotion can play such a critical role. The encouraging of exports will definitely have a multiplier effect in the economy; economic commonsense suggests that export expansion will help stimulate India's domestic economy, and eventually – as more jobs are created – the purchasing power of everyday Indians will surely increase.

'In the diamond business, the magic to becoming big is selling small,' Tushar Kothari, of Rajiv Gems Corporation, said recently as we walked briskly through the lunchtime crowds in Manhattan's midtown diamond district. 'We realized a long time ago that small would be "in", and so we prepared ourselves for the American market. Look at us now.'

Some sight. Capitalizing on the booming demand from Americans for affordable jewellery containing small, brilliant diamonds, the mild-mannered 43-year-old native of India has seen his business climb to annual sales of $25 million. His wealth, accumulated in just eight years, has enabled him to become a prime investor in a New York nightclub and in a travel firm. Among forthcoming acquisitions: a jewellery manufacturing plant and an engineering company in India. And Kothari, who not so long ago was a lowly electronics engineer with the Ford Motor Company in Detroit, has also become the main partner in a venture capital fund in New York.

Not bad for a kid whose forefathers came from the parched and dusty western Indian town of Palanpur, founded in 746 AD, some 350 miles from Bombay. Tushar Kothari is a Jain, a member of an ascetic, non-violent, vegetarian sect of some 4 million people. Many Jains are so opposed to killing in any form that they refuse to swat flies. In India the more orthodox wear white gauze masks so that they will not inhale and kill bacteria.

Various communities in India have traditionally pursued carefully defined occupations. The Punjabis are considered excellent farmers. The Gujaratis are traders and merchants, and the Tamils bureaucrats and administrators. The Marwaris are known as industrialists and moneylenders. The Jains had always served as accountants and administrators to the Moslem *nawabs* of Palanpur. From there it was a fairly easy step in the modern era to become experts in money-management. Ever alert to moneymaking opportunities, some of the Palanpur Jains discovered diamond cutting and trading almost a century ago.

Kothari is a beneficiary of that discovery. He is a self-made success, to be sure, but not out of the ordinary among Indians who sell diamonds in the United States. Along with Kothari, some 200 other Indians – all coming from the Jain community in Palanpur – have quietly worked their way into a position of dominance in America, which accounts for half the world's retail trade in small, polished diamonds. The diamonds they sell are mainly a half-carat each, going down to 400th of a carat – sizes that require extraordinary skill on the part of the cutter.

India, a country of 800 million people, has long possessed the biggest gems and jewellery industry in the world. But now Indian traders like Kothari and his clan deliver more than 50 per cent of the small, brilliant loose diamonds that American wholesalers buy each year – or almost a billion dollars' worth of business, and expanding by as much as 20 per cent annually. They provide more than 75 per cent of the stones used by mail-order catalogue houses and mass-merchandizers in producing jewellery items that retail between $50 and $500 per piece. The most active of these Indian traders pulls in more than $35 or $40 million a year; even the so-called 'briefcase boys' – those lone wolves who work on their feet, not out of heavily guarded diamond-district offices like Kothari – do business worth a million dollars and upwards.

And what is the secret of their success? Cheap but highly skilled labour in India, where rough diamonds bought in London are cut and polished; growing investment in machines and modern cutting methods that include laser technology; a worldwide network, often consisting of extended families, flowing out of Bombay headquarters and even encompassing Israel, with whom India has no diplomatic ties; negligible overheads; skilful pursuit of customers, particularly in such growing sectors as mass-merchandizing; and ruthless price-competition with traditional suppliers from Belgium and Israel.

Success hasn't come easily, of course. The traders started out a decade ago against the backdrop of an industry perception that Indian-cut small diamonds lacked world-class quality. But they convinced American wholesale buyers that Indian-made diamonds were marketable in the United States and could hold their own against stones cut in such traditional diamond centres as Antwerp and Tel Aviv. Indeed, the Indians showed that no one could more cheaply offer small, rounded stones under a half-carat. Their per carat price ranges from $50 to $1,000. (The average price of an Indian-cut diamond is $200 a carat; the figure for a comparable Israeli stone is $460.)

'Today, if you mixed Belgian and Israeli-cut stones with Indian ones, you wouldn't be able to tell the difference,' says Lloyd Jaffe, chairman of the American Diamond Industry Association.

Adds Jeff de Lange, of Haber-Worth Enterprises, who buys diamonds from India and markets them in the form of jewellery in the US: 'When these Indians first started doing business in New York, I thought, They're never going to make it here. Although they had the supply, their stones didn't have the quality and workmanship comparable to Antwerp or Tel Aviv. But now I'm in awe of them. They really improved their product, and they developed their market here with ready inventory and prompt, trustworthy service. The Indians supply us with stones whose price cannot be matched by the others.'

So active are these diamond traders that India has become the world's biggest exporter of small polished diamonds, exceeding Israel in carats sent out each year – and fast closing in on the dollar value of diamonds exported to the United States and other growing markets such as Japan, Italy, West Germany and Hong Kong. Last year, for example, India's diamond exports rose to 6.7 million carats from 5.1 million in 1985. The United States continues to be India's single biggest market. In 1986, the USA imported 2.9 million carats of polished diamonds under a half-carat from India; the value of these stones was almost $800 million. The comparable figures for Israel were 1.6 million carats, with a value of $550 million.

'India long provided the best diamonds to the world's royalty – and now Indians are providing the most affordable diamonds to the world's masses,' says Pravin Mehta, of Occidental Gems in New York. 'This is a perfect marriage of aggressive entrepreneurs and excellent artisans. And this marriage was consummated because we Indians saw a slot for ourselves in the United States. That slot consisted of a market which could cater to middle- and working class Americans who couldn't afford expensive, high-style jewellery.

'When we started out in America, we had nothing to lose,' Mehta, who was among the earliest Indians to begin trading in the United States, continued. 'Small diamonds were the hardest to cut, and the demand then was for the larger stones that the Israelis and Belgians had specialized in. We decided to go in for the roughs, the stones that result in small, polished diamonds under a half-carat. We knew even back then that there would be great growth in the American mass market – that, as affluence among the masses increased, people would be looking for affordable diamonds, not just stones from Tiffany's and Cartier and Harry Winston.'

Arun Bhansali, owner of Eurogems, recalls, however, that Indian traders encountered considerable prejudice from Jewish wholesalers in the United States. 'Since the Indian government loudly supported the Palestinian cause, this aroused a lot of emotions in the Jewish community here,' Bhansali, who was the first Indian diamond trader to set up shop in America back in 1966, says. 'Initially, at least, few Jews liked to do business with me. But I was able to convince them that I wasn't accountable for the actions of the Indian government. And eventually, the fact that I had a good, cheap product to sell, the fact that I delivered on time – this made the difference. I have never again met with prejudice of any kind.'

Today, more than 12 million carats, or 50 per cent of the world's rough diamonds for consumer use such as jewellery, are cut in India each year. Diamond exports constitute the biggest source of foreign exchange for India. India's annual export of $1.6 billion accounts for 25 per cent of the world total value of cut and polished diamonds. Diamond merchants such as Bhansali say that India's diamond exports could climb past the $2 billion mark in another two or three years. Increasingly, diamond cutters themselves are plunging into trading. This gives them higher profitability – as well as a sense of greater self-esteem for having successfully made the transition from cutting factories to the glamorous world of international trading.

Glamorous though that world may be, it certainly isn't without physical risks. Indian traders in the midtown Manhattan diamond district, in Detroit, and in Los Angeles, have been robbed, shot and even killed. This explains why, for instance, the offices of traders such as Tushar Kothari and Pravin Mehta are heavily reinforced with security devices. Despite the security risks in carrying around diamonds, however, Indian traders have refused to carry weapons to protect themselves – although some American traders do indeed carry guns. The Indians cite the precepts of Jainism, a religion that emphasizes non-violence.

Another frequently mentioned risk involves the nature of credit in the business. Unlike the garment industry, which has a rapid turnover, diamond jewellery is considered to be a slow mover in business terms – entailing high capitalization and extended terms of credit. This translates into higher financial risks for traders. The Indians have largely been able to tackle this by aggressively pursuing new customers so as to spread the risk. They have also had to resort to taking out insurance on marginal accounts, and to undertaking more sophisticated methods of credit evaluation. Despite these problems, diamonds are a very lucrative business indeed.

Pravin Mehta's instinct that the mass market for diamond-based jewellery would grow dramatically in the United States was borne out by the sales figures. In 1982, 14.7 million pieces of diamond jewellery were sold in the United States, amounting to $5.7 billion in value; by 1986, Americans would buy 18.3 million pieces, with a value of $10 billion, or just under 50 per cent of the value of total global sales. According to New York's Diamond Information Centre, the value of the 49 million pieces of diamond jewellery sold worldwide in 1986 was $24.6 billion.

Diamonds may be a girl's best friend, but a diamond-buyer's best pal these days is an Indian seller. Largely because of the cheap prices offered by the Indian traders to American wholesalers, the average price of a ring with a half-carat diamond has actually declined in the last seventeen years. The price in 1970 was $799; such a ring retails this year for $399. According to the Diamond Information Centre, such rings constitute the overwhelming share of the diamond-jewellery market – 52 per cent. The rest of the sales consist of necklaces, with a 19 per cent share of the market; earrings, with 20 per cent; bracelets, with 2 per cent; and 5 per cent in assorted miscellaneous items.

But price wasn't the only aspect of the diamond business to be touched by the Indian traders' aggressive salesmanship. So was the style of mass-marketed jewellery. Pravin Mehta notes that American jewellery designers jumped on the idea of easy, affordable accessibility to small, well-cut diamonds. This in turn inspired them to create jewellery with what in the business is known as the 'pavé' setting, and the 'channel' setting. The first type of setting creates the effect of a larger diamond surface through the use of several tiny diamonds; 'channel' setting consists of one diamond in a groove.

And what did these new styles lead to? Such things as tennis bracelets and necklaces – and the introduction of the anniversary ring, now one of the most popular items in the diamond retail business.

Edward Strauzer, head of a $2.5 billion mass-marketing jewellery business called Service Merchandise, says that although women are by far the biggest buyers of diamond jewellery, American men are steadily becoming diamond-oriented. For example, one-eighth of all diamond jewellery sold in 1986 was to males. Strauzer's company buys about $40 million worth of small diamonds from Indian traders each year. Lloyd Jaffe of the American Diamond Industry Association estimates that one-quarter of America's adult males own some form of diamond jewellery. Strauzer emphasizes that mail-order catalogues offering diamond jewellery are increasingly popular with men.

Riding on the coat-tails of India's diamond exports are Indian dealers who are busily selling coloured stones – blue sapphires, garnets, emeralds and rubies. More than 100,000 artisans work on cutting these gems in Jaipur, the capital of India's north-western state of Rajasthan. India now exports about $30 million worth of coloured stones annually, but less than 10 per cent of these exports are to the United States. (According to a report prepared by the Jewellers of America, an umbrella organization representing 12,000 jewellers, total imports of coloured stones and pearls last year was $101 million, with Hong Kong supplying $70 million worth of goods. Retail sales of jewellery containing coloured stones in 1986 was $1.1 billion, up by $100 million from the previous year.)

Will the success of the Indian diamond traders last?

Tushar Kothari, who was until recently president of the Indian

Diamond and Colourstone Association – which represents some 100 Indian traders – says that the main reason for the popularity of Indian diamonds in the American market has been the change in economic and demographic patterns. In other words, the growth in demand for cheaper jewellery has fuelled the demand for cheaper small polished diamonds. The Israelis so far haven't been able to compete in this category with the Indians because of higher labour costs and also because of tightening bank credit and the curtailing of government subsidies to the diamond industry in Israel.

Nevertheless, smaller manufacturers in Israel, seeing the potential in the United States, have begun to step up the production of small brilliants. Similarly, manufacturers in Thailand, China, Malaysia, South Korea and Hong Kong are jumping into the act. But because labour costs in these countries are considerably higher than in India, they may have a hard time in catching up with the Jains of Palanpur.

Ed Strauzer feels that the Indians may still be in for a battle with the newcomers.

Does that faze the Jains?

'We may be non-violent, but we are fighters,' says Pravin Mehta.

Unlike most Third World entrepreneurs who come to the United States to make their fortune, Ramesh Chauhan was already an immensely wealthy man in his native India by the time he set up a tropical fruit-juice business in New York six years ago. His family-owned business, Parle Exports, controlled 60 per cent of India's soft-drinks market, with annual sales of $200 million. Chauhan also had twelve beverage-bottling plants in the Middle East, Africa and Western Europe, with yearly sales of another $50 million.

So why come to America, the Mecca of the soft-beverage business?

'It's good insurance,' the 49-year-old Chauhan says, against political instability and economic downturns in the Third World. Moreover, a physical presence here means improved access to American technology, which benefits his other business interests. And, of course, there is the money to be made. Chauhan's initial investment was $100,000, matching that of his American partner, Dan Dunn, an Ohio-based businessman. They bought a small warehouse in Long Island City, installed equipment of Chauhan's own design (he holds an engineering degree from the Massachusetts Institute of Technology), leased a half-dozen trucks, hired a Berkeley whizzkid named Kartik Kilachand (who is a member of Mensa, the super-IQ society) to manage the business, and charged ahead. Within a year, sales of Chauhan's products totalled a million dollars. This year, sales are expected to climb beyond $3 million.

Chauhan does not compete directly against the giants of the conventional fruit-juice industry, such as the Beatrice Corporation (which makes Tropicana orange juice). He also decided not to tackle the cola market (his Thums Up is the leading cola drink in India). Chauhan concentrates instead on exotic tropical fruits like mango, papaya, guava and passion-fruit, which are popular in largely Spanish-speaking ethnic communities. His flagship brand, called Maaza, is available in ethnic as well as mainstream neighbourhood grocery stores. The product also seems to be catching on with college and high-school students, who are attracted by its low calorie and high fruit pulp content.

Even as he planned expansion in the US and in Britain, Chauhan kept commuting furiously between the United States and India, where he led a drive to prevent PepsiCo Inc. from entering the huge Indian market. Chauhan teamed up with two of his domestic competitors, contending that Pepsi will pose an unfair challenge to them because of its astronomical international resources and marketing advantages. Conceding a 'double-standard' where he feels free to compete in PepsiCo's homeland, Chauhan says that his company hardly poses a life-threat to the cola manufacturer, as PepsiCo would to him in India.

Ramesh Chauhan lost that fight, however. On 19 September 1988, following some three years of controversy, the Gandhi administration announced that PepsiCo would be allowed to establish food-processing plants, soft-drink operations, a centre for agro-research and an export facility in the Punjab. PepsiCo's collaborator would be the Tata Group, and the overall agreement would involve an initial investment of $17 million by the US company, whose annual sales are close to $13 billion. More than 20,000 new jobs would be created in the Punjab as a result of the investment. No doubt, in giving his approval, Rajiv Gandhi saw in this project a way of creating employment for the dissatisfied youths of that border state. Politics, as Ramesh Chauhan has ruefully found out, always influences economics.

For decades India prided itself on the fact that, almost alone among major developing countries, it had not piled up major foreign debts. That seems to be changing fast. Since October 1984, when Rajiv Gandhi became prime minister, India's overall foreign debt has grown from $23 billion to $35 billion.

Talat Ansari, a handsome, amiable New Delhi lawyer, was hired not long ago by the New York law firm of Kelley, Drye and Warren to advise Western clients wishing to do business in Asia. These days, however, the 38-year-old Ansari spends more of his time discussing the implications of India's mounting foreign debt. India, in fact, is already the fifth-biggest Third World debtor (after Brazil, Mexico, South Korea and Argentina). Most of India's outstanding loans are to multilateral institutions, but an increasing portion – some 18 per cent at the end of 1988 – is owed to commercial sources.

The government says that the cost of servicing the external debt was over $2 billion in 1987, or roughly 22 per cent of India's annual export revenues. Ansari believes that debt service is likely to be higher over the next few years. (Gandhi's 1988–9 budget proposed $5.3 billion in new domestic debt and $2.8 billion in foreign borrowings.)

Add to this the government's mounting domestic debt of about $125 billion. The Gandhi administration is thus faced with total annual debt costs amounting to almost 35 per cent of its current annual revenues of $32.3 billion. By comparison, debt service eats up an estimated 16 to 21 per cent of US government revenues.

Now, selling the domestic debt securities is no great problem, although the way it is done piles up future problems. Indian banks were nationalized by Indira Gandhi twenty years ago and are therefore a captive market for government paper. Long-term bonds – some tax-free – are also sold to the public at rates up to 14 per cent annually.

This is the kind of debt creation, especially when combined with prolific money printing, that can lead to runaway inflation. By the government's own admission, the inflation rate in 1988 was 9.8 per cent. Some private economists, however, view that figure with scepticism, claiming that double-figure inflation is already upon India. Each time I visit Bombay's teeming bazaars, for example, prices seem to have soared since the last visit. Mohan Shah says that the 'days of 100 per cent inflation may not be so far away'.

The root cause of the constant debt creation and rising inflation is the same as in Latin America and Israel: a highly unproductive public sector, supported by a hardworking but hamstrung private sector; mounting defence spending ($10 billion for 1988, an increase of $800 million from 1987); a sprawling, sluggish bureaucracy; and a national leadership which knows that state ownership of industry is a disaster but lacks the political courage to tackle the mess.

Since 1947, the government, under the intellectual influence of British Fabian socialists, invested more than $40 billion in some 250 public-sector companies. The net annual return on this? Barely 6 per cent pre-tax, according to Talat Ansari. A recent government estimate showed that of 189 state-owned companies surveyed, only 96 reached 75 per cent of capacity utilization; 48 companies did not even achieve a 50 per cent productivity target.

But instead of privatizing, the government's seventh Five-Year Plan (which began in 1985) provides for additional investment of $138 billion in public-sector enterprises. 'That's a big white elephant out there, doing very little of value for the economy,' says Ansari.

All this casts a dark cloud over the high hopes that many private British and US companies had for investing in India – even though India, under Gandhi, has been more hospitable to foreign investment than preceding governments. Gandhi welcomes such investment in chemicals, heavy machinery, high-technology goods, agro-industries, telecommunications and drugs. But now some of the foreigners are having second thoughts. The flow of equity into India has been less than $150 million a year since Gandhi became prime minister – at a time when China and other rapidly industrializing nations of Asia seem to be getting billions.

Rajiv Gandhi is well aware that the country's economic hopes lie in the private sector. But despite all rhetoric and occasional flashes of administrative resolve, Gandhi seems to be lacking the political will and clout necessary to tackle the bloated, privileged bureaucracy. With the current drift, the Indian economy could degenerate into a nightmare of inflation, unpayable foreign debts and rising domestic unrest.

CHAPTER TWELVE:
INDIA AND THE WORLD

The main hall of the United Nations General Assembly in New York City is massive. Whenever delegates assemble in the auditorium, the scene resembles some great international jamboree – which is exactly what General Assembly sessions often tend to be. The floor becomes a riot of colour and costumes, and the vast chamber resonates with the sound of a thousand tongues. If there can be said to be a collective living-room for the 160-odd nations of the world, then the General Assembly chamber is surely it. At one time or other, virtually every major post-war leader has come here to hold forth on topics ranging from the sublime to the bizarre. There are those who insist that the ghosts of some of those leaders still visit the Assembly Hall – Charles de Gaulle, Nikita Khrushchev, John Fitzgerald Kennedy, Konrad Adenauer, Lester Pearson, Winston Churchill, Harold Macmillan, Jawaharlal Nehru, Kwame Nkrumah, Gamal Abdel Nasser.

Those ghosts may not attend every General Assembly session. That might be a bit too boring these days. It sometimes seems these days that most sessions serve as a diplomatic pulpit for delegates, where rhetorical flourishes are often employed to disguise a lack of substance and thought. But the spirits from the past were surely present when, in late October 1985, heads of government and potentates from all over the world gathered to observe the fortieth anniversary of the founding of the United Nations. The main event, of course, was the birthday party – an extravaganza of banquets, cocktails and soirées. The main attraction, however, was a youthful man from India who had been his country's prime minister for barely a year at that point.

That man was Rajiv Gandhi. Whenever he came to the UN complex during his brief visit to New York, heads would turn and hearts would flutter. He looked handsome in his buttoned-to-the-neck Nehru jacket, he smiled a great deal, he was appropriately deferential to more seasoned world leaders who had come to the UN that autumn, and he made a couple of well-received speeches. Needless to say, media coverage of his trip was extensive and laudatory.

But then he suddenly seemed in a hurry to leave the birthday party – such a hurry, in fact, that his foreign-policy aides were left behind in a New York hotel. Gandhi had a plane to catch, one that made an unscheduled stop in Moscow. Indian officials later claimed that there was no more than met the eye to Gandhi's Moscow stopover. The joint statement issued by him and the new Soviet leader, Mikhail Gorbachev, was nothing out of the ordinary, yet another declaration reaffirming the dedication to global peace and security of the Soviet Union's staunch ally in the Third World, and of India's largest weapons supplier. Both men were reported to have discussed the prospects for the November 1985 summit that Gorbachev and Ronald Reagan had scheduled in Geneva. By being seen consulting with a major Third World figure at a time when President Reagan was hobnobbing mainly with Western Alliance leaders who had attended the UN birthday party, Gorbachev was scoring points in the propaganda battle before the summit.

Gandhi may not have intentionally wanted to become a player in Gorbachev's pre-summit manoeuvres, but his dramatic flight to Moscow pointed to his own concern for Soviet sensitivities, and to his need to reassure Moscow about India's incipient friendship with Washington. Indeed, there had been two Gandhi–Reagan meetings in 1985, and the two men were reported to have developed a warm regard for each other. In flying off to Moscow, Gandhi was nursing India's only reliable ally among the big powers. Moreover, India's relationship with Moscow was then – and certainly is now – enormously popular at home and enjoyed genuine multi-party support. The Soviets are seen as friends who stood by India when it mattered – during India's border conflicts with China and Pakistan. There is no great public clamour, no institutional pressure, no firm lobbying for deepening ties with Washington – and therefore no great compulsion for Gandhi (or any other Indian prime minister) to change the long-established Indian strategy of espousing non-alignment but veering leftwards in foreign policy.

To the casual outside observer, trips by Indian leaders to London or to Moscow or to Washington may mean little. But in the corridors and chancelleries of international power, where nuances of expression are delicately yet thoroughly analysed, the shadings and substance of what India's leaders say do indeed count a great deal. After all, India is not only the second most populous country in the world; it also enjoys unusually high prestige among those 127 countries that constitute the Third World. International politics in our time is as much a struggle for the hearts and minds of these emerging nations as it is a direct struggle for global supremacy for the big powers. Major nations count their pluses and minuses on the world stage on the scorecards of geopolitical influence – and here India ranks high. That is why India's foreign policy pronouncements are a matter of concern for the big powers such as the Soviet Union, the United States and Britain; that is why they frequently solicit India's support on world issues.

As I sat in the press gallery of the General Assembly hall and listened to Rajiv Gandhi during that October 1985 session, it occurred to me that his speech could have been delivered by any one of his predecessors. Nehru might well have said the same things that his grandson did about the pressing need to lessen global tensions; Indira Gandhi could have said precisely what her son said about world peace and security, about disarmament and the need to curb the nuclear arms race, about nonalignment, about development issues, about the yearning of Third World nations to create a better life for their struggling multitudes. Since independence, there has been a striking consistency in India's overall approach to the world.

This approach embraces a number of guiding themes:

• A genuine belief in global nonalignment. At the heart of these are several constructs. First, nonalignment offers India an opportunity to act as a balance between the power blocs of the United States and the Western Alliance on the one side, and the Soviet Union and its allies on the other. Second, nonalignment offers a kind of special protection in that it enables India to refrain from taking sides on geopolitical issues of rivalry between the super-powers. And third, nonalignment is espoused as a worthy cause in itself to advance the political and economic interests of the 'powerless' countries of the world. But nonalignment hasn't necessarily translated into India's silence on global issues. For example, Indian officials have, perhaps much too reflexively, been quick to side with Arab states in their quarrels with Israel. In 1982, when Israel's air force was bombing Beirut, Indira Gandhi issued a strong condemnation – a statement that resulted in virtually every member of the Nonaligned Movement following suit. When the prime minister was later asked by journalists why she spoke out so forcefully against the Israelis, she said that she viewed the Palestine Liberation Organization and the Lebanese as brethren. 'Those who suffer for a cause we truly believe in, suffer for all of us – and we must stand with them whatever the cost.'

- The establishment of India's regional role and dominance in South Asia. By its very size, its ancient culture and its military strength, India's position in the region is very significant. Altaf Gauhar, the distinguished editor of the London-based magazine, *South*, characterizes India as the 'big boy on the block'. Hence, the 1971 war of 'liberation' that resulted in the creation of Bangladesh from East Pakistan; hence, the 1987 treaty with Sri Lanka aimed at ending the civil war between that island-nation's minority Tamils and majority Sinhalese; hence, the November 1988 despatching of troops to the Maldives to crush an attempted *coup* there. There has long been a strong feeling in India's External Affairs Ministry that without a continuing role for India as the region's policeman, there would be considerable outside interference in South Asia.

- The balancing of India's economic and political interests through a carefully calibrated and calculated relationship with the superpowers. This has meant enhanced political relations with the Soviet Union, and significant economic relations with the Western powers. The Russians have been the chief suppliers of military hardware for India (including such items as the MIG-29, the highly sophisticated fighter plane that Moscow has offered to almost no other Third World nation). But since the Russians cannot give India 'breakthrough technology', Delhi has had to turn to the West, and to Japan, for technical and economic assistance. Because its relationship with the United States has been mainly one based on economics, it has been easier for India to condemn or to criticize Washington politically at forums such as the United Nations. And precisely because India relies so heavily on the Soviet Union for military assistance, it has proved virtually impossible for Delhi to condemn such matters as the Soviet invasions of Hungary in 1956, of Czechoslovakia in 1968 and of Afghanistan in 1979. Ironically, though, the interests of the two superpowers converged during India's 1962 border war with China – when Washington and Moscow both helped Delhi substantially by providing military and political support. Both powers thus provided a bulwark against China at a time when Beijing was hostile towards the Russians as well as towards the Americans.

● A strong commitment to international institutions such as the United Nations, which India sees as important mechanisms for settling world disputes and preventing infringement by outside powers on her own areas of geopolitical interest. India has had extraordinary influence in such international forums, and has frequently set the agenda and tone for debates at the UN. Moreover, Indians have traditionally held high positions and perhaps a disproportionate number of posts at international agencies within the UN family. (Indeed, Indians applying for jobs recently at various arms of the UN are being told that there are already far too many Indians in the system!)

Aside from India's historical strengths and geography, what explains the country's conspicuous role on the world stage? The answer to that is simple: both Nehru and Indira Gandhi had a wide-ranging world view that moved them to give much more attention to foreign affairs than most Third World leaders. 'Foreign affairs' was not only a major part of these prime ministers' state duties; the subject was also a key element of their personal intellectual interests. What we have here is an example of how the sheer force of Third World leaders' personality, their cerebral orientation, and international activity, can affect their own role and status – and that of their nations in international and domestic politics. Involvement in 'foreign affairs' has heightened Indian leaders' stature at home, as many Indians like the notion of their leaders consulting with the mandarins of the international community.

But why do other nations, particularly Third World nations, look to India for some strong element of leadership? I put this question recently to Professor Ralph Buultjens. He replied: 'After all, to most of us from the Third World, "India" means more than just India alone. She stands for all those values and cultural traditions that sustain societies from which we come. And so, India's leadership is not only a matter of size and skill, but also a sentimental and civilizational mix which exerts such a strong pull on people who belong to once-colonized societies.'

Many of these once-colonized societies are part of a large grouping known as the Nonaligned Movement (identified widely by its acronym, NAM), which Jawaharlal Nehru helped to found. Indeed, Indira Gandhi, at the time of her death, was the chairman of the grouping, and Rajiv Gandhi inherited the mantle. In 1986, during the twenty-fifth anniversary of the NAM's founding, Gandhi passed the three-year chairmanship to Prime Minister Robert Mugabe of Zimbabwe. I had always thought that NAM had the potential to be a major force in promoting Third World economic development and keeping such issues as child and maternal welfare constantly on the front-burner of the global agenda. But the movement had never quite realized its potential, even though Indira Gandhi had tried to get her fellow leaders to focus more sharply on social and humanitarian issues.

1961

Addressing foreign ministers from NAM nations in Delhi in 1981, Mrs Gandhi said: 'Of great concern to all of us are the wide inequalities and disequilibria in the economic and social structures of the world, and the glaring imbalance between demographic pressures on the one hand, and access to material and technological resources on the other. What should be invested in construction is being channelled into destruction. There is a global waste of talent and resources.

'The solution of today's critical international economic problems needs the total involvement of all nations. Global well-being will be illusory unless the aspirations of developing countries are reflected in the management of the international economy, and in the outcome of international negotiations. No less urgent is the ending of inequalities within our own societies.'

The Nonaligned Movement's primary value has been its growing numerical strength, its role as a collective spokesman for Third World concerns, and its potential moral weight as a pressure group for global disarmament. By the time NAM's 101 member-states met in Harare in 1986, the transition of the movement's leadership from middle-of-the-road India to Marxist Zimbabwe had already evoked concern in Western chancelleries and among many NAM members because of the possibilities for further fractiousness in the movement and a further infusion of leftist ideology.

Indeed, at no point during its troubled lifetime had the movement, whose members represent more than half of the world's population of 5 billion, been more afflicted with malaise, frustration and even political impotency. There were deep divisions in the movement over ideology and tactics, and if there was agreement over anything it was that the movement had gone adrift in recent years, with no clear strategy for action and no sense of political direction. Among some of the movement's influential leaders, in fact, there was pained questioning as to whether the movement, as presently constituted, was really useful, and whether it should survive at all.

And yet, gloomy as the picture was, I felt that the Nonaligned Movement had an unusual and perhaps final opportunity to put together a bold new technocratic agenda that would revive NAM, and bring development issues again to the forefront of the Third World's agenda. The movement had another chance to focus its and the industrialized world's attention on the problems of poverty, overpopulation and infant mortality – and it had the opportunity to catalyze concerted worldwide action to alleviate these interlinked problems. Why? Because the sheer size of its global constituency meant that NAM could effect significant change in Third World countries' development and economic policies. Despite a poor track record of results, which would normally make it inconsequential in world affairs, NAM was still important as a forum for discussion and Third World opinion-making – and as a barometer of superpower influence in the global arena.

That change could only come, I had long felt, if NAM was prepared to re-examine its relationship with the one nation whose technical assistance and expertise are badly needed to ensure further global development. NAM's feisty attitude towards the United States had done a great deal to dilute Washington's enthusiasm for Third World politics, I felt. Yet, simultaneously, many of the states that constituted NAM had become the arenas for American-Soviet rivalry. India had long been a classic case of a country that both superpowers wooed. India's leaders, however, insisted that the country would take no sides. Nevertheless, on the basis of India's votes in such international bodies as the United Nations, many Americans perceived that India's 'nonalignment' was invariably left-leaning.

I felt that if American foreign policy was to achieve its objective of increasing Washington's global influence and limiting Soviet expansionism, a redefined relationship with NAM or some of its more moderate members should be a priority. The confluence of NAM's own crisis of purpose, the context of world politics today, and the economic uncertainties plaguing the Third World, provided a unique opportunity for Washington to win friends and recapture its long-forgotten high standing in the Third World.

I knew that for both sides to take corrective action would be difficult. By the time NAM met in Harare, the movement was divided and disputatious, and its agenda appeared to have no priorities. Moreover, the United States had yet to come to terms with the fact that it could not maintain its highly charged ideological rhetoric and expect to win friends across the board among developing nations. It had to be perceived as muting its verbal pyrotechnics; it had to be seen as willing to push vigorously to completion its practical initiatives for tackling the Third World's major problems like the debt crisis.

NAM itself has been pretty ineffective in alleviating this crisis or in getting the industrialized West to address itself to the underlying causes of the crisis. For more than a decade, nonaligned nations have used a body called the G77 (diplomatic shorthand for the Group of 77, which actually has 127 members, 26 of them – like China, for instance – not belonging to NAM) to raise matters of economic relevance. And perhaps the most dramatic Third World demand lay in the call a decade ago for the establishment of a 'New International Economic Order' (which came to be better known by its acronym NIEO).

What the Third World was proposing under NIEO was a fundamental restructuring of the world economy in order to benefit the poorer countries. Poor countries argued that the existing international economic order was structured to their disadvantage. They maintained that because of the weighted voting structures of the International Monetary Fund and the World Bank, the Third World lacked appropriate influence in these institutions. They claimed that the prices of the primary products that constituted their largest exports had regularly fallen in relation to the prices of the manufactured goods they sought to import from the industrialized countries. The poor states of the Third World insisted that this was primarily due to the monopolistic, oligopolist position of the companies – usually multinational concerns – that purchased their products.

During the mid-1970s, NAM was indeed able briefly to achieve a shift in global debate from an East–West focus to a North–South one, but it was unable to sustain the momentum, largely because the movement simply couldn't draft a clear agenda for economic and politico-social action. While the poor countries vociferously argued that the terms of trade had gone against them, the rich states maintained that any price changes in imports and exports merely reflected the market trends and consumer preferences. The West said that influence in institutions where important decisions were taken had to be related to responsibilities. And consequently, the states that had a major share in world trade and supplied the funds for development assistance should have a determining voice in the IMF and World Bank.

And so, in the years following the hullabaloo over NIEO, the NAM was unable to win any major economic concessions from the West's financial organizations in tackling the debt crisis. The World Bank says that capital-importing developing countries now owe more than $1.3 trillion to Western lending institutions, a fact that results in severely curtailing the availability of Western commercial funds for any meaningful internal development in those nations. Further, the insecure nature of this debt imposes an air of uncertainty over international financial markets; the stability of many Western lending institutions has consequently become linked to the repayment capacities of many almost bankrupt developing countries. (In partial recognition of this, Citibank in effect wrote off $3 billion of its Third World loans in spring 1987, and other major Western lenders to developing countries soon followed suit in writing off some of their loans. Some donor nations, such as West Germany, are also writing off portions of their Third World loans.)

NAM has been unsuccessful in persuading the Western industrialized countries to agree to global negotiations that would correct economic imbalances between rich and poor nations. Nonaligned states are discovering that protectionism is gaining converts in the United States and elsewhere in the West. They are also finding that multilateralism is under siege these days, with the US administration sidestepping cumbersome international bureaucracies in favour of regional or bilateral accords that are more susceptible to political calibration by Washington. With George Bush as president, the contempt for international organizations is unlikely to change. Few Western industrialized countries seem to take the movement seriously; indeed, many officials of the politically conservative administrations of the United States, Britain, and West Germany, for example, speak scornfully of it.

The movement was started to support the post-war struggle against colonialism; to encourage newly independent nations to be neutral in the face of escalating Cold War confrontation between the two superpowers, the United States and the Soviet Union; and to assist the impoverished countries of the Third World to develop their economies and achieve social progress.

Implicit in its founding at the Belgrade Summit of 1961 – when twenty-five states signed NAM's first declaration of peace, disarmament and cooperation – was the recognition that the United Nations had been unable to provide the collective security system promised by its Charter. The movement upheld the cardinal tenets of nonintervention and noninterference in a sovereign state's territory. The movement's founders – among them, Presidents Josip Broz Tito of Yugoslavia, Gamal Abdel Nasser of Egypt and Sukarno of Indonesia, and Prime Ministers Jawaharlal Nehru of India and Kwame Nkrumah of Ghana – intended NAM to provide a moral umbrella for poor nations which were rushing towards modernity. For newly independent nations which wished to make a mark in the world community, NAM held out the possibility of a place in the sun.

But in the eyes of the general Western community, at least, much of the promise of NAM has not been fulfilled. Among ordinary Americans, there is a widespread, and seemingly unshakeable, suspicion that the movement, far from being neutral in the superpower competition, in fact consistently tilts towards the Soviet Union, which, in the words of Fidel Castro of Cuba – a former chairman of NAM – is viewed by many in the Third World as a 'natural ally' of developing countries.

Indeed, it has often seemed that the movement seized on the slightest American folly in international affairs, while its condemnation of the Russians on such matters as the occupation of Afghanistan was relatively mild, if not muted. NAM has failed to resolve on-going conflicts in its own backyard such as the Iran–Iraq war (it took the United Nations to negotiate a ceasefire, which was finally announced in August 1988), the Cambodia imbroglio, and assorted crises in Africa and Central America.

NAM's credibility as an advocate of global peace has been considerably eroded by its inability, despite repeated attempts, to make any headway in resolving such disputes within the Third World family. And here, many critics – including myself – have held that India simply hasn't used its diplomatic and political muscle-power more vigorously in resolving disputes. Given India's long-standing good relations with both Iran and Iraq, for instance, Delhi could have energetically pursued a role as mediator. Precisely because nonalignment is both a shield and a spear for India, Delhi could have used its influence to mobilize world opinion against the terrible Gulf conflict.

NAM was formally born at the Belgrade Summit, which was held between 1 and 6 September 1961. The movement was actually conceived fifteen years before the summit, essentially in the mind of Jawaharlal Nehru. Back in September, 1946, almost a year before India obtained its independence from Britain, Nehru delivered a radio address in which he said: 'We propose as far as possible to keep away from power politics of groups aligned against one another which in the past have led to world wars and which may lead to disaster, on an even bigger scale, in the future.'

Shortly afterwards, Nehru organized a meeting in Delhi for Asian countries to affirm their solidarity and proclaim their vision of the post-war, post-colonial world they planned to build; the Second World War had hastened the decolonization process. Nehru declared at the meeting that Asian nations would no longer be petitioners in foreign chancelleries, nor pawns in the games of the world powers.

'We propose to stand on our own legs and to cooperate with all others who are prepared to cooperate with us,' he said. 'Asia stretches out her hand in friendship to Europe and America, as well as to our suffering brethren in Africa . . . Universal freedom cannot be based on the supremacy of any particular class. It must be the freedom of the common man everywhere, providing him with every opportunity to develop.'

Those were the seeds of the concept that eventually came to be called nonalignment. Nehru's words were uttered at the start of the Cold War, when the two superpowers maintained, in the phrase of the time, 'a balance of terror'. It was a bipolar world, and in the emerging nations of Asia and Africa there were fears about a nuclear holocaust, and there was also mounting concern about the application of the Truman Doctrine of containment of Communism – these new nations saw themselves being dragged willy-nilly into the superpower conflict. For the most part, these former colonial possessions did not wish to accept military alliances with the superpowers or with their former colonial masters. What Nehru advocated was the idea that the new nations could pursue vigorously the axioms of independence, development and peaceful coexistence. Implicit in what Nehru was saying was the notion of neutrality, which John Foster Dulles would later bitterly criticize as being 'immoral'.

It was India that took it upon herself to develop the theme of nonalignment. In the early post-war years, India insisted that the United Nations should be – as Jagat Mehta, a former Indian Foreign Secretary, has put it – a 'universal, nonideological' organization; India lobbied for the admission to the United Nations of Communist China, a country at whose hands it was to suffer a humiliating defeat in a border war in 1962. India warned the West about the consequences of broadening the Korean War. India played a valuable, behind-the-scenes role in the 1954 Geneva Conference on Indochina. And India cautioned the newly decolonized states against taking sides in the superpower rivalry. Through such involvement, India managed not only to gain a world visibility in international affairs, it also set the stage for the eventual adoption of the nonalignment credo of assertive independent positions on world issues.

Nehru saw the new nations of Asia and Africa as a 'moral make-weight to restore the balance in the world', a phrase he used in a conversation in 1954 with Tarzie Vittachi, the Sri Lankan journalist and author. Nehru had travelled to Colombo – the capital of the country then known as Ceylon, now as Sri Lanka – to attend the Colombo Powers Conference. This conference led to the 1955 Bandung Conference, the first summit-level meeting of twenty-nine African and Asian leaders.

What happened at Bandung was to prove extremely useful to the figures who were eventually to found NAM. A debate took place over the concept of 'peaceful coexistence' between the socialist and capitalist systems; there were spirited discussions about the value of national security through external assistance; and, of course, there was a great deal of talk concerning the perceived threats of Communist expansionism. Conference participants opined that nations had the right to choose their sources for economic assistance. And they collectively called on the International Bank for Reconstruction and Development – the World Bank – to offer assistance to the poor nations according to their development needs.

Six years later, in September 1961, Nehru and twenty-four other leaders who had met in Bandung were reunited in Belgrade for what came to be known as the First Conference of the Heads of Governments of Nonaligned Countries. The summit lasted for five days, there were merely five items on the agenda – items that dealt broadly with questions such as nonintervention and the sovereign rights of states – and there was also a 'message' in the final declaration addressed to President John F. Kennedy of the United States and to Prime Minister Nikita Khrushchev of the Soviet Union urging both to start direct negotiations to remove the nuclear threat. Although the final communiqué made an impassioned plea for peace and disarmament, it contained not a word about the Soviet Union's nuclear test explosion, which the Russians set off even while the Belgrade Summit was being held. This omission annoyed President Kennedy.

The late Robert Shaplen of the *New Yorker* has told of meeting a Yugoslav diplomat in Delhi years later who recalled a conversation with Khrushchev just before the Belgrade Summit. The diplomat quoted the Soviet leader as saying: 'You tell Tito that I'm getting ready to build a wall in Berlin and that I'm going to set off a bomb during his conference. Ask him who, then, is more important – his nonaligned movement or the Soviet Union?'

The summit had its discordant notes. President Sukarno of Indonesia urged a confrontational stance towards the United States, which he repeatedly characterized as imperialistic and antagonistic towards developing countries. It was Nehru who held that confrontation with a superpower would do nothing to advance the cause of the nonaligned states, and what was eventually adopted by the summiteers was the Nehru view that the final communiqué should emphasize peace and cooperation. The summiteers left Belgrade without planning to hold another summit. Nonalignment, in their view, was not meant to be an 'anti-bloc bloc'.

But there was to be a subsequent summit, three years later, in Cairo. It was held at a time of a continuing border dispute between China and India, an issue that was dodged by the participants at the Cairo Summit, although it was the first clear-cut test of how NAM members would deal with the thorny question of what to do when a member-state's territory was violated by force. And in evading this question, the nonaligned leaders established a precedent that has haunted the movement – that unless blame could be fairly and squarely placed on 'Western imperialism', intra-Third-World disputes should be played down in the quest for consensus and unity.

It was to be six years before another summit would be held, this time in the Zambian capital of Lusaka. By this time, the membership of NAM had more than doubled, and the summiteers resolved now to meet every three years. Already, a process of institutionalization was taking place, the very thing that the movement's founding fathers had wanted to avoid. In addition to the declarations, the summiteers approved fourteen different resolutions – which were nonbinding and which few took seriously – ranging from issues such as development, disarmament and peace to the question of setting up a 'zone of peace' in the Indian Ocean, and to a suggestion for an international convention on the Laws of the Seas. At Lusaka, too, appeared the first hints of a Third World stand on the need for a North–South dialogue on economic issues.

Economic issues figured prominently at the next summit, which was held in Algiers in September 1973. The question of détente was raised in the deliberations as well, but it was the issue of a Third World State's sovereign rights over its natural resources that generated a lot of debate. Outside NAM precincts, OPEC – the Organization of Petroleum Exporting Countries – had already begun to flex its muscles; the concept of oil as a weapon was well in place. The nonaligned countries hoped that somehow the use of the oil weapon by OPEC would also have simultaneous advantages for Third World countries that relied for valuable foreign-exchange primarily on one-commodity exports. It was, in the event, a vain hope because the oil situation was not replicable for most other natural resources; moreover, the oil-producing states barely assisted the Third World countries, preferring instead to invest their surplus petrodollars in the industrial economies, through which the funds were often recycled at high interest rates to desperately poor nations.

The Algerians put a special stamp on the nonaligned movement, which was that of greater shrillness in articulating economic issues. Their leadership of NAM signalled the accelerated involvement of the Third World with development economics, but in the West this was viewed as a radicalization of the nonaligned movement. At the next summit, in Colombo in 1976, the moderate figures of the movement – including Indira Gandhi – tried to soften NAM rhetoric on economic issues, but the demands escalated nevertheless for the creation of a New International Economic Order (which by now had been approved by the General Assembly of the United Nations).

The 'radicalization' of NAM reached its apogee at the 1979 summit in Havana. Fidel Castro, the activist host, made no secret of his ambition to take NAM more in the direction of the Soviet Union, which he characterized as the 'natural ally' of developing countries. To be sure, he met with resistance – among other people from the late president Tito of Yugoslavia, then in his declining days. In an acclaimed address, Tito called on the movement to 'remain the conscience of mankind' and he warned against a partisan shift. Stronger protest came from Burma, a founding member of the movement: it announced its withdrawal from NAM. Castro was determined to push through a final communiqué that denounced the United States, but it was the last-minute intervention of Yugoslavia, India and a few other Asian states that resulted in a muting of such language to a more even-tempered admonition against all forms of 'hegemony and domination'.

Because Cuba's own political position was at great variance with that of many of NAM's members, the movement slid into three years of near-paralysis. Cuba opposed any NAM attempt to condemn the Soviet invasion of Afghanistan in December 1979. It was not until the Delhi summit of 1983 that the NAM leadership – now having passed to Prime Minister Indira Gandhi, the host of the conference – was able to undertake any meaningful effort to bring the movement back on its rails. Criticism of the West was by no means abjured, but the rhetoric was less strident.

Mrs Gandhi, hardly a foe of the Soviet Union, employed the tactic of highlighting not alleged American imperialism but the questions of development and nuclear proliferation. She pointed out that it was important to trim global defence expenditures: she noted that a single nuclear aircraft carrier cost $4 billion – which was greater than the gross national product of most NAM members. Mrs Gandhi also renewed earlier NAM calls for a new international monetary conference to review and revise the Bretton Woods system on which the post-war global economic structure was constructed. It was a structure, she said, that increasingly discriminated against the developing countries.

Mrs Gandhi's mostly moderate deportment was the most pleasing aspect of the lavish summit, but the most startling episode was a speech by Foreign Minister Sinnathamby Rajaratnam of Singapore. Rajaratnam did not actually deliver the speech but distributed copies to delegates. And with good reason, for had he spoken what he had written, many summiteers would have walked out on him. In retrospect, his was one of the most clear-headed, pithy and unsentimental assessments of the Nonaligned Movement ever. It was also one of those rare times that a delegate had taken on the movement in a frontal assault and questioned NAM's integrity. Of the movement, Rajaratnam said that its 'past is one of which we can be justly proud. Its present condition, however, does it no credit. And finally, if it persists in its present course, its future will be one of shameful oblivion.'

Rajaratnam – who belonged to the Tamil community that long ago migrated to Singapore from India – then went on to criticize the movement's 'self-delusion'. He said that Third World states had less to fear from a return of Western imperialism that from the military ambitions of their own neighbours. He said that pro-Soviet members had become the 'true motor' of the movement. He accused both the United States and the Soviet Union, but especially the latter, of using the ancient technique of proxy wars to gain control of the movement. 'We are witnesses to our own slow-motion hijacking and if we do not wake up to this fact and do something to abort it then the ship of nonalignment and all those who sail in it may wake up one day to find that they have docked in a Soviet port.'

I think that much of this future will depend on how India and the Nonaligned Movement relate to the superpowers in a global context that is currently undergoing such significant changes as *glasnost* and *perestroika* in the Soviet Union, and economic retrenchment in the Third World. This relationship between the Third World and the superpowers must be understood in the context of these shifting changes – as well as in the historical context.

The leaders of NAM may have resisted Fidel Castro's efforts to push their movement more squarely into the Soviet camp, but it is hardly disputable that the Soviet Union enjoys more tolerance than the United States at NAM gatherings. At least a dozen NAM members – including Afghanistan, Angola, Ethiopia and Nicaragua – are openly aligned in political or military terms with the Soviets. More than a quarter of the member-states are ruled by authoritarian governments, mainly of leftist persuasion. While both the United States and the Soviet Union supply considerable quantities of arms to the Third World, Moscow often offers terms – such as barter for coffee from Ethiopia, fish from Mozambique – that are easier on the recipient countries in the short run.

NAM and Indian leaders insist that the movement does not curry favour with the Russians. They say that if the NAM position on issues such as decolonization, the New International Economic Order and Palestine seem similar, that is because Moscow votes with the Third World, not the other way around. NAM leaders point out that the United States votes with the Third World majority at the United Nations some 80 per cent of the time, and that it is only when there are divergences of opinion and voting that Washington chooses to emphasize the different voting patterns between its allies and the Third World majority.

There are significant differences between how Moscow and Washington court NAM. Leaders of the movement say that NAM often comes into voting forums at the United Nations with its position on specific issues already made up at earlier caucuses. But the United States is seen as not paying sufficiently close attention to such small meetings – and so, as one senior NAM official puts it, 'the United States gets slightly startled at the end of the race, and then gets bitter'. It is often a question of technique that has been neglected by the United States. The Russians are generally far more vigilant about how NAM members stand on specific issues. While American diplomats are generally perceived as being neglectful or indifferent towards these small but critical caucuses, Soviet representatives often seem far more energetic and attentive to the concerns of the Third World.

For Washington, the game in Third World voting has often been lost because there has simply been no contest. The Russians and their friends have used NAM differently: for example, Moscow despatched a conspicuously large delegation to the Delhi Summit in 1983; the Russians produced thirty books on nonalignment, which were distributed free of charge to delegates. No comparable Western effort was evident.

In NAM circles, there is resentment over the fact that the popular and official definition of nonalignment in the United States is 'equidistance' from the superpowers, keeping both the Russians and the Americans at a constant symmetrical distance. But in such important Third World states as India, nonalignment, dating back to Jawaharlal Nehru's time, is often defined as 'freedom to act independently in the pursuit of national self-interest', even if it means tilting to one superpower under a given set of circumstances. When accused of pro-Soviet proclivities, many defenders of NAM policies point out that there are inevitably divergences of interest between the United States and the Third World that have led Third World states to align themselves with Moscow.

For example, Indians resented the American embrace of Pakistan, hardly a country fully sharing values of democracy with the United States. India was unable to obtain sophisticated weapons in the 1960s from the United States, even while Washington was stepping up military aid to Pakistan. Indians were also unable to obtain American support for their programme of heavy industrialization. Thus it was that India came to adapt its foreign policy to its development and security needs – which meant turning increasingly to Moscow. This situation continues to be typical of the experience of many Third World states.

Still, it now appears that although the Russians are generally viewed as friends, they are nevertheless seen rather more guardedly among some influential nonaligned nations. This development offers some opportunity for the United States and other members of the Western Alliance to carry more weight in Third World forums.

There are three reasons for this wariness of Moscow in the Third World. First, the invasion of Afghanistan and the subsequent stationing of more than 100,000 Russian troops there showed a brutal side to Soviet behaviour. The invasion highlighted for many Third World states Moscow's readiness to trample on the sovereignty of a nonaligned country. Moscow announced that its troops would start leaving Afghanistan in May 1988 and continue leaving during 1989, but Afghan officials say that Soviet military advisers would remain in this civil-war-torn nation.

Second, the more pragmatic leaders of the Third World say they have some difficulty in seeing in the Soviet Union a reliable source for technology and investment funds that would help them move their countries forward. These leaders contend that the Russians are simply in no position to assist the Third World in alleviating its pressing needs – for example, with debt relief and food shipments, and in providing export markets that would enable beleaguered developing nations to earn the hard currency with which to repay their enormous debts to Western lending institutions. For many Third World nations, the nuclear accident at Chernobyl illustrated the fact that the Russians still do not have a firm grip on the uses of high technology.

And third, there is a perception among some top NAM leaders that the Soviet Union has not made any major moves genuinely to include the Third World in multilateral disarmament negotiations. The NAM's position has long been that disarmament talks should be under multilateral auspices, although NAM leaders have applauded the commencement of bilateral discussions between the Soviet Union and the United States. (NAM leaders point to two existing forums that could be more energetically used for multilateral disarmament talks: the First Committee of the United Nations General Assembly and the forty-member Conference on Disarmament.) NAM's perception is that when the chips are down, the Russians – like the Americans – prefer to play the 'bilateral game'; when it comes to disarmament negotiations, Moscow still acts within the superpower framework.

In contrast to the traditionally favourable standing of the Soviet Union in the Third World, the United States has for a long time been a *bête noire*, at least in the realm of NAM rhetoric. In part, this is due to the legacy of the Dulles–Eisenhower position over the lack of Third World commitment to the United States during the Cold War. Such a lack of commitment was seen as a sign of weakness and sin. Indeed, India was singled out by Washington as an example of fence-straddling.

Thereafter, American involvement in Vietnam, combined with support for Israel and South Africa, inevitably put Washington on the wrong side of NAM. (Washington's support for Israel puts the

United States on the wrong side of NAM because Israel is perceived as an enclave of Western settlement and influence in a 'Third World region'. Exacerbating this perception, of course, is the seemingly intractable question of a homeland for Palestinians.) However, all this could perhaps have been finessed if the United States had exerted the same diplomatic energy in dealing with NAM as the Soviet Union did. For the most part, the United States treated NAM with a studied indifference, bordering on mild hostility, and made few attempts to win friends or influence nations at NAM gatherings.

The American position was perplexing to many NAM states, especially when contrasted with the assiduous courtship lavished on them by the Soviet Union. A telling point is that, twenty-five years after its foundation, NAM's major concerns remain global and the movement still continues to define its agenda largely with reference to superpower actions, motivations and objectives. NAM leaders were offended not long ago when the Reagan administration declined even to give a hearing to the Six-Nation Disarmament Initiative launched by Rajiv Gandhi; in contrast, Mikhail Gorbachev of the Soviet Union was full of public praise for the initiative, even though in reality the Russians did little to advance it.

The United States needs to stop viewing itself as the loyal opposition in United Nations/NAM forums. It should 'join' Third World discussions well before issues come to vote. And while NAM states would certainly not wish Washington to interfere, they would not be averse to more attentiveness on the part of American diplomats. In diplomacy, as in everyday life, it is very humiliating to be dismissed as inconsequential.

With the recent emergence in the Third World of moderate leaders – such as Benazir Bhutto and Rajiv Gandhi – who are deeply committed to democracy and who endorse the usefulness of the market mechanism in their economic policy, this may be an opportune time for the United States and the West to advance its bridge-building with NAM states. Many NAM leaders say that Western policymakers need to look at the Third World through the other side of the telescope: what they are likely to see is a situation where, in an age of spirited nationalism, few countries prefer to be 'aligned' with a superpower. Those who remain aligned do so out of a sense of pressing necessity – like Pakistan, which needs to hang on to external alliances in order, perhaps, to even exist.

The key to better relations between the Third World and the West rests, perhaps more than ever before, with economic issues. Notwithstanding the 19 October 1987 stock market crash – which wiped out more than $500 billion in securities values – the United States remains the largest and single most reliable source of funds in a troubled and uncertain global economic atmosphere for nations in search of capital and markets.

Leaders of many developing countries say that, from a practical point of view, the Russians are largely bystanders in the Third World's grassroots economic development. Of course, the value of Moscow's sponsorship of big hydro-electric projects and steel mills in various poor countries should not be minimized. Professor Padma Desai of Columbia University – an Indian-born expert on Eastern Bloc economics – cites the Bokaro steel plant in India and the Aswan dam in Egypt as instances of US–Soviet aid rivalry: in each case, she says, Washington came to be identified with a massive project of national importance, opted out conspicuously – and the Soviet Union stepped in.

Still, the fact remains that showcase projects such as Bokaro and Aswan are expensive and hard to solicit from donors in today's tightening world economy. Third World states are more concerned with receiving aid in hard currency, and it is here that the US continues to enjoy an edge over the Soviet Union. In 1988, for instance, Washington channelled more than $12 billion to Third World nations in various kinds of foreign aid; the Soviet figure was at least $5 billion below that. With their collective external debt now exceeding $1.3 trillion, and with their revenues from exports stagnating for the most part, many Third World countries are more preoccupied these days with the tricky problem of generating enough cash for domestic economic development and of making payments on their external debt – the vast majority of which is to Western states.

On 7 December 1988, Mikhail Gorbachev went to the United Nations in New York and announced, among other things, that the Soviet Union was now prepared to play an active role in alleviating the Third World's debt crisis. He said that Moscow was prepared to institute a lengthy moratorium – of up to 100 years – on debt servicing by the least developed countries. In some cases, which Gorbachev did not specify, the Russians would even write off debt altogether. Washington has ruled out debt forgiveness, and so Gorbachev's remarks were widely seen as a jibe at the US. The Soviet leader also urged the major creditor countries to undertake various measures to ensure that debt repayment did not destroy Third World economies. In particular, he urged the formation of a specialized international agency that would repurchase Third World debts to commercial and governmental institutions at a discount. And Gorbachev seemed to give a big boost to India's long-proposed idea of consultations under the auspices of the United Nations among leaders of debtor and creditor countries.

The Gorbachev proposals, to be sure, at least partly flowed from his awareness of the importance of 'public relations' in global diplomacy. But I think that it was more than that: Gorbachev seemed to have shrewdly calculated that while arms-control issues may be a priority for Washington and Moscow, the chief concern of most Third World nations these days is debt and development. Gorbachev's idea of debt forgiveness was hardly new, of course. West Germany has already written off tens of millions of dollars' worth of debt owed to its governmental agencies by Third World states, particularly in Africa. Much of the Third World debt to Moscow involved repayment for the arms sold to developing nations. Still, when Mikhail Gorbachev embraced Third World concerns so publicly at the United Nations, it at once made the Soviet Union look like a genuine friend of developing nations. The United States could only sit at the sidelines and listen to Gorbachev steal yet another march on Washington!

When Indira Gandhi visited the United Nations in 1983, she spoke eloquently of how the fundamental realities of international economic life were mirrored in NAM's efforts to change the global economic structure. The nonaligned countries' basic contention concerning their economic situation has not changed greatly since the mid-1970s, when emotions ran high at the United Nations and other forums over the question of the New International Economic Order. Simplistically perhaps, Third World nations invested much hope in the NIEO; this new world economic order was seen by many Third World leaders as an important way to alleviate long-standing problems such as slow economic growth and escalating poverty in developing countries. The NIEO was to be an economic rainmaker!

NIEO was essentially a formalization of the longstanding concerns and demands of the Third World states for a better economic deal. They wanted better trade arrangements with the industrialized West, a greater transfer of technology to pull their backward economics into a post-industrial age, and increased development assistance. When NAM was founded, some of its leaders seemed to hold that political liberty meant automatic economic development and progress. But by the early 1970s, NAM leaders had learned a bitter lesson: that without a strong economic base, political strategies can collapse. Economics had moved to the centre stage of world politics.

The style and level of discourse between the West and the Third World have undergone shifts over the years. For example, in the years immediately after the Second World War, the discourse was on the genteel side – no harangues there. Then, after OPEC flexed its muscles following the Arab-Israeli War of October 1973, the exchanges between the industrialized countries and the Third World became sharper, with the Third World seemingly in a confrontational mood.

Back in the 'Roaring Seventies' – when oil-rich states deposited their rapidly accumulating petrodollars with Western institutions – greedy Western bankers offered easy loans to eager developing nations. These nations, swearing by the earning power of their commodities, then went on a spending spree. Contributing to the mess were the ubiquitous local corruption that plagues the Third World, gross mismanagement of local economies, and burgeoning and unbending bureaucracies that stressed statism, not productive free-market policies. Adding to the mess was the fact that the Third World's principal exports were commodities – and global commodity prices plunged 30 per cent in the last decade alone.

Finally, the Western economies regained their strength in the 1980s and the West overcame the threat of the OPEC oil weapon by stockpiling and developing alternative oil sources and resources. A malaise set in on the Third World. Now its voices are considerably muted, and NAM countries find themselves once again at a loss over how to project a concerted course of action to revive their demands for a greater share of the world economic pie. More and more, nonaligned countries are turning to India to provide new directions for an economic dialogue with the West.

Jagdish Bhagwati, Arthur Lehman Professor of Economics at

Columbia University in New York, says that initially there were 'minimalist' ameliorative demands for changes in the international economic management structure devised at Bretton Woods. Bhagwati adds that there were also 'maximalist' demands, especially after the OPEC-driven oil crisis of 1973, for a major restructuring of this edifice; and then the Third World states were back to seeking 'immediate measures' to confront the common crisis which today centres around debt-relief, food supplies and increased investment. Now many Third World states would be content with accelerated assistance with regard to the management of their awesome external debts, plus a decent portion of development aid.

Professor Bhagwati – who the *Financial Times* has described as the 'doyen' of international economists specializing in trade and protectionism issues – says that the position of poorer countries concerning NIEO can be traced to three factors.

First, a substantial shift occurred in their perception of the gains to be had from economic relations with the industrialized states under the existing rules of the game. These developing countries felt that the industrialized nations of the West enjoyed a death-grip on the world's markets, on technology, on communications and on the media. They felt that, through existing trade arrangements, the West unfairly manipulated the world's pricing system. Many Third World countries were dependent on primary exports, and they also faced obstacles in securing access to Western markets for their manufactured goods.

Second, the Third World countries perceived that, acting collectively, they had sufficient economic and political power to warrant a strategy of effective 'trade unionism' to change the rules of the international game and thereby obtain a larger share of the world's wealth and income. The value of world trade jumped from $60 billion in 1950 to nearly $2 trillion by 1980; to look at it another way, the value of world trade doubled between 1950 and 1960, almost trebled between 1960 and 1970, and trebled again between 1970 and 1973. But most developing countries had remained dependent on a relatively narrow set of exports to spur growth; the major beneficiaries of the growth in global trade were the industrialized countries. Jyoti Shankar Singh of the UNFPA has estimated in a recent study that the volume of industrialized countries' exports rose by 127 per cent between 1960 and 1970, and by an additional 32 per cent between 1970 and 1973. This increase was accomplished by the industrialized countries through use of cheap sources of energy and raw materials, and through a spectacular breakthrough in technological developments. And meanwhile, Third World countries continued to have adverse terms of trade.

Third, the developing countries not only wished their basic economic interests to be safeguarded and enhanced, they also wanted through a new and just international economic order to assert their sovereign rights as members of the world community. The exports of about twelve major non-oil commodities account for more than 80 per cent of the total import earnings of the developing countries. Sharp fluctuations in the world prices of raw commodities, coupled with increased expenditure on the import of manufactured goods from industrialized countries, plus the cost of serving debts to Western financial institutions, have all but wiped out many Third World states' ability to channel substantial amounts of money into their own development. In 1974, the developing countries' debt amounted to $135 billion; by 1985, the figure was touching $1 trillion; at the end of 1988, the figure was $1.3 trillion, according to the World Bank. To this figure, Professor Ralph Buultjens adds $125 billion that the Soviet Union and various Eastern bloc countries owe to Western banks.

On average, 60 per cent of this new debt (and more than 80 per cent in the case of Latin America) was loaned by commercial bankers, who saw marvellous credit opportunities in developing countries. The bankers had billions of petrodollars at their command. Thus, between 1972 and 1979, the indebtedness of the so-called Less Developed Countries (LDCs) increased at an average annual rate of 21.7 per cent. And their indebtedness has kept on increasing. Take the case of China, which in 1981 has almost no external debt. By the end of 1987, it had piled up some $33 billion in foreign debt, making it the world's sixth biggest debtor. In 1986, about 60 per cent of China's $3.3 billion foreign borrowing that year came from Western and Japanese banks.

Coupled with the question of rising external debt of Third World countries is their mounting domestic debt. In India, for example, the 1988 figure was $125 billion. To be sure, many Western industrial nations have vastly larger long-term debts (the federal debt of the United States, for example, is edging past $2.4 trillion). But these Western debts are also secured by vastly richer domestic resources and better access to liquidity.

From the back seat, then, Third World states have wanted to get into the driver's seat. Developing states were hard hit by the dramatic decline in the role of the dollar in the early 1970s; the dollar had been central to the Bretton Woods system as the currency of international trade, and its convertibility into gold was a critical element. After all, nearly 80 per cent of the world's trade was conducted in – or, at least, translated into – the American dollar. With the American trade deficit exceeding $10 billion by 1971, President Richard Nixon suspended the convertibility of the dollar into gold, and the world's major currencies were forced to float against one another.

When Indira Gandhi spoke at the United Nations not long before her assassination about the need for restructuring the global economy to help poor countries, there was a perception among some Western observers that she was calling for something radical. However, demands for a major change in the world's skewed economic system were first voiced at the Bandung Conference of Afro-Asian leaders in 1955. Every summit of the Nonaligned Movement has echoed such demands. At the United Nations, too, the Third World states have broadcast their concerns. But more than three decades after Bandung few, if any, major changes have been instituted where it matters most to the Third World countries – in the trade and aid policies of the industrialized states, and in the global monetary and financial institutions such as the International Monetary Fund (IMF) and the World Bank, where the wealthy industrialized powers retain a dominant controlling voice.

What went wrong with the Third World's strategy to secure such changes? Why did NIEO collapse?

At the heart of the matter is the question of different perceptions of self-interest in the developing world. The evolution of economic development has moved some nations in different directions from others, giving, for example, newly industrializing states in the Third World different sets of concerns from those of the more traditional agricultural economies. Shahid Javed Burki, a senior vice president of the World Bank, and a Pakistani, says: 'The NIEO was neither desirable nor achievable.' In a paper he delivered at a recent meeting in Beijing, Burki said that those associated with NIEO were simply not able to define their positions concerning agenda items. The very concept of NIEO was a romanticized one, and therefore unworkable. It was also doomed to failure because the

Third World, in exchange for a transfer of resources from the wealthy North, wasn't prepared to offer any significant concessions of its own.

Since the NIEO concept was first floated more than a decade ago, the Third World has been unable to agree on specific approaches and responses for negotiations with the West; bickering and sharp dissension are rampant within G77. The G77, the economic coalition of Third World states, tried to 'cut a deal': it supported OPEC's tactic of price hikes and the brandishing of the oil weapon in exchange for the oil cartel's 'willingness to behave as the shock troops' of the NIEO. Indeed, the industrialized West seemed to some extent affected by this tactic, which stemmed perhaps from an exaggerated perception on the part of the South of its own power.

From 1975 to 1977, President Valéry Giscard d'Estaing of France convened in Paris a Conference on International Economic Cooperation. Participants included industrialized states and a selection of Third World countries. The conference followed the format urged by G77: this format linked oil-price discussions to broad proposals on trade, finance, aid, raw materials and the transfer of technology from the North to the South. OPEC had insisted on the participation of developing countries at the conference. The West hadn't really wanted to discuss the North–South issue at the conference; the West had wanted initially to discuss the oil situation with OPEC, perhaps with a deal in mind for longterm price stability.

OPEC then brought in developing countries, largely as a means of gaining legitimacy for its oil-price rises. In exchange for admission to the conference – and the resulting widening of the agenda to include North–South questions – the Third World would give OPEC its endorsement of the oil price rises. The Paris conference, however, was unable to produce any formula satisfactory to all participants and was subsequently overtaken by events. The West was able to absorb successfully the shock of the 1973–4 oil-price rise, and the industrialized states embarked on a massive conservation programme that enabled them to be less frightened of OPEC manoeuvres. Further, Third World leaders felt that their OPEC counterparts were not fully behind the South's set of demands for major restructuring of the world's financial system – a system that had worked well in recent years for OPEC members. OPEC's leverage – and, by extension, that of the developing countries – was diluted. OPEC sought its economic future in

increased links with the West, rather than underwriting a commitment ot NIEO. Petrodollars ended up in London and New York,
rather than in Bangladesh or Malawi or India.

Then in 1979, NAM leaders at the Havana Summit called for
fresh 'global negotiations' between the North and South. Nothing
happened here either: the call did not receive sufficient support to
translate it into reality. By 1981, world oil prices were falling; the
world was entering a terrible recession. And finally, there arrived
the Reagan administration. This administration, in tandem with
politically and fiscally conservative governments in Britain and
West Germany, was unwilling to accommodate the demands of the
Third World for new negotiations, preferring to rely on market
forces rather than on some international planning mechanism to
deal with global economic problems. In fact, the attitude of the
Reagan administration was perceived by NAM and by G77 officials
as being downright hostile to Third World interests.

Earlier, especially during the Carter years, it had seemed to
many in NAM that the United States – which had retreated into
neo-isolationism following the Vietnam débâcle and which had
sought détente with its adversary, the Soviet Union – was prepared
to replace the Cold War with NIEO as the central element of
international life. But after the Soviet invasion of Afghanistan in
1979 and the election to the American presidency the following
year of Ronald Reagan, bipolar realities reasserted themselves.
The Cold War and United States–Soviet Union relations became,
once again, the crucial, pre-eminent issues of the age.

Nowadays many NAM and G77 officials appear alarmed that
under the current conditions of reduced Third World political and
economic strength, the industrialized countries will try to institu-
tionalize Western economic advantages. These leaders cite the
undercutting by the Reagan administration of multilateral mechanisms, including United Nations bodies that could conceivably play
an active role in promoting Third World development – such as
UNCTAD, the United Nations Conference on Trade and
Development.

The Reagan administration called for a widened role for the
World Bank as well as commercial banks in helping alleviate the
debt crisis and in promoting economic development. In a major
speech delivered in October 1985 at the IMF–World Bank meeting
in Seoul, South Korea, the then Treasury Secretary James A.

Baker III – now Secretary of State in the Bush administration – asked commercial banks to continue to lend to fifteen heavily indebted countries, and to increase their exposure by at least 2.5 per cent annually. The banks were asked to contribute some $20 billion over the next three years. Baker also called on the World Bank and other development banks to give more assistance to debtor nations. The World Bank and the Inter-American Development ment Bank were urged by Baker to increase their disbursements to major debtors by about 50 per cent, to $9 billion. The total assistance package would amount to $29 billion.

In addition to the so-called Baker Plan, James Robinson III, chairman of American Express, has come up with a suggestion to create a new debt-relief agency. This agency would be called the Institute of International Debt and Development. Banks would sell their Third World loans to this agency in exchange for long-term institute securities, and the agency would adjust downwards the interest payments of Third World debtors. Arjun Sengupta – formerly economic adviser to Indira Gandhi, and now a top official at the International Monetary Fund – has proposed a special fund financed by the industrialized countries. This fund would be useful in alleviating Third World debts, according to Sengupta.

Japan has announced that it would use its $100 billion trade surplus for enhanced aid programmes, particularly in the ravaged countries of sub-Saharan Africa. Salim Lone, a Kenyan editor of Asian descent who now works for the United Nations in New York, holds out the possibility that massive commercial investment by the Japanese in developing nations could perhaps replace the traditional concept of foreign aid.

Lone points to what the Japanese are doing in India. In 1987, for example, there were nearly a hundred joint-venture agreements signed between various Japanese and Indian companies in such endeavours as thermal power stations and the production of scooters, light commercial vehicles and batteries. The Japanese are also bidding for oil pipelines, and for off-shore drilling contracts. Clearly, they see India as a growing economy and want a share of the increasing economic market.

As Salim Lone suggests, enhanced commercial investment and trade, rather than aid, might well be the means of strengthening Third World economies. And here the Indian situation might well serve as a model.

However, few NAM leaders believe that there will be a dramatic turnabout concerning trade, aid and development in the Bush administration. More and more, NAM and G77 officials are starting to accept the validity of Singapore's assertion that the way to make progress on such issues as trade and aid is not by passing meaningless resolutions seeking global negotiations. A better way, they assert, is by pursuing more market-oriented economic approaches. The Singaporeans, who have seen the benefits of free enterprise and integration into the international marketplace, are calling for greater economic liberalization within the Third World community.

They – along with other developing states interested in more rapid growth, such as India – are urging more South–South trade under a new arrangement called the Global System of Trade Preferences (GSTP). (Supporters of the GSTP point out that there is a significant potential for the expansion of mutual trade between developing countries. Third World countries constitute an import market of about $500 billion, a third of which is catered to by goods and services from Third World suppliers. Also, less than 20 per cent of all imports of manufactured goods in the Third World come from other developing countries.)

But the problem here is that many Third World states feel uncomfortable with the idea of competing with other Third World states. In the Third World, Brazil or India are as much economic giants – and therefore intimidating to smaller developing countries – as, say, the United States or Japan. I think that it is unlikely, therefore, that there will be G77 or NAM unity on economic approaches in the foreseeable future. Some G77 states want such issues as the debt crisis to be tackled on a case-by-case basis – an approach favoured by the IMF. But many African states, hard hit in recent months by famine and falling commodity exports, are seeking a blanket approach to debt relief as part of a wider North–South transfer of resources.

Moreover, there are severe disagreements within G77 over which issues should enjoy pre-eminence in any international debate: India, which has become the Third World's fifth largest debtor (after Brazil, Mexico, Argentina and South Korea), wants to focus on convening a global conference on finance and money; the Africans want to stress development and famine-alleviation measures; the Latin Americans want to concentrate on debt-rescheduling; the newly industrialized countries of East and South-East Asia, such as Singapore, want to emphasize the dangers of protectionism and are calling for lowering trade barriers in the West; and various commodity producers are seeking more stable pricing conditions, especially since dollar prices for non-oil primary commodities in 1985 were roughly 11 per cent lower than in 1980. Economists are predicting that these non-oil commodity prices will fall further. (Oil prices, important for Third World oil-exporting states like Nigeria, Venezuela and Mexico, fell by 16.6 per cent from 1981 to 1985; by 1988, world prices of crude oil had tumbled in seven years from $36 a barrel to barely $10 a barrel!)

It may well be that at some future summit, nonaligned leaders will warm to the idea that Third World economic issues should be negotiated with the industrialized states on a subject-by-subject basis, rather than through a generalized, all-encompassing process. The problem with large-scale global negotiations is that they result in a cornucopia of demands, and political rhetoric often drowns worthwhile discussion of serious economic problems. Indira Gandhi was right in calling for a new Bretton Woods-type summit. Such a summit must be aimed not, as the original one was back in 1944, at restructuring the entire world financial system; but at cogently addressing the critical issues of debt and development. India's unique development experience eminently qualifies it to take a strong leadership role in organizing such a summit. But will the West show up?

The question of just how interested powerful Western countries are in allowing NAM to shape a global economic agenda is especially relevant these days. That is because leaders such as Ronald Reagan and Margaret Thatcher haven't displayed any great enthusiasm for tackling Third World concerns – beyond offering the overall pre-scription of free enterprise to solve developing nations' problems.

And can one blame Reagan, or Bush, or Thatcher, for being dubious about the contributions that NAM could make in setting right the global economy? A strong argument can be made to support the widely held view in powerful Western countries that NAM's usefulness has ended. The movement seems to survive largely on memories of a halcyon era that has forever gone, an age that featured giants such as Jawaharlal Nehru and Indira Gandhi. NAM – unlike, say, ASEAN or the Organization of African Unity

(OAU) – does not maintain a secretariat and a permanent bureaucracy, which makes the implementation of resolutions more random and at the mercy of the diplomatic status and capacity of the state heading the movement.

The movement's litany of failures is long. Its leaders have made some very bad calls concerning modern-day geopolitics and world economics. It has been obvious for many years now that NAM long ago lost its sense of direction, and perhaps even its purpose. The original vision held out by NAM's founding fathers of global solidarity has been overtaken by a myriad disputes within the nonaligned family. Of the 140 or so wars, battles and skirmishes since the Second World War, all but one or two have occurred in territories of NAM states (even though it can be argued – as does Richard Feinberg of Washington's prestigious think-tank, the Overseas Development Institute – that some of these disputes have been 'proxy wars' backed by one or the other of the superpowers). While there may be little internecine disagreement on questions such as the condemnation of the white-minority regime in South Africa, NAM states seem able to agree on few other critical matters facing the world community.

And I think that world audiences have become weary of the movement's conference diplomacy, the extravagance of its summits and the endless rhetoric of its leaders. NAM's summit documents have reflected the tendency of the movement's leadership to be garrulous: the Belgrade Declaration consisted of only 8 pages; the second summit at Cairo produced a declaration of 14 pages; by the time the NAM wound up its Colombo Summit in 1976, its final declaration had expanded to 62 pages. And when Fidel Castro banged the gavel at the end of the Havana Summit of 1979, delegates left with a final declaration of a hundred pages. None of this has enhanced the credibility of the movement, nor heightened its international stature.

While it is tempting to write off the movement as obsolete and valueless, I think that this would be unwise for three reasons:

● The staggering numbers of people who live in the 101 countries belonging to NAM have urgent concerns about their overwhelmingly inequitable lives. These concerns involve poverty, underdevelopment, environmental degradation and the problems of overpopulation, malnutrition and infant mortality. Because NAM represents almost 80 per cent of the world's population of five billion, it can still be a catalyst for concerted international action on these pressing problems.

● In an increasingly interrelated world, the economic and social well-being of Third World states is of growing relevance to the sound political and social health of Western economies. For instance, increased political tension and continued economic deterioration in the Third World would have a violent impact on the West in the form of accelerated illegal migration and terrorism.

● A new generation of Third World leaders is now coming into its own and needs to be given a chance to display its worth. These leaders – such as Rajiv Gandhi – represent a new generation of nonaligned figures: virtually all the founding patriarchs are dead now, and gone too from the scene are second-generation NAM leaders like the late Indira Gandhi and former President Julius Nyerere of Tanzania. Each generation of NAM leaders can be identified with a special set of concerns: the founding fathers wanted the movement to make a political impact; the second generation moved the movement towards economic advocacy; and Rajiv Gandhi's generation wants to make Third World systems deliver the fruits of modernization without the ideological over-tones that affected the policies of earlier NAM leaders.

The newer leaders' reading of the Third World's future is more pragmatic; and they seem to be convinced that unfashionable democracy and faith in the market are better bets for the future of their people than policies flowing from political dialectics. These newer leaders, of course, are relatively inexperienced, and they will need considerable strength and political dexterity to enhance their impact and shape the direction of the movement.

If the movement is to survive, NAM's leadership must chart an entirely different and bold agenda, one that focuses sharply on such pressing issues as debt relief, development and primary health care for children and mothers. The movement has never lacked for ideas; only priorities have been elusive to its leaders. Perhaps NAM should highlight the glaring contrasts between expenditures for destruction and expenditures for development: while the nations of the world spent $1.5 trillion in 1988 on defence, the overall figure for Western aid to Third World development programmes was barely $30 billion.

What NAM can also do now is to transform itself into a movement that focuses on pressing global issues such as overpopulation and the need to promote grassroots development. It need not, of course, abandon its traditional role as a conduit of Third World concerns about nuclear madness. However, if NAM is to be taken seriously by world leaders, it has not only to emphasize advocacy but also to advance specific strategies and action programmes for its own destitute millions.

The movement should more persuasively advocate self-reliance attitudes in Third World societies. In a world of shrinking aid from the West, Third World countries must pull themselves up by the sandal-straps and create better standards of living for their own people – and in a way that is sensitive to their own cultures.

Moreover, with runaway population-growth rates afflicting many black African states, the continent's overall population is expected to double to almost a billion in less than two decades. Non-African Third World states can construct a programme not only for intra-mural technical assistance to the sub-Saharan countries; they can also step up exchanges in agro-technology, light industrial expertise and health care. India has long exported teachers, technicians and physicians to many Third World countries, often through government-sponsored programmes. This is something that, with the glut of doctors and engineers and teachers in India today, Rajiv Gandhi might do even more of.

What we have, then, are roles already cast for a new concept of Third World leadership. The movement need look no further than at some of its newly emerging chieftains for guidance. President Premadasa of Sri Lanka, for example, has launched an inno-vative housing programme for his country's rural and urban poor. under which the government provides low-cost building materials and encourages people to construct their own homes. The sense of proprietorship, and the pride, of the new householders is striking; and such a low-cost programme can easily be replicated in many parts of the Third World, where housing shortages are acute. In Tunisia, the government can take credit for instituting population-control projects that are voluntary, that emphasize female literacy and employment, and that promote child health. In India, the government of Rajiv Gandhi has financed several village projects to revive cottage industries and absorb large numbers of the hopelessly unemployed.

Considering the fact that more than 75 million of the 85 million babies who were added to the world's population last year were born in the Third World, it should be of the utmost urgency that NAM leaders push for a global programme aimed at further lowering the world's still unacceptably high annual population-growth rate. At the current rate of growth, the world's population will double to almost 10 billion in less than thirty-five years. Here NAM can focus world attention on the need to raise resources for family planning, female education and employment, and child-health programmes, and to supplement the diminishing Western funds available to various multilateral agencies. The Nonaligned Movement can put Washington to shame for trimming its traditional support to such agencies at a time when the humanitarian needs of the world could not be greater.

I think that the compass of world power and the structure of global economics are such that the best hope for NAM appears to be in a diminution of political and economic dreams – and to focus on a more specific agenda of technological and social needs for Third World societies. NAM leaders, instead of unleashing more rhetoric that only irritates Western public opinion, should be developing links to sympathetic segments in the West in order to act in tandem in tackling problems like child health, food security, refugee movement, illegal migration, narcotics traffic and terrorism.

In fact, such subjects are already all there on NAM's voluminous cumulative agenda. The challenge now is to pick priorities, then to devise effective ways for action. It takes courage to shed old habits and forge a bold new path. All this necessitates, I think, greater cooperation between the Third World and the West. It requires, too, a rephrasing of the language of discourse.

I believe that the Nonaligned Movement – re-energized by India – has an opportunity to espouse genuine neutrality again by taking up cudgels on behalf of the causes of children and development. The highly charged rhetoric of another era will simply not bring any benefits to the movement or its members in a world that is increasingly mindful of the hard realities of economic and political power. Political morality can be best served today by measures and methods that will create hope out of despair, rather than by words that serviced the expectations of another era. The expectations of today's Indians and their brethren in the Third World are much the same as those of Westerners: a better life. But in countries such as India, a 'better life' doesn't necessarily mean another videorecorder, or an air-conditioner, or even a refrigerator – appliances that one takes for granted in many Western households these days. A 'better life' means better health care, better housing and freedom from hunger. Rajiv Gandhi is learning that his mother's slogan of '*Garibi hatao!*' is still a challenge for India's leaders. It is also a challenge for the mandarins of the Third World.

Nonalignment. Development. The alleviation of extreme poverty. These are all worthy principles and goals that have long formed an essential part of Indian foreign policy. But principles, like rules in a public-school dormitory, do get breached from time to time.

Picture this scene. A crisply cool January morning in Delhi. Prime Minister Olof Palme of Sweden is walking in a heavily guarded garden with his friend and political soulmate, Prime Minister Rajiv Gandhi of India. The talk turns to the bitter war between Iraq and Iran. The year is 1986, and the conflict has already dragged on for six years at a cost of more than $100 billion, and a million lives. Palme is pessimistic that anything could be done by the superpowers to end the war, especially the United States – whose bombing of Hanoi he once likened to Nazi Germany's efforts to exterminate the Jews.

And yes, says Palme, there was another unresolved matter as well – one that directly concerned his country and India. Gandhi, a fellow member of Palme's International Nuclear Disarmament Commission, knows perfectly well what Palme is referring to. He listens carefully as Palme spells out how Sweden would sweeten a deal under which India would buy $1.3 billion worth of howitzers from a failing Swedish weapons manufacturer. To undercut an attractive offer from a French competitor, GIAT, India was offered unprecedented state export credits, which Sweden had previously prohibited for arms deals.

This would be neutral Sweden's biggest export order ever; and the acquisition of the Bofors-made 155mm guns would enable India to shell Lahore, the second largest city in neighbouring Pakistan, from within Indian territory. Sweden, says Palme, badly needs India's business. Its competitors – Austria, the United States, France, Britain and even South Africa – have enough orders to sustain their domestic weapons industries for a long time. But the very survival of Sweden's armaments sector depends on Gandhi's decision, so how about it, my friend?

What followed was a nod, maybe also a nudge and a wink, and most certainly a handshake. Within a month or so, India and Sweden signed the deal, and soon afterwards Sweden started shipping Bofors howitzers at the monthly rate of fourteen. The order guaranteed employment for the company's 5,000 workers for at least another four years. On the day that the deal was signed, Bofors' chairman threw a champagne dinner for all employees and their families at the company's main plant in Karlskoga. There was also much jubilation in Bofors' parent company, Nobel Industries, which was founded by Alfred Nobel, the inventor of dynamite and the man who instituted the Nobel Peace Prize.

And the clincher for the Indian deal? Commissions worth more than $100 million, according to various investigators. Until 1987, Bofors resolutely denied that large payments were made in the howitzer deal. But after energetic research by Swedish journalists, including Bjarne Stenqvist and Bo Andersson of Stockholm's Dagens Nyheter, Bofors came clean – up to a point. It admitted that it had paid about $60 million to its India agents. And for what services rendered was this amount paid? Nobel Industries President Anders Carlberg told me in an interview in mid-1988 that the payments 'weren't bribes or commissions but wind-up costs' paid to Bofors' agents responsible for the India territory.

The payments, Carlberg insisted, were necessitated by an earlier meeting in New York in October 1985 between Palme and Rajiv Gandhi (during the party celebrating the fortieth anniversary of the United Nations). India's need for new howitzers was discussed. Gandhi, said Carlberg, demanded of Palme that there be no middlemen in any future weapons deals between Sweden and India. Palme then relayed the information to Carlberg. As a result, according to Carlberg, he had to wind up a longstanding deal with Bofors' Indian representatives. The $60 million was 'wind-up' money, Carlberg repeatedly insisted, not a commission.

I asked Carlberg who received the money. Each time I put the question, the handsome Swede froze me with his cold steely-blue eyes and then shook his head. 'I am not going to tell you,' he said.

Some Indian publications – most notably the Madras-based daily newspaper, *The Hindu*, and the Bombay-based *Imprint* magazine – have carried out impressive investigations that strongly suggest that Bofors money went to Indian expatriates and companies associated with these people. On 4 November 1988, the Opposition leader

V. P. Singh disclosed that he had evidence of payments by Bofors exceeding $15 million to Swiss bank accounts allegedly held by Indians. Singh, formerly Gandhi's finance and defence minister, and now his deadly political adversary, implied that the bulk of this money was paid to accounts personally controlled by Rajiv Gandhi. The accusation raised another political furor in India. It would be safe to suggest that as long as Rajiv Gandhi remains in power, more such revelations are bound to come from his political opponents.

In late April 1988, India's Joint Parliamentary Committee ruled that Bofors need not reveal the identities of those who received the questionable payments. This predictably touched off a political storm, with Opposition leaders accusing the Congress-dominated committee of carrying out a whitewash, and Gandhi of shielding his friends and associates. The fact is that with a $10 billion annual defence budget, the Indian government is in a position to award a lot of lucrative contracts to foreign suppliers. A middleman by any other name is still a middleman – and bribes by any other name are still bribes. There have long been reports that Congress leaders have secreted vast amounts siphoned from big arms deals. These amounts, according to numerous allegations, are kept abroad and then channelled into India during election time to benefit candidates belonging to the ruling Congress Party. And foreign arms suppliers, ever anxious to develop new business in the Third World, are often only too willing to pay commissions demanded of them: in most cases, of course, these 'commissions' paid to middlemen are factored into the overall amounts billed to the purchasers.

While Swedish law prohibits bribes for arms deals, authorities have long turned a blind eye to such practices, especially at a time when Sweden badly needs export orders and when the international arms bazaar has become a buyer's market. Gandhi has denied that he or any of his associates received bribes from Bofors, although Swedish authorities belatedly began investigating charges that the money was transferred into the Swiss bank accounts of three Indian companies. A month after meeting Gandhi in Delhi in 1986, Palme was murdered as he left a Stockholm cinema by a mysterious assassin. Not long afterwards, Palme was posthumously awarded India's prestigious Jawaharlal Nehru Prize, which is given annually to individuals who promote world peace and nonviolence.

It now turns out that the charismatic Swede was also a strenuous salesman for Swedish arms exports even as he travelled the world declaiming on disarmament. Indeed, when Palme headed a United Nations peace mission to Iran in 1979 – not long before he became prime minister for the second time – he was setting the stage for oil-and-arms deals for Sweden.

Why this surreptitious salesmanship? It is a familiar story, although one that many self-righteous Swedes wish to play down. It was important for Palme to save Sweden's arms industries from the double burden of declining domestic demand and the after-effects of steel-mill closures on regions traditionally housing defence producers like Karlskoga, where Bofors employs 80 per cent of the labour force. Arms exports not only ensured the defence industry's survival, they also paid for important technological research in defence. As a lifelong socialist, Palme believed in full employment – as long as someone else paid for it. And so he worked his charm, first on the Iranians, then on the Indians.

It could hardly have been coincidence, therefore, that in the three years after Palme took office in 1981, Sweden concluded oil deals with Iran amounting to nearly $200 million; oil purchases from Iraq, meanwhile, totalled barely $5.75 million, according to Swedish government estimates. Moreover, Iran bought large quantities of consumer goods from Sweden – more than $500 million worth in 1984 alone. Officially, at least, Sweden was supposed to be neutral in the Iraq–Iran war. And legally, Swedish companies were forbidden to export arms to areas where there were armed conflicts or human-rights violations.

Just around this time, the products of Swedish arms producers – mainly Bofors – were reportedly reaching Iran stealthily. The goods included nearly 1,000 RBS-70 anti-aircraft missiles, which were routed to the Middle East – including Iran – through two Singapore companies, Allied Ordnance of Singapore (AOS), and Unicorn International. Both firms were partly owned by Sheng Li Holding Company, the Singapore Defence Ministry's investment company, or by Bofors. According to Sweden's Bureau of Statistics, tiny Singapore was Sweden's biggest weapons customer between 1977 and 1986, buying $1.40 billion worth of goods, or almost 11 per cent of all Swedish arms exports during the period.

This wasn't the first time that Swedish companies had acted in a questionable fashion in the Third World. Nor was Palme the only Swede connected with arms deals to die in mysterious circumstances. In January 1987, Carl-Fredrik Algernon, director of

Sweden's arms export agency, fell in front of an incoming subway train at Stockholm's Central Station. He had emerged as a key figure in various investigations of Bofors. Witnesses said at first that the 61-year-old Algernon was pushed in front of the train, but the testimony was later recanted. His death has been officially termed an accident, and possibly a suicide. 'Swedes take great pride in their social stability,' says Dr Ian Anthony, an arms expert based in Stockholm. 'These mysterious, unresolved matters perplex them and cause much angst.'

Sweden's current prime minister, Ingvar Carlsson, swore in late September 1987 that stricter rules would be drafted governing weapons exports. There would also be a crackdown on the foreign marketing operations of arms firms, he said, and more rigid monitoring of preliminary contracts between arms producers and potential buyers. The Indians, who feel they got a good deal on the 400 Bofors howitzers, are not about to cancel the deal. As for the alleged bribes, Bofors says that neither Prime Minister Gandhi nor his family were recipients – a statement that the prime minister's political opponents seriously question. It will be quite a while before all the Swedish investigations are completed, and meanwhile Bofors is firmly in business again.

For weapons suppliers, countries such as India are choice customers. And when local governments encourage commission-giving on the part of weapons suppliers, the potential for corruption is awesome. Governments are, after all, supposed to be the guardians of the public welfare. But when governments are in league with shady characters, who remains to protect the public interest? And aren't commissions a theft of public money that might otherwise be spent on economic development for the masses?

The lesson of the Bofors story is that sometimes a combination of a nation's strategic needs and its leaders' human greed, force an unsavoury modification of foreign policy. India is no exception to this. And the Bofors episode has spilled over from being a 'foreign' issue into a highly charged domestic controversy. To put it another way, the harsh realities of Gandhi's foreign policy have dragged India's lofty moral principles into the mud. Indians can now legitimately ask whether there is any difference between the political and financial behaviour of Rajiv Gandhi and his associates, and that of, say, Zaire's corrupt dictator, Mobutu Seko Sese, or the deposed Philippines despot, Ferdinand Marcos.

For Gandhi's wellwishers, it is tempting to describe these accusations as baseless political changes. But India's masses are becoming increasingly conscious of the need for probity in government – and they are not likely to take the same generous view of 'wind-up costs'.

The Bofors case was a glaring example of how developing nations get enmeshed in economic commitments that arise partly as a result of Big Power geopolitics. It can be argued that if the United States hadn't armed Pakistan beyond its legitimate military requirements, India would not have accelerated the arms race on the subcontinent. Of course, Pakistanis could well argue the same case the other way around – just substituting the Soviet Union for the United States!

Notwithstanding India's spirited talk of nonalignment and economic self-sufficiency, the fundamental fact remains that India needs sustained and good relations with the big powers. Consider the following figures: in 1987, nearly 10 per cent of the country's total imports (mainly capital goods, machinery, etc.) of $13.5 billion came from the United States; 8.1 per cent from Britain; 9.6 per cent from West Germany; 12.7 per cent from Japan; 5.3 per cent from the Soviet Union; and 9.4 per cent from other industrial countries excluding the above. And the exports from India? Of nearly $10 billion worth of gems, commodities, tea, coffee, leather, textiles, etc., nearly 20 per cent went to the United States; 14.9 per cent to the Soviet Union; 10.7 per cent to Japan; 10.6 per cent to the Common Market countries; 5.9 per cent to West Germany; and 5.9 per cent to Britain.

With the United States being the biggest trading partner of India, you would think that relations between the two countries would be more affable. But the relationship has been, at best, ambiguous. At the heart of this is India's attempt to prevent the extension of American power around the world – power that Indian officials see as being intimidating to small and medium-sized countries. Of course, there is also the historical resentment over the US selection of Pakistan as the cutting edge of Washington's South Asia policy. Squaring off against this historical animus is the mounting Indian desire for American technology.

And so, since Rajiv Gandhi became prime minister, Delhi has been a bit more flexible towards Washington, even though the latter hasn't always reciprocated. A significant aspect of Rajiv

Gandhi's foreign-policy efforts has been the encouragement he has given to private individuals to promote India's image and ideas abroad.

For instance, a close Gandhi associate, Kamal Dandona, a New York-based businessman, makes it a point to develop personal ties with influential legislators in order to convey India's views in Washington better. Taking time off from his electronic-goods business, Dandona – a former employee of Air India – helped form the Indian National Congress of America. In 1986, he organized a successful campaign to ensure that Washington would not sell sophisticated AWAC planes to Pakistan. Dandona brought hundreds of US-based Indians by bus to Washington to convince Congressmen that the electronic surveillance aircraft would pose a grave security threat to India.

Just as Kamal Dandona helps Indian policy-makers through his private contacts, Prakash Shah is instrumental in enhancing the awareness of the American business and corporate communities concerning investment opportunities in India. Shah has his own flourishing management business, but donates a great deal of his time to the India Chamber of Commerce of America in New York, of which he is the executive director. Among other activities, Shah and the organization's full-time director, Patricia Erdman, host tours of the US for Indian industrialists, introducing them to the titans of American industry. They regularly arrange seminars where Indian officials and businessmen make sales pitches for foreign investment in India. 'Economics is a key, but often over-looked, element of a nation's foreign policy,' says Mohan Shah, a businessman who has long been a supporter of Rajiv Gandhi.

Then there is Janki Ganju, 'Mr India' himself, a longtime fixture on the Washington scene. Ganju, a portly, silver-haired *bon vivant*, has been a lobbyist for India for more than three decades. He has often persuaded important journalists and Congressmen not ordi-narily kindly disposed towards India, to be more accommodating and attentive to India's political and economic needs. He does this by assiduously cultivating contacts on Capitol Hill and in the American executive branch. He also entertains frequently at his home, preparing savoury dishes himself from his native Kashmir. As a result, Ganju has developed key alliances in Washington; many a putative crisis in Indo-American relations has been private-ly resolved because of his informal diplomacy. As his businessman friend Mohan Shah often says, the thought of Washington without Ganju is like curry without spice.

And there is Asoka Dutt, who for the last three decades has been a prominent part of the highly competitive public-relations scene in New York. Dutt, who was personally close to both Nehru and Indira Gandhi, is currently engaged in promoting India's image before media audiences in the US. He sponsors appearances by Indians on American television and radio shows, and at various educational and cultural institutions, in order to present aspects of India that foreign audiences might not ordinarily be familiar with – such as Indian classical dance, music and literature. These appearances have proved highly popular. Dutt selects articulate and attractive Indians (not necessarily officials) who are escorted to TV and other outlets around the US by his assistant, Twilla Duncan, a savvy American who knows the Third World well. Miss Duncan coaches these Indians about media techniques and about how to talk effectively before American audiences. And the purpose of all this? Not only to promote an awareness of India, but also to promote Indian tourism.

The 'diplomacy of personality' as exemplified by people such as Dandona, Ganju, Shah and Dutt is possible, of course, in societies whose political systems are open to such persuasion. It is inconceivable that these men would work or flourish in, say, Moscow. But then, relations between the Soviet Union and India do not lend themselves to crisis-management. Indeed, the Soviet Union enjoys a status in Delhi that it possesses in virtually no other major Third World country. Originally, tacit alliance with Moscow was seen by Indian policy-makers as a balance against US interests in the region. But the relationship has become far more deep and complex than that. In 1971, for instance, the two countries signed a treaty of peace, friendship and cooperation. Since then, the Soviet Union has been steadily importing more consumer goods from India; and India has been buying more military hardware from Moscow. Indeed Soviet aircraft, submarines, tanks, and other weapons systems have become the mainstay of India's armed forces.

Since Gorbachev rose to power, he has already visited India several times. In late November 1988, for example, he announced in Delhi that the Soviet Union would extend to India about 3.2 billion roubles in credit to cover the Soviet construction of two nuclear reactors to produce electricity for southern India, and other non-nuclear energy projects. With such gestures continually emanating from Moscow, together with large-scale cultural and educational exchange programmes, it will be difficult to dislodge the Russians from a very special place in the minds and hearts of Indian officials, if not necessarily those of ordinary Indians.

A cordial relationship with the Kremlin also helps Delhi to blunt threats from indigenous communists. During Gorbachev's November 1988 visit to India, for instance, he did not meet Indian communist leaders, as he did during his 1986 trip. With these gestures, Gorbachev seems to be taking out political insurance that India's public reaction to Soviet adventures and misadventures in the international arena will be, at the worst, moderate. The Soviet connection is very valuable to India, so Delhi is unlikely to criticize Moscow too strongly, but Indians are concerned that the Russians will improve their relationship with Beijing and Islamabad to their own detriment. India is also concerned about how its relationship with the Soviet Union would fit into the new framework resulting from internal structural and policy changes in Gorbachev's 'new' Soviet Union.

If India's relationship with the Soviet Union is remarkable, then perhaps even more extraordinary is India's nexus with Britain. This is a relationship between a former master and slave who now treat each other as fully equal members of the comity of nations. Despite occasional political hiccups – such as the question of immigration to the UK – the relationship between India and Britain continues to be a model for former colonial bosses and subjects. Indeed, as time recedes, even the colonial relationship develops the glow of nostalgia which engenders a residual affection.

More than forty years after that 'freedom at midnight', this remains a relationship more lodged in friendship and affection than that between any other imperial and subjugated country. Amicable personal relations between successive leaders of the two countries partly explains this relationship; for instance, Mrs Gandhi developed an unusual and unlikely friendship with the ideologically very different Mrs Thatcher. And Rajiv Gandhi maintains a cordial connection with No. 10 Downing Street. When Mrs Gandhi was assassinated, Prime Minister Thatcher flew to Delhi for the funeral, a gesture that was applauded and admired by tens of millions of

Indians who did not seem as impressed by the other world dignitaries who had also flown to Delhi to pay their last respects to the 'Empress of India'.

A key aspect of the India–Britain relationship has been the fact that India has not nationalized substantial British investments, unlike many other newly independent Third World countries that appropriated British commercial assets after gaining freedom. Trade and financial relationships have prospered, moreover, perhaps because Indian and British businessmen understand each other's commercial ways better than most other players in a two-way commercial traffic. Cricketing ties between the two countries also help. Stars such as Ian Botham are as much household names in India as they are in Britain.

Moreover, the million-strong Indian community in Britain has, for the most part, adapted well to its new home; and it has played an important though unobtrusive role in British society. A great deal of credit for strengthening 'Indo-British relations' in Britain itself must go to people like Swraj Paul, an industrialist, and Rajpal Singh Chowdhury, an entrepreneur and publisher. These men strenuously lobby the British Establishment, and host well-publicized dinners to commemorate such occasions as India's Republic Day. And they make sure that their channels of communication with British politicians – and particularly the Foreign Office – are always kept open. The aggregate impact of such activities is that formidable goodwill towards India is generated in influential British circles. Chowdhury's glossy magazine, *Kohinoor*, regularly featured articles that encompass a broad range of subjects – from art to politics to history – concerning the two countries. Because of Chowdhury's personal access to Rajiv Gandhi and his influence in Delhi society, he enjoys added respect in his adopted home base of London.

The activities of people like Paul and Chowdhury, to be sure, attract criticism. Paul was accused of being a money-manager for Indira Gandhi; Chowdhury's detractors contend that he is developing a cult of personality. However, my own feeling is that their individual efforts go a long way towards strengthening India's ties with countries such as Britain – countries that matter significantly in India's bilateral relationships and whose own influence in world affairs is considerable. Perhaps private diplomacy may even be more effective in the long run than Foreign Office pronouncements or long-winded speeches by Indian cabinet ministers at the United Nations.

As with Britain, India's relationships with Western European countries have a strong degree of warmth and an increasing element of economic benefit. This has in turn translated into growing trade ties. The relationships have been cemented with many construction and weapons contracts being awarded to European companies. Sonia Gandhi's Italian heritage has been an unstated but important factor in strengthening such ties. As Europe grows into closer union with the approach of 1992, it is likely that its relationship with India will increase in importance because they will both represent medium-sized powers lodged between major superpower blocs of the world. Political wags explain Rajiv Gandhi's special interest in Western Europe as offering a clue to his 'exile option' if things go sour in Indian politics for him.

On balance, it is clear that India's consistency in foreign policy has paid important dividends – although not always to the liking of Western policy-makers. To them, India's pronouncements on world affairs often seem self-righteous, moralistic and preaching – a charge that has some validity, of course. You only have to sit through a committee session at the United Nations to be persuaded about the pompousness of many Indian officials. However, such loftiness must be perceived as an abrasive shield behind which an old culture seeks to hide some of its domestic failures and insecurities. India has no more of a monopoly of moral values than any other Third World country or industrialized nation, but India officials have yet to fully accept this.

Still, I think that the management of India's policies in foreign affairs by successive prime ministers, starting with Jawaharlal Nehru, has been largely consistent over the years and has contributed significantly to the country's enhanced status in world affairs. These policies, although modified from time to time by the personal relationships of India's leaders with foreign leaders, are likely to be maintained whatever the political complexion and creed of future Indian governments.

EPILOGUE:
THE ASIAN CENTURY

Almost from the start of his stewardship, Rajiv Gandhi recognized that it would be important for India to build better political and trade ties with the economic success stories of Asia: Japan, Singapore, South Korea and Malaysia, in particular. Rajiv saw those countries as offering several lessons for India in economic management – regardless of the fact that they were so culturally different, smaller and more domestically manageable. Although India had already become the world's tenth biggest industrial power by the time Rajiv succeeded his mother as prime minister, the country's annual exports and *per capita* income were not growing rapidly. And India's moribund bureaucracy was severely retarding economic growth.

Gandhi, a firm believer in free enterprise, had seen how the Asia–Pacific region had led the world in economic growth. Some of these economic giants had few natural resources; the engine of their growth was an unfettered private sector. In 1987, for example, the real gross domestic product (GDP) growth for Japan was 4.9 per cent; Hongkong, 13.5 per cent; Singapore, 9.8 per cent; Thailand, 7.1 per cent; Taiwan, 12.3 per cent; South Korea, 12.2 per cent; Malaysia, 6 per cent; and China, 9.4 per cent. The figure for India was about 4 per cent.

What could be done to stimulate economic growth? How could India become a genuine economic giant – a 'tiger', as Singapore, South Korea, Taiwan and Hongkong were each being widely called? Asia's economic tigers would almost certainly sustain their drive well into the next century; indeed, it may well be that the twenty-first century will become known as 'the Asian century', just as the twentieth has been termed 'the American century'.

With Japan's fantastic advance in technology and accumulation of investment capital, China's enormous and inexpensive labour pool, and the resources of the Pacific Basin, it seems almost inevitable that the global centre of economic gravity will shift to East and South-East Asia in the next generation. The linchpin of this scenario will of course be Japan, whose economic dynamism has already profoundly affected world markets (its trade surplus in 1988, for example, was almost $100 billion). But the economic slipstream of the new Nipponese giant will undoubtedly uplift all the economies in the area. The conditions for this great leap forward are already evident in the economic indices of the region.

How could India aspire to be a leading player of this emerging era? Gandhi knew that by most conventional measurements, India's economic performance since independence was remarkable. In 1947, Rajiv's grandfather, Jawaharlal Nehru, inherited a country that had experienced economic stagnation, and declining *per capita* income and *per capita* foodgrain production. Nearly 85 per cent of India's people lived in villages and were involved in traditional, low-productivity agriculture. The industrial sector was small and not globally competitive. Barely 15 per cent of the population was literate. Nutritional levels were appalling, communicable diseases were rampant and infant-mortality rates were among the highest in the world. Average life expectancy at birth was less than thirty-five years.

By 1988, India had come a long way in promoting industrialization, spreading literacy and widening the availability of health care and education. Life expectancy is now close to sixty years. One of the most significant accomplishments was the creation of a cadre of highly skilled men and women in the physical and social sciences, engineering, management, public administration and the arts. Says the World Bank's senior vice-president for operations, Moeen A. Qureshi: 'Such trained manpower is the envy of other developing countries. It should be an example to some industrialized countries as well.' In fact, India is said to have the biggest cadre of technical manpower in the world, after the United States and the Soviet Union.

And yet, Rajiv Gandhi realized, Indians by and large widely seemed uneasy about their future. The goal of eliminating poverty seemed as distant in 1988 as it was back in 1947. The number of people living in absolute poverty was put by the World Bank at nearly 300 million! The fundamental reasons for the persistence of poverty are largely two: the continued high population-growth rate; and the fact that, despite the impressive industrial and technological advances, the Indian economy hasn't grown fast enough or long enough to provide above-subsistence income opportunities for the poor – especially the very poor.

India's population trebled between 1901 and 1986. It took 65 years for the 1901 population to double but within the next 20 years the population had increased by a further 30 per cent. In less than 35 years, India is likely to double its present population of 800 million people. The accelerating population growth has, of course, steadily increased the density of population. In 1981, for example, population density was 208 people per square kilometre in India, while in Asia as a whole the figure was 95 people per square kilometre. The figure for Western Europe was 98; for the United States, 15; and for Africa – where annual birth rates are among the highest in the world – the population density figure was 16 per square kilometre.

The population-growth rate and the density figures have had crippling impacts on India's economic performance. The World Bank estimates that if the real gross domestic product (GDP) had increased annually at the rate of 5 per cent since 1947 – rather than between 1 and 3 per cent – Indians' *per capita* income would today be almost 50 per cent higher. And if the annual population-growth rate had been just half a percentage point lower, *per capita* income today would have been 60 per cent higher. Lost opportunities, lost dreams.

Most Westerners find it difficult to comprehend the notion that 300 million Indians live in abject poverty. But look at it this way: the figure is almost the combined population of Britain and the United States. It would even be appropriate, given this mind-numbing number of poor people, to wonder why India hasn't had its own violent revolution. In fact, Indians have been extremely tolerant of their lot in life. They have also been, excessively so, tolerant of their leaders' shortcomings. Time and again, they have overlooked corruption, weaknesses of character, authoritarian tendencies, ineptitude. Indians have given their leaders, particularly from the Congress Party, more second and third chances than they deserved.

And sadly, this tolerance hasn't resulted in a worthy response from India's leaders. These *netaas* – the Hindi word for homespun leaders, a word sometimes used in sarcasm – haven't responded to this tolerance with greater concern for poor people's plight but with greater venality.

As Rajiv Gandhi completes his first term in office his report card, on balance, is one of good intentions and mixed performance. A second chance for Rajiv? Can we expect him to improve on his political and economic performance?

A 'second chance' would depend on the people's view of who can best deliver results with regard to the agenda facing the nation. And a second chance would mean not only winning elections but also revitalizing the political and bureaucratic system – in short, girding the national loins. There is a greater popular consciousness that things have gone wrong in the body politic, and there is mounting awareness of just who has been responsible for the many problems of India.

Looking ahead, what are the realistic changes and improvements that can renew hope for India's aspiring masses? Such an agenda for India would perhaps include the following:

● Stimulation of the economy in order to generate more productivity, create more wealth and better distribute income. There must be accelerated dismantling of the bureaucratic Licence Raj. There must be greater competition for Indian industry. Opportunities for foreign investment must be widened. In our world of increasing global interdependency, India cannot afford impediments to competition in domestic markets. As Ashok Birla says, India's industrialists simply must shape up. Virtually all modern-day economic 'miracle' stories from West Germany to Singapore have been created from the primacy of exports. Moreover, every one of these 'miracle' countries has had highly educated populations – and thus there is the need to accelerate literacy programmes in India.

● The elimination of 'socialism' from the national dictionary. Marxist philosophy, however mildly applied in national economic policy, has proved to be a prescription for disaster all over the Third World. Indian politicians often argue that a completely 'free' economy would lead to abuses. Well, the situation could hardly worsen beyond the excesses and abuses of statist bureaucracy that Indian-style 'socialism' has created. Moreover, the government can always play a better regulatory and monitoring role. But, as the late Ludwig Erhard – the West German chancellor and architect of his country's extraordinary post-war economic recovery –

once said, if you let the men and money loose, prosperity will follow.

● Trimming the gargantuan bureaucracy. In India, 'socialism' has too long stood for statism. And the most privileged Indians have been the politicians who proclaimed socialism in the first place, and the upper-echelon bureaucrats who profited by the proliferation of the licence system. Bureaucracies breed corruption. Today it is often impossible even to get into a bureaucrat's office without greasing the palm of his peon. But the peon charges you just a handful of rupees; the paper-pushers inside the comfortably air-conditioned offices in Delhi secretariats and state capitals demand considerably more – even foreign-currency payments.

● Instituting genuinely honest and accountable government. When Rajiv Gandhi became prime minister, the Indian press instantly gave him a sobriquet: 'Mr Clean'. Everyone expected him to rid politics of the peculation and thievery that had become rampant. And, indeed, some of Gandhi's early moves were heartening: he got rid of some ministers who were considered corrupt; he drafted a bill that made it virtually impossible for members of Parliament to switch parties for reasons of expediency; he vowed to cut down on election expenses because such costs fuel corruption and enhance the clout of frequently illegal political contributions. But then things settled back into 'politics as usual'. So much so that once-trusted friends and allies such as Arun Singh and Arun Nehru left the government, and Rajiv's circle, in disgust. Now Gandhi surrounds himself with men of small stature and sycophantic dispositions. Indeed, the two national politicians who these days enjoy high national repute for personal honesty and integrity belong to the Opposition: V. P. Singh of Uttar Pradesh, and Ramakrishna Hegde of Karnataka. In fact, in an action possibly unprecedented in Indian public life, Hegde resigned as his state's chief minister in 1988 after newspaper disclosures concerning a dispute about the illegal bugging of officials' phones in Karnataka.

● Satisfying the needs and expectations of India's growing middle class. This means encouraging more consumer industries, creating wider employment opportunities, promoting higher education in the small towns and rural regions of India, and giving them an opportunity to participate in financial gains. A strong middle class strengthens the economy. Consumer spending by the middle class rose by 20 per cent in 1988, after rains ended a three-year drought. A growing economy means more jobs. One of India's most astute industrialists, Dhirubhai Ambani, recognized the yearning of the middle class for participating in the economy's growth. Ambani, once a petty clerk, started his Reliance Group to manufacture textiles, synthetic fabrics, chemicals and engineering goods. He began issuing shares in order to raise capital – and now more than 2 million Indians hold Reliance stock, making Ambani's flourishing company the world's third or fourth biggest in terms of the total number of shareholders.

• Emphasizing grassroots development projects. This would especially include encouraging private voluntary civic organizations that are rapidly sprouting all over the country to tackle effectively the problem of poverty and other social concerns. Many of these groups are stimulating popular awareness of environmental hazards such as acid rain in large cities where industries are concentrated. Private groups are promoting handicrafts and other cottage industries in rural areas, thereby creating badly needed jobs for artisans. Other groups are working vigorously to promote female literacy and employment. Female literacy, in fact, is frequently the key to smaller families, as is female employment.

• Promoting an enhanced secular social agenda. This means that national leaders must act forcefully to reduce communalism – particularly the increasing religious tensions between Hindus and Moslems. Unfortunately, the Gandhi administration has at times shamelessly pandered to Moslems in order to win votes: it recently banned Salman Rushdie's new novel, *The Satanic Verses*, because some Moslem extremists were offended by the London-based writer's references to the Prophet Mohammed. Earlier, Gandhi bowed to Moslem fundamentalist demands that Moslem women should not be subjected to civil laws concerning divorce but to traditional Islamic tenets. Through such compromises, the government has set into motion a process where secularism will be irreparably eroded.

• Developing a better working relationship between the central government and India's states. Gone for ever are the days when one party – specifically, the Congress – can control national as well as local administrations. As N. T. Rama Rao says, if the limbs are strong, so will the entire body politic be. Rajiv Gandhi, unlike his mother, seems to appreciate this thought. His accord in Mizoram state, where an armed rebellion had been waged by local tribes for nearly two decades, was a genuine act of statesmanship. Gandhi persuaded the Mizoram rebels to give up their arms in exchange for free elections. Indeed, the local rebel chief, a man named Laldenga, then became the state's chief minister (only to resign later). Another Gandhi triumph was the Assam Accord, in another eastern border province like Mizoram. Here the tensions were between tribal people from the hill areas and the natives of the plains. Again – as with the Punjab – the prime minister held successful negotiations, which led to elections that a non-Congress party won. In 1988, Gandhi secured assurances of cooperation from the virulent Gurkhaland National Liberation Front, which enjoyed the support of more than 600,000 Gurkhas – the fierce warrior tribe that fought so valiantly in the British army in several wars and colonial adventures. The Gurkhas were given assurances that they'd be allowed to form their own Hill Council to look into local grievances. The common thread in all these developments was Gandhi's willingness to coopt local leaders, not to engage them in confrontation. Rajiv Gandhi is not often given credit for his determination to create better relations with regional opponents. Yet Gandhi must also bear the responsibility for the almost universally quick collapse for every one of these promising breakthroughs.

• Mobilizing young people to participate in the delivery of services to rural regions and urban slums. More than 50 per cent of India's population is under twenty-five years of age. Why not a national programme, a sort of domestic 'peace corps', under which college students or even high-school kids spend part of their academic year in villages? There are some states that do promote such schemes; but a nationwide programme would be highly effective in binding together the nation's different communities. The young people could assist in a variety of projects such as road-building, teaching, educating rural folk about sanitation and hygiene. In a country where there is little geographical mobility, a national job programme of this kind would also serve to educate the young about lifestyles in various states – states that might be as foreign to them as other countries.

• Creating better relations with neighbouring nations. Regional harmony is often the precursor of strengthening international relations. The Sri Lanka Accord of 1987 was meant to resolve the bitter civil war in that island-nation, and Rajiv Gandhi mediated with compassion and with a willingness to use India's influence where appropriate. Sadly, the internal situation deteriorated, making India's original action counterproductive. India needs to work out a more amicable relationship with Bangladesh, with whom there has been a long-standing feud over river waters, and with other neighbours.

• Resolving the China dispute. In December 1988, Gandhi made a dramatic visit to China. Relations between the two countries have been troubled since border clashes broke out in the 1950s. In 1962, India and China went to war – and the Chinese thrashed the Indians, seizing sizeable chunks of Indian territory in the process. Moreover, the Chinese have fomented agitation among several tribes in India's border states. The visit by Gandhi was the first in twenty-nine years by a leader of either nation: the last high-level visit was made by the then prime minister Chou En-Lai to Delhi in 1960. China insists that the McMahon Line – the 700-mile border drawn up by the British in 1914 in what is now the Arunachal Pradesh region of India – was imposed unilaterally. Indeed, Beijing refuses to recognize this border. India, for its part, wants the Chinese to return 14,500 square miles of Ladakh's Aksai Chin region, which they captured during the 1962 war. A pity, this dispute. It has caused so much grief over the decades. Perhaps with improved relations, the two countries might even increase their trade, which currently stands at about $145 million annually. Here are two ancient lands both undergoing modernization. Conflict between them involves 40 per cent of the world's population. Why not march towards the future in cordiality and cooperation?

Such an agenda can only become workable if another dimension is added. No material programme can work in India unless there is a revival of that spirit of commitment which distinguished India's Freedom Movement. India, more than any other Third World land, is a nation sensitive to spiritual influences. Mahatma Gandhi and the other founding fathers of modern India understood this; they used these forces to sustain their more practical policies. The agenda for tomorrow must seek to mobilize these intangibles and draw from the immense psychological and spiritual resources of Indian culture. Unless it does so, the most sophisticated of modern plans will not engender the sense of national discipline and sacrifice for the common good that is the essential ingredient for the alchemy of progress.

To write about India is, finally, to care even more deeply about India. Some of my acquaintances in India ask me occasionally – and with barely suppressed sneers – how I, an expatriate Indian, could presume to write about a country so large, diverse and distant from the place where I make my home, New York.

I have been privileged to be a journalist for more than two decades, enjoying a front-row seat in the arena of contemporary affairs. Not often does a journalist get personal tutoring on such a complicated subject as poverty and development and it was my good fortune that I did.

The early tutorials came from my parents. This parental education was much too brief, however. I can now think of so many questions to ask my parents about their experiences. But we borrow our parents from the cosmic reservoir only for a very short time, and when they are gone, they are gone.

My mother died not long ago, barely ten months after my father passed away. A close family friend, who helped with the funeral arrangements, asked what my mother's life meant to me. He said that perhaps I should one day explain to my young son the nexus between my mother and myself because it was important that children understand what went into the making of their parents, what the threads and seams were that joined the generations. During the funeral, sitting by myself on a bench in a Bombay crematorium watching the flames from my mother's pyre blaze into the clear blue December sky, I grasped for the connections between her life and mine.

As I watched my mother's body crumble into ashes, it occurred to me that there were perhaps many of my generation who, in their anxiety to develop nuclear families and escape the smothering traditionalism of their parents' societies, fled so fast from their backgrounds that they often failed to comprehend where they had come from. How important it was to understand, it seemed to me, why it was that some escaped being part of the world's 'silent crisis' of poverty, deprivation and unnecessary death, while others did not. Was it simply *karma*, the accident of birth?

In my mother's case, she never forgot her roots. She was born a Hindu in the village of Chauk in Maharashtra, a state in the

Western region of India. She was the youngest of two surviving daughters and a son of an obscure Indian Army subaltern, Ramchandra Pradhan. Seven Pradhan children died in their first year, the victims of tetanus or diarrhoeal infections or diphtheria. My mother herself had suffered from an attack of poliomyelitis.

As an adult my mother never returned to Chauk; she always refused to show me her birthplace, which was a hovel in a village elder's backyard. The three children, after the death of their father, were shunted from one relative's home to another. My mother told me that she and her siblings were frequently made to work as servants, cleaning toilets and scrubbing floors. The children were often abused by irascible relatives, but they suffered in silence because to complain would have meant eviction.

The early years of my mother's marriage to my father were hard. He was a struggling solicitor in Bombay; she was a teacher, and also worked on her doctoral thesis. Their first child, a boy, died within hours of being born. The baby was barely two pounds at birth; babies born that size are much more likely to die than infants weighing at least 5.5 pounds. My mother told me that she often blamed herself for the death of this child because she was unable to get proper nutrition: my parents were so consumed by the demands of holding down several petty jobs just to earn a handful of rupees that they didn't pay sufficient attention to pre-natal care.

I was born in 1948, almost a year after India obtained its independence from Britain. My mother spent an excruciating day in labour, and finally the physicians performed a caesarian to get me out. A few days later, a tumour was discovered in my skull; then I fell victim to an infection that apparently resulted from unhygienic hospital conditions. On two occasions in my first year, my mother told me, I came close to death on account of respiratory and diarrhoeal problems. But my parents were determined not to lose another child. I became the object of close attention and constant affection. I lived.

Many of my childhood memories are of my mother's various political, literary and community activities.

One such memory is of the night my mother was elected from the Dadar constituency to the Bombay Municipal Corporation, the equivalent of a city council in a Western metropolis. I remember being in an old car that was part of a procession. Drums rolled and conch shells were sounded. The music of *shehnai*, Indian clarinets, was in the air. Sweetmeats were distributed. I remember my father patiently explaining to me the electoral process, and I can still remember my mother's tears of joy.

Yet her political life was less fulfilling than she would have liked. Although she was active in the ruling Congress Party, she was not included in the Maharashtra state cabinet, which had been her ambition; she felt that in government she would have been even more useful in promoting women's rights and children's welfare. But my mother did not display her private wounds in public. Instead, she accelerated her literary and social work. She churned out scores of novels, plays and short stories. She wrote radio scripts and film documentaries.

Long before I heard United Nations experts expound on the subject 'children first!' I heard my mother passionately speak out about children at countless forums in India. Her message – unconventional at the time – to poor women was always: nothing is pre-ordained, it is possible to unshackle oneself from poverty. A better lot for children was possible, too. But for any national change to occur and for progress to be sustained, Third World governments had to continually commit economic and political resources in order to eradicate poverty.

Growing up as a son of a woman of letters, I was always surrounded by books and by literary people. My mother would take me to the homes of these writers, and they would visit our home. Their discussions were often about crushing poverty, high infant-mortality, and the low economic status of women in India. Some of these writers – including my mother – had started visiting various Asian and African countries that were about to unshackle themselves from their British or French colonial rulers. In those days – the early and mid-1950s – Indian writers, educators and sociologists were becoming increasingly interested in other poor societies. They wanted to understand the social dynamics there, and also to see if the still-evolving prescriptions for social and economic progress in India could be replicated elsewhere in post-colonial states. And so the talk in our living-room was also about the development priorities of these soon-to-be-independent nations. I was too young to understand everything that was discussed, of course, but through osmosis I must have absorbed some of our friends' concerns.

There was also the political traffic through our home. Among my childhood memories are those of visits by local politicians. Some of these men and women became my mother's allies in her campaigns for children's rights and women's causes. She established women's organizations to promote the development of literary skills among women. She started local agencies to push for better child care, and for better health facilities for pregnant women and new mothers. Sometimes accompanied by my father – who supported her projects with great zest and often with his personal funds – she travelled to distant rural areas.

One such assignment involved visiting a village not far from Bombay to prepare a report on health care for children. I must have been six or seven years old then, and my mother took me along for the ride. She suggested that I donate some old toys to the local children, which I immediately resented and resisted.

'What is one less toy for you?' my mother said. 'You'll be meeting children who don't even know what toys are.'

Not long ago, my son Jaidev and I happened to be walking past a slum in Delhi. It was a chilly winter evening, it had just rained, and some people were warming themselves in front of a fire that had been lit in a tin drum in a muddy courtyard. This area of shacks and shanties nestled in the shadows of grand edifices occupied by the élite of democratic India. Most of the children wore faded clothes, and some of them had sores on their skins. Their elders looked emaciated and weary. It was a feature-page scene of Third World hopelessness, and my son was instantly intrigued.

'Who are they?' he asked.

'They are just people,' I said. 'Just like you and me.'

'But we don't live like this,' Jaidev said.

'That's because we are luckier,' I said.

'Can I share something with them?' my son, then eight years old, said.

'Yes, you can,' I said, both startled and exhilarated. Of course, by 'sharing', Jaidev, in his innocence, meant giving of some of the good things of life he enjoys. However, I would like to think that this also meant a sincere concern for the more unfortunate – an attitude we must all hope will be reflected in a special sensitivity in tomorrow's generation.

What seemed to echo in Jaidev was my mother's spirit. I hope he sustains his precocious concern for the underprivileged of India when he grows up. If my son reaches out to those far less fortunate than him, he will be part of a cycle that was sparked by an extraordinary woman from a tiny village in India.

That is why – despite the daily discouraging headlines – I am hopeful for the India of today and tomorrow. I like to think that there are millions of Jaidevs in the country where both he and I were born. The hopes and dreams of India's founders have only been partially fulfilled over the last four decades. Fully to translate those dreams into reality is the task of today's generation and the one to which my son belongs.

These dreams were foreshadowed by the visions of India's founders. If the nation-building ideas of Mahatma Gandhi and Jawaharlal Nehru are not made a reality, India could implode into a nightmare of a broken country and broken dreams, never to rise in a cohesive form again. If political chaos and economic deterioration accelerate, the centrifugal forces of communalism – and maybe even communism – encouraged by regional good-for-nothings may prove too powerful for any central authority to withstand. If corruption continues to eat into the very soul of India's political structure, the country's governmental institutions will doubtless collapse. If the fruits of economic progress are not distributed meaningfully and with a strong driving sense of social justice, neither the charm and charisma of Rajiv Gandhi, nor the mythology of the Nehru–Gandhi dynasty, will be enough to hold India together.

But if the political leaders and ordinary Indians work at nation-building in a committed, sustained and energetic way, I believe that India can genuinely become a moral, political and economic giant in the global community. This can be said for Indians: they are resilient, and they are resourceful. The national leadership hasn't sufficiently tapped these extraordinary qualities. The leadership doesn't need to keep redefining India's dreams. The path towards the future was charted with sharp clarity more than four decades ago. It's the navigation that matters, and that's where India has frequently been let down by its helmsmen.

The vision so wonderfully articulated by Jawaharlal Nehru at the time of independence, that time when India made its 'tryst with destiny', is still valid. The Asian century – the Indian century – beckons this remarkable country, an ancient land of continuity and change.

India, Indians and India's wellwishers all over the world will celebrate in 1989 the birth centenary of Nehru. Anniversaries are a time of remembrance and reflection; the wisdom and vision of India's great leader remain a beacon for the nation he helped create. Not long ago, I was talking to Professor Ralph Buultjens, whose personal links with the Nehru family date back to his early youth. He recalled visiting Nehru many years ago in Delhi. Nehru, who had a fondness for young people, spoke of the challenges before India, which was then a very new independent nation.

'We are engaged in a desperate race – a race between achieving progress and heading off violent revolution,' the prime minister said to Buultjens. 'Our people are immensely tolerant, but there are limits even to their patience. If we do not succeed in giving them the basics of life and offering them realistic hope, they will throw us out – and they will be right to do so.'

Ralph Buultjens recalls that the conversation took place one very cold morning in October. He can still recall the grave expression on Nehru's handsome face. And he recalls how deeply moved he was as the prime minister spoke to him.

It is now well over a generation since that conversation occurred, but what Jawaharlal Nehru said on that cold October morning is no less true today. Nehru's caution and challenge to his countrymen still resonate, louder than ever before, and with greater urgency than the much simpler time when he talked of his dreams for a truly great India.

GLOSSARY

ACCHA: Okay!

ACHKAN: a long coat buttoned up to the neck, usually worn on formal occasions.

ADIVASI: a tribal or aboriginal person.

AGNI: fire; ancient Aryan god of fire.

AHIMSA: non-violence; originally a Jain concept, reinterpreted by Mahatma Gandhi as a political doctrine.

ARAAY: I say!

ARYAN: Indo-European language group of tribal peoples who invaded and conquered north India thousands of years before the birth of Christ.

ASHRAM: a hermitage.

AYAH: a nursemaid, or maid servant.

AZAD: free.

BAAS: Enough!

BABU: a somewhat disparaging term for a clerk or lowly official.

BACHHAA: literally, 'child'; used to mean naive.

BADMASH: a rascal or rogue.

BAGH: a garden.

BANDH: a total strike, these days generally accompanied by violence.

BANIA: a Hindu merchant caste, originally from the western state of Gujarat.

BANYAN: the traditional holy Indian tree, usually old and huge.

BEGUM: honorific for a Moslem woman, usually a noblewoman.

BHANG: Indian hemp.

BIDI: a cheap Indian cigarette in which the tobacco is rolled in leaves instead of paper.

BRAHMAN: a member of the highest Hindu priestly caste.

BRINJAL: aubergine.

BUDDHA: Enlightened One; Gautama Buddha, the former Prince Siddharta, was the founder of Buddhism.

BURKHA: a long veil, usually used by conservative Moslem women.

BURRA: literally, big.

CANTONMENT: a military station, or community.

CHAPPRASI: an office boy, or servant.

CHOR: thief.

CHOTTA: small.

CHOWKIDAR: a security guard, usually nightwatchman.

COOLIE: a manual labourer.

CRORE: 10 million; a crore of Indian rupees is equivalent to a million American dollars, at current exchange rates.

DACOIT: a bandit; the hotbed of banditry has long been in the Chambal Valley in central India.

DARSHAN: literally, a glimpse; an audience with a holy man; audiences with Indira Gandhi were often called *darshan*.

DARZI: a tailor.

DHOBI: a washerman.

DHOTI: a white garment worn like a sarong and drawn up between the legs in the manner of a loincloth.

DOWRY: usually a cash payment given by a bride's family to the bridegroom at the time of marriage.

DURBAR: a royal court.

DUREE: a rug.

FAKIR: a mendicant, usually someone living on charity.

FIRINGHI: usually a put-down term for a white.

FLEETFOOTS: canvas shoes, usually the sort worn for tennis or jogging.

GARIBI: poverty.

GHATS: steps leading into a river, such as the Ganges in Benares; also a word used as a synonym for hills.

GHEE: clarified butter used in cooking and for religious ceremonies.

GHERAO: literally means to surround; a form of protest perfected by leftist unions in West Bengal who would surround a factory and refuse to let the management out until their demands were met.

GOONDA: a bad character, or hooligan.

GURKHA: one of the class of Nepalese mountain people who have long served with distinction as mercenaries in the British and Indian armies.

GURU: a spiritual adviser, a saint, or a mentor.

GYMKHANA: a club.

HARAMI: a person who does harm, or evil.

HARIJAN: a member of the 'untouchable' class; means 'child of God', a term used by Mahatma Gandhi to characterize untouchables, many of whom still live in overwhelming poverty and suffer from social discrimination.

HARTAL: a local strike, usually a wildcat or lightning strike.

JAI: victory.

JIHAD: Moslem holy war.

KAFFIR: infidel.

KALI: the mother goddess.

KARMA: the Hindu doctrine that holds that every deed, good or bad, entails certain consequences that may appear during successive incarnations of the soul. It is sometimes called the doctrine of retribution.

KHADI: homespun cloth; Gandhi advocated the wearing of *khadi* garments as a form of protest against British colonial rulers under whom India became a lucrative market for British textiles; *khadi* is cool and comfortable, and thus ideal in India's heat and dust. *Khadi*, or *khaddar*, has long been the symbol of allegiance to the Congress Party.

KHANSAMA: a cook.

KIRPAN: a dagger carried by many Sikhs.

KOTWALI: a local police station.

KURTA: a long, loose tunic, usually worn with pyjama trousers.

LAKH: 100,000 units, such as a lakh of rupees.

LATHI: a stave, carried by Indian policemen and used as a baton to disperse crowds.

LOK: people; the lower house of the Indian Parliament is called the Lok Sabha, or Assembly of the People.

LUNGI: a sarong-like wrap, favoured in the Tamil south.

MAHARAJA: king; also Raja.

MAHATMA: great-souled one; the honorific by which Mohandas Gandhi, founder of modern India, was widely known.

MALEE: a gardener.

MANDAPAM: the central shrine of a temple.

MANTRA: a Hindu hymn or psalm.

MAYA: an illusion.

MEMSAHIB: European married woman, from 'madam-sahib'.

MITHAI: greasy Indian sweetmeats, usually offered at auspicious times.

MORCHA: a protest march.

MULLAH: a Moslem religious or social leader.

MUNNAH: a young son, or sometimes daughter.

NAGAR: a city.

NATARAJA: 'King of the Dance'; one of the names by which Shiva, a Hindu god, was known.

NAUTCH-GIRL: a dancing girl.

NAWAB: a nobleman, usually a Moslem; also, nabob.

NETA: a leader.

NIRVANA: the goal of salvation, or eternal liberation, to which Buddhists aspire.

PAAN: a betel leaf, highly favoured as a digestive; usually available with a variety of savoury fillings, and sometimes with narcotics.

PADDY: rice in the husk.

PAKISTAN: Land of the Pure.

PANCHAYAT: an Indian village council originally supposed to consist of five elders.

PANCH SHEEL or PANCH SHILA: the so-called 'Five Principles of Co-existence' first enunciated in the preamble to the Sino-Indian treaty of 1954 on trade with Tibet. The principles are: mutual respect for each other's territorial integrity and sovereignty; nonaggression; noninterference in each other's internal affairs; equality and mutual advantage; and peaceful coexistence and economic cooperation. The treaty has now lapsed, but the principles are frequently cited by Indian policy-makers in their dealings with other nations.

PARSI: a descendant of Zoroastrian Persians who migrated to India as religious refugees after the Arab invasion of Persia in the eighth century AD. The Parsis are now concentrated in Bombay; an enterprising community, many Parsis are engaged in commerce and the professions. India's most famous Parsi is Zubin Mehta, conductor of the New York Philharmonic.

PEON: a go-fer, or office boy.

POOJA: a holy ritual, the Hindu form of mass.

PRASAD: a religious offering, usually a sweet dish, blessed by the gods.

PUKKA: 'the real thing', or the 'real McCoy'; or solid.

PUNKAH: a large cloth fan, usually worked by servants pulling a cord attached to a wood frame.

PURDAH: literally, curtain; but commonly means a form of segregation of the female in a conservative Moslem household.

RAJ: literally, kingdom or empire; used in such expressions as the 'British Raj'.

SADHU: a holy man, usually a wandering mendicant.

SAHIB: respectful term for 'sir'.

SARDAR: sobriquet for a Sikh; *sard* is usually the derogatory term.

SATI: outlawed Hindu ritual where widow burned herself on her husband's funeral pyre.

SATYAGRAHA: literally, 'force of truth' or 'soul force'; nonviolent civil disobedience originally used by Mahatma Gandhi as a weapon against the British, now employed for political and economic causes.

SEPOY: old term for a soldier.

SHAKTI: strength.

SHETHJI: word used to address a wealthy person, or a 'big man'.

SHIKAAR: a hunt, usually for tigers or elephants.

SIKH: literally, a disciple; a member of the martial religious community that sprang up in the Punjab in the sixteenth century in the time of Moslem rule as a reformist monotheistic sect. The founders of Sikhism borrowed heavily from both Islam and Hinduism. Sikhism's holiest shrine is the Golden Temple in Amritsar.

SWAMI: a saint, or spiritual leader.

SWARAJ: independence.

TAMASHA: a spectacle; generally a word used to connote farce.

TAMIL: a member of the largest linguistic group in south India. Tamils are also found in Sri Lanka, Burma, Malaysia and Singapore. The word also denotes their language, the oldest and most highly developed of the southern Indian Dravidian tongues.

TIFFIN: literally, box; means lunch, usually a packed lunch for white-collar workers.

TIKKA or TILAK: forehead mark of red paste, or vermilion, worn by Hindu women, usually to denote married status.

TONGA: a two-wheeled pony cart.

VAKIL: regent; also, lawyer.

VARNA: the ancient word for caste, signifying the four traditional Hindu social divisions: the Brahmans, or priests; Kshatriyas, or warriors and administrators; the Vaishyas, or traders and merchants; and the Sudras, or labourers; the 'untouchables' were traditionally outside the caste system.

WAH: Wow!

YAMA: Vedic god of death.

ZAKAT: Islamic income-tax, imposed on Moslems only.

ZAMINDAR: landowner; popular usage denotes someone who exploits.

BIBLIOGRAPHY

Abbas, K. A., *Indira Gandhi: Return of the Red Rose* (Bombay: Popular Prakashan, 1966)

Ahluwalia, B. K., and Ahluwalia, Shashi, *Martyrdom of Indira Gandhi* (Delhi: Manas Publications, 1984)

Akbar, M. J., *India: The Siege Within* (Harmondsworth, UK: Penguin Books, 1985)

—— *Nehru: The Making of India* (London: Viking, 1989)

Alexander, Michael and Anand, Sushila, *Queen Victoria's Maharajah: Duleep Singh, 1838–1893* (London: Weidenfeld and Nicolson, 1980)

Ali, Tariq, *An Indian Dynasty: The Story of the Nehru–Gandhi Family* (New York: G. P. Putnam's Sons, 1985)

Allen, Charles and Dwivedi, Sharada, *Lives of the Indian Princes* (London: Century Publishing, 1984)

Asher, Robert E., *Developing Assistance in the Seventies: Alternatives for the United States* (Washington, DC: The Brookings Institution, 1970)

Ayres, Robert L., *Banking on the Poor: The World Bank and World Poverty* (Cambridge, Mass.: MIT Press, 1983)

Azad, Maulana Abdul Kalam, *India Wins Freedom* (New York: Longmans, Green, 1960)

Baig, M. R. A., *The Muslim Dilemma in India* (Delhi: Vikas Publishing House, 1974)

Bairoch, Paul, *The Economic Development of the Third World since 1900* (Berkeley: University of California Press, 1975)

Barnds, William J., *India, Pakistan and the Great Powers* (New York: Praeger, 1972)

Basham, A. L., ed., *A Cultural History of India* (New Delhi: Oxford University Press, 1975)

Bauer, P. T., *Equality, the Third World, and Economic Delusion* (London: Weidenfeld and Nicolson, 1981)

Bence-Jones, Mark, *The Viceroys of India* (London: Constable and Co., 1982)

Bhagwati, Jagdish, *The Economics of Underdeveloped Countries* (New York: World University Library/McGraw-Hill Book Co., 1966)

Bhatia, Krishan, *The Ordeal of Nationhood* (New York: Atheneum, 1971)

—— *Indira* (New York: Praeger, 1974)

Birla, K. K., *Indira Gandhi: Reminiscences* (Delhi: Vikas Publishing House, 1987)

Blaise, Clark and Mukherjee, Bharati, *Days and Nights in Calcutta* (New York: Doubleday and Co., 1977)

Bobb, Dilip and Raina, Asoka, *The Great Betrayal: Assassination of Indira Gandhi* (Delhi: Vikas Publishing House, 1985)

Bose, Mihir, *The Aga Khans* (London: World's Work, 1984)

—— *A Maidan View: The Magic of Indian Cricket* (London: George Allen and Unwin, 1986)

Bowles, Chester, *Ambassador's Report* (New York: Harper & Row, 1954)

—— *Promises to Keep* (New York: Harper & Row, 1972)

Brata, Sasthi, *India: Labyrinths in the Lotus Land* (New York: William Morrow & Co., 1985)

Brecher, Michael, *Nehru: A Political Biography* (Oxford: Oxford University Press, 1959)

Bright, J. S., *Indira Gandhi* (Delhi: New Light Publishers, 1984)

Buultjens, Ralph, *Windows on India* (New York: Express Books, 1987)

Cameron, James, *An Indian Summer* (London: Macmillan, 1973)

—— *Point of Departure: An Autobiography* (London: Arthur Barker, 1967)

Campbell-Johnson, Alan, *Mission with Mountbatten* (London: Robert Hale, 1951)

Chaudhuri, Nirad C., *Autobiography of an Unknown Indian* (London: Macmillan, 1951)

—— *The Continent of Circe: Being an Essay on the Peoples of India* (New York: Oxford University Press, 1966)

—— *To Live or Not to Live* (Delhi: Indian Book Co., 1973)

Chopra, V. D., Mishra, R. K. and Singh, Nirmal, *Agony of Punjab*. (Delhi: Patriot Publishers, 1984)

Clark, William, *From Three Worlds: Memoirs* (London: Sidgwick and Jackson, 1986)

Collier, Richard, *The Great Indian Mutiny: A Dramatic Account of the Sepoy Rebellion* (New York: E. P. Dutton, 1964)

Collins, Larry and Lapierre, Dominique, *Freedom at Midnight* (New York: Simon and Schuster, 1975)

Coolidge, Olivia, *Gandhi* (Boston: Houghton Mifflin, 1971)

Coomaraswamy, Ananda K., *The Dance of Shiva* (New York: H. Wolff, 1957)

Coomaraswamy, Radhika, *Sri Lanka: The Crisis of the Anglo-American Constitutional Traditions in a Developing Society* (Delhi: Vikas Publishing House, 1984)

Correa, Charles, *The New Landscape* (Bombay: The Book Society of India, 1986)

Critchfield, Richard, *Villages* (New York: Doubleday/Anchor, 1983)

Crocker, Walter, *Nehru: A Contemporary's Estimate* (New York: Oxford University Press, 1966)

Das, Durga, *India: From Curzon to Nehru and After* (London: Collins Publishers, 1969)

Davies, Philip, *Splendours of the Raj* (Harmondsworth, UK: Penguin Books, 1987)

Desai, Morarji, *The Story of My Life* (Delhi: Macmillan, 1974)

Desai, Padma, *The Bokaro Steel Plant: A Study of Soviet Economic Assistance* (Amsterdam: North-Holland Publishing Co., 1972)

Eck, Diana L., *Benaras, City of Light* (New York: Alfred A. Knopf, 1982)

Edwardes, Michael, *The Myth of the Mahatma* (London: Constable Books, 1986)

Erikson, Erik H., *Gandhi's Truth* (New York: Norton, 1969)

Etienne, Gilbert, *India's Changing Rural Scene 1963–1979* (Delhi: Oxford University Press, 1982)

Fischer, Louis, *The Life of Mahatma Gandhi* (New York: Harper & Row, 1950)

Fishlock, Trevor, *India File* (London: John Murray, 1983)

Forster, E. M., *A Passage to India* (New York: Harcourt Brace Jovanovich, 1965)

Galbraith, John Kenneth, *Ambassador's Journal: A Personal Account of the Kennedy Years* (Boston: Houghton Mifflin, 1969)

—— *John Kenneth Galbraith Introduces India* (London: André Deutsch, 1974)

Gandhi, Indira, *On People and Problems* (London: Hodder and Stoughton, 1983)

Gandhi, Mohandas Karamchand, *The Story of My Experiments with Truth: An Autobiography* (Boston: Beacon Press, 1970)

Gardner, Brian, *The East India Company* (London: Rupert Hart-Davis, 1971)

Garland, Nicholas, *An Indian Journal* (Chicago: Academy Chicago Publishers, 1986)

Gascoigne, Bamber, *The Great Moghuls* (New York: Harper & Row, 1971)

Glyn, Anthony. *The British: Portrait of a People* (New York: G. P. Putnam's Sons, 1970)

Greer, Germaine, *Sex and Destiny: The Politics of Human Fertility* (New York: Harper & Row, 1984)

Gross, John, *Rudyard Kipling: The Man, His Work and His World* (London: Weidenfeld and Nicolson, 1972)

Gupte, Pranay, *The Crowded Earth: People and the Politics of Population* (New York: W. W. Norton, 1984)

—— *Vengeance: India After the Assassination of Indira Gandhi* (New York: W. W. Norton, 1985)

Hangen, Welles, *After Nehru Who?* (London: Rupert Hart-Davis, 1963)

Harrison, Paul, *Inside the Third World* (London: Penguin, 1979)

—— *The Third World Tomorrow* (London: Penguin, 1980)

Harrison, Selig S., *India, the Most Dangerous Decades* (Princeton: Princeton University Press, 1960)

Hazarika, Sanjoy, *Bhopal: The Lessons of a Tragedy* (Delhi: Penguin Books, 1987)

Hibbert, Christopher, *The Great Mutiny: India 1857* (New York: Viking Press, 1978)

Hiro, Dilip, *Inside India Today* (London: Routledge and Kegan Paul, 1978)

Hobbs, Lisa, *India, India* (New York: McGraw-Hill, 1967)

Hutheesing, Krishna Nehru, *Dear to Behold: An Intimate Portrait of Indira Gandhi* (New York: Macmillan, 1969)

Illustrated Weekly of India, ed. Pritish Nandy (Bombay: Times of India Publications)

Imprint, monthly magazine published by R. V. Pandit, Bombay

India Today, news magazine, edited and published by Aroon Purie, Delhi

Iyer, Pico, *Video Night in Kathmandu and Other Reports from the Not-So-Far-East* (New York: Alfred A. Knopf, 1988)

Jackson, Richard L., *The Non-Aligned, the UN and the Superpowers* (New York: Praeger, 1983)

Jaipal, Rikhi, *Nonalignment: Origins, Growth and Potential for World Peace* (Delhi: Allied Publishers, 1983)

Jha, Prem Shankar, *India: A Political Economy of Stagnation* (Bombay: Oxford University Press, 1980)

Jiwa, Salim, *The Death of Air India Flight 182* (London: Star Books, 1986)

Johnson, B.L.C., *Development in South Asia* (New York: Penguin Books, 1983)

Johnson, Paul, *Modern Times: The World from the Twenties to the Eighties* (New York: Harper & Row, 1983)

Joshi, Chand, *Bhindranwale: Myth and Reality* (Delhi: Vikas Publishing, 1984)

Jung, Anees, *Unveiling India: A Woman's Journey* (Delhi: Penguin Books, 1987)

Kapur, Rajiv A., *Sikh Separatism: The Politics of Faith* (London: George Allen and Unwin, 1986)

Karanjia, R. K., *The Mind of Mr Nehru* (London: George Allen and Unwin, 1960)

—— *The Philosophy of Mr Nehru* (London: George Allen and Unwin, 1966)

Kaye, M. M., *The Far Pavilions* (New York: St Martin's Press, 1978)

Keay, John, *Into India* (London: John Murray, 1973)

Kennedy, Paul, *The Rise and Fall of the Great Powers* (New York: Random House, 1988)

Khan, Mohammed Ayub, *Friends Not Masters: A Political Autobiography*, (Oxford: Oxford University Press, 1967)

Khosla, G. D., *Indira Gandhi* (Delhi: Thomson Press, 1974)

Kothari, Rajni, *Politics in India* (Boston: Little Brown & Co., 1970)

Lapierre, Dominique, *City of Joy* (New York: Doubleday, 1985)

Lewis, John P., *Quiet Crisis in India: Economic Development and American Policy* (Washington: The Brookings Institution, 1962)

Malgonkar, Manohar, *A Bend in the Ganges* (London: Hamish Hamilton, 1964)

—— *The Devil's Wind* (London: Hamish Hamilton, 1972)

—— *The Garland Keepers* (Delhi: Vision Books, 1986)

Masani, Minoo, *Is J. P. the Answer?* (Delhi: Macmillan, 1975)

Masani, Shakuntala, *The Story of Indira* (Delhi: Vikas Publishing House, 1974)

Masani, Zareer, *Indira Gandhi: A Biography* (London: Hamish Hamilton, 1975)

—— *Indian Tales of the Raj* (London: BBC Books, 1987)

Mason, Philip, *The Men Who Ruled India* (London: Jonathan Cape, 1985)

Maxwell, Neville, *India's China War* (New York: Pantheon Books, 1970)

Mehta, Gita, *Karma Cola: Marketing the Mystic East* (New York: Simon and Schuster, 1979)

Mehta, Ved, *Portrait of India* (Delhi: Vikas Publications, 1971)

—— *Walking the Indian Streets* (Delhi: Vikas Publications, 1972)

—— *The New India* (New York: Penguin Books, 1978)

—— *Mamaji* (New York: Oxford University Press, 1979)

—— *The Ledge Between the Streams* (New York: W. W. Norton, 1984)

Menon, K. P. S., *The Flying Troika: The Political Diary of India's Ambassador to Russia, 1952–61* (New York: Oxford University Press, 1963)

Menon, V. P., *The Story of the Integration of the Indian States* (Calcutta: Orient Longmans, 1956)

—— *The Transfer of Power in India* (Princeton: Princeton University Press, 1957)

Mohan, Anand, *Indira Gandhi: A Biography* (New York: Hawthorn Books, 1967)

Moorhouse, Geoffrey, *Calcutta* (New York: Harcourt Brace Jovanovich, 1971)

—— *India Britannica* (London: Harvill Press, 1983)

—— *To the Frontier* (London: Hodder and Stoughton, 1984)

Moraes, Dom. *A Matter of People* (New York: Praeger, 1974)

—— *Voices for Life* (New York, Praeger, 1975)

—— *The Great Cities: Bombay* (Amsterdam: Time-Life Books, 1979)

—— *Mrs Gandhi* (Delhi: Vikas Publishing House, 1980)

Moraes, Frank, *Indira Gandhi* (Delhi: Directorate of Advertising and Visual Publicity, 1966)

Morris, James, *Pax Britannica* (London: Faber & Faber, 1968)

—— *Heaven's Command* (New York: Harcourt Brace Jovanovich, 1973)

—— *Farewell the Trumpets* (New York: Harcourt Brace Jovanovich, 1978)

Morris, Jan (with photographs and captions by Simon Winchester), *Stones of Empire: The Buildings of the Raj* (New York: Oxford University Press, 1983)

Mukerjee, Hiren, *The Gentle Colossus: A Study of Jawaharlal Nehru* (Delhi: Oxford University Press, 1986)

Myrdal, Gunnar, *Asian Drama: An Inquiry into the Poverty of Nations* (New York: Twentieth-Century Fund, 1968)

—— *The Challenge of World Poverty* (New York: Pantheon Books, 1970)

Naipaul, Shiva, *Beyond the Dragon's Mouth* (London: Hamish Hamilton, 1984)

—— *An Unfinished Journey* (London: Hamish Hamilton, 1986)

Naipaul, V. S., *An Area of Darkness* (London: André Deutsch, 1964)

—— *The Overcrowded Barracoon* (London: André Deutsch, 1972)

—— *India: A Wounded Civilization* (New York: Alfred A. Knopf, 1977)

—— *Finding the Centre* (London: André Deutsch, 1984)

Nanda, B. R., *The Nehrus: Motilal and Jawaharlal* (London: George Allen and Unwin, 1962)

—— *Mahatma Gandhi: A Biography* (New York: Baron, 1965)

Narayan, R. K., *My Days* (Delhi: Orient Paperbacks, 1986)

Nayar, Kuldip, *India: The Critical Years* (Delhi: Vikas Publications, 1971)

—— *The Judgment: Inside Story of the Emergency in India* (Delhi: Vikas Publishing House, 1977)

—— and Singh, Khushwant, *Tragedy oj Punjab: Operation Bluestar and After* (Delhi: Vision Books, 1984)

Nehru, Jawaharlal, *Autobiography* (London: Bodley Head, 1936)

—— *The Discovery of India* (New York: John Day, 1946)

—— *India's Freedom* (London: Unwin Books, 1965)

Newby, Eric, *Slowly Down the Ganges* (London: Picador Books, 1983)

Nossiter, Bernard, *The Global Struggle for More: Third World Conflicts with Rich Nations* (New York: Harper & Row, 1987)

Pandit, Vijayalakshmi, *Prison Days* (Calcutta: Signet Press, 1945)

—— *The Scope of Happiness: A Personal Memoir* (New York: Crown, 1979)

Parasher, S. C., ed., *United Nations and India* (Delhi: Indian Council of World Affairs, 1985)

Paul, Swraj, *Indira Gandhi* (London: Heron Press, 1984)

People magazine, edited by John Rowley and published by the International Planned Parenthood Federation, London

Piramal, Gita and Herdeck, Margaret, *India's Industrialists* (Washington, DC: Three Continents Press, 1986)

Raghavan, G. N. S., *Introducing India* (Delhi: Indian Council for Cultural Relations, 1983)

Rajagopalachari, Chakravarti, *The Mahabharata* (Bombay: Bharatiya Vidya Bhavan, 1951)

—— *The Ramayana* (Bombay: Bharatiya Vidya Bhavan, 1951)

Reeves, Richard, *Passage to Peshawar* (New York: Simon and Schuster, 1984)

Rushdie, Salman, *Midnight's Children* (New York: Alfred A. Knopf, 1980)

—— *The Satanic Verses* (New York: Viking, 1988)

Sahgal, Nayantara, *Prison and Chocolate Cake* (New York: Alfred A. Knopf, 1954)

—— *Indira Gandhi: Her Road to Power* (New York: Frederick Ungar Publishing Co., 1982)

Sarkar, Jadunath, *India Through the Ages* (Calcutta: Sangam Books, 1979)

Savarkar, Vinayak Damodar, *The Indian War of Independence: 1857* (Delhi: Rajdhani Granthagar, 1986)

Scott, Paul, *The Raj Quartet* (New York: William Morrow, 1976)

Sen Gupta, Bhabani, *The Fulcrum of Asia: Relations Among China, India, Pakistan and the USSR* (New York: Pegasus, 1970)

Seton, Marie, *Portrait of a Director: Satyajit Ray* (London: Denis Dobson, 1971)

Shaplen, Robert, *A Turning Wheel: Thirty Years of the Asian Revolution* (London: André Deutsch, 1979)

Sharada Prasad, H. Y., *Indira Gandhi* (Delhi: Ladybird Books, 1985)

Sheean, Vincent, *Lead, Kindly Light* (London: Cassell, 1950)

—— *Mahatma Gandhi: A Great Life in Brief* (New York: Alfred A. Knopf, 1970)

Sheth, N. R., *The Social Framework of an Indian Factory* (Manchester: Manchester University Press, 1968)

Shourie, Arun, *Mrs Gandhi's Second Reign* (Delhi: Vikas Publishing House, 1983)

Singh, Karan, *Contemporary Essays* (Bombay: Bharatiya Vidya Bhavan, 1971)

Singh, Khushwant, *India: A Mirror for its Monsters and Monstrosities* (Bombay: IBH Publishing Co., 1969)

—— *The Sikhs Today* (Bombay: Orient Longmans, 1967)

—— *Train to Pakistan* (London: Chatto & Windus, 1956)

—— *We Indians* (Delhi: Orient Paperbacks, 1982)

—— *Delhi: A Portrait* (with photographs by Raghu Rai) (New York: Oxford University Press, 1983)

—— *The Sikhs* (with photographs by Raghu Rai) (Delhi: Rupa and Co., 1984)

Singh, Patwant, *The Struggle for Power in Asia* (London: Hutchinson, 1971)

—— and Malik, Harji, *Punjab: The Fatal Miscalculation* (Delhi: published by Patwant Singh, 1985)

Singh, S. Nihal, *My India* (Delhi: Vikas Publishing House, 1982)

Smith, Hedrick, *The Power Game: How Washington Really Works* (New York: Random House, 1988)

Spear, Percival, *A History of India* (London: Penguin Books, 1970)

Sunday, weekly news magazine, edited by Vir Sanghvi and published by Ananda Bazar Patrika Publications, Calcutta

Thapar, Romila, *A History of India* (London: Penguin Books, 1966)

Theroux, Paul, *The Great Railway Bazaar: By Train Through Asia* (Boston: Houghton Mifflin, 1975)

Trevelyan, Raleigh, *The Golden Oriole: Childhood, Family, and Friends in India* (London: Secker and Warburg, 1987)

Tully, Mark and Jacob, Satish, *Amritsar: Mrs Gandhi's Last Battle* (London: Jonathan Cape, 1985)

Vadgama, Kusoom, *India in Britain* (London: Robert Royce, 1984)

Walvin, James, *Passage to Britain: Immigration in British History and Politics* (London: Penguin, 1984)

Wanniski, Jude, *The Way the World Works* (New York: Touchstone Books, 1983)

Watson, Francis, *A Concise History of India* (London: Thames and Hudson, 1979)

Wiles, John, *Delhi is Far Away: A Journey Through India* (London: Paul Elek, 1974)

Willcoxen, Harriet, *First Lady of India: The Story of Indira Gandhi* (New York: Doubleday, 1969)

Wirsing, Giselher, *The Indian Experiment* (Delhi: Orient Longman, 1972)

Wolpert, Stanley, *A New History of India* (New York: Oxford University Press, 1977)

World Commission on Environment and Development, *Our Common Future* (Oxford: Oxford University Press, 1987)

Ziegler, Philip, *Mountbatten: A Biography* (New York: Alfred A. Knopf, 1985)

INDEX

Also available in Mandarin Paperbacks

BENAZIR BHUTTO

Daughter of the East

Beautiful and charismatic, the daughter of the only popular leader Pakistan has ever produced – President Bhutto, hanged by General Zia in 1979 – Benazir Bhutto, Pakistan's first woman Prime Minister, has achieved a status approaching that of a royal princess.

From her upbringing in one of Pakistan's richest families, the shock of the contrast of her Radcliffe and Oxford education, and her subsequent politicisation and arrest after her father's death – she spent nearly five years in detention – Benazir Bhutto's life has already been full of drama.

Transformed by suffering into a tireless political leader, she has donned her father's mantle with that iron determination which has astonished observers throughout the world. Her own story, presented here with strength and simplicity, is an inspiring one as she sets out to bring about the necessary change without compromise which she desires for Pakistan.

'An unusually (for a political memoir) moving and challenging account of a brave woman, a martyred family and a heroic country struggling to maintain the spirit of freedom in the face of savage repression.' *Sunday Times*

'Benazir has certainly been tested in the flame, and not found wanting . . . A deeply moving saga of love, drama and heroism.' *Evening Standard*

A Selected List of Non-Fiction Available from Mandarin Books

While every effort is made to keep prices low, it is sometimes necessary to increase prices at short notice. Mandarin Paperbacks reserves the right to show new retail prices on covers which may differ from those previously advertised in the text or elsewhere.

The prices shown below were correct at the time of going to press.

☐	7493 0000 0	**Moonwalk**	Michael Jackson	£3.99
☐	7493 0004 3	**South Africa**	Graham Leach	£3.99
☐	7493 0010 8	**What Fresh Hell is This?**	Marion Meade	£3.99
☐	7493 0011 6	**War Games**	Thomas Allen	£3.99
☐	7493 0013 2	**The Crash**	Mihir Bose	£4.99
☐	7493 0014 0	**The Demon Drink**	Jancis Robinson	£4.99
☐	7493 0015 9	**The Health Scandal**	Vernon Coleman	£4.99
☐	7493 0016 7	**Vietnam – The 10,000 Day War**	Michael Maclear	£3.99
☐	7493 0049 3	**The Spycatcher Trial**	Malcolm Turnbull	£3.99
☐	7493 0022 1	**The Super Saleswoman**	Janet Macdonald	£4.99
☐	7493 0023 X	**What's Wrong With Your Rights?**	Cook/Tate	£4.99
☐	7493 0024 8	**Mary and Richard**	Michael Burn	£3.50
☐	7493 0061 2	**Voyager**	Yeager/Rutan	£3.99
☐	7493 0060 4	**The Fashion Conspiracy**	Nicholas Coleridge	£3.99
☐	7493 0027 2	**Journey Without End**	David Bolton	£3.99
☐	7493 0028 0	**The Common Thread**	Common Thread	£4.99

All these books are available at your bookshop or newsagent, or can be ordered direct from the publisher. Just tick the titles you want and fill in the form below.

Mandarin Paperbacks, Cash Sales Department, PO Box 11, Falmouth, Cornwall TR10 9EN.

Please send cheque or postal order, no currency, for purchase price quoted and allow the following for postage and packing:

UK — 55p for the first book, 22p for the second book and 14p for each additional book ordered to a maximum charge of £1.75.

BFPO and Eire — 55p for the first book, 22p for the second book and 14p for each of the next seven books, thereafter 8p per book.

Overseas Customers — £1.00 for the first book plus 25p per copy for each additional book.

NAME (Block Letters) ....

ADDRESS ....

....